SOCIALIST PLANNING

SOCIALIST PLANNING

Michael Ellman
Professor of Economics
University of Amsterdam

Second edition

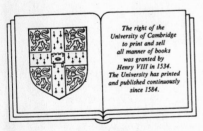

The right of the
University of Cambridge
to print and sell
all manner of books
was granted by
Henry VIII in 1534.
The University has printed
and published continuously
since 1584.

CAMBRIDGE UNIVERSITY PRESS

CAMBRIDGE
NEW YORK   PORT CHESTER
MELBOURNE   SYDNEY

Published by the Press Syndicate of the University of Cambridge
The Pitt Building, Trumpington Street, Cambridge CB2 1RP
40 West 20th Street, New York, NY 10011, USA
10 Stamford Road, Oakleigh, Melbourne 3166, Australia

First published 1989
Reprinted 1989

Printed in Great Britain at the University Press, Cambridge

British Library cataloguing in publication data

Ellman, Michael
Socialist planning – 2nd ed. – (Modern
Cambridge economics). 1. Communist countries. Economic planning
I. Title. II. Series
338.9'009171'7

Library of Congress cataloguing in publication data

Ellman, Michael
Socialist planning / Michael Ellman. – 2nd ed.
  p.   cm. – (Modern Cambridge economics)
Bibliography: p.
Includes index.
ISBN 0 521 35345 9. ISBN 0 521 35866 3 (pbk.)
1. Economic policy. 2. Comparative economics. 3. Marxian
economics. 4. Central planning. 5. Communist countries – Economic
policy. I. Title. II. Series.
HD82.E52 1988
335.43–dc19   88-16850 CIP

ISBN 0 521 35345 9 hard covers

ISBN 0 521 35866 3 paperback

CE

SERIES PREFACE

The modern Cambridge Economics series, of which this book is one, is designed in the same spirit as and with similar objectives to the series of Cambridge Economic Handbooks launched by Maynard Keynes soon after the first World War. Keynes' series, as he explained in his introduction, was intended 'to convey to the ordinary reader and to the uninitiated student some conception of the general principles of thought which economists now apply to economic problems'. He went on to describe its authors as, generally speaking, 'orthodox members of the Cambridge School of Economics' drawing most of their ideas and prejudices from 'the two economists who have chiefly influenced Cambridge thought for the past fifty years, Dr Marshall and Professor Pigou' and as being 'more anxious to avoid obscure forms of expression than difficult ideas'.

This series of short monographs is also aimed at the intelligent undergraduate and interested general reader, but it differs from Keynes' series in three main ways: first in that it focuses on aspects of economics which have attracted the particular interest of economists in the post Second World War era; second in that its authors, though still sharing a Cambridge tradition of ideas, would regard themselves as deriving their main inspiration from Keynes himself and his immediate successors, rather than from the neoclassical generation of the Cambridge school; and third in that it envisages a wider audience than readers in mature capitalist economies, for it is equally aimed at students in developing countries whose problems and whose interactions with the rest of the world have helped to shape the economic issues which have dominated economic thinking in recent decades.

Finally, it should be said that the editors and authors of this Modern Cambridge Economics series represent a wider spectrum of economic doctrine than the Cambridge School of Economics to which Keynes referred in the 1920s. However, the object of the series is not to propagate particular doctrines. It is to stimulate students to escape from conventional theoretical ruts and to think for themselves on live and controversial issues.

v

our task is to study the state capitalism of the Germans, to spare *no effort* in copying it and not to shrink from adopting dictatorial methods to hasten the copying of it. Our task is to hasten this copying even more than Peter hastened the copying of Western culture by barbarian Russia, and did not refrain from using barbarous methods in fighting barbarism.

V. I. Lenin (*'Left wing' childishness and the petty-bourgeois mentality*)

A number of countries have built socialism for decades. Socialism, however, has turned out to be a great deal more complex than our generation imagined. We had thought that once [a workers'] Party assumed power and applied the principle 'to each according to his work', we could go on and build communism and all the problems would be solved. This has not been the case in practice.

S. Carillo, General Secretary of the Spanish Communist Party (*Beijing Review* August 24 1981)

Socialism was born as the negation of capitalism, of exploitation, of bourgeois morality. Consequently, the new society was imagined as a romantic-ideal type, without flaws or contradictions. Misfortunes and blemishes were ascribed to the notorious 'survivals of capitalism'. If only things were so simple. The manifest advantages of socialism created the illusion that it was not susceptible to the appearance of negative tendencies, to the influence of petty bourgeois characteristics. The objective laws of socialism were often analysed outside the context of world development. In many respects the forecasts about the development of the capitalist system, about the limits of its vitality and ability to survive, were over-simplified.

A. N. Yakovlev (Secretary, CC CPSU) (*Vestnik AN SSSR 1987* no. 6)

CONTENTS

List of figures	*page*	viii
List of tables		ix
Preface to second edition		xi
Glossary		xii
Important dates		xiv
1 The need for planning		1
2 The traditional model		17
3 The reform process		53
4 Planning agriculture		92
5 Investment planning		131
6 Planning the labour force		173
7 Planning incomes		209
8 Planning consumption		233
9 Planning international trade		266
10 Results of socialist planning		298
Bibliography		332
Index		359

FIGURES

1.1 The prisoners' dilemma.   *page* 6
4.1 The cause of unemployment: the neoclassical view.   94
4.2 The tribute model.   97
5.1 Feasible consumption paths.   133
5.2 The convergence of aspirations and feasibilities.   134
5.3 Absorptive capacity and the optimal rate of investment.   136
5.4 Feldman's first theorem.   142
5.5 The choice of technique.   153
5.6 Technical progress and the Dobb-Sen criterion.   155
6.1 A planning labour balance.   203
8.1 Changing relative prices to improve welfare.   241
8.2 A shortage preserving supply curve.   249
9.1 The pre-capitalist economy.   267
9.2 Multilateral trade.   279
9.3 Bilateralism with the export constraint operative.   279
9.4 Bilateralism with soft commodities.   279
9.5 Exports and the economic mechanism.   291
9.6 Imports and the economic mechanism.   292
10.1 International dynamic efficiency 1958–68.   307
10.2 Dynamic efficiency in China in 1952–78.   308

TABLES

2.1 Time taken to construct thermal electricity stations completed in the USSR in 1959–62. *page* 32

2.2 The creation of automated management systems in the USSR. 43

4.1 Marketed output of basic wage goods, USSR 1928–32. 105

4.2 Improvements in the Soviet diet, 1950–76. 107

4.3 Collectivisation and grain extraction, USSR and China. 111

4.4 Productivity of Chinese agricultural labour in grain output. 115

4.5 Per capita food availability in China. 117

4.6 Rate of growth of Chinese agricultural production. 118

5.1 Division of Soviet industrial production between consumer and producer goods. 139

5.2 Division of Chinese industrial production between light industry and heavy industry. 140

5.3 Share of consumer goods in industrial output in selected countries. 141

5.4 Feldman's two theorems. 143

5.5 Consumption paths on various investment strategies. 144

5.6 Industrial implications of different macro-economic growth rates. 146

5.7 Construction periods and economic institutions. 161

5.8 Construction periods in Hungary and Japan. 163

5.9 Plans and outcome for the Kuznetsk Combine. 166

6.1 Urban unemployment in China. 180

6.2 Gross investment as a proportion of net material product. 183

6.3 State employment in the USSR. 185

7.1 Ratios of income per head in selected countries. 217

7.2 Elite occupational groups in the USSR in 1970. 218

7.3 Distribution of income in selected capitalist and socialist countries. 219

8.1 Personal consumption plan for China for 1981–5.   234
8.2 USSR daily nutritional norms.   236
8.3 Actual and normative food consumption in the USSR
     and actual food consumption in selected countries.   237
8.4 USSR rational wardrobe and 1961 US Heller budget
     clothing stocks.   238
8.5 Polish consumption structure in 1967.   239
8.6 Social cost – retail price ratios (Poland in 1970).   240
8.7 Pressure and suction compared.   253
8.8 Social indicators of the state socialist countries (ranks
     of indicators).   258
8.9 Consumption of pure alcohol in the USSR per person
     of 15 years old and over.   262
9.1 CMEA – population of members at the end of 1985.   275
9.2 Foreign trade of CMEA members by trade bloc in 1970
     and 1983.   277
9.3 Price differences in Hungary's exports to CMEA coun-
     tries in the mid 1960s.   281
9.4 Growth of CMEA trade.   283
10.1 Average growth of rates in the EEC and CMEA.   301
10.2 A dynamic comparison of the Soviet and US
     economies.   302

PREFACE TO SECOND EDITION

The first edition of this book evidently fulfilled a useful purpose, since it has become widely used throughout the world. In view of this, it seemed desirable to bring out a second edition to take account of the substantial changes that have taken place since the mid seventies when the first edition was written. Although the structure of the book remains basically unchanged, alterations have been made both in the empirical and theoretical sections. On the empirical level, account has been taken of the radical economic changes in China together with the huge increase in accurate information about that country, the Polish crisis of 1979–82, the virtual Soviet stagnation of 1976–85 and the first steps of *perestroika*. On the theoretical level, account has been taken of the chief contributions of the systems and behavioural approaches and also of new developments within Marxism-Leninism. I have tried to combine accurate and up to date information, the latest theoretical ideas, relevant historical material, a survey of the chief contributions to understanding, and my own ideas, all set against the reality of the state socialist countries. Due to space limitations, it has been impossible to analyse a number of interesting and important topics, such as monetary and financial relations and the price system. I am grateful to T. Bauer, J. de Beus, G. Biessen, P. Boot, W. Brus, T. Buck, E. Dirksen, J. Drewnowski, P. Ellman, S. Estrin, P. Hanson, H. Jager, D. Lane, P. Nolan, B. Simatupang, W. Swaan and H. J. Wagener for helpful comments on draft chapters.

MICHAEL ELLMAN
Amsterdam University
October 1987

GLOSSARY

CC The Central Committee of the Communist Party.

CCP The Chinese Communist Party.

Classical Marxism Marxism 1881–1914.

CMEA The Council for Mutual Economic Assistance (often known as Comecon). Its members are, Bulgaria, Cuba, Czechoslovakia, the German Democratic Republic (GDR), Hungary, Mongolia, Poland, Romania, Vietnam and the USSR.

CPSU The Communist Party of the Soviet Union.

Economic model (or *mechanism*) The system of ownership and allocation in an economy. Examples are, *War Communism* (q.v.), *NEP* (q.v.) or the *traditional model* (q.v.). (Economic model is the Polish terminology, economic mechanism the Hungarian terminology.)

The 11th Congress The Eleventh Congress of the CCP was held in 1977. This Congress confirmed the appointment of Hua Guofeng as Party Chairman, of Deng Xiaoping as one of the Vice-Chairmen, and the condemnation of the 'gang of four' (q.v.).

'Gang of four' Wang Hongwen, Zhang Chunqiao, Jiang Qing (Mao Zedong's fourth and last wife) and Yao Wenyuan. Fell from power after Mao Zedong's death in 1976.

GLF Great Leap Forward.

Gosplan The USSR State Planning Commission, the central planning organ.

Great Patriotic War The Soviet term for the Soviet-German war 1941–5.

GPCR Great Proletarian Culture Revolution.

Liberal Adherent to the teachings of Adam Smith and Milton Friedman. Not to be confused with contemporary US political usage.

NEM The New Economic Mechanism introduced in Hungary from 1 January 1968.

NEP New Economic Policy is the term used to describe the economic model which existed in the USSR in the 1920s.

OGAS 'Nation-wide automated management system for the gathering and processing of information for accounting, planning and control of the national economy', i.e. departmental management information and control systems which are compatible with one another.

Perestroika (literally 'reorganisation', 'reorientation', 'reconstruction', or 'rebuilding'). Official term used in the USSR to describe economic changes under Gorbachev.

Productive forces The technology, skills and resources available to society.

Productive relations The relationship between people in the process of production, eg the exploitation of the workers by the capitalists in the Marxist model of capitalism.

R&D Research and Development.

Taylorism Organisation of the labour process which separates planning from execution. Founded by US engineer F. W. Taylor. Basis of 'scientific management'.

Traditional model Term used in this book to describe the economic model developed in the USSR in 1930–4 and subsequently adopted for shorter or longer periods throughout the state socialist world.

The 20th Congress The 20th Congress of the CPSU was held in 1956. At this Congress the First Secretary made a report 'On the personality cult and its consequences'.

The 22nd Congress The 22nd Congress of the CPSU was held in 1961. At this Congress a resolution was passed to remove the body of J. V. Stalin from the Lenin Mausoleum.

War Communism Term used to describe the economic model which existed in the USSR in 1918–21.

IMPORTANT DATES

15th century	Portuguese ships enter the Indian ocean. Spanish assault on the Americas begins.
16th century	Growth of Portuguese trade with Africa, Ceylon, Indonesia and Brazil. Portuguese Empire created. Spain conquers Mexico, Peru and the Philippines. Demographic catastrophe in Mexico.
1568–1648	1st bourgeois revolution. Dutch Republic becomes an independent state. Amsterdam becomes the commercial capital of the world.
1640–88	2nd bourgeois revolution. England prepared for commercial expansion.
18th century	Heyday of the slave trade. Britain overtakes the Dutch Republic.
1688–1815	Britain and France struggle for commercial mastery of the world. Britain emerges victorious. British rule established in India, Canada, Australia, New Zealand and South Africa.
1776	Continental Congress issues Declaration of Independence.
1787	United States Constitution drafted.
1789	1st pure bourgeois revolution begins in France.
1780–1820	Industrial revolution in Britain.
1815–1914	Industrial revolution spreads across Europe and North America. Transcontinental railways built. Industrialisation of war. Conquest by European countries and the United States of Central Asia, Vietnam, nearly all Africa and the remainder of North America.
1839–42	1st Opium War.
1848	*Communist manifesto* published. Year of revolutions.
1850	*Address of the Central Committee to the Communist League* written.
1856–60	2nd Opium War.

1861–8	Last bourgeois revolution. Slavery abolished in USA. Conditions for free scope for capitalism created in USA.
1867	*Capital* vol. 1 published.
1868	Meiji Revolution
1917	October Revolution.
1918–20	Russian civil war.
1921–2	Famine in Russia.
1921–8	New Economic Policy in Russia.
1928–	Five Year Plans in USSR.
1929–53	Stalin's dictatorship in USSR.
1929–32	Collectivisation of agriculture in the USSR.
1932–3	Bottom of the Great Depression. Mass unemployment in Europe and North America. Ruin of many primary producers. Widespread bank closures in the USA. Victory of National Socialism in Germany. Famine in USSR.
1937–8	Mass arrests in USSR.
1937–45	Japanese–Chinese war.
1941–5	Second World War.
1945–	Decline of Britain.
1945–9	Division of Europe into US and Soviet spheres.
1946–7	Last famine in USSR.
1947–55	USA establishes world-wide network of military bases.
1947	Britain withdraws from India.
1948	Soviet–Yugoslav split.
1949	People's Republic of China established.
1950	Korean war begins.
1950–2	Land reform in China.
1952–73	Cyclical boom in capitalist world.
1953–7	First Five Year Plan in China.
1953	USA overthrows Mossadeq regime in Iran.
1954–73	Volume and price of oil exports develop satisfactorily for importers.
1956	20th Congress of the CPSU. Anglo–French–Israeli invasion of Egypt. Soviet invasion of Hungary.
1957	USSR launches world's first artificial satellite. 100 flowers movement in China.
1958	Great Leap Forward in China.
1959	Victory of Castro in Cuba.
1959–61	Economic crisis in China. Three bad harvests, famine and industrial recession.

1960	USSR withdraws technicians from China.
1961	22nd Congress of the CPSU.
1961–73	USA wages war in Vietnam, Laos and Cambodia.
1962–6	Socialist education movement in China.
1964–6	Debate on alternative economic mechanisms in Cuba.
1965–9	Abortive economic reform in USSR.
1965–6	White terror in Indonesia.
1966–8	Cultural Revolution in China.
1966–70	Maoist–Guevarist economic mechanism in Cuba.
1968	NEM introduced in Hungary. USSR invades Czecho-slovakia.
1968–late 1970s	Liberal opposition in USSR.
1969	Serious Sino–Soviet border clashes.
1970s	Extensive imports of technology from capitalist world by state socialist countries. Development of East–West production cooperation agreements. Creation of trans-ideological enterprises.
1973	Internal opposition and the USA successfully destabilise *Unidad Popular* in Chile. Murder of Allende.
1975	Recession in capitalist world. Victory of state socialism in South Vietnam, Laos and Cambodia. Mass sending down in Cambodia. Disintegration of Portuguese Empire.
1976	Death of Mao Zedong and defeat of 'gang of four'.
1977	11th Congress of the CCP. New economic management system introduced in Cuba.
1977–8	Serious Kampuchean (Cambodian) – Vietnamese border clashes.
1978	Mini Great Leap Forward in China.
1978	(December) CC initiates economic reform in China.
1979–84	Decollectivisation of agriculture in China.
1979	Vietnamese invasion of Kampuchea. Chinese invasion of Vietnam. Soviet invasion of Afghanistan. Murder of Amin. Special Economic Zones established in China. Economic crisis in the CMEA countries. Revolution in Iran.
1979–80	Oil prices develop satisfactorily for exporters.
1979–83	Economic stagnation in the USSR.
1980	Widespread strikes in Poland. Polish Government formally accepts independent trade unions.
1981	(December) Martial law declared in Poland.

1982   Run on Hungarian central bank by foreign banks. Mexico unable to meet its external commitments. International debt crisis. Bottom of recession in capitalist world.

1984   (October) Chinese economic reform extended to the towns.

1984–5   Economic boom in China.

1985   Failure of monetary reform in Vietnam.

1985–   Gorbachev's *perestroika* in the USSR.

1987   Individual economic activity and non-agricultural cooperatives permitted in the USSR. 'Resignation' of Hu Yaobang as General Secretary of the CCP. Campaign against 'bourgeois liberalisation' in China.

1987   (June) Soviet CC approves new Law on the State Enterprise.

1987   (October) 13th CCP Congress.

1988   (January) New Soviet Law on the State Enterprise begins to come into effect.
          (June) 19th CPSU Conference.
          (July) New Soviet Law on Cooperatives comes into effect.

1

THE NEED FOR PLANNING

The reasons for state control and direction of the economy can conveniently be considered from the standpoint of two schools of thought and one historical process.

The liberal view

An outstanding early representative of this school was Mandeville. The conclusion of his famous (1724) was that the book had demonstrated:

that neither the friendly qualities and kind affections that are natural to man, nor the real virtues he is capable of acquiring by reason and self-denial, are the foundations of society: but that what we call evil in the world, moral as well as natural, is the grand principle that makes us sociable creatures, the solid basis, the life and support of all trades and employments without exception: that there we must look for the true origin of all arts and sciences, and that the moment evil ceases the society must be spoiled, if not totally dissolved.

He expressed this thought both in prose and also in verse, in his well-known description of the hive, analogous to human society:

> There every part was full of vice
> Yet the whole mass a paradise.
> Such were the blessings of that state
> Their crimes conspired to make them great.

This idea played a major role in Adam Smith's great work *The Wealth of Nations*. There is the well-known passage in which Smith argued that 'It is not from the benevolence of the butcher, the brewer or the baker that we expect our dinner, but from their regard to their own interest. We address ourselves, not to their humanity but to their self love, and never talk to them of our own necessities but of their advantage.' At another point he refers to the 'invisible hand' which ensures that individuals pursuing their own selfish ends collectively act in a socially rational way. From Adam Smith's day to the present a large part of the teaching of elementary economics has been devoted to explaining and expounding this doctrine of the strange virtues of private vices. Traditionally students have come along to lectures on economics concerned about the great problems of poverty, inequality and unemployment. Their teachers have taught them to readjust their vision, and instead of these evils to see in the market system a socially rational process for combining individually rational decisions into socially rational ones.

En passant, one should note that the process by which the acceptance of a new theory replaces what one previously 'saw' by an entirely new set of observations, is not the absurdity that it might seem at first sight. After all, a central part of Marxist economics is concerned with replacing one vision of the labour contract by another. Before studying the Labour theory of Value one may 'observe' a mutually beneficial process whereby a worker obtains a wage in exchange for working a certain number of hours for an employer. After one has learned the Labour Theory of Value one 'sees' a process of exploitation whereby the worker sells his labour power and the employer obtains surplus value. Such a transformation may seem odd to a vulgar positivist, who imagines that there exist so called 'facts' independent of our theories. On the other hand, to someone who accepts the doctrine of Sextus Empiricus and of Popper according to which 'there are no empirical propositions, only theoretical ones' it seems entirely normal.

In some quarters there appears to lurk the view that Ricardo was some kind of 'progressive', a proto Marx. After all, we are told, his theory of the rate of profit is different from, and free from the justificationist bias of, later writers. In addition his theory recognised the class nature of capitalist society and the reality and importance of class conflict. All this is undoubtedly true. It is very important to bear in mind, however, that this same David Ricardo fully accepted Adam Smith's doctrine of the invisible hand. If one looks, for example, at the chapter on wages in *The Principles* one finds the proposition that, 'Like all other contracts, wages should be left to the free and fair competition of the market, and should never be controlled by the interference of the legislature.' This certainly contrasts dramatically with Marx's analysis of the 10 hours Act!

In the late nineteenth century the classical economists, with their concern with growth and distribution, gave way to the neoclassical economists, with their concern with the efficient allocation of resources and the mathematical demonstration both of the invisible hand doctrine and also of the 'exceptions' to it.[1] One of the most eminent of the neoclassical economists was Walras, whose views on this matter are clearly set out in the following extract from *The principles of pure economics* (1954 edn p. 255 italics added):

Production in a market ruled by free competition is an operation by which services can be combined and converted into products of such a nature and in such quantities as will give the greatest possible satisfaction of wants within the limits of the double condition, that each service and each product have only one price in the market, namely that price at which the quantity supplied is equal to the quantity demanded, and that the selling price of the products be equal to the cost of the services employed in making them.

Besides their 'rigorous', mathematical 'proof', of the invisible hand doctrine, the masters of the neoclassical school, such as Marshall and Pigou, were, of course, very much concerned with the 'exceptions' to the general rule that leaving things to the market is best, such as monopoly, increasing returns, consumer's surplus and externalities.

In the 1930s there took place, under the impact of the great depression, what in Cambridge England is known as the 'Keynesian revolution'.[2] The incorporation of Keynes' teaching within the accepted corpus of economic theory led to the well-known division of economic theory into two halves, *micro* and *macro*. What did *micro* economics teach? That the price mechanism leads to the efficient allocation of resources, of course. What did *macro* economics teach? That unless the Government pursues just the right sort of stabilisation policy either we will have serious unemployment, or serious inflation, or possibly both together. The curious coexistence of *micro* and *macro* reflected a society in which the overall regulation of the economy was in the hands of the state, whereas concrete production and distribution decisions were in the hands of private firms. *Macro* economics performed the technocratic role of discussing some aspects of the central regulation of the economy. *Micro* economics continued the very important ideological role which invisible hand doctrines have had since Adam Smith incorporated Mandeville's paradoxical notion into his powerful analysis of original accumulation. It was used to adjust the vision of those who are so benighted that they 'observed' poverty, inequality and unemployment.

[1] Generations of economics students have been taught both the 'proof' of laissez faire doctrines and the standard list of 'exceptions'. How many of the teachers have explained how it is possible to 'prove' a doctrine which is obviously false?

[2] This phrase is used to describe the emergence and acceptance of the doctrines of Keynes' *General Theory*, although adherents of Hobson, Myrdal, Kalecki and Currie might dispute their originality, and Marxists, or indeed anyone living outside the very cloistered world of Cambridge in the 1920s and 1930s, their 'revolutionary' character.

What is the relationship between *micro* and *macro*? In the early 1950s it was assumed that they could easily be combined into the 'neoclassical synthesis'. This was the belief that if the state ensured macro-economic equilibrium and growth by macro-economic policy, the market mechanism could be relied on to ensure the efficient allocation of resources. Events in the 1960s and 1970s (the increased rate of inflation in the homelands of capitalism, the declining rate of profit, the decline in productivity growth, increased labour militancy, the crisis of the welfare state, the oil price shocks and associated demands for a new international economic order) undermined this faith. On the policy level this led to the abandonment of *macro* by politicians at the end of the 1970s. On the theoretical level it led to numerous publications seeking to relate *micro* and *macro*, or to replace *macro* by other doctrines (monetarism, new classical macro economics, supply side economics).

Besides developments in the material world, there are also three developments in the intellectual world which have emphasised the special case nature of the invisible hand doctrine. I have in mind developments within welfare economics, game theory and general equilibrium analysis.

Welfare economics as developed by writers such as Pigou was largely concerned with analysing the conditions under which the market would, or would not, lead to maximum welfare. It stressed that, under conditions of technological externality, the market solution would normally be non-optimal. The usual conclusion drawn from this was that the state should intervene in order to improve efficiency, via taxes, subsidies and other regulatory devices. It was assumed that whereas market decisions were often socially irrational (e.g. because of externalities) Government decisions, which took account of all costs and benefits, would be socially rational. As Hahn (1974 p. 37) put it, it was concluded that 'the Government can in principle always do as well and often better than the market'. For writers in this tradition, planning is a substitute for the market which is likely to be more successful in achieving the same aims, the maximisation of consumer satisfaction, because it takes account of all the relevant factors (e.g. externalities).[3] Hence the widespread recommendation that decisions on major investment projects should avoid reliance on market prices and purely business rationality and

[3] The unsatisfactory conclusion of Pigovian welfare economics from a liberal standpoint gave rise to a liberal critique of it, to the theory of property rights, and to an economic analysis of the political process (new political economy/public choice theory/economics of politics).

instead make use of shadow prices and take account of social costs and benefits. The market, for writers in this tradition, is important and useful, but only for the production of private goods produced under conditions of constant or increasing costs and without significant externalities. Furthermore, welfare economics revealed a painful dilemma for liberals in the claims that could be made about the market economy. If utility was assumed to be a cardinal magnitude (as nineteenth-century utilitarians normally conceived of it) and if the law of diminishing marginal utility was assumed, then welfare economics provided powerful arguments for redistribution in favour of the poor. On the other hand, if utility were assumed to be ordinal, the socialist dangers latent in welfare economics could be reduced but so would be the claims that could be made about the merits of the market economy. Pareto-optimality is a very *weak* claim – a society in which some people are dying of starvation and others living in luxury may be Pareto-optimal but it is not very attractive.

Von Neumann and Morgenstern in their (1944) opened up a new field of theoretical investigation in economics, game theory.[4] Subsequent research in this field uncovered a far-reaching proposition which, from an invisible hand point of view, appeared a paradox. Under certain circumstances the interaction of isolated individuals, each making individually rational decisions, may result in a situation which is not only socially irrational but also worse for each individual than an alternative which was open to him but which he consciously declined! This proposition is known, for reasons which will appear shortly, as 'The prisoners' dilemma'. The simplest method of explaining it is by way of example.

Consider the following situation. Two suspects have been arrested. The police have enough evidence to ensure that each one would receive on trial a light sentence, e.g. one year. They would very much like, however, to strengthen their case by obtaining confessions. Accordingly they decide to interrogate each prisoner separately and offer him the following deal. If he confesses, they tell him, and the other prisoner does not, then the prisoner who does confess will receive only three months. If he does not confess, and the other prisoner does, then the prisoner who did not confess will get ten years. If he confesses and so does the other, he gets five years. The situation is set out in figure 1.1.

Take prisoner 1 (the situation is symmetrical for both prisoners). If

---

[4] Whereas the 'marginalist revolution' had been concerned with applying seventeenth-century mathematics to economics, the 'von Neumann revolution' applied twentieth-century mathematics to economics.

Figure 1.1 *The prisoners' dilemma*

		Prisoner 2	
		Not confess	Confess
Prisoner 1	Not confess	1 year each	10 years for 1 and 3 months for 2
	Confess	3 months for 1 and 10 years for 2	5 years each

he does not confess, the worst possible outcome for himself would be that he would receive a ten year sentence (in the event that 2 caves in). If he does confess, the worst possible outcome for himself is that he receives a five year sentence (if 2 also confesses). Accordingly, if prisoner 1 is a cautious person who, when making choices, chooses the least bad of the worst possible outcomes, he will confess. The same argument applies to prisoner 2. Accordingly, the outcome will be that each prisoner will receive a five year sentence. In the event, however, that neither prisoner had confessed, each would have received only a one year sentence (because of the lack of evidence). Each decision maker has made an individually rational decision, but as a result both are worse off than if they had both made an alternative decision which each one considered and rejected.

Each individual prisoner would be better off if some force other than his own immediate self-interest (such as Republican loyalty, working-class solidarity, the state, or belief in the golden rule) compelled him not to confess. This 'paradoxical' situation has resulted from a combination of the decision rule adopted (striving to avoid the worst possible outcomes, i.e. the maximin criterion), the fact that the decisions are made in isolation (i.e. that it is a non-cooperative game), and that the total sentence received depends very much on the decisions made (i.e. that it is a non-constant-sum game).

This startling (from an invisible hand point of view) result has been interpreted by Runciman and Sen (1965) as an elucidation of Rousseau's concept of the 'general will' and his idea of the advantages to the members of society of their being 'forced to be free'. Many writers have found Rousseau's concepts absurd or meaningless, but the prisoners' dilemma is a situation in which the general will is clearly distinct from and superior to the outcome that would result from atomistic decision making. Pursuing this line of argument, one can say that, if Mandeville's doctrine is the 'liberal paradox', the prisoners' dilemma is the 'totalitarian paradox'. From this point of view one can say that the difference between 'liberal democracy' and 'totalitarian democracy' (Carr 1945 pp. 5–19, Talmon 1952, 1957 and 1960) is that, while both make the value judgement that social choices ought to be based on individual preferences, liberal democracy assumes that individual preferences are both unconcerned with, and independent of, the choices of other individuals whereas totalitarian democracy assumes that the decision-making process normally corresponds to the 'prisoners' dilemma' situation.[5]

If the second internal intellectual discovery which undermined invisible hand doctrines was in the field of game theory, the third was in the field of general equilibrium analysis, the branch of economics which was widely assumed to have demonstrated in a 'rigorous', 'scientific' way the validity of the assertion by Walras quoted above. During the 1950s and 1960s there was a great deal of research into general equilibrium analysis. According to two leading workers in this field (Arrow and Hahn 1971 p. vii) the purpose of this research was to ascertain the conditions under which Adam Smith's assertion about the invisible hand is valid. The main result of this immense body of research has been to emphasise how very stringent these conditions are. The general equilibrium model focuses attention on trade rather than production; ignores the central role of labour; treats prices as guides to efficient allocation rather than as a reflection of the mode of production, the distribution of the national income and the methods of production; treats competition as a socially rational process for ensuring efficient allocation rather than as a mechanism for fostering technical progress or as a cost-increasing factor; emphasises the equilibrating role of markets and neglects the disequilibrating role of markets; ignores information other than price information; approaches all decision making from the standpoint of maximisation; focuses attention on the combination of individually rational choices into socially rational choices while neglecting the possibility of individually rational choices combining into socially irrational choices; neglects the role of increasing returns in manufacturing; concentrates on auction markets; treats the quantity of resources and

[5] The invisible hand doctrine is not entirely inapplicable in a Prisoners' Dilemma situation. If the game is played an indefinite number of times, if the future weighs heavily with the players, and if each player begins by cooperating and then reciprocates what the other player did (the tit for tat strategy) then the invisible hand will ensure a stable state of cooperation to attain the socially rational outcome. The invisible hand doctrine is inapplicable if the game is played a finite number of times, the future does not weigh heavily or a turn the other cheek strategy is adopted.

the effectiveness with which they are used, rather than the level of effective demand, as the determinants of the level of output; considers an economy without a past and with a certain future; plays down the difference between a barter and a monetary economy ... Indeed, according to Hahn (1974 p. 36), an eminent general equilibrium theorist often referred to as a supporter of 'orthodox' or 'neoclassical' economics, general equilibrium analysis, by emphasising the stringency of the conditions necessary for Mandeville's doctrine to hold, has demonstrated that the Mandeville-Smith world 'cannot serve as a description of an actual economy in which prices are never fully known and economic agents are ceaselessly adjusting to new circumstances'. The same author has also argued in his (1973 p. 330) that 'the vulgarizations of General Equilibrium theory [i.e. the view that General Equilibrium theory is a descriptive theory of the world in which we live and hence that Mandeville's doctrine is valid in our world] which are the substance of most textbooks of economics are both scientifically and politically harmful'. The knock out blow to the idea that general equilibrium analysis was a descriptive theory of an (ideal) economy was given by Weintraub (1985), the author of which was a keen defender of the general equilibrium approach. He argued that the general equilibrium approach was not a descriptive theory but the hard core of a particular research programme. Theories inspired by it might be relevant to particular economic problems, but the idea that a particular economy ought to be assessed by or transformed into the one modelled by what had traditionally been described as general equilibrium theory was shown to be senseless. The result of a century's work in the Walrasian tradition has been that the Mandeville-Smith assertion about market economies has been replaced by a scientific research programme. Scientifically this was an advance but for liberals it was an important ideological retreat.

The Marxist view

The Marxist analysis of capitalism rejects the liberal view that capitalism is a socially rational system. It argues that only a planned socialist economy can be socially rational. It stresses two advantages which a planned socialist economy has over an unplanned capitalist economy. First, the absence of the anarchy of production, and secondly the absence of class conflict. On the first point a classical Marxist text, Bukharin and Preobrazhensky (1969 edn pp. 88–9), argued that

under capitalism the production and distribution of goods is quite unor-
ganized; 'anarchy of production' prevails. What does this mean? It means
that all the capitalist entrepreneurs (or capitalist companies) produce
commodities independently of one another. Instead of society undertaking to
reckon up what it needs and how much of each article, the factory owners
simply produce upon the calculations of what will bring them most profit and
will best enable them to defeat their rivals in the market. The consequence
often is that commodities are produced in excessive quantities ... There is no
sale for them. The workers cannot buy them, for they have not enough
money. Thereupon a crisis ensues. The factories are shut down, and the
workers are turned out into the street. Furthermore, the anarchy of production entails a struggle for the market; each producer wants to entice away
the other's customers, to corner the market. This struggle assumes various
forms: it begins with the competition between two factory owners; it ends in
the world war, wherein the capitalist states wrestle with one another for the
world market. This signifies, not merely that the parts of capitalist society
interfere with one another's working, but that there is a direct conflict
between the constituent parts.

*The first reason, therefore, for the disharmony of capitalist society is the anarchy of
production, which leads to crises, internecine competition, and wars.*

A major achievement of capitalism was that it introduced the idea
of economic rationality or efficiency, the use of given resources to
produce the maximum output, or the achievement of given goals with
minimum effort. In the Marxist view, under capitalism this rationality is confined to individual firms and does not extend to society as a
whole. What is rational for a firm may be irrational for society as a
whole. Individual firms may dismiss workers to raise efficiency and
save costs, regardless of the fact that whether or not they work and
produce an output the workers have a claim on the output of society
(e.g. via unemployment benefits) and that the unemployment may
itself generate social costs (e.g. ill health or riots).

On the second point the same text (pp. 89 and 119–20) explains
that a major

*Reason for the disharmony of capitalist society is to be found in the class structure of that
society.* Considered in its essence, capitalist society is not one society but two
societies; it consists of capitalists, on the one hand, and of workers and poor
peasants, on the other. Between these two classes there is continuous and
irreconcilable enmity; this is what we speak of as the *class war* ... [Under
socialism, on the other hand] there will have ensued the liberation of the vast
quantity of human energy which is now absorbed in the class struggle. Just
think how great is the waste of nervous energy, strength, and labour – upon
the political struggle, upon strikes, revolts and their suppression, trials in the
law-courts, police activities, the State authority, upon the daily effort of the
two hostile classes. The class war now swallows up vast quantities of energy
and material means. In the new system this energy will be liberated; people

will no longer struggle one with another. The liberated energy will be devoted to the work of production.

It is for these two reasons, to overcome the anarchy of production and class struggle characteristic of capitalism, that socialists have traditionally argued for a socialist planned economy. It is hoped in this way to establish a rational society, a society in which social objectives (e.g. full employment, or an equitable distribution of opportunities and income) are achieved in an efficient way.

Experience of socialist planning has shown that the Marxist classics had an oversimplified conception of the functioning of a socialist planned economy. Hence, while retaining the traditional idea that social rationality requires conscious social regulation and control, Marxist-Leninist doctrines about a socialist planned economy have evolved considerably in recent years. This evolution has resulted from developments in both the socialist and capitalist countries, theoretical reflection on those developments and political struggle. This evolution affects such matters as the most efficient organisational forms for agriculture, the merits of the non-state sector, the relationship between state ownership of the means of production and social ownership of the means of production, the importance of feedback mechanisms in economic and political life, the role of prices and markets in a socialist economy, the significance of conflicting social groups in determining economic policy and economic results under socialism, the role of economic planning in a socialist economy and the kind of economic planning appropriate for a socialist economy. At appropriate places later in this book, attention will be drawn to some of these developments in Marxism-Leninism.

The global industrialisation process

The division between advanced and backward countries has been a major feature of the world economy since West European military technology overtook and surpassed that of all other parts of the world in the sixteenth century (Cipolla 1965). This division widened still more after the industrial revolution. The advanced countries were in Western Europe and subsequently in certain overseas territories which they colonised. The backward countries comprised the rest of the globe. Historically speaking, this division is very recent. When Marco Polo visited China, he was most impressed by Chinese civilisation, which manifestly compared extremely favourably with that of mediaeval Western Europe. Within a historically very short period the Europeans used their military superiority to overrun what is now Latin America, and colonised Africa and much of Asia. China probably only escaped colonisation because of rivalries between the potential conquerors.

This predatory behaviour by the advanced countries aroused intense anxiety in the surviving independent countries, the leaders of which realised that if they were to retain their independence it was necessary for them to catch up with the advanced countries. This fact was keenly appreciated by Japan's rulers after the Meiji Revolution and by Russia's rulers during Witte's tenure of office.

This historical background is absolutely indispensable for understanding the nature of economic planning in the state socialist countries. With some exceptions (such as the GDR and the Czech lands) the socialist countries are backward countries, and a major task of their economic institutions and policies has been to facilitate the essential task of catching up with the advanced countries.

The fact that they are backward countries is not an accident but has a definite theoretical explanation. According to classical Marxism, the socialist revolution is a result of the contradictions of capitalist society. Hence, those people and political parties which wished to organise socialist revolutions in precapitalist societies, simply showed their ignorance of the laws of motion of society discovered by Marx. This view was made explicit in Plekhanov's famous polemic with the narodniks in the 1880s. Nevertheless, the Bolsheviks, and all subsequent Communists ultimately came in practice to accept a different view. This was first formulated by Marx in 1850 and repeated by Lenin in 1905.[6] It is the view that Communists should strive for power and build socialism even in countries which were not yet developed capitalist countries, i.e. the theory of the 'permanent revolution'. The significance of this theory, as explained by its chief theorist (Trotsky 1930 p. 15), is that it

demonstrated that the democratic tasks of backward bourgeois nations in our epoch lead to the dictatorship of the proletariat, and that the dictatorship of the proletariat places socialist tasks on the agenda. This was the central idea of the theory. If the traditional view held that the road to proletarian dictatorship ran through a lengthy democratic period, the doctrine of permanent revolution asserted that *for the backward countries the road to democracy leads through the dictatorship of the proletariat.*

This analysis makes it clear that Communist dictatorship is only relevant for backward countries and quite irelevant to the advanced

[6] The classic texts are the *Address of the Central Committee to the Communist League* (1850) and *Two tactics of Social-Democracy in the democratic revolution* (July 1905) and 'Social-Democracy's attitude to the peasant movement' (September 1905).

industrial countries. It also explains why the Euro-Communist parties, which operate in advanced industrial countries, abandoned the aspiration to establish dictatorships of the proletariat. Since they operated in advanced countries which already had democracy, policies advocated for pre-democratic backward countries were absolutely irrelevant. Whether in fact the route advocated by Trotsky leads to the goal he postulated, is considered in chapter 10.

The fact that the state socialist countries are backward countries desperate to catch up, partly explains why it is that, instead of executing the legacy of Marx, of constructing an egalitarian, non-market, society with a truly human organisation of the labour process and an end to the division of labour and the exploitation of man by man, they have in fact been mainly concerned with executing the legacy of Peter the Great and the Meiji Revolution. That is to say, with the accelerated import of foreign techniques in order to preserve national independence, and, in the words of Lenin which have been taken as a motto for this book, of 'using barbarous methods in fighting barbarism'. The reasons why socialist planning has not come about in the advanced industrial countries are twofold. First, in these countries capitalism has led to a huge and historically unprecedented increase in real wages, a development not foreseen by Marx. Secondly, the experience of socialist planning has not appeared superior to that of capitalism. This book considers, implicitly throughout, and explicitly in the final chapter, whether the latter view is in fact correct.

The fact that Soviet economic policy was largely concerned with catching up, for military reasons, was clearly explained by Stalin at the very beginning of socialist planning. In a famous speech delivered in 1931 and reprinted in his (1955b pp. 40–1) he explained the imperative need to press on with rapid industrialisation regardless of the obstacles.

It is sometimes asked whether it is not possible to slow down the tempo somewhat, to put a check on the movement. No, comrades, it is not possible! The tempo must not be reduced! On the contrary, we must increase it as much as is within our powers and possibilities. This is dictated to us by our obligations to the workers and peasants of the USSR. This is dictated to us by our obligations to the working class of the whole world.

To slacken the tempo would mean falling behind. And those who fall behind get beaten. But we do not want to be beaten. No, we refuse to be beaten! One feature of the history of old Russia was the continued beatings she suffered because of her backwardness. She was beaten by the Mongol khans. She was beaten by the Turkish beys. She was beaten by the Swedish feudal lords. She was beaten by the Polish and Lithuanian gentry. She was beaten by the British and French capitalists. She was beaten by the Japanese barons. All beat her – because of her backwardness, because of her military backwardness, cultural backwardness, political backwardness, industrial backwardness, agricultural backwardness. They beat her because to do so was profitable and could be done with impunity. You remember the words of the pre-revolutionary poet: 'You are poor and abundant, mighty and impotent, Mother Russia.' Those gentlemen were quite familiar with the verses of the old poet. They beat her, saying: 'You are abundant', so one can enrich oneself at your expense. They beat her, saying: 'You are poor and impotent', so you can be beaten and plundered with impunity. Such is the law of the exploiters – to beat the backward and weak. It is the jungle law of capitalism. You are backward; you are weak – therefore you are wrong; hence you can be beaten and enslaved. You are mighty – therefore you are right; hence we must be wary of you.

That is why we must no longer lag behind.

In the past we had no fatherland, nor could we have had one. But now that we have overthrown capitalism and power is in our hands, in the hands of the people, we have a fatherland, and we will uphold its independence. Do you want our socialist fatherland to be beaten and to lose its independence? If you do not want this, you must put an end to its backwardness in the shortest possible time and develop a genuine Bolshevik tempo in building up its socialist economy. There is no other way. That is why Lenin said on the eve of the October Revolution: 'Either perish, or overtake and outstrip the advanced capitalist countries.'

We are fifty or a hundred years behind the advanced countries. We must make good this distance in ten years. Either we do it, or we shall go under.

This orientation of socialist planning to the building up of military might is one of the reasons why the USSR and other state socialist countries, unlike Japan, have failed to catch up with the leading capitalist countries in the civilian sector. Military programmes are a burden on the economy. Failure to take full advantage of the opportunities offered by the world market has an adverse effect on growth and the quality of production.

Summary

From the eighteenth century onwards a central feature of liberal economics was the view that a decentralised market economy was bound to be more efficient than a state directed economy. As a result both of developments in the economy and of intellectual developments taking place during the elaboration of the theory, it became clear that market processes and market outcomes have both positive and negative aspects. Marxists have traditionally argued in favour of socialist planning on the grounds that this enables society to over-come both the anarchy of production and the class war inherent in the capitalist mode of production, and to establish a rational mode of production. Existing state socialist economies have to be seen against the background of both liberal and Marxist theories with their analyses of the characteristics of a rational economic system; their historical experiences; and the imperative need to catch up with the most advanced countries, especially in the crucial field of military power.

SUGGESTIONS FOR FURTHER READING

THE LIBERAL VIEW

M. Friedman, *Capitalism and freedom* (Chicago 1977).
F. Hayek, *Law, legislation and liberty* vols. I & II (Chicago 1973 & 1978).

WELFARE ECONOMICS

A. C. Pigou, *Socialism versus capitalism* (London 1937).
W. J. Baumol, *Welfare economics and the theory of the state* (London 1952).
H. van den Doel, *Democracy and welfare economics* (Cambridge 1979).
E. J. Mishan, 'Pangloss on pollution', *The Swedish Journal of Economics* (March 1971), reprinted in P. Bohm & A. V. Kneese (eds.) *The economics of environment* (London 1971).
E. J. Mishan, 'The postwar literature on externalities', *Journal of Economic Literature* (March 1971).
A. K. Sen, 'The moral standing of the market', *Social Philosophy and policy* vol. 2, no. 2 (Spring 1985).

GAME THEORY

R. Axelrod, *The evolution of cooperation* (New York 1984).

GENERAL EQUILIBRIUM ANALYSIS

J. Kornai, *Anti-equilibrium* (Amsterdam 1971).
E. K. Hunt & J. G. Schwartz (eds.), *A critique of economic theory* (London 1972).
E. R. Weintraub, *General equilibrium analysis* (Cambridge 1985).
M. C. Toruno, 'Appraisals and rational reconstructions of general competitive equilibrium theory', *Journal of Economic Issues* vol. XX, no. 1, (March 1988).

THE MARXIST VIEW

F. Engels, *Anti-Dühring* (1st edn 1878) part III, chapter 2.
N. Bukharin & E. Preobrazhensky, *The ABC of Communism* (1st edn 1920, Penguin edn with introduction by E. H. Carr, London 1969).

J. Stalin, *Economic problems of socialism in the USSR* (Moscow 1952).

L. V. Kantorovich, *The best use of economic resources* (Oxford 1965).

N. Ya. Petrakov, *Kiberneticheskie problemy upravleniya ekonomikoi* (Moscow 1974).

T. I. Zaslavskaya, 'Creative activity of the masses: social reserves of growth', *Problems of Economics* vol. XXIX, no. 11, March 1987

Sun Yefang, 'What is the origin of the law of value?', *Social Sciences in China* vol. I, no. 3 (1980).

Xue Muqiao, *China's socialist economy* (2nd edn Beijing 1986).

GLOBAL INDUSTRIALISATION

K. Marx & F. Engels, *The Communist Manifesto* (1st edn 1848) chapter 1.

A. Gerschenkron, *Economic backwardness in historical perspective* (New York 1965).

J. Stalin, 'The tasks of business executives', *Works* vol. 13 (Moscow 1955).

J. Berliner, 'The economics of overtaking and surpassing', in H. Rosovsky (ed.) *Industrialisation in two systems* (New York 1966).

M. Morishima, *Why has Japan 'succeeded'?* (Cambridge 1982).

J. Petras, *Capitalist and socialist crises in the late twentieth century* (Totowa NJ 1984).

S. Gomulka, *Inventive activity, diffusion and the stages of economic growth* (Aarhus 1971).

D. Holloway, *The Soviet Union and the arms race* (New Haven & London 1983).

2

THE TRADITIONAL MODEL[1]

CHARACTERISTICS OF THE TRADITIONAL MODEL

The traditional Soviet planning system was adopted in the USSR in 1930–4 in a haphazard unplanned way as a tool of rapid industrialisation and as a reaction to the economic crisis of 1931–3. Once adopted, however, it remained fundamentally unchanged for decades, although some relatively limited changes did take place. It succeeded the moneyless, fully planned model of 1929–30, which in turn had succeeded the mixed economy model of the 1920s. Under the impact of the great depression in the capitalist world, the widely accepted image of exceptionally rapid economic development in the USSR in the 1930s, and the position of the USSR within the international Communist movement, it became in the 1930s a trivial orthodoxy of the international Communist movement and widely accepted outside it, that this model, combining national economic planning, state ownership of the means of production and rapid economic growth, was a rational and equitable form of economic organisation and represented a more advanced economic system than capitalism. It came to be very widely believed that this model represented the realisation of the Marxist goal of establishing a socialist planned economy, a higher mode of production than capitalism.

After the Second World War the model was adopted throughout

[1] This model is variously described in the literature as 'planned', 'centralised', 'centrally planned', 'centrally managed', 'centralised pluralism', 'decentralised monolithism', 'the bureaucratic economy', 'the command economy', 'the shortage economy' etc. In previous writings I have used the term 'the administrative economy'. Since this model has now been officially rejected in most of the countries which introduced it and remains important mainly as an inheritance from the past which influences the present, a new terminology is necessary emphasising the historical nature of the model. One possibility would have been 'the Stalinist model'. This, however, focuses attention on only a part (1929–53) of the period when the model was applied. Furthermore, some characteristic features of the Stalin period (massive reliance on repression, tying of workers to their place of work, enormous income inequalities) turned out not to be permanent features of the model. Hence the term 'traditional model' has been chosen.

the state socialist world, first in Eastern Europe (1949–53) then in China (1953–7) and then in countries such as Vietnam and Cuba. There were naturally some differences between countries in the application of the model. For example, in Poland agriculture was never predominantly collectivised. Nevertheless, there were some important features of the model common to all these countries. Moreover, aspects of the model (e.g. national economic plans, the stress on state ownership of the means of production, the restrictions on the operation of the price mechanism and a negative attitude to private enterprise) were widely copied throughout the world.

According to the Polish economist Brus (1972 chapter 3) perhaps the most famous and influential of its analysts, the main features of the traditional model are as follows:

1 It is centralised. Practically all decisions (except for individual choice in the fields of consumption and employment) are concentrated on the central level.
2 The hierarchical nature of plans and the vertical links between different parts of the economic apparatus. This means that the whole economy is organised as a complex mono-hierarchical system in which higher organs give orders to lower ones which disaggregate them and pass them on to their inferiors.
3 The imperative nature of the plans. This means that the plans take the form of instructions, binding on the lower organs, rather than, say, forecasts which the enterprises are free to accept or reject as a basis for their decision making (as in so-called indicative planning).
4 The predominance of economic planning and calculation in physical terms. The central role in the system is played by the physical allocation of commodities and the attempts by the planners to ensure that these physical allocations are consistent (i.e. that the planned allocation of each commodity is not incompatible with its planned production).
5 The passive role of money within the state sector. As a result of the predominance of physical allocation, money plays a subsidiary role. For example, to obtain wanted commodities, it is far more important to have an allocation certificate than to have money (which can often be obtained automatically for plan purposes).

In a well-known paper, the US economist Grossman (1963) picked out the following key features of the traditional model:

1 Individual firms produce and employ resources mainly as a result of instructions from higher bodies (this corresponds to Brus's third characteristic).
2 The hierarchical nature of the economy (this corresponds to Brus's second characteristic).
3 The authoritarian political system in which it is embedded.
4 The bulk of the planning work is concerned with ensuring the consistency of the plans.
5 The planning is primarily physical planning (this and the previous feature together correspond to Brus's fourth characteristic).

Conceptualising a complex historical reality as an (institutional) model is inevitably influenced by the author's theoretical background, empirical knowledge and classification used. The present author regards the main features of the traditional model as:

1 state ownership of the means of production,
2 political dictatorship,
3 a mono-hierarchical system,
4 imperative planning,
5 physical planning.

Consider each in turn.

State ownership of the means of production

In the traditional model, the dominant form of ownership is state ownership. The state owns the land and all other natural resources and all the enterprises and their productive assets. Collective ownership (e.g. the property of collective farms) also exists, but plays a subsidiary role and is expected to be temporary. In due course, it is expected to be transformed into the higher form of state ownership. Private property in the means of production (e.g. animals and tools used on the private plots of collective farmers) also persists on a small scale in some sectors, but is frequently subject to official campaigns directed against it (e.g. during the cultural revolution in China). The only fully accepted kind of private property is that in consumption goods, but even here the state sector receives priority. Those who use state owned consumption goods (e.g. housing) normally receive greater benefits from them (because of their higher quality) than those who rely on privately owned consumption goods.

State ownership of the means of production is justified on three grounds. First, that it is necessary for national economic planning.

Secondly, that it is the highest form of social ownership of the means of production. Thirdly, that it enables consumption goods to be allocated in accordance with the deserts principle.

State ownership of the means of production allows the state to allocate resources to key national economic tasks. For example, the state can minimise the resources devoted to financial and other 'non-productive' services,[2] and allocate massive resources to heavy industry, scientific research, education and regional development. In this way it can accelerate growth and create the conditions for overtaking and surpassing the capitalist world. The frittering away of resources in capitalist countries, which fail to mobilise many of the resources available (unemployment, low participation rates, unused capacity) and the high mobilisation of resources under the traditional model, are well known.

The class struggle which according to Marxists is one of the fundamental contradictions of capitalism, is ultimately based, according to Marxism, on the division of society between the owners of the means of production and the proletarians who do not own the means of production and have to sell their labour power to the capitalists. In order to overcome this contradiction, Marxists advocate the socialisation of the means of production. In the traditional model, socialisation is identified primarily with state ownership. As the Constitution of the USSR puts it (articles 10 and 11), 'The foundation of the economic system of the USSR is socialist ownership of the means of production in the form of state property (belonging to all the people) and collective farm-and-co-operative property ... State property, i.e. the common property of the Soviet people, is the principal form of socialist property.'

With state ownership of the means of production and of their products, the state is able to allocate consumer goods in accordance with the contribution that individuals have made to building up the new society. As the widow of the top economic policy maker and administrator in the Polish People's Republic in 1949–56 explained (Toranska 1987 p. 28) in answer to a question about the exceptionally early retirement permitted for a number of formerly prominent party leaders:

[2] In the traditional model national income accounting takes the form of MPS (material product system) rather than SNA (system of national accounts) accounting. The major difference between the two is that the former only includes material production and excludes 'non-productive' services such as medical care, education and (usually) passenger transport. This difference in methodology is one of the reasons why the national income statistics of countries with the traditional model are non-comparable with the national income statistics of countries not applying the model.

It was all according to the law. There are legal provisions for such privileges for activists. After all, socialism is built on the principle of equality before the law, not total equality for everyone. And the law clearly states that those who have rendered services to the Polish People's Republic have certain privileges. They used to be certified by special ID cards; those have gone out of use now, but the custom has been retained. A very appropriate rule.

Asked about the numerous villas enjoyed by Bierut (the Polish leader up to 1956) she replied:

Well, was he supposed to stifle in three rooms? Everyone has to have appropriate living conditions guaranteed according to his rank and burden of responsibility. The time of total equality may come, but not until communism; under socialism you can't have a minister earning and living like a shopkeeper, mainly because then no one would want to be a minister. In socialism everyone should be given not an equal share, but a share according to his deserts.

Political dictatorship

The political system in which the traditional model is embedded is a dictatorship, that is a system in which the ruling group impose their will on society and deal with opposition (real and imaginary) by repression. This dictatorship was originally known as the 'dictatorship of the proletariat'. This formula expressed the idea that it was a dictatorship of the proletariat, by the proletariat, for the proletariat. Although the formula 'dictatorship of the proletariat' was abandoned in the USSR under Khrushchev, along with the Stalinist terror which it had been used to legitimate, it was retained elsewhere. For example, in China it was still orthodox in the mid 1980s.

Since naturally the proletariat as a whole cannot exercise a dictatorship, it must be exercised by some representative body. In the traditional doctrine, that body is the Communist Party. As the Chinese Constitution puts it (article 2, constitutions of 1975 and 1978), 'The Communist Party of China is the core of leadership of the whole Chinese people. The working class exercises leadership over the state through its vanguard, the Communist Party of China.'

The dictatorship has important economic consequences. For one thing, it makes disasters more likely. Because feedback is suppressed by censorship and repression, it is much easier than would otherwise be the case to pursue policies which have disastrous consequences, such as the collectivisation of agriculture. Even when these policies lead to famine, the extent of the famine can be hidden by censorship and control over movement. The leadership has an interest in hiding the extent of the famine so as not to undermine the image of the Glittering Future to which the party is leading society. It is not an accident that the worst famines of the twentieth century have been in China and the USSR (see chapter 4).

More generally, by simultaneously politicising all decisions and eliminating feedback mechanisms, the dictatorship generates specific forms of waste. These are basically of two types. There is waste resulting directly from counter-productive central policies, and waste resulting from unintended (by the leadership) responses by local officials and the population at large to central policies. Examples of the former range from the economic crisis of 1931–3 in the USSR, the economic crisis of 1958–62 in China, and the economic crisis of 1979–82 in Poland, to the decline in labour productivity in Cuba in the 1960s and the poverty and unemployment in Vietnam in the 1970s and 1980s.

An example of the second kind of waste, that resulting from the unintended response of local officials and the population at large to central policies, is provided by the reaction to the 'non-labour incomes' campaign of 1986 in the USSR under Gorbachev. As a result of this, the food and housing situations in a number of Soviet cities worsened. Some local officials began preventing the delivery of food products grown on private plots to the market in order to prevent the earning of 'non-labour incomes'. At the same time, people became afraid to let out spare rooms in their flats in case local officials treated the rent as 'non-labour income'. At the time when the national leaders were making great efforts to improve the food and housing situations, the unintended responses to their own policies were making them worse!

The dictatorship is reflected in socialist planning thought in the important principle of 'partymindedness'. The principle of party-mindedness means that the plan is a concrete expression of party policy. It must look at all problems from a party point of view. This principle is of great importance in all the state socialist countries. A major reason why economic reform proved abortive in the USSR in the 1960s was because, as one State Planning Commission official put it (Krylov 1969), 'in practice it means a weakening of the role of the socialist state and the party of the working class in the management of the economy'. The partymindedness of planning is ensured, *inter alia*, by party control over appointments and promotions. The State Planning Commission (Gosplan in the USSR) itself is under the supervision of the department of planning and finance organs of the

CC. Other departments of the CC (e.g. the department of heavy industry, the department of defence industry, the agricultural department, etc.) supervise particular branches of the economy, controlling in particular appointments and policy. Party control over appointments in the economic apparatus is simply one example of the *nomenklatura* system (Voslensky 1984) at work.[3]

The principle of partymindedness is also very important for published economic statistics. For example, in 1969–85 the Soviet statistical handbooks omitted data on prices on the collective farm markets (which previously had been regularly published). The intention, presumably, was to hide the significant degree of inflation which the USSR experienced in the Brezhnev period. Similarly, publication of Soviet infant mortality statistics stopped in 1974 and resumed again only in 1986. The reason, clearly, was that Soviet infant mortality in the late Brezhnev period was rising and that to have acknowledged this in published official statistics would have violated the principle of partymindedness. Similarly, in Poland in the 1970s the Government sometimes deliberately falsified statistics to mislead the public. Such lies included exaggerating the number of dwellings completed in a year by including in the annual figures also the number of dwellings to be completed in the first quarter of the following year, deliberately giving a lower figure for investment than the actual investment costs, or falsely publishing a higher figure for coal exports in a year than actually exported in that year by also including exports in January of the following year. Similarly, Chinese statistical practice has made extensive use of stratified non-random sampling which generates unrepresentative data which has been used to illustrate the success of this or that current official policy (Travers 1982). While useful for official propaganda, the data thus derived should not be confused with that derived from a proper random sampling procedure.

A mono-hierarchical system

The result of combining state ownership of the means of production with political dictatorship is to create a 'mono-hierarchical' system. This term describes an economy in which the various economic

[3] The *nomenklatura* is both the list of appointments in the gift of a particular party committee and of the persons qualified to fill them. By '*nomenklatura* system' is meant the system in which all significant posts are filled by the appropriate party committee by persons on the list of the appropriate party committee, regardless of whether or not the post concerned is formally appointive or elective. The *nomenklatura* system is one of the most important ways by which the party implements the dictatorship.

hierarchies (industrial, labour, financial, supply, banking, internal and external trade, investment, agricultural, technical progress, national, regional and local) are ultimately all responsible to the party leadership. The central economic bodies may be numerous and disunited, the local bodies numerous and at odds with each other and with the central bodies, but ultimately authority flows from the centre to the periphery, in accordance with the principle of 'democratic centralism'.

The mono-hierarchical nature of the traditional model means that vertical relations of hierarchy and subordination dominate horizontal relations of contract and exchange. Hence the (normal) absence of competition and the dominant role played by the fulfilment of evaluation criteria imposed from above, rather than use criteria insisted on by customers.

Imperative planning

Planning in the traditional model primarily takes the form of orders, binding on the recipient, as in any army or civil service. Characterising planning in the traditional model, Stalin long ago observed that 'our plans are not forecasts but instructions'. Whereas in some models planning takes on an 'indicative' form, or is merely political or external (e.g. to impress aid givers), in the traditional state socialist model it takes the form of instructions binding on the participants in the economy. The characteristic feature of the 'planned economy' in the traditional model is that economic activity proceeds in accordance with instructions from above. This identifies planning with the bureaucratic allocation of resources.

In the traditional model, the plans are largely long lists of output targets. They are operationalised by two procedures, listing the corresponding investment projects to be completed, continued or initiated, and 'breaking down' the plan to individual enterprises (via intermediate organisations such as the ministries). 'Breaking down' the plan means disaggregating the plan to link national targets with the productive activity of individual enterprises. These lists and the 'broken down' production targets become instructions binding on the relevant bodies. (In accordance with the important 'address principle', in the traditional model to each plan target there corresponds an organisation or address, responsible for carrying it out. This ensures the imperative character of the plans.)

Physical planning

Planning in the traditional model is primarily an activity that takes place in physical terms. That is, it is concerned with allocating tonnes of this, cubic metres of that, etc. rather than being primarily concerned with allocating financial flows. Most planning work is concerned with calculating material balances, that is balance sheets in physical units of particular goods, in order to try and ensure a balance between the need and availability of particular goods (Levine 1959, Ellman 1973 chapter 1). There are material balances for the production and distribution plans, labour balances for the labour plan, fuel-energy balances for the plans of the energy sector and financial balances for the financial plan. A major innovation in Soviet planning in the 1960s involved the introduction into planning work of a new type of integrated balances, input-output.

In the traditional model, the economy is partially demonetised. Although money exists, and there are financial flows corresponding to the real flows, the former are subordinated to the latter. For all economic actors, it is far more important to obtain an allocation certificate for scarce inputs than money. Money can always be obtained from the budget or banking system for planned production, but planned production is often impossible, or gravely hampered, by shortages of necessary physical inputs. Similarly, for individual consumers, the possession of money, although important, is far from sufficient to acquire desirable consumer goods. The latter (e.g. housing) are often rationed and allocated by official organs in accordance with bureaucratic criteria (e.g. place in the hierarchy) quite independent of the possession of money. Similarly, in the traditional model, there are many 'planned loss' enterprises. These are enterprises which are expected by the plan to make losses. These losses are automatically covered by the state budget and have no adverse economic effects on the enterprise. As Stalin explained to the first US workers' delegation (1927), 'the extraction of profit is neither an aim nor a motive force of our socialist industry'. Reverting to this question after two decades of experience of the traditional model, he stated in *Economic problems of socialism in the USSR* (1952) that in a socialist planned economy profitability must be considered 'not from the standpoint of individual plants or industries, and not over a period of one year, but from the standpoint of the entire national economy and over a period of, say, ten or fifteen years'.

According to the traditional doctrine, the survival of money and financial flows in a socialist planned economy is something of an anomaly which will in due course disappear. Stalin assumed that in the higher phase of communism, when collective ownership would have disappeared and state ownership become universal, goods would circulate on the basis of direct product exchange (i.e. physical exchange without the intermediation of money).

WASTE AND UNPLANNED ACTIVITY IN THE TRADITIONAL MODEL

There is an extensive literature, with important contributions by Liberman (1950), Berliner (1957), Kornai (1959), Bergson (1964), Xue Muqiao (1981 and 1986) and Grossman (1988), describing and explaining the waste and unplanned activity in the traditional model. Perhaps the most important issues dealt with in this literature are: the dictatorship over needs, the difficulties with innovation, the long construction and running in periods, the instability of the plans, the second economy and the third economy.

The dictatorship over needs

Experience has shown that, instead of the traditional model ensuring the fulfilment of social needs, the traditional model prevents the satisfaction of social needs. The resulting situation has been described by Fehér, Heller and Markus (1983) as a 'dictatorship over needs'. Similarly, N. N. Slyunkov, a Soviet CC Secretary, has described it as 'dictation by the producer to the consumer' (*Pravda*, 13 June 1987). This situation results from a number of factors.

Bureaucratisation

Both empirical and theoretical analysis emphasises the role of bureaucratisation under socialism. On the basis of the experience of War Communism, Kritsman (1924 p. 143) argued that '*The basic distortion* of the internal relations of the proletarian-natural economic system *was* its *bureaucratism*'. Similarly, in the course of his well-known theoretical analysis of the economics of socialism, Lange (1937) stated that 'the real danger of socialism is that of a bureaucratisation of economic life, and not the impossibility of coping with the problem of allocation of resources'.

In the traditional model, bureaucratic considerations (risk aversion, quarterly plan fulfilment, bounded rationality, subservience to superiors) take precedence over economic considerations (costs, markets). Hence cost control, technical progress and customers, suffer. As the German author Bahro (1978 p. 222) argued, 'the essential obstacle to economic dynamism [in the traditional model] consists in the fact that right down to the factory director and head of department, the laws of bureaucratic behaviour time and time again take precedence over economic rationality, which in *this* connection, at least, would be the higher criterion'.

Personal consumption problems

A very important feature of the traditional model is its adverse effect on personal consumption. Aspects of this are:

widespread shortages and queues. The long time devoted to shop-ping, the intermittent supply of basic consumer goods and the long waiting lists for durables such as housing and cars are notorious features of the traditional model,

a very limited assortment of goods and services, with many imported goods and some very important services, such as repairs to housing and consumer durables, being almost unavailable in the legal economy,

poor quality and availability of food products,

poor quality of manufactured consumer goods, and

slow introduction of new consumer goods.

These topics are discussed further in chapter 8.

Production for plan rather than use

In a system of imperative planning, the main job of the enterprises is to carry out orders from above. It is for this that they are judged. Whether or not the output meets the wishes of consumers is for the enterprises a matter of indifference. Hence under the traditional model there is often a substantial gulf between the volume of output and its usefulness. The discrepancy between the impressive pro-duction figures and the meagre volume of consumer satisfaction derived from them, had become a very sore point in the USSR by the 1980s. As Abalkin (1987 p. 14), the Director of the Institute of Economics of the USSR Academy of Sciences, very sensibly observed:

According to the data for 1985 we produced 788 million pairs of shoes and the USA, West Germany, England and France taken together, 700 million pairs. Moreover, their population is one and a half times that of the USSR. We do not need so many shoes. Furthermore, the kind of shoes that many enterprises are currently producing, we also do not need. There is no need to plan the output of shoes. Let the enterprises produce those shoes, which the consumers need, and which they order via the wholesale trade.

The fact that state control over the economy can cause a divergence between what is produced and what is actually needed, is not a twentieth-century discovery. It was already well known two thousand years ago. It was for example discussed in the famous *Discourses on salt and iron* which record a debate in the first century BC in China on the state monopolies of salt and iron. In this debate, popular representatives pointed out that the state monopoly of iron led to a situation in which, instead of producing iron tools suitable for the situation in particular places, only standard tools were produced. These were often not suitable for farming needs. They argued for the abolition of the state monopoly so as to ensure the provision of suitable tools at reasonable prices.

Wasteful criteria

The fact that the traditional model is one of physical planning means that the assessment of the work done by enterprises often depends on their meeting physical plan targets, e.g. output measured in tons. These assessment criteria often stimulate waste (Nove 1958). For example, a Chinese textile enterprise, for which quality, defined as the absence of imperfections, was an important target, achieved this very efficiently by cutting out all imperfections so that every length of cloth was dotted with holes (Donnithorne 1967, p. 160)! Waste is also generated when aggregated criteria in prices are used, e.g. gross output. For example, the central planners, concerned with maximising output, often ignore the cost of output and its usefulness. Although the USSR has overtaken the USA in the production of a number of important intermediate goods, they are often produced less efficiently, and the volume of final products derived from them is often lower, than in the USA. In some of the experiments which preceded the Kosygin reform it was found (Khanin 1967) that instructing clothing factories to produce according to the requirements of shops led to a fall in the growth rate. This did not signify that the experiments were a failure. It simply resulted from the fact that, when given a choice, the shops ordered a wider assortment of clothes than the planners would have ordered. As a result production runs were shorter and there was less 'output' (measured in constant prices rather than in units measuring consumer satisfaction).

The ministries are primarily concerned with plan fulfilment and hence sometimes ignore proposals which would raise national economic efficiency but which might jeopardise a ministry's plan, such as the construction of specialised enterprises to provide low-cost components for enterprises belonging to several ministries (Selyunin 1968). The enterprises are primarily concerned with securing a low plan for the production of goods with which they are familiar. They have little incentive to pay attention to the needs of customers, to innovate or to ensure the most efficient use of the resources which they have. Xue Muqiao (1981 p. 198) has explained, for example, that in China:

> Many enterprises produced large amounts of sub-standard products because they devoted exclusive attention to quantity and neglected quality. In the last two decades, the quality of many products has not improved but worsened. Although the targets for output and output value were over-fulfilled, great losses were caused to the state and the people. For instance, the quality of tractors was so poor that they often lay idle after the peasants spent much of their savings to buy them. The cost of farm production rose, while agricultural labour productivity remained the same.

Slack plans

A notorious feature of the traditional model is the tendency by enterprises to strive for a slack plan, i.e. a plan which provides for the production of less output than possible and/or the use of more inputs than necessary. Socialism is supposed to have eliminated the contradiction between the productive forces and the productive relations which Marxists consider to be the reason for the inevitable downfall of capitalism. The fact is, however, that under state socialism too there is a conflict between the socio-economic system and the development of production. This has long been regarded as undesirable by many Soviet economists, and a major feature of the Kosygin reform of 1966–9 was a new incentive system designed to motivate enterprises to aim at taut plans. The Kosygin reform failed in this respect because of the prevalence of administrative uncertainty, the system of incentives for managerial personnel and the risk-averting behaviour of Soviet managers.

Rationing of producer goods

The waste which results from the rationing of producer goods was already familiar to observers of War Commission. Kritsman (1924 pp. 102–3) argued that both capitalism and the administrative economy are inefficient, but that their inefficiency takes different forms. Whereas under capitalism there are difficulties with sales and the accumulation of stocks with producers, under the administrative economy there are difficulties with supply and the accumulation of stocks with users.

No surpluses can accumulate with the producers, since the product is not superfluous in an absolute sense; as a matter of fact, if such a surplus is formed, it will be immediately allocated when the first demand for it is announced. The multitude of independent allocating organisations, however, unavoidably causes situations in which, for example, an organ demanding paraffin lamps gets all the necessary lamp-chimneys (100 per cent) from one economic organisation, but only 60% of the holders from another, 50% of the wicks from a third one, and only 20% of the burners from a fourth. In this case 4/5 of the lamp chimneys, 2/3 of the holders and 3/5 of the wicks will prove to be superfluous and lie wasted. A month later, the burners, so much needed by the first user, will lie unused with another organ needing paraffin lamps. Similar cases are unavoidable with fuels, raw materials, and various complementary materials.

This type of waste persisted throughout the whole history of the traditional model, in all the countries in which it was introduced. For example, a Soviet estimate (*Khozyaistvennaya* 1968 p. 36) suggested that in the mid 1960s 25 percent of all working time in the USSR was being lost through difficulties with the supply system.

The effects of the rationing of producer and consumer goods are considered further in chapter 8.

The residual principle

An important aspect of the traditional model is the leading links principle. This means that, at any given moment, the efforts of the planners, and the allocation of material and human resources, are directed to achieving the plan goals in certain priority sectors, the leading links. Precisely which sectors are the leading links naturally varies over time. In the USSR, in the 1930s the leading links were iron and steel and heavy engineering, in the 1940s armaments, in the 1950s steel, coal and oil, in the 1960s chemicals and natural gas, and in the 1970s and 1980s agriculture and electronics.

The mirror image of the leading links principle is the residual principle. This means that the non-priority sectors have to take what is left after the leading links have had what they require. The residual principle tends to have a harmful effect on services crucial for the welfare of the population, such as medical care, housing and retail trade.

Misallocating prices

In the traditional model, prices are determined by state organs on a cost-plus basis, and are fixed for lengthy periods. Prices are important not as guides for enterprise decision making but as a means of aggregating physical data and for financial control. This system is a logical part of the traditional model, but it is not conducive to the efficient allocation of resources, technical progress and quick reaction to changing circumstances. It encourages the use of expensive inputs to produce goods the enterprises are familiar with. It discourages cost reduction, innovation, adaptation to new developments and the satisfaction of consumer needs. There is an extensive literature giving examples of this and analysing their causes (Nove 1968 chapters 4 and 8, Bergson 1964 chapters 4 and 8, Zielinski 1967, Berliner 1976 part II).

The prices of consumer goods are normally fixed in a way that contributes to the frequent state of widespread shortages which lowers real incomes below the level which would be technically attainable (see chapter 8).

Difficulties with innovation

It is well known that the state socialist countries have experienced rapid technical progress over long periods of time. They have shown rates of increase of labour productivity and changes in assortment that compare not unfavourably with those of the leading industrial economy of the nineteenth century (the UK) and of the twentieth century (the USA). On the other hand, this has required very high rates of investment (by international standards), has not been unique in the post Second World War world and did not prevent economic stagnation in the CMEA (and in some CMEA member states economic crisis) in the early 1980s. Furthermore they have tended to copy, rather than originate, new technology, and in the 1960s, 1970s and 1980s had great trouble in modernising the product-mix of existing plants, and more generally, in reducing the technology gap between themselves and the leading capitalist countries. According to a classic study (Amann 1977), despite the great emphasis placed in Soviet planning on technical progress, the technological gap between the USSR and the leading capitalist countries in the mid 1970s was substantial and had not diminished in the previous 15–20 years. By the mid 1980s, the slowdown in Soviet growth, combined with the rapid technical progress in the West, had led to the problem of reducing the technology gap being replaced with the problem of preventing the technology gap widening.

Factors hindering innovation have included, the hostility of the authorities to unrestricted intercourse with the capitalist world and especially to the free movement of people, the state monopoly of foreign trade, the risk-averting behaviour generated by the system,

Table 2.1 *Time taken to construct thermal electricity stations completed in the USSR in 1959–62*

Period of construction (years)	No of thermal stations
5– 7	8
8–10	8
11–13	8
14–15	2

Source: Krasovsky (1967), p. 52.

the centralisation of initiatives, the emphasis on economies of scale even where this conflicts with rapid changes in assortment, the separation of research from development, the stress on cutting costs of the producers of equipment rather than on service to customers, and the emphasis at all levels of the economic hierarchy on quantitative plan fulfilment (Berliner 1976).

Long construction and running-in periods

A well-known and much-discussed aspect of the investment process in countries with the traditional model is that the construction and running-in periods of new plants tend to be excessive both relative to planned periods and also relative to international experience. An example is set out in table 2.1. Other examples are given in chapter 5.

   These lengthy construction periods are one of the results of the system of investment planning (see chapter 5).

Instability of the plans

A characteristic feature of enterprise plans which has a severe adverse effect on the work of enterprises, is their instability (Smekhov 1968, Xue Muqiao 1981, p. 118). The operational (quarterly and annual) plans of enterprises are often altered repeatedly during the course of the 'planned' period, sometimes even retrospectively. The instability of the plans is a permanent feature of the 'planned' economies.

The second economy

By the 'second economy' is usually understood that part of the economy resulting from private production and/or (re)distribution.

Attempts have sometimes been made to abolish it (e.g. the USSR in 1918–21 and 1930, China in 1958–9 and the Cultural Revolution, Kampuchea in the late 1970s). The results of such attempts have always been very adverse for popular welfare and have always ultimately been abandoned. Even when part of this sector (e.g. the private plots of collective farmers) is legalised, other parts often remain criminalised. The extent of criminalisation varies over time and between countries. The long-run tendency has been to reduce the area of criminalisation. The second economy provides goods, services and income for the population which the state sector is unable, or unwilling, to provide.

The third economy

By the 'third economy' is understood transactions between state enterprises which are unplanned but which are entered into in order to achieve the goals of the plan. Such transactions arise because it is often impossible to fulfil an enterprise plan with the planned (or actually available) inputs. This sector is extensive in all countries with the traditional model. It is normally tolerated by the authorities (indeed an important role in it is often played by local party officials) since otherwise the economy could scarcely function.

CAUSES OF WASTE AND UNPLANNED ACTIVITY IN THE TRADITIONAL MODEL

The fundamental cause of the waste, inefficiency and 'anarchic' phenomena described on pp. 26–33, in the author's opinion, is a theoretical one. It is the inadequate nature of the theory of rational social decision making implicit in the traditional Marxist-Leninist theory of planning. In the USSR, there is a long tradition of publishing critical articles describing particular examples of waste and blaming them on particular bureaucrats. Experience has shown, however, that the publication of critical articles, or the replacement of one bureaucrat by another, are entirely inadequate to eliminate the problems. The difficulty lies deeper. As E. G. Liberman (1970 p. 74) argued:

We sometimes wrongly, without the necessary bases, blame gosplans, ministries and supply-marketing organisations for misunderstandings, disproportions, losses in production and the violation of the interests of consumers. When one encounters so many people making mistakes, it is necessary to look for the reason not in their individual qualities, but in that system, or more precisely in that 'theory', which conceives of planning as the management from the centre of an all-embracing extremely detailed nomenclature of commodities.

The theory of rational social decision making implicit in the traditional Marxist-Leninist theory of planning is inadequate because it ignores the fundamental factors of partial ignorance,[4] inadequate techniques for data processing and complexity. The limitations of Marxist-Leninist theory are different from, but parallel to, those of neoclassical theory. Marxist-Leninist theory concentrates on vertical links and instructions, while neoclassical theory concentrates on horizontal links and prices. Neither theory, by itself, is adequate as a basis for economic policy, although both theories have much to say that is of interest.

Partial ignorance

If (as in some models) the central authorities had perfect knowledge of the situation throughout the economy (and also adequate techniques for processing it and transmitting the results) then they would be able to calculate efficient plans and issue them to the periphery. In fact, the central authorities are partially ignorant of the situation throughout the economy and this is a major factor explaining the phenomena described on pp. 26–33, which are so unexpected from a traditional Marxist-Leninist point of view.

For example, the problem of slack plans arises from the fact that the necessary information is largely concentrated in the hands of the periphery, and the data available to the centre is heavily dependent on the data transmitted by the periphery. Since the social situation is not one in which the value of selfless work for the good of the community has been widely internalised, the problem of motivating people on the periphery to submit socially rational plan suggestions arises. (The actual social situation is one in which officials strive to avert risk and avoid responsibility, and obedience to instructions from above is highly valued by superiors.) The fact that subordinate members of an administrative hierarchy are more interested in defending their own interests than in the general interest, and the failure of the authorities to reconcile fully the two, is a permanent problem of the traditional model. It derives its importance from the inability of the central authorities to concentrate in their hands all the information necessary for the calculation of efficient plans and from the complexity of the decision-making process (see below).

[4] This term is taken from Loasby (1976). It is preferred to 'uncertainty' because the latter is often used in a restricted, technical, sense in economics.

Another example is the criterion problem, which largely results from the fact that the central authorities lack the information necessary to issue all the enterprises with all-embracing efficient plans and are only able to issue them with certain plan targets and certain criteria.

Likewise, one of the causes of the dictatorship over needs is the partial ignorance of the authorities. In many cases, the conflict between 'production for plan' and 'production for use' results not from any conflict between 'planners' preferences' and 'consumers' preferences', but from the fact that the planners know neither what the consumers prefer nor what the real production possibilities of the enterprises are. That knowledge is concentrated in the hands of the distribution network and the enterprises.

Similarly, one of the reasons why the rationing of producer goods is a cause of inefficiency is because the organisations that do the rationing are ignorant of where the goods would be of most value to the national economy.

An analogous situation exists with respect to misallocating prices. If the planners had sufficient information and time to make socially rational decisions throughout the economy, and enterprises simply carried out their instructions, then the problem of misallocating prices would not exist.

Also, the third economy arises from the fact that the central planners do not possess the detailed knowledge about the stocks, production possibilities and production needs of every enterprise that (together with perfect techniques for data processing) would be necessary to obviate the need for it.

Partial ignorance about the future is the main reason why the repeated attempts to calculate long-term plans have never led to more than the production of documents that speedily became irrelevant. After a short time it became obvious that the main current problems were not those considered in the plan.

The partial ignorance of the planners is of two types. First, ignorance which is created by the planning process. Secondly, ignorance which is unavoidable. The first type of ignorance has three causes. Subordinates may transmit inaccurate information, the process of transmitting information may destroy some of it, and the addressees of information may not receive it. Consider each in turn.

It is well known that in any bureaucracy (Downs 1967 p. 77), 'Each official tends to distort the information he passes upwards to his superiors in the hierarchy. Specifically all types of officials tend to exaggerate data that reflect favourably on themselves and to minimize those that reveal their own shortcomings.' This explains such phenomena as the exaggeration of agricultural output figures in the USSR, which Khrushchev and Gorbachev criticised, and in China during the Great Leap Forward. It also explains the exaggeration of input requirements and the underestimation of output possibilities that is a normal part of the process of planning and counterplanning by which plans are drawn up.

The tendency by officials to distort the information they transmit upwards can be minimised in three ways, by strict supervision, by appropriate incentives, and by avoiding the need for the information. Strict supervision (by the party, a control commission, statistical and financial agencies) is a standard method used in the traditional model to reduce information distortion. It is not without cost. Inappropriate incentive systems (for example for plan fulfilment and overfulfilment) can generate distorted information, and alternative incentive systems are often experimented with. An example of avoiding the need for the information was the partial and experimental replacement of the indent method of determining material requirements by mathematical methods in the USSR in the 1970s.

An example of how the process of transmitting data may destroy some of it is provided by the aggregation problem. During the process of planning there is aggregation by commodities, enterprises and time periods. All three introduce errors (Ellman 1969a). Aggregation errors can be reduced by following suitable aggregation criteria or by enlarging the detail of the plan, but are unlikely ever to be eliminated.

Another example of how socialist planning can create ignorance is provided by what the cognitive theorists of decision making refer to as 'the assumption of a single outcome calculation'. This refers to the fact that the decision-making process often 'does not match the uncertain structure of the environment in which events might take a number of alternative courses. Rather, it imposes an image and works to preserve that image.' Hence, 'Pertinent information may enter the decision-making process or it may be screened out, depending on how it relates to the existing pattern of belief ... That information which is threatening to established belief patterns is not expected to be processed in a fashion wholly dominated by the reality principle' (Steinbruner 1974, p. 123).

The classic example, of course, is Stalin's surprise at the German invasion of 1941, despite the advance information transmitted by Sorge and others, resulting from his screening out of information that threatened an established belief pattern. Similarly, Gomulka was surprised at the outcome of his policy of self-sufficiency in grain, despite warnings by economists, such as Kalecki, of its likely adverse effects (Feiwel 1975 chapter 19).

Not only may decision makers screen out accurate information, but they may also suppress its sources. For example, the reaction of the Polish leadership to discussion of the Five Year Plan 1966–70 was not only to ignore the suggestions made (whose correctness was shown by subsequent events), but also to take 'exceptionally violent action' (Brus 1973, p. 107) against the leading discussant. Similarly, one of the causes of the problems of Soviet agricultural policy between the wars was the screening out of accurate information about, for example, the size of harvests and of marketed output, and of the importance of proper crop rotation, and the suppression of the leading specialists in agricultural statistics and agronomy. More generally, the screening out of information provided by specialists (and sometimes their suppression) because the political leadership distrusted the specialists, regarding them as 'not our people' and politically unreliable, has often been a source of avoidable ignorance in the state socialist countries. It is one of the wastes resulting from the dictatorship.

Once accurate information has been screened out and its purveyors suppressed, reliance may be placed on people who are in fact not competent in the area concerned. As the Hungarian economist Jánossy (1970) noted, the Stalin era was characterised not only by suspicion of specialists but also by confidence in non-specialists. For example, in working out investment plans, reliance was often placed on engineers not competent in the area concerned, let alone in calculating and evaluating costs. As a result some extraordinarily expensive projects were designed and executed.

Moreover, once accurate information has been screened out, and its sources suppressed, an entirely fanciful picture of reality may play a major role in the perception of decision makers. This is especially easy if there is a strict pre-publication censorship of all publications and only material supporting the illusions of decision makers can be published. For example, it is well known that at the end of Stalin's life his policies were having a very negative effect on agriculture in the USSR and throughout Eastern Europe. One reason for this was that, as Khrushchev pointed out in his report to the 20th Congress of the CPSU, 'On the personality cult and its consequences', Stalin's perception of the agricultural situation largely derived from films which portrayed a quite illusory picture of rural prosperity. 'Many films so pictured collective farm life that the tables were bending from the weight of turkeys and geese. Evidently Stalin thought that it was actually so.'

A major feature of developments in the CMEA countries after the death of Stalin was a reduction in the ignorance of decision makers. The publication of statistical data was substantially increased. Numerous scientific research institutes were set up. New, policy-related disciplines such as mathematical economics, sociology and demography grew up. Constraints were generally relaxed, and in some countries and in some periods the use of these new possibilities for policy-related research was actively encouraged. Serious discussions were held on policy questions (for example, the Soviet discussions of the 1960s and 1980s about economic reform).

Nevertheless, the partial ignorance of the decision makers, which they themselves had created, still played a major role in developments, as Polish events dramatically showed. In Poland in 1970–80 attempts to increase the price of food twice had to be withdrawn (December 1970 and June 1976) and twice led to the fall of the party leader (December 1970 and September 1980) as the authorities reacted to popular feeling. Their ignorance about likely popular reactions resulted from the non-existence of institutions for conveying the views of the workers to the leadership,[5] the unwillingness of subordinates to convey unpalatable facts to their superiors, the screening out by decision makers of unpalatable information and the suppression of those who provided it.

Some ignorance is just unavoidable. The nature of economic life is such that the economy is continually being affected by events that were not foreseen when the plan was drawn up. This is particularly obvious with respect to harvest outcomes, innovations,[6] either technological or managerial/organisational, international affairs and demographic factors. This ignorance about the future can be reduced, for example by establishing institutes for research into the

---

[5] According to the transmission belt theory, the function of trade unions is just the opposite. A partial substitute is provided by the state security organs. (By the 'transmission belt theory' is meant the view, explicitly formulated by Stalin, that the function of trade unions in a socialist economy is to serve as a transmission belt which conveys the views of the leadership to the workers.)

[6] An example of the way in which unforeseen technical innovations can prevent socialist planning working smoothly, was given by Zhou Enlai in his report to the 8th Party Congress (1956). He observed of China's economic plans that, 'Even if they are fairly accurate at the moment when they are drawn up, they may be thrown out of balance by unforeseeable factors. For instance, in 1956, when the utilisation rate of the open-hearth and blast furnaces was raised as a result of the introduction of new technology, the supply of ores and coke failed to catch up.' (This type of disruption can be reduced by holding adequate stocks.)

international conjunctural situation or demography, but it can never be eliminated. As Keynes (1937 pp. 213–14) observed,

the expectation of life is only slightly uncertain. The sense in which I am using the term, is that in which the prospect of a European war is uncertain, or the price of copper and the rate of interest twenty years hence, or the obsolescence of a new invention, or the position of private wealth holders in the social system in 1970. About these matters there is no scientific basis on which to form any calculable probability whatever. We simply do not know.

Keynes, of course, drew far-reaching conclusions from the importance of ignorance.

Not only are the central decision makers unavoidably partially ignorant, but the attempts to concentrate all relevant decision making in their hands is costly. It is costly in two ways. First, large numbers of people and considerable specialised equipment are required. Secondly, the erroneous view that social rationality can be attained by calculating a central plan which is then faithfully executed may reduce the responsiveness of the country to new information and hence generate waste. Lerner (1975 p. 214) has argued that

a distinguishing feature of a system with centralised control is a high degree of *rigidity* of the structure, because adaptation, to both random changes and changes caused by the evolution of the system and of the environment, does not take place in the individual parts of the system but only in the central control point. Centralised control permits stabilisation of a system over a long period, suppressing both fluctuations and evolutional changes in the individual parts of the system without reconstructing them. However, in the final analysis, this may be damaging to the system because contradictions between the unchanged structure of a system and changes associated with evolution increase to global dimensions and may require such a radical and sharp reconstruction as would be impossible within the framework of the given structure and would lead to its disintegration.

Similarly Beer (1969 p. 398) has noted that 'adaptation is the crux of planning, although it is not its ostensible object. The ostensible object of planning – a realized event – happens from time to time as a fall-out of the planning process which passes it by. The real object of corporate planning is the continuous adaptation of the enterprise towards continuing survival.' Because of partial ignorance, Loasby (1976 pp. 136–7) has argued that

large organisations, if they are to prosper, may have to reject determinism in favour of free will. Delegation may be used, not to programme choice, but to encourage initiative. Amid the uncertainties and chances of war the initiative, or lack of it, shown by subordinate commanders has often proved decisive. Nelson both demonstrated such initiative as a subordinate and fostered it as a commander; and Slim, rating as 'one of my most helpful generals' the Japanese commander at Kohima who missed a great opportunity by conforming to his orders, praised his own subordinates 'for their ability to act swiftly to take advantage of sudden information or changing circumstances without reference to their superiors'.

The assumption that all relevant data have already been processed at the centre and that the duty of all subordinates is to carry out the plan may simply result in wasteful and socially irrational responses to the changing situation because subordinates are barred from socially rational responses and the centre lacks the information.[7]

It is because of partial ignorance that feedback mechanisms are so important in economic control. They enable the economy to respond smoothly in the event of unforeseen disturbances. Examples of what happens in the absence of adequate feedback mechanisms are the shortages and queues for consumer goods mentioned in the second part of this chapter. These partly result from the absence of the two feedback mechanisms, flexible prices and flexible quantities, which balance supply and demand under capitalism.

A major weakness of the traditional Marxist-Leninist theory of planning (and of the institutions based on that theory) is that it failed to take any account of ignorance, despite its fundamental importance. It also failed to take account of stochastic, as opposed to deterministic, processes. It assumed a perfect knowledge, deterministic world, in which unique perfect plans can be drawn up for the present and the future. In fact, we live in a world in which we are partially ignorant about the past, the present and the future, and in which stochastic processes are important, and our theories, institutions and policies must take account of this. In this respect the traditional Marxist-Leninist theory of planning suffers from the same weakness as

---

[7] As Crozier (1964 p. 190) has observed, the result of the decision-making process which characterises bureaucracies is that the 'People who make the decisions cannot have direct first hand knowledge of the problems they are called upon to solve. On the other hand, the field officers who know these problems can never have the power necessary to adjust, to experiment and to innovate.' The Maoists were very much concerned with overcoming both these problems. To give the cadres direct first hand knowledge of the problems, they used cadre participation in manual labour and sending down. To give the field officers the necessary power, they transferred to them considerable authority to implement central policies. Participation in manual labour, however, reduced the gains from specialisation and the division of labour and hence reduced output and economic growth. In addition, the national policies pursued by the Maoists were in many respects counter productive (see chapter 4).

traditional neoclassical price theory.[8] This may be ironical, but it is scarcely surprising, since both are nineteenth-century theories which ultimately derive from classical physics, a theory in which ignorance and stochastic processes play no part, and whose success turned it into an extraordinarily influential research programme. The Laplacean demon has long been expelled from physics. It is time to exorcise him from economics too.

Inadequate techniques for data processing

The time has not yet come when the giant computing machines of the Central Planning Board, supplied with all the necessary information by the Central Statistical Office, can take over from where the mechanism of the market system has left off.   W. Leontief (1971 p. 20)

The inadequacy of the techniques used to process such data as are available is the main reason for the instablity of the plans and one of the reasons for the long construction periods. The planning techniques currently used (material balances and input-output) are such that the current plans are always inconsistent (Ellman 1973 chapter 1). As the inconsistencies come to light during the planned period, it is necessary to alter the plan so as to allow the economy to function. A typical example of an inconsistency leading to the alteration of a plan is the impossibility of fulfillilng a plan because of the lack of a necessary input. When the production plan affected is that of a construction site then this naturally delays completion of the project. Although some plan alterations are made formally by the responsible bodies (e.g. the ministries) others are made informally by the affected enterprises (the third economy).

This problem can be dealt with, to some extent, by improving the planning techniques. For example, a major innovation in investment planning in Eastern Europe in 1960–75 was the calculation of optimal investment plans by means of linear programming and related techniques. This was an improvement in planning techniques because the investment plans drawn up in this way were more likely to be feasible. The plans drawn up by the traditional methods were often not feasible, which is one of the explanations of the chronic long

---

[8] The reason why according to Pigovian theory 'the Government can in principle always do as well and often better than the market' (Hahn 1974 p. 37), is because the model it analyses, like the traditional Marxist–Leninist one, is a deterministic one which takes no account of the fundamental factors of partial ignorance, inadequate techniques for data processing and complexity. Hence it is unable to discuss the real advantages of markets from an efficiency point of view, dispersal of initiatives and simplicity. (For examples see Ellman 1969b pp. 342–3.) Empirical work on the technology gap and innovation in Soviet industry has emphasised the importance of dispersal of initiatives for technical progress.

construction periods. This new technique also gave the possibility of doing variant calculations. For example, when the 1976–90 plan was being worked out in the USSR it was decided to compile the optimal plans for the development of each industry in four variants. Two variants differed according to the value used for the norm of investment efficiency, and two according to the volume of consumption assumed. In this way it was possible to study the sensitivity of the optimal location and output decisions to variations in the key parameters. Although this new technique was an improvement on the old ones, its use was far from sufficient to ensure the realisation of efficient investment plans. Problems with the new technique included, the insufficient availability of the necessary data, the unrealistic nature of some of the assumptions (e.g. constant returns to scale), the need to coordinate the calculation of optimal plans for all the industries with each other and with the macro-plan variables, and the fact that the results of the calculations were often not accepted. The improvement of techniques is a continuous process in which further improvements can always be made.

It sometimes happens that major innovations in planning techniques about which high hopes are held, simply fail to achieve the objectives of those who introduce them. For example, during the 1960s, input-output was widely introduced in planning in the European state socialist countries. It was the first mathematical technique to be introduced in socialist planning, and high hopes were held by many about the benefits that would flow from using it. It was widely expected that it would eliminate the problem of inconsistent plans because the use of input-output enables consistent plans to be calculated. In fact, however, this turned out to be erroneous. Input-output, like material balances, is quite unable to resolve the problem of drawing up consistent plans for all the centrally planned commodities. This did not mean that the new technique was useless. On the contrary it turned out to be very useful for the calculation of pre-plan variants and as a source of information. The problem it had been introduced to solve, however, remained unresolved.

Not only may new techniques fail to solve the problems they were introduced to solve, but experiments with them may simply underline the losses caused by the use of administrative methods. A well-known example was provided by the use of linear programming in the USSR in the 1960s to calculate minimum cost transport schemes.[9] Another example was the Soviet programme for automat-

[9] 'This is not a complicated task. Many articles and books have been written and not a few dissertations defended, but almost no freight is shipped by the optimal schemes.

Table 2.2 *The creation of automated management systems in the USSR*

	1971–5	1976–80	1981–5
Number of automated management systems introduced	2,309	2,374	3,565
of which			
automated management systems for enterprises	838	389	296
automated management systems for technological production processes	564	1,306	2,611
automated management systems for territorial organisations	631	454	339
automated management systems for ministries and departments	168	92	60
automated data processing systems	108	133	259

Source: *Narodnoe khozyaistvo SSSR v 1985g* (Moscow 1986) p. 77.

ing planning and management. In order to improve the techniques of central planning an immense research programme was launched in the USSR in the 1970s aimed at establishing a 'nation-wide automated system for the gathering and processing of information for accounting, planning and control of the national economy'.[10] This was intended to be an interconnected system of management information and control systems that would enable the planners to control in an efficient way the entire national economy. It was analogous to the well-known work undertaken by S. Beer in Chile under the *Unidad Popular*.

Experimental work on the development of ASUs[11] in the USSR began in the Eighth Five Year Plan (1966–70). In this period 414 ASUs were introduced in various parts of the economy. In the Brezhnev period massive resources were devoted to the programme as table 2.2 indicates.

By the 1980s, there was widespread scepticism in the USSR about the usefulness of the widespread introduction of ASUs in the economy (Lebita and Orfeev 1984, Kushnirsky 1982 pp. 119–26).

Why? Simply because the transport organisations are given plans based on ton kilometres. One can establish computer centres, and conceive superb algorithms, but nothing will come of it as long as the transport organisations reckon plan fulfilment in ton kilometres.' (Belkin and Birman 1964.)

[10] Known from its Russian initials as OGAS.

[11] ASU is an abbreviation for *Avtomatizirovannaya sistema upravleniya*. The literal translation is 'automated management system'. The equivalent English language concept is 'management information and control system'.

This largely resulted from the failure to achieve the earlier exaggerated hopes about the returns to be obtained from the introduction of
ASUs in the economy. Much of the impetus for the ASU programme
in the Brezhnev period came from the idea that the automation of
planning and management was likely to be an effective alternative to
economic reform as a means of substantially improving economic
efficiency. Experience showed that this was not the case because the
traditional model generated systemic barriers to the widespread
dissemination of technical progress throughout the economy. For
example, as Academician Nesterikhin (1982) pointed out, the USSR
when developing computers has been able to gain the benefits neither
of competition and grass roots initiative nor of the concentration of
resources on national programmes. Centralisation has prevented the
formation of dynamic new enterprises to exploit the ideas and
initiatives of bright engineers and scientists. On the other hand,
centralisation has been unable to prevent 'branch creativeness'.
From the late 1960s to the mid 1970s Soviet industry produced 138
different kinds of computers, mostly repeating the same basic ideas.
Only after the CMEA in 1969 decided upon cooperation in producing the ES series of computers (based largely on the IBM 360) did a
unified technology policy become more of a reality in the USSR.
Although the OGAS entirely failed as an alternative to economic
reform, it was not entirely useless. The ASUs for regulating technological processes were often quite useful.

Complexity

One of the rarely mentioned economic wastes of Soviet-type command
systems has been this destruction of élan vital, a production input for which
there is no close substitute.   V. Holesovsky (1968 p. 547)

Complexity is used here to describe the fact that decision making is
dispersed over numerous individuals and organisations. The dispersal of decision making is a normal and necessary reaction to the
difficulties of collecting and processing in one spot all the data
necessary for rational social decision making. It creates, however,
numerous problems.

   One of the reasons for the inconsistency of the current plans, which
in turn is a major cause of their instability, is precisely that the
planning of production and supply for the entire national economy is
regarded as too complicated for any one organisation, and accordingly is split up among many organisations. This creates numerous
coordination problems (Ellman 1973 pp. 24–5).

Similarly, the fact that in the traditional Soviet planning model, planning in the sense of the compilation of plans and checking up on their fulfilment, was split between two organisations, Gosplan (the State Planning Committee) and TsSU (the Central Statistical Administration) created numerous problems. For example, the introduction of input-output into Soviet planning in the 1960s was hindered by the two organisations using different commodity classifications.

The dispersal of decision making over various organisations ensures that it will be affected by what Downs (1967 p. 216) has termed the Law of Interorganisational Conflict. This states that *every large organisation is in partial conflict with every other social agent it deals with.*

The traditional Marxist-Leninist theory of planning assumes that all the decision makers in an economy form a 'team', that is, a group of persons working together, who have identical goals. In fact the decision makers form a 'coalition', that is, a group of persons working together who have some, but not all, goals in common.[12] An example of the results of this is that subordinate organisations (ministries, local party committees) often begin the construction of plants the building of which is in their interest (because it makes them less vulnerable to the behaviour of other organisations, or increases the output of 'their' product) even though the initiation of such construction projects may slow down other construction projects and hence have a negative effect on national goals. This is a normal phenomenon in countries with the traditional model and is one of the explanations of the chronic long construction periods. Similarly, the second economy partly arises because of the gulf between the goals of the centre and the goals of individual members of society (it is also partly a result of the partial ignorance of the planners about both the detailed needs of the population and the real production possibilities of the enterprises). While the planners are often primarily concerned with major defence and investment projects, individuals are frequently more concerned with their own consumption and that of their family and the prospects for maintaining or increasing it. Hence their activities aimed at achieving these goals (the second economy).

The fact that decision making is dispersed between organisations which have some, but not all, goals in common, creates the need for higher level bodies to guide lower level ones to socially rational decisions, i.e. the criterion problem.

It is because decision makers form a coalition and not a team that

---

[12] This was extensively discussed in the Czechoslovak literature of the 1960s and the Soviet literature of the 1980s.

incentives, both negative and positive, moral and material, play an important motivating role in ensuring the necessary output of work. Of course, there are certain groups of the population that may work well to meet national requirements independently of their own material rewards.

There can be no doubt that on the highest level of Cuban political leadership and economic management, as well as on other levels, including the lower ones of educational, scientific, medical and artistic activities, true inner dedication to the interests of the community does, in fact, prevail. In most instances, moreover, it is combined with a deeply ingrained 'instinct of workmanship'. The Cuban programs of health, education and social welfare seem major accomplishments, especially in view of the limited resources available for investment in them.   (Leontief 1971 p. 22).

Nevertheless, the whole experience of the state socialist world indicates that motivating people to work well to achieve the goals laid down in the national plan is a complex and difficult issue which has not so far been solved in an entirely satisfactory manner anywhere. From an analytical point of view the whole problem only arises because, contrary to traditional Marxist-Leninist expectations, many people, even in economies where the means of production are nationalised and there is a national economic plan, are guided not by an internalised need to fulfil the plan but by other motivations. In other words, they constitute a coalition and not a team. The failure to motivate adequately the labour force was the main cause of the falls in labour productivity in Cuba in the 1960s, in Soviet agriculture in the aftermath of collectivisation and in Chinese agriculture in the aftermath of the Great Leap Forward. In fact, it has been an important source of waste throughout the whole history of state socialism. This question is considered further in chapters 4 and 6.

An important criterion for officials in any organisation is risk aversion. Risk aversion is one of the explanations both of bureaucratisation and of the failure of the incentive system introduced in the Soviet economy as part of the abortive Kosygin reform of 1966–9. Why risk aversion is one of the causes of bureaucratisation has been well described by Downs (1967 p. 100). In order to avoid the risk of making a decision that might subsequently be criticised, officials rely mainly or wholly on the established rules and regulations. This may generate 'red tape' and socially irrational decisions, but it is likely to provide the relevant official with a satisfactory answer in any subsequent inquiry.

As for the failure of the Kosygin reform of 1966–9,

It is easy to see that for risk averting enterprise management, even under the reform, plan underfulfilment and an increase in the plan, are asymmetrical. The loss from each one per cent of underfulfilment (reprimands, inspection by higher bodies, loss of managerial bonuses, reduction in the enterprise incentive funds) is much greater than the gain from each one per cent by which the plan is increased (30% or more of the marginal increments to the enterprise incentive funds and marginal increments to the managerial bonuses). Hence risk aversion is another reason why the new system failed to lead to the universal adoption of taut plans.   (Ellman 1977 p. 33)

The fact that decision making is dispersed among a coalition, whose members are not allowed, in many cases, to charge for their output, is also one of the causes of bureaucratisation. The reason for this is that it brings into operation what Downs (1967 p. 188) has termed the Law of Non-Money pricing. This states that *organisations that cannot charge money for their services must develop non-monetary costs to impose on their clients as a means of rationing their outputs*. Hence, much of the irritating behaviour of bureaucrats often represents a means of rationing their limited resources so that they will be available to those truly anxious to use them. It is precisely because non-market organisations tend to breed bureaucratisation that in the traditional model repeated, but not very successful, efforts are made to strengthen the commercial aspects of the behaviour of production units. For example, there is much stress on commercial accounting or businesslike management (*khozraschet*). Hence, when during the 1970s in the USSR numerous chief administrations of ministries were transformed into industrial associations, they were supposed to make more use of commercial accounting (*khozraschet*) than had the former chief administrations.

Risk aversion and localised criteria are important factors hindering technical progress. Innovation is hindered by a system in which quarterly plan fulfilment is so important and where the external effects of the innovation are of little importance to most decision makers.

The importance of the dispersal of decision making in ensuring that even a state owned non-market economy would not necessarily be socially rational, was familiar already to acute observers of War Communism. More than half a century ago, Kritsman (1924 p. 116) observed that

If we consider the economy as a whole ... we come to the conclusion that in our proletarian-natural economy *exploitation and the market were overcome without overcoming the anarchy of economic life* ... As is well known, commodity economy is anarchic economy. It would, however, be incorrect to conclude from this that a non-commodity economy, i.e. a natural economy, is necessarily a non-anarchical, i.e. a planned, economy . . . For an economy to be anarchic it is necessary and sufficient for there to be a multiplicity of (independent) economic subjects.

With the advantage of over half a century's extra experience we can add to Kritsman's observation the twin points, that the dispersal of decision making is inevitable and permanent (because of partial ignorance and inadequate techniques for processing information) and that an economy with dispersal of decision making may be, but is not necessarily, socially irrational.

IS THE TRADITIONAL MODEL A PLANNED ECONOMY?

The actual course of economic development in countries with the traditional model often differs sharply from that which was planned. This is shown both by the phenomena discussed in the second part of this chapter and by a number of macro-economic developments. For example, neither the Polish depression of 1979–82 nor the Soviet stagnation of 1979–82 were consciously planned. Furthermore, the plans are often only available late, and frequently altered. Hence the question arises, in what sense are the economies of countries with the traditional model 'planned'?

This question has been examined on both a historical and theoretical level. On the historical level, after a very detailed analysis of the actual practice of Soviet planning in the Stalin period, Zaleski (1980 p. 484) concluded that, 'The priority of management over planning has been the dominant feature of the Soviet economy since Stalin's time. Since management is highly centralised, this feature is characteristic of the entire model. Therefore it seems more nearly correct to call the economy "centrally managed" rather than "centrally planned".'

On the theoretical level, a number of authors have argued that 'planning' as it exists in the traditional model is not 'planning' in the Marxist sense. This is an argument which unites New Left (Ticktin 1973, Bettelheim 1986) and New Right (Roberts 1971). It is not planning in the Marxist sense because it is not socially rational (as shown in the second part of this chapter it is actually rather wasteful) the 'anarchy of production' has not been abolished (as shown by the existence of the second and third economies) the actual course of development often diverges from the plans and money and commodities have not been eliminated. The relationship between plan and outcome naturally differs between sectors (the weather and the world market being notoriously 'unplannable') over time and between countries. The fact that there is often a substantial gulf between what is planned and what actually happens is easy to understand from the perspective of systems theory. The plan is only one of the factors (and often not a very important one) in determining outcomes. Other important factors which also help to determine the outcome are the behaviour of the entities in the system (e.g. ministries, enterprises and households) and the economic environment. Hence, from the standpoint of systems theory, there is no reason to expect economic life to be determined solely by the plans.

Realisation of these facts has led to the development of new terms to describe what were formerly (and still are in some circles) referred to as the 'centrally planned economies'. Various authors have used such terms as 'centrally managed', 'centralised pluralism', 'decentralised monolithism', the 'bureaucratic economy', the 'administrative economy', or the 'shortage economy' to describe the system. What is fundamental to this system is not the plan, but the role of the administrative hierarchies at all levels of decision making; the absence of control over decision making by the population, either through the political or economic process; the social order in which it is embedded; its economic problems in the fields of technical progress and the provision of private goods; and its successes in the fields of industrialisation,[13] build up of military might, provision of public goods, full employment (generally) and stability (normally).

The difference between plan and outcome also directs attention to planning not as a means of attaining certain objectives, but as a rationality ritual in the sociological or anthropological sense. As a rationality ritual it has two aspects, giving significance to human life and legitimising the ruling group. It does the first by conveying the illusion that the waste which we think we 'observe' in countries with the traditional model is actually part of a rational system. It does the second by ascribing to the priests (planners, economists and other technicians) and the rulers they serve, the function of bringing order out of chaos, of leading society to the Glittering Future.

[13] Experience in this respect has been mixed. In third world countries such as Vietnam and Cuba, the traditional model entirely failed to lead to industrialisation. Even where industrialisation has been more successful (e.g. the USSR) it has been a rather conservative industrialisation which has lagged behind the leading capitalist countries in many respects. Unlike Japan, none of the state socialist countries have caught up with the industrialised countries of Western Europe and North America. (The GDR *began off* as part of a country which for decades had been one of the leading industrial countries.)

CONCLUSION

The main features of the traditional model are state ownership of the means of production, political dictatorship, a mono-hierarchical system, imperative planning and physical planning. The model exhibits widespread waste, inefficiency and 'anarchy'. The fundamental reason for the waste, inefficiency and 'anarchic' aspects of the traditional model is theoretical, namely the omission from the traditional Marxist-Leninist theory of planning of some essential aspects of reality. They are partial ignorance, inadequate techniques for data processing and complexity. Hence the economies of countries with the traditional model are not 'planned' in the Marxist sense of a socially rational economic system. Nor are they 'planned' in the technocratic sense that the plan alone determines the outcome. An important function of planning is to serve as a rationality ritual.

SUGGESTIONS FOR FURTHER READING

THE TRADITIONAL MODEL

M. Lewin, 'The disappearance of planning in the plan', *Slavic Review* vol. 32, no. 2 (June 1973).

E. Zaleski, *Planning for economic growth in the Soviet Union 1918–32* (Chapel Hill N.C. 1971).

W. Brus, *The market in a socialist economy* (London 1972).

G. Grossman, 'Notes for a theory of the command economy', *Soviet Studies* vol. XV, no. 2 (October 1963).

W. Brus, *Socialist ownership and political systems* (London 1975) pp. 32–62.

WASTE, INEFFICIENCY AND 'ANARCHY' IN THE TRADITIONAL MODEL

J. Kornai, *Overcentralization in economic administration* (London 1959).

A. Nove, 'The problem of success indicators in Soviet industry', *Economica* (1958).

J. Kornai, *Economics of shortage* vols. A & B (Amsterdam 1980).

F. Fehér, A. Heller & G. Markus, *Dictatorship over needs* (Oxford 1983).

W. Brus & T. Kowalik, 'Socialism and development', *Cambridge Journal of Economics* vol. 7, no. 3/4 (September/December 1983).

W. Zafanolli, 'A brief outline of China's second economy', *Asian Survey* vol. XXV, no. 7 (July 1985).

G. Grossman (ed.) *Studies in the second economy of the Communist countries* (Berkeley 1988).

CAUSES OF THE WASTE, INEFFICIENCY AND 'ANARCHY' IN THE TRADITIONAL MODEL

F. Hayek, 'Economics and knowledge', *Economica* vol. IV, no. 13 (February 1937).

F. Hayek, 'The use of knowledge in society', *American Economic Review* vol. XXXV, no. 4 (September 1945).

R. P. Mack, *Planning on uncertainty* (New York 1971).

M. Ellman, *Planning problems in the USSR* (Cambridge 1973) chapter 1.

A. Tretyakova & I. Birman, 'Input-output analysis in the USSR', *Soviet Studies* vol. XXVIII, no. 2 (April 1976).

L. Kantorovich, M. Albegov & V. Bezrukov, 'Towards the wider use of optimizing methods in the national economy', *Problems of Economics* vol. XXIX, no. 10 (February 1987).

M. Ellman, 'Economic calculation in socialist economies', *The new Palgrave: A dictionary of economics* vol. 2 (London 1987).

H. R. van Gunsteren, *The quest for control* (London 1976).

H. Simon, *Administrative behaviour* (3rd edn New York 1976).

A. S. Tannenbaum *et al.*, *Hierarchy in organisations* (San Francisco 1974).

M. Crozier, *The bureaucratic phenomenon* (Chicago 1964).

A. Downs, *Inside bureaucracy* (Boston 1967).

L. Johansen, 'The bargaining society and the inefficiency of bargaining', *Kyklos* vol. XXXII, no. 3 (1979).

IS THE TRADITIONAL MODEL A PLANNED ECONOMY?

E. Zaleski, *Stalinist planning for economic growth, 1933–1952* (Chapel Hill N.C. 1980).

J. H. Wilhelm, 'The Soviet Union has an administered, not a planned, economy', *Soviet Studies* vol. XXXVII, no. 1 (January 1985).

E. Neuberger & W. J. Duffy, *Comparative economic systems: A decision-making approach* (Boston 1976) chapter 2.

H. H. Ticktin, 'Towards a political economy of the USSR', *Critique* 1 (spring 1973).

C. Bettelheim, 'More on the nature of the Soviet system', *Monthly Review* (December 1986).

P. C. Roberts, *Alienation and the Soviet economy* (Albuquerque 1971).

P. Rutland, *The myth of the plan* (London 1985).

3

THE REFORM PROCESS

the destiny of the changes is a result of two conflicting tendencies – to preserve the continuity of the political system, and to enhance the efficiency of the economic system. In effect the shape of the reform becomes inconsistent, reflecting the contradictions in the interactions between politics and economics.

Rychard, A. (1980 p. 70)

INTRODUCTION

The problems of the traditional model have been well known for many years. A variety of strategies have been attempted for overcoming them. The Maoists argued that the way to overcome them was by internal political struggle, decentralisation to local political authorities and self-sufficiency. In the GDR, reliance was placed in the 1970s and 1980s on the reorganisation of industry into vertically integrated combines run by technocrats and with a considerable say in the plan compilation process. In the USSR under Brezhnev, stress was laid on the automation of planning and management, improved planning of technical progress, the reorganisation of industrial management and, in the heyday of detente, import of technology, including turn-key factories. By the late 1980s, however, the predominant reaction to the problems of the traditional model was that of economic reform. By 'economic reform' will be understood a major institutional change that replaces the traditional model of a socialist economy by an alternative model of a socialist economy that combines centralised state decision making with a market mechanism.

The need for economic reform was argued for many years by economists such as Brus (Poland), Kornai (Hungary), Xue Muqiao (China) and Nemchinov, Petrakov, Zaslavskaya, Popov and others (USSR). They argued that the experience with the traditional model showed the need to make the transition to a new model which would combine centralised state decision making with the market mechanism. According to the reformers, the market should be seen

53

not as the negation of planning but as an instrument that could be used to achieve efficiently some of the goals of the plan. The reformers hoped to combine the advantages of socialism (abolition of exploitation, socialisation of the major economic decisions, full employment, price stability, social security, an equitable income distribution, economic growth) with the advantages of the market (abolition of shortages and queues, efficient use of intermediate products, innovation and rapid technical progress, attention to personal consumption). More generally, the reformers hoped to combine the informational, incentive and feedback functions of the market, with overall control by the centre. Not only did these arguments generate a lively economic literature, but in certain periods in certain countries they were very controversial politically. The censorship, dismissal from appointments, and menial jobs were among the instruments used to suppress the reformers.

Economic reform began in Yugoslavia in 1950–1, was discussed in Poland and Hungary in the mid 1950s, introduced in Czechoslovakia in 1967–9, in Hungary from 1968, in China from 1978, and attempted in the USSR in 1966–9 and from 1988. By the late 1980s, the once controversial arguments of the reformers had been partly accepted by the authorities in countries accounting for virtually all the population of the state socialist world.

In view of the important differences between the countries that have embarked on the process of economic reform and their varied experience of the reform process, a short summary of some of the reform experiences is given below.

SOME CASES

Yugoslavia

The traditional model of socialist planning was introduced in Yugoslavia in 1946–50. Its introduction (and also the economic blockade by the Cominform[1] which began to take effect in 1949–50) led to a big increase in investment, particularly in industry, an increase in industrial output, especially of producer goods, a poor performance by agriculture, a modest increase in national income, and a sharp fall in real wages and per capita consumption.

[1] The Cominform (in full: Communist Information Bureau) was created in 1947 and dissolved in 1956. It was a partial successor to the Comintern (in full: Communist International) which had been dissolved in 1943, as an organisation which united, and through which the USSR controlled, the international Communist movement.

The poor results of the traditional model, combined with the need to seek internal social support for a polity under threat from hostile external forces, and to differentiate the Yugoslav economic system from the traditional model prevailing in the Cominform countries, led to radical institutional changes in 1950–1. The scope of central planning was greatly reduced (being mainly confined to investment), a system of workers' self-management was introduced, and the forced collectivisation of agriculture came to an end (see chapter 4). This more decentralised model functioned in approximately 1952–65.

These reforms were quite successful in raising living standards and increasing the legitimacy of the authorities. Nevertheless, this new model experienced both systemic and conjunctural problems. On the systemic level, investment, foreign trade, inflation and employment all gave rise to considerable difficulties. For example, spokesmen for the more developed republics argued that national investment planning meant that they were being made to subsidise less developed regions and that this was undesirable, leading to higher costs and lower returns than would otherwise be the case. Under Yugoslav conditions of significant differences, and often hostility, between republics, transferring authority from the centre to the republics has the effect of defusing tension between the national and local power elites. On the conjunctural level, the Five Year Plan for 1961–5 was unsuccessful. It was abandoned in 1962 in response to the recession of 1961–2. The upswing of 1964 ended in a massive inflation and large balance of payments deficit. The reaction by the leadership to this combination of systemic and conjunctural problems was to implement a new round of economic reforms (often referred to as the 1965 reform). This reform was implemented in 1964–7 and chiefly affected investment and foreign trade, the chief areas of central control retained in the decentralised model.

From 1965 to the early 1970s, Yugoslavia purported to have a largely market economy with only sporadic federal intervention. Referring to the situation in 1970, one well informed observer (Granick 1975 p. 468) wrote that 'the Yugoslav economy is run along Adam Smith lines to a degree which is quite unusual for Europe as a whole'. Other writers, however, suggest that the role of non-market regulation in this period was substantial. It soon became obvious that the post 1965 system too was unable to generate socially rational outcomes. Emigration in search of work abroad grew. Unemployment, inflation and the balance of payments deficit all remained high. Subsequent comparative studies of micro-economic efficiency (Sapir

1980) and macro-economic stability (Burkett 1983) in the periods
before and after the 1965 reform are unfavourable to the latter period.
Flaherty (1982 p. 141) has concluded that, 'Reform, reacting to the
experiences of the 1950s, consistently underestimated the risks of
decentralisation and liberalisation, moving from one non-viable
strategy to another.'

The combination of political (nationalist movements in Croatia
and Kosovo), conjunctural (inflation and balance of payments
deficits) and systemic, problems gave rise to a further round of
institutional changes leading to the adoption of what following
Burkett (1986) may be termed the bargaining model. This model,
which has lasted up to the time of writing, was introduced by
constitutional amendments in 1971 and consolidated by the adoption
of a new constitution in 1974. The most important feature of this
constitution was the far reaching power granted to the six republics
(Serbia, Croatia, Slovenia, Bosnia-Herzegovina, Macedonia and
Montenegro) and two autonomous provinces (Kosovo and Vojvo-
dina). As far as the economy was concerned, the most important
results of the adoption of the new model were twofold.

First, was the fragmentation of the national market into eight
sub-markets, each with its own taxes, foreign exchange system,
investment policy, and regulations of all kinds. At a time when the
EEC was integrating the economies of its member states, and the
CMEA was attempting to implement its programme of economic
integration (see chapter 9), Yugoslavia adopted an economic system
which promoted the economic disintegration of the country. The
result has been wasteful investments (each republic strives to develop
a wide range of industry regardless of likely costs of production), loss
of economies of scale and potential gains from specialisation, and
unnecessary costs (resulting from the need to meet the requirements
of the various republics).

Secondly, was the development of bargaining as the key factor in
economic decision making. Bargaining, of course, existed long before
the early 1970s. What is new about the period since 1971–4 is the
importance it has attained. In an institutional context in which
central authority has been so weakened, bargaining has emerged as
the key mode of decision making. Since each of the eight republics/
provinces has a veto right and cannot be overruled, national decision
making requires a long and difficult process of consensus forming/
horse trading. This naturally is viewed favourably by the political
leadership in each republic/province, which is the main beneficiary
from the system and its chief supporter. Bargaining, however, is a

very inefficient decision making system (Johansen 1979, v.d. Doel 1979 chapter 3).

In the late 1980s, the Yugoslav economy was characterised by a deep economic crisis with both conjunctural and systemic aspects. On the conjunctural level, the most important elements were the foreign debt and the onerous debt service ratio, the high inflation, falling real wages and real consumption, and unemployment. On the systemic level, the main issue was the viability of the bargaining model and, more generally, of all the institutions created in Yugoslavia since the Second World War. The depth of the crisis, the prolonged failure of the authorities to resolve it, and the international importance of the 'Yugoslav model' led to a wide discussion both in Yugoslavia and outside it, as to the cause/s of the crisis.

Some writers ascribed the crisis to the system. For example, Sirc (1979 pp. 242–6) treated the institutions of workers' self-management as being the chief cause. Similarly, Županov (1983) sees the roots of the crisis in the contradiction between the role of a firm in a market economy and institutions partly derived from Marx's notion of an 'association of direct producers'. Similarly, the implication of Burkett (1986) was that the problems were largely a result of the bargaining model and could be cured either by a greater reliance on market forces or more centralisation.

Other writers laid more stress on the policies that have been pursued and on the policy preparation process. For example, analysing the reasons for the failure of the reform of 1965 to achieve the anticipated results in the field of foreign trade, Flaherty (1982 p. 142) concluded that, 'planning and patience were the requirements for success, but reform tended to neglect both in favour of quick remedies from the imposition of the "discipline" of the market'. Similarly, Vacić (1986 p. 17) has stressed that 'an efficient apparatus for the formulation and implementation of current economic policy is needed for timely decision making at the national level'.

Other authors laid the blame on the environment. Some years ago, official spokesmen used to blame the unstable world economy (oil shocks, high real interest rates, low rates of growth of imports by trade partners, etc.). By the mid 1980s, this argument was no longer very convincing, for three reasons. First, Yugoslavia had received substantial advantages from the outside world (remittances from *gastarbeiter*, loans from overseas lenders). Secondly, in precisely the same international environment, numerous countries had done much better than Yugoslavia. Thirdly, to the extent that Yugoslavia was vulnerable to external factors (e.g. high interest rates) this was largely a result of earlier policies of the authorities (e.g. the substantial loans contracted in the 1970s). Unofficial thinkers tended to see the domestic political system as the root cause of the problems. At the Fourth Congress of Yugoslav Political Scientists held in Belgrade in June 1984, there was widespread agreement with the view that (Vacić 1986 pp. 16–17) 'The basic cause, and therefore the main characteristic, of the crisis of Yugoslav society is the crisis in the ideological and political sphere; the economic crisis actually plays the smallest role.' The conclusions drawn from this proposition were various. Some people called for full liberal freedoms and/or an end to the power monopoly of the League of Communists of Yugoslavia and/or greater centralisation, an end to the confederal system and an enhancement of the role of Serbia. One outcome of the latter line of argument would be constitutional amendments (or a new constitution) to strengthen federal decision making and the position of Serbia. A more dramatic outcome would be a military coup on Polish lines.

A particularly important environmental problem for Yugoslavia are the conflicting interests and aspirations of the various nationalities which make up that country. This has played a key role in the evolution of its economic and political system and is a crucial background factor explaining the crisis. Bargaining may be an inefficient decision-making system, but it is at any rate a non-dictatorial method of resolving objectively existing conflicts of interest.

Agreement on *the* cause/s of the crisis is scarcely likely, because of the conflicting interests at stake, the difficulty of proving some and rejecting other propositions about such a multi-faceted phenomenon as a general crisis, and also because of methodological difficulties concerning the meaning of 'cause' in a policy-related subject such as economics.

One of the features of the Yugoslav experience which has given rise to wide international interest is the institution of 'workers' self-management'. This has been officially treated in Yugoslavia as the realisation of an important part of the Marxist legacy. It contributes, according to this interpretation, to the overcoming of alienation by replacing private ownership and the social division of labour by free associations of producers. At one time, this interpretation was also widely repeated outside Yugoslavia. Is this in fact the real significance of 'workers' self-management'? According to a classic study by Granick (1975), the main significance of self-management (i.e. the decentralisation of decision making) under Yugoslav conditions is that it contributes to defusing nationality conflicts. It does this by reducing the role of political factors in decision making and enhancing those of 'purely economic' factors which it is more difficult to blame on the privileged position or illwill of a particular nationality. As far as the role of the workers is concerned, in Granick's interpretation, this is not so much to manage the factories (in fact this is done by the managers) but to legitimise a market economy in a country ruled by a League of Communists with Marxism-Leninism as its official doctrine. Other writers suggest that 'workers' self-management' is a real economic phenomenon whose effects, in some interpretations, are one of the causes of the crisis (e.g. because of the allegedly inflationary tendencies of 'workers' self-management'). The economic effects of 'workers' self-management' under Yugoslav conditions is an interesting and controversial topic which has given rise to extensive empirical work (e.g. Estrin 1984).

Poland

Poland has a rich experience with discussions of economic reform and attempts to introduce economic reform. The discussions have been on a high theoretical level and have had an international impact. This has been due to the outstanding contributions of a number of Polish economists (e.g. Lange, Brus and Kalecki), the relatively weak censorship and the massive popular opposition to the Party and the traditional model.

The first national economic plan which reflected the traditional model was the Six Year Plan 1950–5. It led to a massive increase in investment, especially industrial investment, a massive increase in industrial output, especially of producer goods, a big increase in national income and employment, a modest increase in agricultural output and a significant decline in real wages in 1950–3 (prior to the more pro-consumption policies of 1954–5 initiated by the post-Stalin Soviet leadership).

The unsatisfactory outcome of the Six Year Plan, combined with Khrushchev's report to the 20th Congress of the CPSU 'On the personality cult and its consequences' (February 1956), the workers' revolt in Poznan (June 1956) and the disarray in the ruling elite (Bierut, the Polish leader in the Stalin period, died in March, Gomulka, who had been condemned for 'right wing and nationalistic deviation' in 1948, came to power in October) created in the autumn of 1956 excellent conditions for a radical break with the traditional model. Three radical documents were quickly drafted, published for public discussion and then passed into law. They were, government regulation no. 704 (10 November 1956) providing the state industrial enterprises with substantial autonomy, the Workers' Council Act establishing workers' councils as the managing bodies of enterprises, and the Enterprise Fund Act establishing the principles and rules of profit sharing. The two Acts were formally adopted by the Polish Parliament on 19 November 1956. In addition, the partial collectivisation of agriculture was ended and an accommodation with the Church was arranged. In May 1957 the Economic Council (an official advisory body which had been established in 1956 and which included the leading academic economists) adopted a comprehensive reform blueprint. By this time, however, the wind had veered. As it turned out, the only two lasting results of the 'Polish October' were the partial decollectivisation of agriculture and the recognition of the Church. The economic reform was soon emasculated. (The Economic Council itself was disbanded in 1963 following a steady erosion of its role.)

The most controversial aspect of the reform was the position of the workers' councils. The reason for this was primarily political. It threatened a basic feature (a mono-hierarchical system) of the traditional model. If actually realised, it would have replaced the appointment of managers by party officials and their responsibility to party officials (the *nomenklatura* system) by autonomous firms independent of the party-state apparatus. This would have greatly weakened the power of the party-state apparatus and created an important social group independent of it. Hence in the medium run it might have threatened yet another of the main features of the traditional model, the political dictatorship.

After October 1956, the new party leadership, which shared with its predecessors a commitment to the mono-hierarchical system and the political dictatorship, and whose social basis was formed of groups who benefited from them, quickly 'normalised' the non-agricultural economy. By 1958, the workers' councils had been fully incorporated into the party-state apparatus. As for the documents on decentralising decision making, reducing the role of physical planning and increasing the role of market relations, they remained just documents. The reasons for this are controversial. Some writers (e.g. Nuti 1979 p. 257) stress economic factors and other writers (e.g. Brus 1985a) stress political factors. On the economic level, as Brus points out, in 1954–8 real wages grew rapidly, even without substantial non-agricultural reforms. This naturally undermined the perceived need for them. Furthermore, as Nuti points out, in 1958–9 there was an investment boom in Poland, the extent of which appeared to signal the problems of decentralisation and the control of which appeared to require renewed centralisation. The political factors are quite clear. The Polish party leadership, an unpopular minority group ruling a hostile country, was permanently afraid that liberalisation might get out of control and threaten their power monopoly. As the once prominent party leader J. Berman pointed out, when explaining why the party was so cautious about liberalisation (Toranska 1987 p. 350), 'One can ask whether we were right to use brakes in implementing it, to do it slowly and gradually, to phase through the process of liberalization. But why did we do this? We did it because we were afraid, afraid of what broke out in 1956 and 1980 but could have broken out already in 1954. Poland is a Pandora's box.'

In the early 1960s there was a widespread discussion throughout the CMEA about the limitations of the traditional system and the need for reforms. This found its echo in Poland in the form of limited changes announced in 1964–5. These were also partly a response to the low growth of real wages in the early 1960s. The changes were 'within system' changes rather than a radical reform, and failed to have any significant impact.

The next attempt at reform came in the mid 1970s with the reorganisation of Polish industry into large firms (Nuti 1977). The first of the new units appeared in 1973, but within a couple of years institutional reform had ceased to have any significance. Popular opposition had been bought off with large consumption increases and local officials given a free hand to initiate grandiose investment projects (both paid for by foreign credits).

The legal recognition by the authorities in 1980–1 of the independent trade union 'Solidarity', combined with the rapidly deteriorating economic situation in 1979–82, once more placed economic reform on the political agenda. This despite the fact that the crisis had been primarily caused by the macro-economic policy of the authorities rather than by the traditional model. An official Reform Commission reported in June 1981; its report was adopted by the Party Congress in July 1981 and served as a basis for laws passed in the autumn of 1981. These were supposed to come into force, to the extent that they did not contradict martial law regulations, from January 1982.

What effect did these measures have on the actual running of the economy? It rapidly became obvious that they had not led to a rational synthesis of central planning and market processes. Rather there developed in Poland in the mid 1980s a system which has been

described as one of 'authorisations and bargaining', where (Simatupang 1988)

the center and the enterprises are constantly negotiating over the scope of
'government orders' or 'operational programmes', material supplies, taxes
and grants, subsidies and investment. The results of the negotiating process
are often specific to individual enterprises or industrial sectors. The role of
vertical bargaining and individual norms prevented the emergence of a
built-in market mechanism in the state industrial sector.

Although the traditional model was no longer fully functioning, the
system which did exist was a hybrid which no one had ever
advocated. Attempts by the authorities to implement economic
reforms were hampered by popular opposition to the costs of a
market system (hard work, income insecurity, price increases,
unemployment), Poland's massive foreign debts, the economic
incompetence of the leadership, popular hostility to a military
dictatorship which had presided over a very sharp fall in living
standards and the eternal fear of Polish Communists of going too far
and hence cutting off the branch they were sitting on. For Jaruzelski,
as for Berman, 'Poland is a Pandora's box.' The poor performance of
the hybrid Polish model in terms of living standards and public
services (such as medical care and housing) undermined public
interest in and support for economic reform as a means of overcoming
the problems of 'real socialism'. By the mid 1980s, economic reform
in Poland was being kept alive mainly by external forces, the IMF
(see chapter 9) and Soviet *perestroika*. Among the Polish people
extreme privatisation prevailed. After three decades of talk about
economic reform, what some reformist Communist intellectuals had
striven for in 1956 increasingly appeared unrealistic. The notion that,
under Polish conditions, it was possible to combine the political
dictatorship with extensive reliance on market mechanisms appeared
very naive.

An interesting and important issue raised by Polish experience
concerns the relationship between economic reform and economic
policy. Has too much attention been given in Poland to economic
reform and too little to economic policy? Already in 1957, Kalecki
argued (*Trybuna Ludu* 3 February) that the problems of the Six Year
Plan were not caused primarily by the model but by the excessive and
inefficient investment programme and by the additional defence
expenditure caused by the deteriorating international situation at the
beginning of the 1950s. The traditional model, according to this line
of reasoning, was not an independent *cause* of the problems but a *result*
of the planners trying to finish key investment projects and obtain the

resources necessary for rearmament in an environment of acute shortages of the necessary resources. Hence, the chief way to over-come the problems was to adopt more sensible policies, in particular to reduce the share of investment in the national income and to raise the efficiency of the investment process. The view that too much attention has been given in Poland to economic reform and not enough to economic policy has also been argued by Chawluk (1974).

There is much to be said for this line of argument. The main social and political problem of the Six Year Plan (the sharp fall in real wages in 1950–3) was overcome in 1954–8, not by reforming the economic mechanism but by changing economic policy (a more sensible policy in agriculture, a reduction of the share of investment in national income, more attention to consumer interests). The crisis of 1970 (which forced the resignation of the then Party leader) was largely a result of policies which had been criticised by Kalecki already in 1964 (see chapter 2 p. 37) but which had been endorsed by the leadership. The deep economic crisis of 1979–82 was primarily a result of another policy failure, the inability of the authorities to preserve internal and external economic equilibrium in the 1970s. In the 1980s, when considerable official efforts were devoted to imple-menting the various stages of the economic reform, the main economic needs of the country were successful policies to stimulate agriculture and exports.

Although there is much good sense in this argument, it should not be taken too far. There is a close relationship between the economic model and economic outcomes. In the three sectors particularly important for Poland in the 1980s, agriculture, consumption and foreign trade, it is notorious that the traditional model has severe adverse effects on economic outcomes (see chapters 4, 8 and 9). It is difficult to conceive of successful agricultural and hard currency export promotion policies, and eliminating shortages of consumer goods, within the traditional model.

Hungary

Serious work on criticism of the traditional model and the design of an alternative, began in the Institute of Economics of the Hungarian Academy of Sciences in 1953–5. A classic fruit of this research was Kornai (1959) the English translation of a thesis defended in 1956. This combined a critical description of the traditional model with ideas for reform. A detailed reform blueprint was prepared in 1957. The political atmosphere following the Soviet military intervention of

1956, however, was not compatible with a radical economic reform. After the Kadar administration consolidated power, however, and after the discussions throughout the CMEA had legitimatised the idea of economic reform, a comprehensive economic reform was initiated in Hungary from the beginning of 1968 – the New Economic Mechanism (NEM). The ideas underlying it were not new, but the changed political climate now made it possible to implement them.

The essence of the NEM was the abandonment of imperative planning and physical planning. The central bodies continued to compile plans. Instead, however, of breaking them down into detailed physical targets binding on particular enterprises, they attempted to realise them by means of financial levers (e.g. prices and taxes) which in principle were uniform for an entire sector or for the whole national economy. Looked at from the standpoint of the enterprises, the essence of the NEM was that current production planning and the rationing of producer goods were swept away. Enterprises were in principle free to determine their own production programmes on the basis of orders from customers and to obtain the inputs they needed by freely negotiated purchases from suppliers. In making their decisions they were supposed to be guided by profitability and by the financial parameters set by the centre. Hungarian institutions have not remained unchanged since 1968. In 1973–8 there was a renewed stress on the use of administrative measures, followed by renewed waves of reform from 1979 onwards.

The main successes of the NEM have been agriculture and the private sector. In Hungary in the mid 1980s there was an abundance of food available and the country was a net food exporter. This had been achieved mainly by providing the agricultural enterprises with much more autonomy than they had in the traditional model and by encouraging the private sector (see chapter 4). The private sector has been encouraged not only in agriculture but also in the non-agricultural sector (notably in construction and services). It has been estimated that in Hungary in 1984 one third of all working time was spent in the private sector, which accounted for 56 per cent of the output of new dwellings and the overwhelming majority of repair and maintenance services (Kornai 1986 p. 1707). (The private sector consisted mainly of the part-time activity of state sector employees, genuine cooperatives and self-employment. Large-scale private enterprise remained illegal.)

As far as the state sector is concerned, although the traditional model was abolished, it was not replaced by a market mechanism but by a mixture of bureaucratic and market processes. Bauer (1983a) has referred to this system as 'neither plan nor market'. It was not planning in the traditional sense, since breaking down the plan to individual enterprises and the rationing of producer goods had both been abolished. Neither was it a real market system. Competition was weak and there was a monopolistic market structure. Prices, markets and profits were only of limited importance for state enterprises. They had to concern themselves at least as much with the views of their hierarchical superiors, with social and political expectations, with current official policy and with the constantly changing official regulators (e.g. prices, price forming rules, charges for the use of resources, taxes etc.).

Kornai (1986 p. 1715) has described the reformed system in the following way: 'the Hungarian economy is a symbiosis of a state sector under indirect bureaucratic control and a nonstate sector, market oriented but operating under strong bureaucratic restrictions. Coexistence and conflict exist between the social sectors in many ways and all the time.'

In the late 1980s, the Hungarian economy exhibited a number of serious negative phenomena, both social and economic. On the social level the chronic housing problem, the very long hours of work (resulting from the second and third jobs of state economy employees), alcoholism, morbidity and poverty were all serious problems. On the economic level, stagnant or declining real wages throughout the 1980s (at any rate if state sector income only is considered), inflation, balance of payments deficits and growing foreign debts were all major problems. In 1987 the growing external debts were increasingly alarming economists and politicians, while the Government's plans for tax changes (the introduction of personal income tax and value added tax) and actual and anticipated inflation and job insecurity were increasingly alarming the public.

Hungarian experience illustrated the importance for popular welfare of economic policy. In the mid 1980s, Hungary (unlike the other CMEA countries) shielded personal consumption from the worst effects of macro-economic stagnation by drastically slashing investment (see chapter 6). In the same period, it also protected personal consumption by running a current account deficit (like Poland in the 1970s). It was the pro-consumer economic policy, plus the successful agricultural and private sectors, that most distinguished Hungary from the other CMEA countries in the mid 1980s.

The GDR

Unlike Yugoslavia, Poland and Hungary, the arguments for economic reform have had little lasting impact in the GDR. (The 'new economic system' of 1964–8 was terminated at the end of the decade in view both of the problems of implementing it and of the new political situation created by the 1968 events in Czechoslovakia.) Instead, the GDR has concentrated on improving planning and streamlining industrial management. Efforts have been made to improve the quality of planning by strengthening the role of the Five Year Plans and by involving the firms themselves more in the planning process. Industrial management has been streamlined by a process of amalgamating enterprises into vertically integrated firms (combines) with capable managers.

In Marxist-Leninist planning theory, the basic plan is the Five Year Plan. It is this which is intended to shape the structure of the economy, focus the work of all persons in the economy, and make substantial progress in achieving the objectives of the party. Great efforts were made in the 1970s and 1980s throughout the CMEA to ensure that this was actually so. (Traditionally, the main operational plans have been the annual plans and those for even shorter periods such as quarters, months, ten days, and 24 hours.) In the GDR, at any rate, this seems to have been achieved (Boot 1982). Whereas in the 1950s, annual planning had predominated, from 1971–4 the Five Year Plans became of much greater importance. In the latter period, the annual plans depended much less on actual performance in the previous year and much more on the Five Year Plan.

In the traditional model, the plans were worked out by a process of planning and counterplanning, i.e. of administrative iteration. The centre issues control figures, the periphery receives the control figures and on their basis submits plan suggestions to the centre. In the light of these suggestions the centre issues revised control figures. Having received them, the periphery submits revised suggestions, and so on. This process is sometimes described as 'plan bargaining'.

Planning and counterplanning is not confined to an exchange of documents. A former Soviet planner has described (Kushnirsky 1982 p. 66) how in the USSR in the final stages of compiling a draft plan, 'Representative delegations from all ministries and republic gosplans begin the siege of Gosplan. Day after day, ministers and chairmen of republic gosplans, accompanied by their retinues, arrive at Gosplan with arguments, diagrams, calculations and tables with the sole purpose of obtaining more resources. Gosplan preserves a certain amount of resources for such situations, which of course is not enough to satisfy everyone.'

An important feature of GDR planning, is the crucial role played in this process of administrative iteration by the firms (combines) themselves. Aided by their informational advantage, their small number, and their acknowledged capable managers, the firms use their strong position relative to the ministries to make a major input into the planning process (Granick 1975 p. 211, Boot 1983).

Enterprises in the GDR are grouped into combines. These are large (often vertically) integrated firms, headed by capable managers and with important rights in the field of foreign trade. Combines such as Carl Zeiss Jena and Robotron are well known for their engineering capability and the quality of their products. A well-known US specialist in international management comparisons has stated that his impressions of GDR top industrial management were (Granick 1975 p. 215) 'quite favourable'. He was impressed by their apparent willingness both to assert and to delegate authority. He was also impressed by the willingness of the authorities to dismiss politically acceptable but technically inefficient managers and their attention to career planning for managers.

In the mid 1980s, the GDR was a stable welfare state with the highest living standards in the CMEA. Its macro-economic perform-ance was marked by steady growth and stable prices, at any rate as measured by official statistics. These statistics overstated its actual performance. Nevertheless, compared to the other CMEA countries, its achievements were real and impressive. Although some problems of the traditional model (e.g. widespread shortages) existed also in the GDR, the population was at any rate spared the sharp falls in living standards experienced by Poland and Romania, the long hours, sharply rising prices and uncertainty about the future which characterised Hungary, and the massive retail price increases threat-ened by Gorbachev for the USSR. (Compared to the FRG, on the other hand, the achievements of the GDR were much less impressive.)

What explains this combination of relative success with an absence of economic reform in the traditional sense of combining central planning with a built-in market mechanism? There appear to be three reasons. First, some aspects of the traditional model have in fact been changed. The greater role of the Five Year Plans, the greater role of the firms (combines) in the plan compilation process, and the authority of the firms (combines) in the economy are all new. If the GDR is not an example of economic reform, it is at any rate an example of a modified, rationalised and technocratic version of the traditional model. Secondly, the environment is especially favourable for the traditional model. This is a result of several factors. For one thing, in the GDR the traditional model was planted in an old industrial region with substantial numbers of scientists, engineers and skilled workers. The population was already accustomed to industrial society. Hence the model was able to inherit the traditions of scientific and technical expertise, skilled labour, hard work and the efficient operation of bureaucratic structures that have long existed in what had previously been central Germany. For another, the period of full Stalinism in the GDR was very short. For another, the country has financial and trade links with West Germany which are of great benefit. For example, in the early 1980s, when it had a very difficult external debt situation, it obtained loans guaranteed by the West German authorities. Furthermore, its trade with the West benefits from 'intra-German' trade which in effect gives the GDR privileged access to the EEC market. Thirdly, the policies pursued in the GDR have been reasonably sensible. The GDR has neither generated prolonged internal and external disequilibrium (like Poland in the 1970s and 1980s) nor protected domestic consumption by accumulating large foreign debts (like Hungary in the 1980s) nor depressed living standards in the attempt to repay foreign debt quickly (like Romania in the 1980s) nor wasted huge investment resources on projects with a low, marginal or negative return (as in the USSR under Brezhnev).

The relative importance of these three reasons in explaining the relative success of the GDR is a matter for debate and there is no consensus among observers.

The 'paradoxical' (from the standpoint of liberal economics) fact that the GDR appears to have done so well compared to countries such as Yugoslavia and Hungary has given rise to an interesting discussion about the appropriate criteria for assessing the relative performance of socialist economies. Kornai (1988), for example, has argued that in assessing economic reform experiences a one-sided attention has been given to conventional macro-economic criteria at the expense of a criterion such as individual freedom. As far as the freedom of the individual to spend her/his money freely on the goods she/he really wants, or the freedom of individuals who want to work for themselves or set up a business or work in a non-state enterprise, is concerned, this according to Kornai is clearly much greater in Hungary than in the GDR. The greater extent of individual freedom, according to his values, makes the Hungarian economic system of the mid 1980s superior to the GDR system. A number of other criteria for assessing socialist economic systems are considered in chapter 10.

China

The traditional model was introduced in China in the 1950s. For example, the First Five Year Plan (1953–7) was modelled on Soviet experience. This applied both to its strategy (emphasis on heavy industry) and to the principles underlying its method of implementation (e.g. one-man management). Similarly, the institutions characteristic of the traditional model, such as the organisation of agriculture in collective or state farms and the state monopoly of foreign trade (see chapter 9), were also introduced.

In the wake of the 20th Congress of the CPSU and China's experience with the traditional model, the Chinese leadership recognised that policy changes would be necessary. For example, in Mao Zedong's 1956 speech *On the ten major relationships* he argued, *inter alia*, that it was necessary for China to pay greater attention to agriculture and light industry, not to squeeze the peasants too hard, to give greater power to local organs, make less use of repression, not to slavishly copy the USSR and to admit weaknesses. Mao's views had considerable impact on the level at which economic decisions were made. Nevertheless, although Soviet economic policy was much criticised in Maoist China, many of the policies actually implemented in Maoist China, e.g. the high share of investment in the national income, the concentration of resources on heavy industry, and the suppression of small-scale private economic activity, were characteristic of the traditional model. Furthermore, the methods and procedures of economic planning remained similar to the traditional model until the major reforms of the mid 1980s. In addition, the Maoist variant of the traditional model was characterised by an even greater reliance on the use of administrative methods than was the case in the CMEA countries after 1956. This was particularly important in the fields of labour and consumer goods.

Since 1956, the USSR has had a fairly free urban labour market (although moving to 'closed' cities such as Moscow is difficult and not to work in the state or collective sector is in general illegal). Workers are free to resign and enterprises compete for workers. In China on the other hand, at least up to the mid 1980s, there was virtually no free labour market within the state sector and most labour was allocated administratively. This system (which has certain resemblances to the Japanese system of life-long employment for male employees in the big-firm sector, to the direction of labour in the UK in the Second World War and to the system prevailing in the USSR in 1940–56) had important consequences. It meant that material incentives were much less important for the efficient allocation of labour. The Chinese labour force was allocated to its place of work and the allocation was enforced by the rationing of consumer goods. It also meant that fear of the sack could not be used to discipline the workers and to raise labour productivity. Furthermore, in the Maoist period, large numbers of people (e.g. school leavers) for whom there were no urban jobs, were directed to the countryside. These matters are considered further in chapter 6.

Basic consumer goods are rationed in China and have been since the early days of the People's Republic. This has facilitated both egalitarian distribution and control over population movement. The number of commodities covered by rationing and the extent to which goods can be obtained on the free market outside the rationing system, has varied sharply over time and between places. In the Maoist period, rationing was extensive and the free market greatly restricted.

Economic reform emerged on the political agenda at the end of 1978 as a result of the coming to power of the victims of the cultural revolution, the poor results achieved by the Maoist variant of the traditional model, in particular in the fields of living standards and the modernisation of production and the poor results of Hua Guofeng's mini Great Leap forward in 1978. In 1978 living standards were low, real wages had not increased for two decades (indeed, according to official statistics, average real wages in 1977 were 17 percent less than they had been twenty years earlier) and poverty was widespread. Furthermore, the technical gap between Chinese production and that of dynamic Asian countries such as Japan, South Korea, Hong Kong, Taiwan and Singapore, was growing. Instead of overtaking the advanced capitalist countries, China was in danger of falling further behind them. The investment boom of 1978 turned out to be no panacea. It raised investment to a level in excess of the absorptive capacity of the economy and generated macro-economic disequilibrium.

The most dramatic changes in the Chinese economic system which have been implemented up to the time of writing were in the field of agriculture (see chapter 4) and external economic relations, and the least significant in large-scale state industry.

In agricultural policy, the main landmarks in the reform process were the Central Committee meeting of December 1978, which raised state procurement prices for agricultural products and initiated what turned out to be a process of decollectivisation in agriculture, and the Circular of the Central Committee of the Chinese Communist Party on rural work during 1984 (document no. 1 1984) which endorsed the system of state tenancy which had emerged in the countryside. In external economic relations, the main landmarks were the introduction of the import-led growth policy in 1978, the beginning of large scale and open foreign borrowing in 1979, the decision to establish Special Economic Zones in 1979, the opening of the Shenzhen Special Economic Zone in 1980, a relaxation in 1983 of the tax and tariff rules applicable to foreign investments, and the opening of a number of coastal cities to foreign investment in 1984.

Indeed, by the mid 1980s, the openness of the Chinese economy to the world market, although far less than would have been the case in a purely market economy, was truly remarkable in the light of the traditions both of state socialism and of China. By 1987, China was a member of both the IMF and the World Bank and had received a positive response to its expressed interest in joining GATT. Help had been requested and received from the leading capitalist countries and their international agencies in areas ranging from the conduct of a national census to the education of graduate students. Foreign help was being encouraged for investment in basic sectors (e.g. energy and transport) and stimulating exports played a key role in national economic planning. As the Proposal (adopted in September 1985) of the CC for the Seventh Five Year Plan (1986–90) clearly stated (paragraphs 41 and 42),

The key to implementing the open policy with an increased use of foreign funds and imported technology is to increase foreign exchange earnings through exports. To accomplish this, which is of paramount importance in our modernization programme, we must adopt strategies which meet the demands of the international market and correspond to China's domestic conditions ... Except for a few major commodities vital to the national economy and the people's everyday life, whenever there are conflicts between exports and domestic sales, priority should be given to the needs of exports.

The monopoly position of the Ministry of Foreign Trade and its specialised foreign trade corporations had been relaxed. A number of provinces and municipalities had acquired rights in the foreign trade field. In addition, some enterprises had been granted autonomy in foreign trade decisions. The effect of all these measures was to make the possibilities offered by foreign trade of great importance in the Chinese economy and something felt directly by many enterprises which were no longer completely insulated from the world market by the state monopoly of foreign trade.

The reform process has not been a steady movement in one direction, guided by a leadership conscious in advance of the path to be followed. On the contrary, it has seen false starts, retreats, and initiatives from below. One false start was the February 1978 version of the Ten Year Plan (1976–85), with its huge investment programme and massive import requirements. It was soon abandoned, and in 1979 and 1980 many of the import contracts were cancelled. Significant retreats were the working session of the CC in December 1980, which halted the reform experiment because of macro-economic disequilibria which had emerged, and the extension of rationing in December 1987. Initiatives from below have been particularly important in agriculture, where they provided the main impetus for decollectivisation. They also provided the main impetus for the rapid growth and success of the village and township enterprises (see chapter 4) which was such a feature of the 1980s. As Deng Xiaoping (1987) honestly observed, 'this result was not anything that I or any of the other comrades had foreseen; it just came out of the blue'. The only constant factors during the reform process have been a willingness by the leadership to experiment and to learn from mistakes, the continued importance of political factors (such as the Deng Xiaoping's personal support for economic reform, campaigns against 'spiritual pollution' in 1983 and against 'bourgeois liberalisation' in 1987, and the stress on grain production by those sceptical about reform) and the goal of transforming China into an economically advanced country as soon as possible.

After a decade of economic reform, its most striking successes concerned living standards, economic growth and the modernisation of production. In 1979–85, average per capita consumption rose by 8.6 percent per annum, an outstanding achievement for such a huge and backward country. In the same period, the net material product (the MPS equivalent of the national income) rose by 8.8 percent per annum. In the mid 1980s, when many other countries were experiencing economic decline, stagnation or slow growth, China was experiencing a spectacular boom. Moreover, by 1987, China's annual exports of goods had reached about 38 billion US dollars, with about two thirds of them being manufactures, rather than primary products.

Although the experience of economic reform appeared basically favourable (despite serious inflation and extensive corruption), the future remained uncertain. Future political changes, inadequate foreign exchange earnings, poor economic management, inflation, corruption, underemployment or unemployment, the stagnation of agriculture after the once-and-for-all gains of decollectivisation, the inefficient investment planning system, world recession, energy shortage, the unsatisfactory price system, the absence of a labour market, the failure to link work and pay in the state sector, and so on – singly or in combination – could blow China off course. The violent political oscillations in 1949–87 were a warning of what was possible.

USSR

The first attempt at economic reform in the USSR took place in 1965. It followed the poor economic performance of the early 1960s (in 1963, according to the CIA, Soviet GNP actually fell slightly), Khrushchev's criticism of Stalin's policies at the 22nd Party Congress (1961), a wide public discussion of the need for reform and the fall of Khrushchev (1964). The new leaders hastened to announce new policies in agriculture and a reform of the urban sector. Although the reintroduction of the economic ministries was a lasting result of the reform announced by Kosygin in September 1965, the promised greater independence of enterprises and the gradual transition to wholesale trade, remained just promises. In 1969, partly as a result of problems of implementing the reform (Kushnirsky 1982) and partly as a result of the close connection which the 1968 Czechoslovak events had shown existed between economic and political reforms, the marketisation aspect of the reforms were reversed. Twenty two years after the 1965 reform, speaking at the June 1987 meeting of the Supreme Soviet, Prime Minister Ryzhkov referred to the 'sad experience of the 1965 reform', after which 'everything returned to the old ways, only perhaps in a worse form'.

The next attempt at economic reform began in 1986 and was part of Gorbachev's *perestroika* campaign. This aimed at overcoming the 'pre-crisis' situation (this was Gorbachev's own description) in which the USSR found itself in the mid 1980s. By a 'pre-crisis' situation Gorbachev meant a situation which, if not resolved, would inevitably be followed by a real economic crisis, for example the one which took place in Poland in 1980–2. This pre-crisis situation was characterised by economic stagnation, internal disequilibrium, an increasing lag in economic and technological development behind the developed capitalist countries, and widespread drunkenness, corruption, misuse of official positions and indifference to the public good.

An important part of *perestroika* was a radical change in economic policies. The policy of 'stability of cadres' was replaced by wholesale sackings of senior officials and massive promotions of new blood. Investment policy was significantly changed. More emphasis was placed on the need to modernise the engineering sector, and the scheme to reverse the direction of flow of a number of giant rivers flowing into the Arctic ocean was abandoned. So-called 'non-labour incomes' were attacked, two and three shift working extended and a dramatic war waged on alcohol use. Vigorous efforts were made to raise the quality of production, both by the introduction of a state quality control system which provided for external quality control for industrial products and by the widespread and vigorous evaluation of the work of individuals throughout the economy. Andropov's discipline campaign was continued. Although important for *perestroika*, these measures did not constitute an economic reform, i.e. a change in the economic model. What did constitute an attempt to introduce an economic reform were the law on individual economic activity (November 1986), the law on cooperatives (May 1988), the law 'On the State Enterprise' (June 1987) and the official advocacy of a substantial expansion of the family contract and lease contract systems in agriculture in 1987–88.[2] These measures affected three features of the traditional model, imperative planning, physical planning and state ownership.

The law 'On the State Enterprise' came into force on January 1 1988. The original intention was that the new procedures prescribed by it would be introduced throughout the economy in 1988–9 and the necessary accompanying changes in planning, prices, the financial and banking systems would be introduced in 1988–90. It was at first officially hoped that, in 1991 when the new Five Year Plan would begin, the new economic mechanism would be fully in operation. The detailed decrees issued soon after the June (1987) Plenum, concerned with 'implementing' the law approved by it, however, made it clear that this timetable was overoptimistic. For example, not only was the transition from the rationing of all producer goods to wholesale trade intended to be phased in over a 4–5 year period, but even in 1992 it was envisaged that 20–25 per cent of turnover would still be rationed!

[2] A 'family contract' or 'family commitment' is an arrangement between a small group, usually one or two families, and an official organisation such as a collective or state farm. The group obtains the right, for a certain period, to use a certain patch of land or to look after a certain number of animals. In return it commits itself to deliver an agreed quantity of products to the official organisation either at regular intervals or at the end of the contract/commitment period. In a 'lease contract' the contract/commitment runs for a number of years.

The law 'On the State Enterprise' was clearly a compromise between those who wanted to abolish imperative planning and physical planning altogether, and those who wanted to retain elements of them. According to the letter of the law, imperative planning was completely abolished, but physical planning was only partially abolished. The reason for this was that, although compulsory annual and Five Year Plans prescribed from above were formally abolished, the enterprise Five Year Plans had to be partly based on 'control figures' received from Gosplan and the ministries ('control figures' are aggregated plan targets) and state orders. These would presumably remain largely in physical units. What would actually happen from 1988 remained to be seen. The system envisaged by this law had important features in common with the New Economic Mechanism introduced in Hungary in 1968 (although the Soviet law gives a greater role to physical planning, and its 'implementation' is to be phased in over a lengthy period) and the October 1984 decision of the Chinese CC about the reform of Chinese industry.

The law 'On individual economic activity', the new cooperatives, and the family and lease contracts in agriculture, also challenged another feature of the traditional model, state ownership. Although legally speaking, the family contract system in agriculture was based on state ownership (means of production and land were only leased to the family groups) control over the use of these factors of production would be largely in the hands of the families concerned. This combination of state ownership and private control also existed under NEP, when legally speaking, all land belonged to the state. (Of course, the state was much more strongly entrenched in the countryside in the late 1980s than it had been under NEP.) Another way in which the ownership rights of the state were affected by the new laws concerned appointments. The law 'On the State Enterprise' introduced a system of elections of enterprise directors and the heads of sub-units within enterprises or associations by the work force. Formally speaking, the hierarchical superiors (e.g. the ministry) had only the right to accept or reject the elected person, but could not appoint their own candidate. In practice, however, it seemed that this would be likely to leave the *nomenklatura* system unaffected or even strengthened. The election would normally be under the control of the enterprise party committee and be about as meaningful as elections for Soviet organs. Indeed, one of the features of the new law, was that it strengthened the position of the party committees relative to the ministries. This was more a reorganisation within the bureaucratic apparatus, than a meaningful reform.

At the time of writing, the outcome of the second Soviet attempt at economic reform was uncertain. Its scope was limited, there were a large number of economic and social problems that could derail it and evident disagreement within the leadership about how to proceed. Nevertheless, the leadership and its advisers were conscious of the experience of other countries, of the internal problems to be expected and the urgent need to achieve concrete results. Gorbachev's *perestroika* had a number of positive features compared with Kosygin's reform. It was launched from the party secretariat rather than from the prime minister's office and thus had much greater political weight behind it. It recognised that economic reform was not a purely technical matter but had important social and political implications, affecting the position of different social groups and the Soviet political system. It was accompanied by a stress on the need for political changes if the economic measures were to be a success (this led to some real changes such as the recognition of unofficial social organisations and the partial and limited tolerance of unofficial political demonstrations). In addition, the leadership was not afraid to challenge long-established theoretical propositions (e.g. concerning state ownership – see chapter 10) and historical falsifications (e.g. concerning the 1930s).

LESSONS OF REFORM

On the basis of the experiences of those countries which have embarked on the reform process, and of the international discussion about that experience, it is possible to draw a number of lessons. These concern, the order in which reforms should be introduced, the conditions for a successful economic reform, the regulation illusion, investment planning, entrepreneurship, ownership and market socialism.

The order of reforms

Izvestiya for 1 June 1985 contained an interview with Academician Zaslavskaya, a leading Soviet reformer. Part of it read as follows:

Academician Zaslavskaya. 'For success in improving economic relations we need a well thought out economic strategy which allows people interested in raising the economy to a qualitatively new level to manifest themselves and which gives no-one the possibility to block the essential reconstruction.'
Journalist. 'A strategy, surely requires also the choice of initial tasks, their allocation over time? Which branch of the economy should be the pioneer?'

Academician Zaslavskaya. 'In my opinion, agriculture. This has been proved by the experience of the socialist countries which have undertaken economic reforms. The agroindustrial complex is the most suitable for the introduction of new relations. It is the most sensitive to economic forms of management and the most flexible. Its priority is determined also by the fact that agricultural products are a basic social need.'

This view, that economic reform should begin with agriculture and has a good chance of succeeding in agriculture, is based on the success of economic reform in agriculture in Hungary and China. This success contrasts sharply with the very limited success of economic reform in large-scale state industry in all the countries that have embarked on economic reform.

Another sector in which Hungarian and Chinese experience has shown that rapid and substantial results can be achieved, is the small-scale private and cooperative sector, particularly in small-scale construction, repairs and other service activities.

Hence by the late 1980s, it had become part of the conventional wisdom that economic reform should begin in agriculture and the small-scale private and cooperative sectors, and had most chance of substantial and rapid results there. The reason for this difference between farming and small-scale services on the one hand, and large-scale state industry on the other seems to be as follows. In the individual/family/cooperative sector economic reform provides an environment in which the 'natural' desire of an individual to earn more to support his/her family leads to more output. The participants in this sector are principals and react directly to economic incentives. In the large-scale state sector, however, the situation is fundamentally different. There the key role is played by managers at various levels. These are not principals, but bureaucrats in a complex bureaucratic apparatus. Hence for them the expectations of their superiors (who appoint and dismiss them), the campaigns waged by their superiors, the favours they can obtain from them, and their own desires for expansion of their own empires and for promotion, are often more important than satisfying the needs of customers. What is evidently required if economic reform is really to take hold in large-scale state industry is the transformation of managers into entrepreneurs.

Conditions for a successful economic reform

The conditions for successful economic reform have been widely analysed (e.g. Group 1985, Knaack 1984, 1985, Ellman 1988b). Particularly important factors would appear to be, a supportive political environment, a compatible macro-economic situation, micro-economic consistency, appropriate institutional changes and the comprehensive nature of the reform.

Successful economic reform requires a favourable political situation. In 1921 Lenin introduced the NEP in a society in which the Whites had been defeated and the need for a compromise with the peasantry was self-evident. Within a few years its success had given it massive support, despite its problems. Similarly, Gorbachev's *perestroika* benefited from the personal support of the top leader, and the widespread recognition throughout Soviet society of the unsatisfactory nature of the results achieved with the traditional model. On the other hand, the Kosygin reform of 1965 was terminated in 1969, partly as a result of the new political situation created by the 1968 events in Czechoslovakia. In China, the coming to power after 1977 of the victims of the Cultural Revolution, created a favourable political climate for reform.

It is important that the macro-economic situation should be compatible with economic reforms. This means that widespread shortages and tension in many markets, caused by ambitious plans of the authorities, or overenthusiastic reaction to the reforms by the lower bodies, should be avoided if possible. Otherwise, for example, more freedom in price setting may contribute more to inflation than to the efficient allocation of resources. The role of macro-economic equilibrium in preventing inflation when enterprises have more scope in decision making has been noted by Chinese writers (Group 1985 p. 31). Similarly, giving more authority to republics, cities, associations and enterprises to initiate investment projects may simply lead to a general fall in the efficiency of investment as too many projects are started and each one takes too long to complete. Hence economic reforms at the micro level (e.g. affecting price formation and investment authority) must be combined with macro-economic policies of harmonious growth (in place of rush), monetary restraint and policies to stimulate competition and harden the budget constraint. (Gorbachev's attempt to combine economic reform with growth acceleration was one of the factors weakening the chance that his economic reform would be a success.) Similarly, the share of heavy industry and defence in total output must not be too great otherwise the consumer goods necessary to make money incentives a reality will not be available.

By micro-economic consistency is meant the need for the different parts of the reformed economic mechanism to mesh with each other. For example, using profit as a guide to efficiency only makes sense with an appropriate price system. Hence the attention usually given as part of economic reform to rationalising the price system. Similarly, decentralising (some) investment is only possible if the rationing of producer goods has been (at least partially) replaced by wholesale trade. Decentralising decision making will only give the desired results when there is a general buyers' market. As a group of Chinese specialists has observed (Group 1985 p. 31): 'Otherwise, a return to the centralized administrative managing system is likely to occur if there is an overall shortage of commodities and materials, and the model [of a planned economy with a built-in market mechanism] would hardly be realized.' One aspect of a buyers' market is an absence of monopolies (Kurashvili 1985 p. 70). Competition between state owned enterprises is bound to be difficult at first. In this connection, non-state enterprises and international trade can play a useful role in generating competitive pressures.

Hungarian experience in the 1970s showed that when an economic reform takes place in an unchanged administrative framework (i.e. with the same ministries, state committees etc.) there is a tendency for the higher bodies to brake the reform by behaving much as before. Hence it seems likely that a serious reform will normally be accompanied by a drastic reorganisation of the intermediate level bodies (ministries etc.). This question has been extensively discussed by Kurashvili (1982, 1983a, 1983b, 1985). He has argued (1983a p. 38) that 'alterations in the situation of the enterprises cannot be implemented other than by a simultaneous alteration in the management of the branches of the economy'. The reasons for this is that (ibid.) the branch ministries 'were and remain organs for the direct management of their "objects", embodying the maximum centralisation of management, bearers of the command style. This is in their blood, and it is difficult to imagine that they can change their nature.' The need, as part of reform, to eliminate most of the branch ministries and strengthen regional ties, has also been argued by a group of Chinese specialists (Group 1985 p. 29). It is important to note that, although administrative changes are normally an important part of serious economic reform, administrative changes by themselves do not constitute a serious economic reform.

On the basis of experience in the CMEA countries, it has long been argued that a successful economic reform should be a comprehensive reform affecting all spheres of economic life. There is a long history in the state socialist countries of piecemeal changes in the system of planning and economic management which are introduced with high hopes but which fail to achieve very much. In Hungary the idea emerged in the 1950s that the traditional model formed an integrated economic mechanism, with characteristic advantages and disadvantages, and that if it were desired to overcome the disadvantages what was required was an alternative economic mechanism (Kornai 1959). This view has also been endorsed by Chinese specialists (Group 1985 p. 18):

the objectives, measures and results of reform differ from country to country and all possess their own specific features. One bit of experience worth noting and summarizing is that countries which adopt thoroughgoing reform measures have all achieved marked results, while those that only try to patch up and improve things have gained very few results and have even invited new contradictions. The reason is simple. An economic reform is intended to change the basic specifications and principles of motion of the economic system, it is a transition from one economic model to another. If the economic reform is confined within the basic framework of the original model – to attempting local improvements of certain details – there can be no possibility of thoroughly solving the original problems, and moreover . . . new and insurmountable problems may arise because such localized improvements clash with the original basic framework.

Failure to recognise the need for a comprehensive reform is likely to prevent partial changes working as intended. For example, an important aspect of the Kosygin reform of 1965 was the attempt to introduce incentives for adopting taut plans. This did not achieve its objective because of the retention of aspects of the traditional system, for example the view that inferiors should carry out orders and the formula for determining current managerial bonuses which gave effect to this view, and institutions and behaviour which encouraged risk aversion by enterprise management (Ellman 1977). Similarly, the 1979 alteration in Soviet success indicators was unsuccessful because of supplier dominance and information overload, two key aspects of the traditional model (Hanson 1983). Incentives, success indicators, the price system, the state budget, the availability of consumer goods, a buyers' market, the non-state sector, competition, the system for appointing managers, the existence of branch ministries etc. etc. are all linked together. To introduce partial changes in an otherwise unreformed economic mechanism is likely to prevent the changes from having the desired effect.

On the basis of the experience of China, further generalisations about the extent to which the reforms must be comprehensive have been made (Liu 1987). It is clear, for instance, that in a third world country major improvements can take place in agriculture even without a successful reform in industry. Nevertheless, even in a third world country (and still more so in a more advanced country where agriculture is more dependent on industrial inputs) the failure to implement a comprehensive economic reform throughout the economy can limit the potential opened up by economic reform in agriculture (e.g. by leading to an adverse development of agricultural prices relative to those for industrial products, and/or to the inability to obtain necessary industrial inputs).

The regulation illusion

The regulation illusion (Antal 1979, 1982, Kornai 1986) is the idea that enterprise behaviour can easily be controlled by the planners by manipulation of certain regulators (e.g. prices, taxes, loans etc.). With the help of certain carefully designed regulators controlling wages, prices or enterprise net income, the reformers hope that it will be possible to steer the enterprises in a socially rational direction. Experience has shown that this is much more difficult than many economists have traditionally believed. Indeed, experience shows that this traditional belief of many economists is, to a considerable extent, an 'illusion'. The reasons for this seem to be as follows:

The enterprises react to a whole complex of economic, social and political factors. Change in just one of the economic regulators is likely to be too weak a signal to have the desired effect.

It is impossible to develop a completely watertight system of rules and regulations. The enterprises generally learn how to use the letter of the rules to avoid their intention. (This is analogous to how Western firms and individuals learn to use tax regulations to achieve their own objectives, rather than those of the authorities, by judicious avoidance measures.)

The reaction of the enterprises may be different from what the designers of the regulations expected because the goals of the enterprises are other than those hoped for by the planners. For example, the planners may assume that the enterprises are profit maximisers and design their regulators accordingly. The enterprises, however, may be more interested in growth than in profits.

The critique of the regulation illusion, which was developed by Hungarian economists reflecting on the experience of their country, is analogous to the rational expectations critique of the Keynesian belief in the easy controllability of the economy.

Investment planning

In older writings on economic reform, it used to be assumed that
current decisions should be decentralised to the enterprises, but that
investment should be planned. In this way it was hoped to combine
micro-economic rationality (resulting from the behaviour of the
enterprises) with macro-economic rationality (resulting from wise
planning of investment by the planners). Experience has shown that
this dichotomy is neither viable nor rational.

It is not viable for two reasons (Kornai 1986 p. 1729). 'On the one
hand the bureaucracy is not ready to restrict its activity to the
regulation of investment. On the other hand, the autonomy and
profit motive of the firm become illusory, if growth and technical
development are separated from the profitability and the financial
position of the firm and are made dependent only on the will of the
higher authorities.'

It is not rational because investment planning is not a purely
technical process in which omniscient planners weigh up all possible
alternatives with the help of perfect criteria. It is a socio-political
process in which powerful individuals and interest groups fight to get
'their' favourite investment projects first adopted and then completed (see chapter 5).

Hence, for Kornai (1986) the neat division between current
decisions, to be left to the market, and investment, to be left to the
planners, is an example of naivety.

Entrepreneurship

In the early stages of reform, reformers, often influenced by illusions
derived from general equilibrium analysis, gave great weight to
prices as carriers of information and guides to efficiency. They were
surprised to discover that in large-scale state industry, the reaction
by managers to price signals was often non-existent or sluggish.
Furthermore, the large-scale state sector failed to show much dynamism even when imperative planning and physical planning were
abolished and firms themselves given much more autonomy. This
gradually led to the widespread rehabilitation in the countries
undergoing a reform process of Austrian notions of competition and
the Austrian stress on the role in market economies of the entre-
preneur. Competition is a process in which rivals compete against
each other with some winning and others losing. The losers suffer
(demotion, salary cuts, unemployment, bankruptcy). The picture

depicted by general equilibrium theory in which prices automatically guide everyone to the social optimum is a poor guide to competitive market processes. A key role in the competitive process is played by entrepreneurs who react quickly to market possibilities, taking initiatives and risks.

How can entrepreneurship be stimulated in a socialist economy? This question has given rise to a lively discussion in countries such as Hungary and China. The Hungarian economist Liska has proposed the large-scale leasing of state enterprises to private individuals, who would act as entrepreneurs and be responsible for managing them. (Leasing to private individuals of state productive assets already exists on a significant scale in Hungary in the sphere of small-scale services, e.g. restaurants and retail trade.) Similarly in China in the late 1980s the idea of leasing large state enterprises to entrepreneurs who would be responsible for running them in a profitable way and for providing the state with a good financial return on its assets was being discussed. This would be a generalisation of the system of leasing state or collectively owned land to private individuals which has been so successful in agriculture and small-scale services (see chapters 4 and 8).

It is important to note that, under certain circumstances, entrepreneurship can be socially harmful. Entrepreneurship can be directed towards criminal activities, tax evasion, tax avoidance, rent seeking, power seeking ... To create and maintain an institutional system which encourages entrepreneurship for socially useful activities and discourages it for socially harmful activities, is a difficult task. So far the state socialist countries have taken only the first steps in this direction.

Ownership of the means of production

State ownership of the means of production is an important feature of the traditional model. It has been traditionally treated by all Communists and most socialists as a major advantage of socialism, wiping out classes and creating the conditions for national economic planning. Experience with economic reform, however, shows that state ownership hinders the development of real market relationships.

State ownership has traditionally meant that the state appoints the managers whose careers are entirely dependent on the opinions of them held by the relevant higher bodies. They are therefore naturally much more interested in the opinions held about them by the higher bodies than in satisfying their customers, reducing their costs, introducing new products etc. This contributes to what Brus has termed 'the negative selection of cadres' (i.e. selection on the basis of obedience, loyalty, subordination, conformity etc.).

For this reason, it is difficult to imagine a serious economic reform without a weakening of the *nomenklatura* system. This, of course, is a crucial political issue. In Poland in 1981 under pressure from the trade union Solidarity a (paper) compromise was reached whereby the directors of certain key national enterprises would continue to be nominated by the state organs, but the directors of the remaining enterprises would be chosen by the workers. In Hungary in 1985/6 as part of the development of the reform process, significant changes were made in the rules governing the appointments process. The state enterprises were divided into three groups. The first group, employing about a third of all employees and mainly in the energy, oil refining, public utility and defence sectors, retained the traditional system. The second group, employing about two thirds of all employees, had an enterprise council (partly elected by the employees and partly nominated by the director). This council appoints the director after advertising the post, subject to a veto by the relevant party and state bodies. The third group, consisting of small enterprises and employing only about 2–3 percent of all employees, introduced a type of workers' self-management with directors chosen by a secret ballot of all employees. Similarly, the 1985 World Bank study of China's economy called for boards of directors, independent of the Government, to run enterprises. Similarly, the Soviet 1987 law 'On the State Enterprise' introduced election of directors (see above). In Brus's terminology, what is at stake in all these measures, is a socialisation of the means of production which transfers important rights over them out of the hands of the party-state apparatus to wider social groups. In Adler-Karlsson's terminology, what is at stake is transferring one function of ownership, operative management, out of the hands of the party-state apparatus. The fact that economic reform is not a purely technical question but is, *inter alia*, concerned with the decision-making rights of various social groups, is one of the reasons why it is such a sensitive issue.

Besides drawing attention to the adverse effects of state ownership on the large-scale sector, the experience of economic reform has also drawn attention to the benefits of collective and private ownership. One of the features of economic reform has been the increased scope given to collective ownership, e.g. the greater freedom for cooperatives in agriculture and services. This has brought substantial benefits in the form of extra output and more jobs and income. Another feature has been the legalisation of small-scale private ownership in countries such as Hungary and China and this too has generated substantial economic benefits in terms of output and income. The limits which should be set to cooperative and private economic activities under socialism is a controversial issue in all the socialist countries. They fluctuated over time and between countries and remained a permanent subject of discussion.

Market socialism

The idea of 'market socialism', i.e. of combining state ownership of the means of production with a market mechanism, was developed by economists in the inter-war period. Experience of economic reform has shown that this is a distinctly problematic concept, given what has been written above about the regulation illusion, investment planning, entrepreneurship and ownership. The classic writers on market socialism combined an inadequate understanding of market processes with a lack of understanding of the consequences of state ownership.

PLANNING AND THE REFORM PROCESS

The question is often asked, what is the role of planning in the reformed model and how does it differ from that in the traditional model? This question can be analysed either on the basis of *a priori* arguments, or on the basis of actual experience. It should be noted, however, that up to now no stable reformed model has been developed anywhere. Hence empirical generalisation can only concern itself with the role of planning in economies going through the reform process and not with the role of planning in a final reform model.

The role of planning in a reformed economic mechanism was first discussed in the state socialist world in the Polish literature of the 1950s and early 1960s. In his well-known book published in Polish in 1961 and translated into English as *The market in a socialist economy* (1972), Brus argued in favour of a 'planned economy with a built-in market mechanism'. This amounts to a combination of centralisation and indirect centralisation.[3] The range of problems covered by

[3] By centralisation is meant decision making at the centre, e.g. by the national Gosplan or a national ministry. By decentralisation is meant decision making by

central planning in the model of a planned economy with a built-in market mechanism is similar to that in the traditional model, although some indices in the former are less detailed, especially for output assortment. The main difference between the models is in their methods of plan implementation. The former makes extensive use of indirect centralisation, the latter relies primarily on direct centralisation. The Polish discussion of the 1950s about the economic model was both extensive and has had an international influence.

With the benefit of 30 years hindsight, it is possible to see that, despite its great merits, Brus's original model combined the regulation illusion with a misunderstanding of the nature of investment planning, failure to perceive the need for entrepreneurship and the problems of state ownership, and inadequate attention to the collective and private sectors.

Generalising on the basis of countries which are some way along the reform process, three important changes in planning stand out. They are, the greater role of indirect centralisation and of macro-economic planning and the reduced scope of the plan.

Experience has shown that in some sectors the Brus idea of indirect centralisation, of implementing the plan not by means of instructions but by means of manipulating economic levers such as prices, is entirely feasible and socially desirable. The classic example is agriculture, where farmers respond quickly to changes in prices and profitability. Implementing the agricultural plan by manipulating prices and other financial levers (e.g. the terms on which credits are made available) has turned out to be much more efficient than the attempt to implement agricultural plans by coercion (see chapter 4).

In the traditional model, the plans are largely long lists of output targets. They are operationalised by two procedures, the lists of the corresponding investment projects to be completed, continued or initiated, and 'breaking down' the plan to individual enterprises (via intermediate organisations such as the ministries). Once countries embark on the reform process, however, it becomes necessary to reduce the role of these micro-economic targets in the plan and expand the role of macro-economic strategy. As the Chinese premier Zhao Ziyang noted in his speech on the Proposal of the CC for the

individuals, local authorities and firms whose decisions are entirely independent of the wishes of the central authorities. By indirect centralisation is meant decision making by individuals, local authorities and firms which produces decisions which are exactly the same as those which would have been made at the centre, had the centre had the necessary information, because the centre has determined the criteria (e.g. profit maximisation or party policy) and the parameters (e.g. prices or party directives and newspaper articles) which lower level decision makers use.

Seventh Five Year Plan at the September 1985 party conference, 'One of the document's distinct features is its emphasis on development strategy and on principles and policies, which represents an important new approach to planning. It allows us to concentrate our attention on essential contradictions in economic work and on key problems in economic development.'

Bobrowski (1956 p. 83) correctly noted that in the USSR when the traditional model was introduced, 'The problem of the limits of useful planning was regarded as non-existent.' It was simply assumed that the greater the area of economic life regulated by the plan, and the greater its detail, the better. It is now generally realised that this was an illusion from the standpoint of economic efficiency, and that an economic plan that does not attempt to cover everything may be more effective in achieving social goals. For example, in Hungary and China in the late 1980s a large part of economic activity took place outside the plan framework to the great benefit of popular living standards.

An important possible development in planning which has not happened anywhere, but which was discussed in Hungary in the late 1980s, concerns the democratisation of planning. The Hungarian politician Nyers, well known as the Politburo member responsible for the introduction of the NEM, argued for instance in the Hungarian Parliament in September 1987 for a planning system in which not only would Government agencies draw up plans but also independent economists and organisations (e.g. research institutes or social organisations) would draw up counter or alternative plans. These various plan variants would then be widely debated before one or another variant (not necessarily the officially formulated one) would be adopted. It is not an accident that Nyers also made it plain that he was against the political dictatorship and in favour, in the future, of a multi-party system for Hungary.

CONCLUSION

Economic reform is a long and difficult process with an uncertain outcome. It has not yet led to the establishment of a stable and successful economic system anywhere. Experience with the reform process illustrates the importance for economic outcomes not only of the economic system but also of economic policy and of the economic environment. It also shows that, given a favourable economic environment and sensible economic policies, economic reform is not necessary for high living standards and a welfare state. It also shows

how important for the conclusions reached about the success of
economic reform are the assessment criteria that are used. It also
draws attention to the crucial importance of political factors in the
reform process. One such factor is the control by the party-state
apparatus of the means of production. Experience of the reform
process enables generalisations to be made about the order in which
sectors lend themselves to reform, the conditions for a successful
reform, the regulation illusion, investment planning, entrepreneurship, ownership and market socialism. Planning in countries
undergoing the reform process differs from planning in the traditional model by its greater use of indirect centralisation, its greater
stress on macro-economic issues (rather than micro-economic ones)
and its reduced scope. An important political issue raised for
planning by the reform process is the democratisation of planning.

SUGGESTIONS FOR FURTHER READING

INTRODUCTION

T. Koopmans & J. M. Montias, 'On the description and comparison of economic systems', A. Eckstein (ed.) *Comparison of economic systems* (Berkeley 1971).

W. Brus, *Socialist ownership and political systems* (London 1975) chapter 4 ('The prospects for socialisation in the future').

M. Nuti, 'The contradictions of socialist economies: a Marxist interpretation', R. Milliband & J. Saville (eds.) *The Socialist Register 1979* (London 1979).

R. Knaack, 'Dynamic comparative economics: lessons from socialist planning', A. Zimbalist (ed.) *Comparative economic systems* (Boston 1984).

M. Kalecki, *Selected essays on economic planning* (Cambridge 1986).

CASES

Yugoslavia

L. Tyson, *The Yugoslav economic system and its performance in the 1970s* (Berkeley 1981).

H. Lydall, *Yugoslav socialism* (Oxford 1984).

L. Sirc, *The Yugoslav economy under self-management* (London 1979).

D. Flaherty, 'Economic reform and foreign trade in Yugoslavia', *Cambridge Journal of Economics* vol. 6, no. 2 (1982).

S. Estrin, *Self-management: Economic theory and Yugoslav practice* (Cambridge 1984).

J. P. Burkett, 'Stabilization measures in Yugoslavia', *East European Economies: Slow growth in the 1980s* vol. 3 (JEC, Washington DC 1986).

Poland

J. Drewnowski, 'The central planning office on trial', *Soviet Studies* vol. XXXI, no. 1 (January 1979).

J. G. Zielinski, *Economic reforms in Polish industry* (London 1973).

D. M. Nuti, 'Large corporations and the reform of Polish industry', *Jahrbuch der Wirtschaft Osteuropas* vol. 7 (Munich 1977).

S. Gomulka & J. Rostowski, 'The reformed Polish economic system 1982–83', *Soviet Studies* vol. XXXVI, no. 3 (July 1984).

W. Brus, 'The political economy of Polish reforms', *Praxis International* vol. 5, no. 2 (July 1985).

Hungary

P. Hare, H. Radice & N. Swain (eds.) *Hungary: A decade of economic reform* (London 1981).
T. Laky, 'The hidden mechanism of recentralization in Hungary', *Acta Oeconomica* vol. 24, nos 1–2 (1980).
M. Tardos (ed.) 'Hungarian enterprise behaviour, Parts I & II', *Eastern European Economics* vol. XXI, nos. 3–4, vol. XXII, no. 1 (1983).
E. Szalai, 'The new stage of the reform process in Hungary and the large enterprises', *Acta Oeconomica* vol. 29, nos. 1–2 (1982).
T. Bauer, 'The Hungarian alternative to Soviet-type planning', *Journal of Comparative Economics* vol. 7, no. 3 (September 1983).
J. B. Hall, 'Plan bargaining in the Hungarian economy: an interview with Dr. Laszlo Antal', *Comparative Economic Studies* vol. XXVIII, no. 2 (Summer 1986).
J. Kornai, 'The Hungarian reform process', *Journal of Economic Literature* vol. XXIV, no. 4 (December 1986).

GDR

G. Leptin & M. Melzer, *Economic reform in East German industry* (London 1978).
P. Boot, 'The end of predominantly annual planning in the German Democratic Republic', *The ACES Bulletin* vol. XXIV, no. 3 (Fall 1982).
P. Boot, 'Continuity and change in the planning system of the German Democratic Republic', *Soviet Studies* vol. XXXV, no. 3 (July 1983).

China

Xu Dixin *et al.*, *China's search for economic growth* (Beijing 1982).
Liu Guoguang & Wang Ruisun, 'Restructuring of the economy', chapter 2 of Yu Guangyuan (ed.) *China's socialist modernisation* (Beijing 1984).
S. L. Shirk, 'The decline of virtuocracy in China', J. L. Watson (ed.) *Class and social stratification in post-revolutionary China* (Cambridge 1984).
M. Ellman, 'Economic reform in China', *International Affairs* vol. 62, no. 3 (Summer 1986).
Wang Jue, Han Kang & Lu Zhongyuan, 'On China's system of a socialist planned market and the way to its realization', *Social Sciences in China* vol. VIII, no. 2 (1987).
'Chinese economic reform: how far, how fast?', *Journal of Comparative Economics* vol. 11, no. 3 (September 1987).

USSR

M. Ellman, 'Seven theses on Kosyginism', *De Economist* no. 1 (1977). Reprinted in M. Ellman, *Collectivisation, convergence and capitalism* (London & New York 1984).

F. I. Kushnirsky, *Soviet economic planning, 1965–1980* (Boulder 1982).

P. Hanson, 'Success indicators revisited', *Soviet Studies* vol. XXXV, no. 1

A. Nove, ' "Radical reform", Problems and prospects', *Soviet Studies* vol. XXXIX, no. 3 (July 1987).

'A symposium on reorganization and reform in the Soviet economy', *Comparative Economic Studies* vol. XXIX, no. 4 (Winter 1987).

LESSONS

'On the model for the reform of China's economic structure', *Social Sciences in China* vol. VI, no. 1 (March 1985).

Liu Guoguang *et al.*, 'Economic reform and macroeconomic management: commentaries on the international conference on macroeconomic management', *Chinese Economic Studies* vol. XX, no. 3 (Spring 1987).

Wang Liming & Li Shirong, 'Probing the question of the state's right of ownership of enterprises under the system of ownership by the whole people', *Social Sciences in China* vol. VIII, no. 2 (1987).

Dong Fureng, 'Socialist countries diversify ownership', *Beijing Review* no. 40 (1987).

T. Bauer, 'The second economic reform and ownership relations', *Eastern European Economics* vol. XXII, nos. 3–4 (1984).

T. Bauer, 'Reform policy in the complexity of economic policy', *Acta Oeconomica* vol. 34, nos 3–4 (1985).

W. Brus, 'Socialism – feasible and viable?', *New Left Review* (September–October 1985).

W. Brus, 'Market socialism', J. Eatwell, M. Milgate & P. Newman (eds.) *The new Palgrave* vol. 3 (London 1987).

4

PLANNING AGRICULTURE

Another thing we have learned from experience is the importance of developing agriculture. As long as the people are well fed, everything is easy, no matter what may happen in the world.

Deng Xiaoping (1984 p. 384)

THE CASE FOR COLLECTIVISM

The case for collective, rather than private, ownership and management of land, is simply one specific aspect of the general socialist argument for socialism rather than capitalism. Comparing socialist with capitalist agriculture, Marxists have traditionally considered that the socialist form has four important advantages. First, it prevents rural exploitation, that is, the emergence of a rural proletariat side by side with an agrarian capitalist class. Secondly, it allows the rational use of the available resources. Thirdly, it ensures a rapid growth of the marketed output of agriculture. Fourthly, it provides a large source of resources for accumulation.[1] Consider each argument in turn.

Writers such as John Stuart Mill (1891), Doreen Warriner (1969) and Michael Lipton (1974) advocate organising agriculture on the basis of peasants or smallholders operating efficient, family-sized farms. On the basis of theoretical and empirical analysis Marxist researchers have traditionally argued that this 'solution' to the agrarian problem is illusory. As Engels explained in his famous essay *The peasant question in France and Germany* (1894), 'we foresee the inevitable ruin of the small peasant'. The reasons for this are both

---

[1] The third and fourth arguments are often conflated. This is a serious source of confusion. It is entirely possible for the marketed output of agriculture to grow rapidly but for agriculture not to provide resources for industrialisation (for example if the marketed output is used to feed a repressive apparatus or is exported in exchange for armaments). Conversely, it is entirely possible for rapid industrialisation to be accompanied by a decrease in the net transfer of resources from agriculture (for example if the increase in industrial inputs in agriculture exceeds the increase in the marketed output of agriculture).

social and technical. The former were clearly explained by Lenin in *The development of capitalism in Russia* (1956 edn p. 172), his classic study of Russian rural society in the 1890s. He found that in the Russian countryside:

all those contradictions are present which are inherent in every commodity economy and every order of capitalism: competition, the struggle for economic independence, the snatching up of land (purchasable and rentable), the concentration of production in the hands of a minority, the forcing of the majority into the ranks of the proletariat, their exploitation by a minority through the medium of merchant capital and the hiring of farm-workers. There is not a single economic phenomenon among the peasantry that does not bear this contradictory form, one specifically peculiar to the capitalist system, i.e. that does not express a struggle and an antagonism, that does not imply advantage for some and disadvantage for others. It is the case with the renting of land, the purchase of land, and with 'industries' in their diametrically opposite types; it is also the case with technical progress in farming.

In addition, the Marxist-Leninist tradition lays considerable emphasis on the economies of scale which exist in agriculture as in industry. It also stresses the importance of technical progress, and the need for large units to take full advantage of it. The efficient use of tractors and other machinery may require land holdings larger and more consolidated than many peasant holdings. All these factors ensure that the peasant, like the artisan, forms part of a mode of production which is destined to be wiped out by the higher labour productivity of large-scale production. Despite their theoretical opposition to it, the Bolsheviks did in fact implement a distributivist land reform in 1917–18, in order to gain political support at a crucial moment. Bolsheviks saw in the outcome the results that Marxist theory would lead one to expect, the emergence of a stratified society in which rich peasants employing wage labour coexisted with an increasing number of poverty stricken labourers.[2] Abdel-Fadil's (1976) sees in the aftermath of the distributivist Egyptian land reform of the 1950s a similar outcome.

The capitalist organisation of agriculture often coexists with substantial rural unemployment and underemployment. Why is this? There are three standard explanations, neoclassical, Keynesian and Marxist.

The neoclassical explanation concerns the marginal product of labour. This is illustrated in figure 4.1. DD' is the demand curve for

[2] This view of Soviet rural society in the 1920s was strongly challenged both at the time and subsequently. According to Shanin (1982 p. 199) the Bolshevik understanding was 'a misleading conception of rural society'.

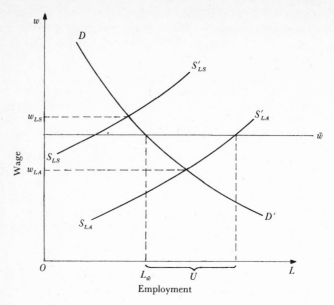

Figure 4.1 The cause of unemployment: the neoclassical view

labour. It is determined by the marginal product of labour. The supply curve of labour is given by SS'. In an economy where labour is scarce relative to land and other means of production, the supply curve is $S_{LS}S'_{LS}$ and the equilibrium wage is w_{LS}. In an economy where labour is abundant relative to the means of production the supply curve is $S_{LA}S'_{LA}$. The equilibrium wage is w_{LA}. Suppose the actual wage is $\bar{w}$ (e.g. because of custom, subsistence needs or the law). Then employment will be $L\bar{w}$ and unemployment will be U. The cause of the unemployment is the excessively high level of wages. Wage labour is an inefficient mode of labour organisation when the marginal product of part of the labour force that wishes to work at the prevailing wage rate is less than that wage. It is for this reason that narodniks argue that peasant farming is more efficient than wage labour in labour surplus economies. Whereas under wage labour, labour will only be employed till the marginal product of labour equals the wage rate and the remainder of the labourers will be unemployed, under peasant farming labour will be performed until the marginal product of labour is zero. As a result, in conditions of labour abundance, under peasant agriculture output will be higher (because more work is performed) and unemployment much lower (both because greater work is performed and because it is spread among family members) than under capitalist agriculture. If under-employment exists in peasant agriculture, the neoclassical view is that it must be caused by the zero marginal product of labour resulting from the abundance of labour relative to means of production.

The Keynesian view emphasises the role of effective demand in determining unemployment. If effective demand is too low relative to the availability of labour, then unemployment will result. The way to deal with it is to raise the effective demand for food products, e.g. by an income redistribution which diverts demand from imported luxuries to food, or by grants to poor consumers.

The Marxist view is that unemployment in capitalist agriculture (as in capitalist industry) is an inevitable result of the capitalist mode of production. Marx explained in volume 1 of *Capital* (1961 edn p. 642) that, in agriculture, the General Law of Capitalist Accumulation is that

As soon as capitalist production takes possession of agriculture, and in proportion to the extent to which it does so, the demand for an agricultural labouring population falls absolutely, while the accumulation of the capital employed in agriculture advances, without this repulsion being, as in non-agricultural industries, compensated by a greater attraction. Part of the agricultural population is therefore constantly on the point of passing over into an urban or manufacturing proletariat, and on the look out for circumstances favourable to this transformation ... But the constant flow towards the towns presupposes, in the country itself, a constant latent surplus-population, the extent of which becomes evident only when its channels of outlet open to exceptional width. The agricultural labourer is therefore reduced to the minimum of wages, and always stands with one foot already in the swamp of pauperism.

The function of the unemployed under capitalism is to depress wages[3] and ensure labour discipline.[4] The Marxist view is that under socialism, on the other hand, there is no social requirement for not using labour, and an obvious social need to employ all the available people.

Besides irrational use of labour, capitalist and pre-capitalist agri-

---

[3] The reserve army of unemployed ensures that (ibid. p.620) 'The rise of wages [during the boom] ... is confined within limits that not only leave intact the foundations of a capitalistic system, but also secures its reproduction on a progressive scale.'
[4] The reserve army of unemployed ensures that the employed workers (ibid. p.636) 'submit to over-work and to subjugation under the dictates of capital'.

culture is often marked by the irrational use of land and other inputs. The causes of this can be analysed analogously.

During the process of economic development the growing urban population requires an expanding supply of agricultural products. If the marketed output of agriculture does not grow then the supply of labour to industry is likely to be adversely affected. Communists have traditionally considered that the capitalist organisation of agriculture is likely to be less efficient in mobilising agricultural output for industry than the socialist organisation of agriculture.

Marxists have traditionally expected collectivist agriculture to supply a major share of the resources required for rapid accumulation. In a speech at the July 1928 Plenum of the Communist Party's Central Committee, Stalin analysed the question of the origin of the resources required for Soviet industrialisation. He began by considering capitalist industrialisation.

In the capitalist countries industrialisation was usually effected, in the main, by robbing other countries, by robbing colonies or defeated countries, or with the help of substantial and more or less enslaving loans from abroad.

You know that for hundreds of years Britain collected capital from all her colonies and from all parts of the world, and was able in this way to make additional investments in her industry. This, incidentally, explains why Britain at one time became the 'workshop of the world'.

You also know that Germany developed her industry with the help, among other things, of the 5,000 million francs she levied as an indemnity of France after the Franco-Prussian war.

One respect in which our country differs from the capitalist countries is that it cannot and must not engage in colonial robbery, or the plundering of other countries in general. That way, therefore, is closed to us.

What then remains? Only one thing, and that is to develop industry, to industrialise the country with the help of *internal* accumulations ...

But what are the chief sources of these accumulations? As I have said, there are only two such sources: firstly, the working class, which creates values and advances our industry; and secondly the peasantry.

The way matters stand with respect to the peasantry in this respect is as follows: it not only pays the state the usual taxes, direct and indirect; it also *overpays* in the relatively high prices for manufactured goods – that is in the first place, and it is more or less *underpaid* in the prices for agricultural produce – that is in the second place.

This is an additional tax levied on the peasantry for the sake of promoting industry, which caters for the whole country, the peasantry included. It is something in the nature of a 'tribute', of a supertax, which we are compelled to levy for the time being in order to preserve and accelerate our present rate of industrial development, in order to ensure an industry for the whole country ...

It is an unpalatable business, there is no denying. But we should not be

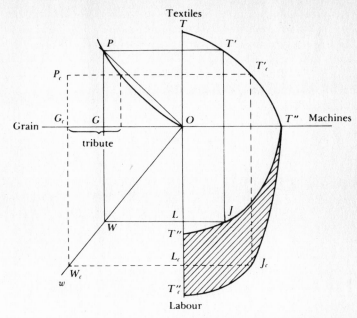

Figure 4.2 The tribute model

Bolsheviks if we slurred over it and closed our eyes to the fact that, unfortunately, our industry and our country cannot *at present* dispense with this additional tax on the peasantry.

Stalin's idea of the terms on which the marketed output of agriculture can be obtained, as a constraint on the rate of industrialisation, and of a tribute levied on agriculture as a source of resources for industrialisation, is illustrated in figure 4.2.

Figure 4.2 illustrates an economy with two sectors: industry and agriculture. Industry produces two goods, machines and textiles. It does this using machinery and workers. Workers are paid in grain which can only be obtained from the peasants who work in the agricultural sector. They exchange grain for textiles. The amount of grain supplied depends on the peasants' offer curve of grain for textiles. The amount of grain so obtained, and the wage rate in industry, simultaneously determine the labour force in industry in the subsequent period. Time is discrete.

The north-east quadrant shows the production possibility curve in industry. It is technically determined. At time (1), with initial stocks of machines and grain, the planners must choose a point on it – an output mix of machines and textiles. To produce at T would ensure that the peasants were well dressed, but entail zero production of machines, i.e. zero investment in industry. To produce at T'' would provide the maximum possible addition to the capital stock in industry, but would lead to the dissolution of the industrial labour force, and zero production in industry at time (2). The planners have to balance these considerations when choosing. Whatever point is chosen (say T') determines investment in industry and the stock of textiles available for sale to the peasantry.

These textiles are sold to the peasants and realise a quantity of grain (say OG) determined by the peasants' offer curve. (The slope of the vector from the origin to P gives the price ratio of the two goods.) The quantity of grain realised determines the point reached on the Ow line. The slope of the Ow line in the south-west quadrant is the grain wage of labour in industry, which is socially determined. The quantity of grain obtained from the peasants determines the point reached on the Ow line (say W) and hence the size of the labour force (OL) in time (2). The south-east quadrant shows the relationship between the labour force and the increment to the capital stock available for production in the industrial sector at time (2) for different choices of output mix at time (1). Given T' (and thus P, G, W, L and J) the production possibility curve TT'' for subsequent periods can be determined.

The model shows the initial capital stock, technology, the terms on which the peasants will sell grain and the real wage rate, simultaneously constraining growth. Assume that the rate of growth so determined is below that desired by the party. Then one way of raising the rate of growth is by the use of coercion to levy a tribute on the peasantry, i.e. to force them off their offer curve to point P_c. This is shown by that part of the figure in dashes. The transition from peasant agriculture to collectivist agriculture is assumed to raise grain procurement to OG_c. This enables more workers to be employed in industry, than with peasant farming, while simultaneously production of textiles is lower and investment higher. This enables the desired higher growth rate to be attained. In the figure, the additional combinations of labour and investment available in period (2) as a result of collectivisation is shown by the shaded area in the south-east quadrant.

Summary

Marxists have traditionally considered that peasant farming is not a viable way of organising agriculture. Comparing capitalist agriculture with socialist agriculture, Marxists consider that the latter has four important advantages. First, it prevents rural exploitation. Secondly, it allows the rational use of the available labour and other resources. Thirdly, it ensures a rapid growth of the marketed output of agriculture. Fourthly, it provides a large source of resources for accumulation.

PROBLEMS OF COLLECTIVISM

In this section five problems of collectivist agriculture will be considered, economies of scale, labour incentives, the use of collective farms for taxation, inequality, and the use of administrative methods.

Economies of scale play an important role in Marxist-Leninist arguments about why peasant farming is not a viable way of organising agriculture. Experience, however, has shown that agriculture is fundamentally different from industry in that organising workers in large productive units does not in general raise productivity. As Joan Robinson (1964a p. 1) has explained:

For the deployment of labour, a rather small scale is required. Workers are spread out over space so that discipline is hard to enforce; an incentive wage system is not easy to arrange or administer; there has to be a great diffusion of managerial responsibility; every field is different, every day is different and quick decisions have to be taken. For getting work out of the workers a peasant family is hard to beat. Discipline and responsibility are imposed by the pressing incentive to secure the family livelihood.

This is the main explanation of the abundant evidence (Dorner 1972 p. 120) that 'output per unit of land is inversely related to farm size'. As Lipton (1974 p. 289) has noted,

Part of this relationship is spurious (because holding size is usually smaller on good soil), but much of it survives even in micro studies where the soil quality can be held constant. Small family farms can saturate the land with plenty of labour per acre, as there is little else for the labour to do (except perhaps at seasonal peaks). Large commercial farms must supervise labour and pay it the full market price, which is likely to rise if they buy too much of it. Another and more surprising fact is that, as Colin Clark has often emphasised, all the careful micro work shows that *capital* per acre also increases as farm size declines ...

Where labour is abundant relative to land, the efficient utilisation of scarce resources requires small, not large, units, a finding paradoxical from a Marxist-Leninist standpoint. Where there is a high labour-land ratio, the main production problem of agricultural development is to raise land productivity and not labour productivity. Hence in labour-abundant farming there is a smaller gain from organising labour in large units than there is in industry, where factories raise labour productivity by the division of labour (and also by strict supervision, which is not possible in a spatially dispersed activity such as farming). The gains from the division of labour in agriculture are also limited by the sequential nature of much agricultural work. Raising land productivity is largely a matter of the application of modern inputs such as improved seeds and artificial fertilisers.

In addition, there are also managerial diseconomies of scale in agriculture. The efficient large-scale organisation of labour requires efficient planning, administration and bookkeeping work which is unnecessary under peasant farming where each peasant organises his own work himself. The extent of this managerial diseconomy of scale depends on two factors. First, the size of the organisation. The bigger it is, the more serious the problem. Secondly, the educational level of the farmers. An important cause of the adverse effects of organising Chinese agriculture into communes in 1958 was the large size of the workforce per commune, in a society in which the majority of farmers were completely illiterate. They were incapable of handling even the simplest bookkeeping.

Although, in the area of the efficient deployment of agricultural labour, the Marxist–Leninist thesis of the advantages of large-scale organisation is invalid where labour is abundant relative to land, there are important areas in which the Marxist–Leninist thesis of the importance of economies of scale is correct. For example, transport and marketing. Furthermore, when land is scarce, the efficient use of land of different qualities requires specialisation, which is incompatible with peasant farming in the strict sense of the term. But specialisation is compatible with small holder farming – small-scale farming whose output is destined for the market – and with large-scale capitalist farming. Also, the division of land into fragmented plots, and the use of land for boundary lines, are common sources of waste in agriculture when there is private ownership of land. Obviously investment in irrigation, water control and land reclamation may require very large-scale organisations, as in the irrigated areas of Soviet Central Asia or the river valleys of China or the United States.

To establish effective labour incentives for collective agriculture is a difficult but very important task. In the USSR, where collectivist agriculture was first established, it was organised on what was virtually a feudal pattern. Work on the communal fields was enforced by coercion and paid almost nothing. The livelihood of the farmers was gained from their private plots, the right to which depended on their performance of labour for the collective farm. This system did produce an increased supply of basic wage goods for the towns, but only at the cost of a low level of labour productivity and very high costs of production in agriculture. In addition, more than half a century after the transition to collective farming the Soviet Government was still unable to provide the population with a continuous supply of high quality foods – fresh fruit and vegetables and meat. The absence of adequate labour incentives was a serious problem in Chilean agriculture under the land reform carried out by the Christian Democrats in the late 1960s. It was assumed that the consciousness of the villagers had been so transformed that material incentives could be neglected. As Lehmann (1974 p. 95) has observed, for this to have worked,

> there would have to be a high level of morally based co-operation among the *asentados*, in the absence of an effective material incentive. In practice, however, it was common to hear the argument that there is no point in a man working hard if another spends his time drinking. My interviews with workers and *asentados* in 1969, show a very clear concern for a fair return to physical effort expended in work. Thus, where there is a lack of trust among co-operators they prefer to turn their energies to the family economy where such a return is more secure.

In China, the need to increase material incentives was a major reason for decollectivisation in 1979–84.

The collectivist labour incentive system in Maoist China suffered from two major problems: private income and the allocation of collective income. In the late 1960s and 1970s at least 25 percent of the peasants' personal income came from the private sector. Here the link between work and income was direct. Work in this sector was therefore more attractive to the peasants than work in the collective sector. As for work incentives in the collective sector, there were two problems. First, part of the output was not distributed to those who had produced it, but used for taxes, investment, to support cadres and for other purposes. Secondly, of that part which was available for peasant consumption, a substantial amount was distributed in the form of a ration which was allocated according to family size and age structure. In poor areas, this basic grain ration swallowed up the bulk of the output available for distribution. Hence, in poor areas, labour incentives for work in the collective economy were weakest. It is therefore not surprising that decollectivisation began in those areas and spread from there to the rest of the country.

A serious threat to the success of collectivist agriculture (from the standpoint of the welfare of the villagers and the levels of productivity and output) is its treatment by the Government primarily as a source of taxation. A major purpose of Soviet collectivisation was precisely to raise rural taxation, or as Stalin put it in the passage already quoted, to levy a 'tribute' on the peasantry (see also Stalin 1955a pp. 52–9). This policy did provide the state with an increased supply of basic wage goods (bread, potatoes and cabbage). It also, however, contributed to a high-cost agriculture and chronic urban shortages of quality foods. Similarly, in China the failure of average rural incomes to rise significantly under collectivisation was a major cause of decollectivisation in 1979–84.

From a socialist perspective, a major problem of collectivist agriculture is that its introduction and maintenance may be based on crude coercion and be incompatible with the transition to a society which is egalitarian and under social control. Collectivisation in the USSR was largely a matter of the application of state power to crush peasant farming, and was necessarily accompanied by widespread deportations. It created a hierarchical society, employing an unparalleled apparatus of repression and with a concentration of power akin to that of the Roman Empire. In China the Great Leap Forward led to an enormous increase in work done, most of which was wasted, and a dramatic fall in output. The inequality between those who had to do the extra work and those who inspired the Leap, and the lack of social control over the decisions taken, were extreme.

The decollectivisation of agriculture in Yugoslavia in 1950, the ending of partial collectivisation in Poland in 1956 and decollectivisation in China in 1979–84 were not signs of a widespread desire for the hard work, long hours and insecurity of peasant farming. They were signs of the failure of a collectivist agriculture primarily concerned with establishing and maintaining control by the state and its officials over the peasants, to satisfy the needs and wishes of the rural population. In 1961, Chen Yun made an investigation of the real situation in Xiaozheng Commune of Qingpu county (near Shanghai). The peasants had both criticism and praise for the party's agricultural policies (Chen Yun 1961 p. 156).'Their criticisms and complaints', Chen wrote in a letter to Deng Xiaoping, 'may be summarized as the following four: first, they do not have enough to eat; second, the cadres at the grass-roots level set high quotas arbitrarily in disregard of realities, and they have failed to participate regularly in work and have led privileged lives; third, the cadres have given wrong orders in production and refused to make self-criticisms; and fourth, because collective production has not been organized well, the peasants lack enthusiasm – while by contrast, they show great enthusiasm for private plots and sideline production.' It is scarcely surprising that, when in 1979–82 the political pressure from the centre for the institutional arrangements which had contributed to this situation weakened, spontaneous decollectivisation should take place.

A major negative aspect of collectivist agriculture in many countries is the use of administrative methods, such as instructions from above, rather than economic methods, such as price and tax policy, where the latter would be more efficient. The consequent growth of bureaucracy and decline of local initiative has been simply a dead loss to society.

During the 1980s, the problems of collectivist agriculture were recognised in the practice of many state socialist countries and also led to important theoretical developments. There was a recognition by Marxist–Leninist theorists in the 1980s of the dangers of creating excessively large farms and of the losses resulting from the use of administrative methods. There was also a recognition of the economic and social advantages, in some situations, of petty commodity production and of the merits of using economic methods. This resulted from the experience of the state socialist countries and theoretical reflection on that experience. Important works which incorporated this new perspective were Bogomolov (1984) and Zhou and Du (1985). The former recognised that household agricultural production could be efficient under certain circumstances, attracting into production resources (e.g. small buildings, remote areas of land or the time of pensioners) otherwise not available to the state. It specifically recognised that such production was not necessarily technically backward and grossly inefficient. On the contrary, it could produce additional output at low cost, quite unlike the state sector with its high investment, high waste, high costs and low returns. It also specifically recognised that directive planning of agriculture could disorganise it and that indirect planning via manipulation of prices and other financial regulators was often more efficient. Zhou and Du (1985) argued that, because of important differences between the labour process in agriculture and in other sectors, the gains from the division of labour in agriculture were less than in industry. Therefore, they argued, the factory model, based on division of labour and close supervision, was inappropriate to agriculture.

Summary

There are five main problems of collectivist agriculture. First, the absence of some of the economies of scale postulated by Marxism–Leninism. Secondly, the need to design an effective system of labour incentives. Thirdly, the use of collective farms by the state primarily as instruments of taxation and control of the rural population. Fourthly, the extreme inequalities and lack of social control over decision making, to which it can lead. Fifthly, the use of administrative methods where economic methods are more efficient. Some account was taken of these problems by Marxist–Leninism and Marxism–Leninism–Mao Zedong Thought in the 1980s.

THE COERCIVE MODEL

The model

In *The Wealth of Nations* Adam Smith analysed 'previous accumulation', i.e. the accumulation the existence of which is a precondition for self-sustaining capitalist growth. Taking this notion as his starting point, Marx in Part VIII of *Capital* Volume 1 analysed 'the so-called original[5] accumulation'. He stressed two factors, the creation of new relations of production (the employment of propertyless labourers by capitalists) and the use of force. ('In actual history', wrote Marx in *Capital* Volume 1 chapter 26, 'it is notorious that conquest, enslavement, robbery, murder, briefly force, play the great part ... The history of the [original accumulation] ... is written in the annals of mankind in letters of blood and fire.') During the Russian Civil War some Bolsheviks adapted Marx's concept to Soviet conditions and analysed 'original socialist accumulation'.

As interpreted, for example, in Bukharin's famous work *The economics of the transition period* (1920 pp. 101–2) original *socialist* accumulation has in common with original *capitalist* accumulation primarily the use of coercion to create a labour force. As such the concept provided a convenient rationalisation of party economic policy

[5] Marx used the phrase 'ursprüngliche Akkumulation'. In the Moore-Aveling translation of *Capital* this is rendered as 'primitive accumulation'. Some writers, such as Gerschenkron and Sweezy, refer to 'original' or 'primary' accumulation, and this, as Pollit (1971) has noted, is the better translation.

Table 4.1 *Marketed output of basic wage goods, USSR 1928–32**
(millions of tonnes)

	1928	1929	1930	1931	1932
Grain	8.3	10.2	17.9	18.8	13.7
Potatoes	4.1	5.5	8.8	9.1	8.4
Vegetables	1.1	1.5	2.5	3.2	2.3

* Mass collectivisation in the USSR began in the autumn of 1929.
Source: Ellman (1975)

during the Civil War, for example the militarisation of labour and the use of force to obtain agricultural products. During NEP the concept was used by Preobrazhensky in the course of his well-known analysis of Soviet economic growth.

In the mid 1920s the idea of 'original socialist accumulation', i.e. of socialist construction by means of coercion against the peasantry, was decisively rejected by the party. In a well-known paper of 1925 (*Bol'shevik* No. 8) Bukharin argued that it was unnecessary and even harmful to the economy to carry on class warfare by administrative methods. If a 'St. Bartholomew's massacre' were organised for the village bourgeoisie, the socialist state would lose large resources for economic growth, which could otherwise be exploited for its purposes through channels of taxation and the banking system. In the late 1920s, however, under the influence of the increasing difficulties with grain procurements and the criticism of party policy by the Left, views within the party changed.

In his speech in July 1928, quoted above, Stalin announced his acceptance of the need to levy a 'tribute' on the peasantry to provide resources for investment. At the end of 1929 he launched the policies of dekulakisation, collectivisation and taking grain.[6] These policies required the use of coercion on a large scale, over many years. The logic of Stalin's policy was analysed above.

The outcome

The collectivisation of agriculture in the USSR did lead to a sharp increase in the marketed output of basic wage goods (bread, potatoes and cabbage). This is shown in table 4.1. This increase in marketed output was not a result of increased production, but of the state

[6] For a description of the latter, see Lewin (1974).

taking products which would otherwise have been eaten by livestock or the rural population. Hence there was a catastrophic drop in livestock numbers in 1929–32 and a famine in 1932–3.[7]

The collectivisation of agriculture in the USSR also provided a substantial increase in the urban labour force. The mass deportations from the villages, together with the sharp drop in animal products and grain supplies per capita, severely depressed rural living standards and drove millions of villagers to the towns.

Although the state did obtain an increased supply of basic wage goods as a result of collectivisation, the supply of livestock products fell sharply. Furthermore, the state had to provide substantial resources for agriculture. A significant share of Soviet investment since 1929 has always been devoted to agriculture. Much of this investment has been wasted. Collectivisation itself meant that much of the investment in tractors was simply required in order to offset the disinvestment in animal traction power caused by the state taking the grain which was needed to keep the animals alive. In addition, the very sharp increase in food prices on the free market meant that much of the squeeze on living standards was transferred to the working class. According to the Soviet researcher Barsov (1974 p. 96), the amount of unequal exchange was higher in 1913 than in any year of Soviet power, and higher in 1928 (i.e. prior to collectivisation) than in the late 1930s (i.e. after collectivisation). Barsov's findings suggest

[7] The number of deaths from the famine of 1932/3 and the population deficit resulting from it (i.e. deaths + decline in births) are controversial. This primarily results from the poor state of Soviet demographic statistics for this period. There were censuses in 1926, 1937 and 1939. The results of the 1937 census were suppressed because of its inconvenient results. The accuracy of the 1939 census is uncertain. The 1926 census, although relatively good, was also imperfect. Both birth and death rates for the early 1930s are uncertain. Furthermore, there were a number of other demographic disturbances between 1926 and 1939 which affect the estimates, such as dekulakisation and the arrests of 1937–8. In addition, for many authors, these estimates have an important political significance. A plausible estimate of the number of excess deaths (i.e. deaths in excess of those to be expected under normal circumstances) in 1926–39 of those already alive in 1926 is about 5 million. The population deficit in 1939 of those who were born (either actually or potentially) after 1926 naturally depends on the counter-factual assumptions made about fertility and mortality. Since a wide range of assumptions is possible, there is a wide range of possible estimates, from zero to 18 million. The medium fertility medium mortality figure is 9.4 million. It is not possible to divide this population deficit accurately between excess deaths and reduced births due to lack of reliable data. It seems unlikely, however, that the number of excess deaths in this cohort was less than 3 million. Hence total excess deaths in 1926–39 were probably not less than 8 million. The total population deficit in 1939 is larger because it also includes children who were not born in this period. The great majority of the excess deaths and shortfall in births in 1926–39 were a result of famine, food deficiency diseases and dekulakisation. The repression of 1937–8 was a relatively small cause.

Table 4.2 *Improvements in the Soviet diet, 1950–76*

Product	Per capita consumption in 1976 as percentage of	
	1950	Norm
Meat and fat	215	68
Milk and milk products	184	78
Eggs	348	72
Fish and fish products	263	101
Sugar	361	105
Vegetable oil	285	85
Fruit and berries	336	33
Vegetables and melons	169	59
Potatoes	49	123
Bread and bread products	82	128

Source: E. M. Agababyan & Ye. N. Yakovleva, *Problemy raspredeleniya i rost narodnogo blagosostoyaniya* (Moscow 1979) p. 142.

that collectivisation did *not* lead to an increased net transfer of commodities from agriculture. Hence Stalin's 1928 implicit argument for collectivisation, based on the idea that it would lead to an increased net transfer of commodities to industry, seems to have been wrong, at any rate in the Soviet case.

The actual process of accumulation which took place in the USSR during the first three Five Year Plans differed in three important respects from that analysed in Preobrazhensky's book *The new economics*. First, there was no increase in unequal exchange between agriculture and industry. Secondly, the fall in urban real wages (what Trotsky had earlier termed 'the self-exploitation of the working class') played an important role in financing the increase in accumulation. At the end of the First Five Year Plan, real wages per worker were only about half of what they had been at the beginning of it. The decline in working class living standards, however, was much less than the decline in real wages, because of the big increase in the urban participation rate (e.g. the abolition of urban unemployment during the First Five Year Plan). By the end of the Second Five Year Plan, urban per capita consumption was above that at the beginning of the First Five Year Plan. Thirdly, the whole process was based on coercion rather than use of the price mechanism.

After Stalin's death, the coercive model was gradually abandoned in the USSR and Eastern Europe. The reason for this was the adverse effect of the model on output and on the availability of quality foods in the towns. According to US specialists (Millar 1977), in 1951–75 total Soviet agricultural output grew at not less than 3.4 percent per annum. The population in this period grew only 1.4 percent per annum, so that per capita output grew at c. 2 percent per annum. This was a very satisfactory performance, and one much better than in many other countries. Besides this quantitative improvement, there was also a qualitative improvement with a significant increase in the output and consumption of high quality products. Some data is set out in table 4.2.

Table 4.2 shows very clearly the sharp improvement in the Soviet diet in the third quarter of the twentieth century. Per capita consumption of fish and meat more than doubled, milk and milk products nearly doubled and vegetables rose by two thirds. At the same time, the per capita consumption of potatoes halved and that of bread also fell. Nevertheless, even in 1976, per capita consumption of fruit, vegetables and meat were still significantly below the norms (for the use of norms in consumption planning see chapter 8).

Considered historically, the most important achievement of post-Stalin agricultural policy has been to eliminate famines in the USSR. Famines were endemic in Tsarist Russia. The USSR has experienced four famines, in 1921–2, 1932–4, 1941–3 and 1946–7. In addition, throughout the period 1931–52 Soviet people were dying of starvation or food deficiency diseases. (In the 1930s the USSR experienced a major malaria epidemic largely arising from food shortages.) As a result of the progress of the Soviet economy since the end of the Great Patriotic War, it seems entirely likely, however, that the famine of 1946–7 will be the last famine ever in Russia/USSR (save only in the wake of nuclear war). This is an achievement of fundamental importance in a country traditionally prone to famines.

The reasons for this impressive performance appear to be, a huge increase in modern inputs (e.g. chemical fertilisers and machinery), an improvement in the economic position of the farmers (whose real incomes have increased enormously in this period), an increase in the sown area and a more consumer-oriented economic policy. The latter is manifested by the fact that since the late 1960s the USSR has been investing in agriculture on an enormous scale, and that since the early 1960s it has been prepared to buy grain in large quantities from abroad, as is done by some West European countries.

Nevertheless, Soviet agriculture in the third quarter of the twentieth century suffered from four problems. First, its low initial level (largely resulting from the policies pursued in the previous quarter century). Secondly, the fact that it was a high cost agriculture, requiring massive inputs of land, investment and labour. Thirdly, output, especially of grain, fluctuated sharply from year to year. Fourthly, the investment, labour and price policies pursued in the distribution sector (see chapter 8) were not favourable to the general availability of good quality food.

In 1975–85 the performance of Soviet agriculture was very disappointing and led to massive food imports, widespread shortages and local rationing in some parts of the country in the 1980s. This resulted from prolonged adherence to non-market clearing prices, errors of economic policy (such as heavy investment in agro-industrial livestock complexes for red meat production and harmful irrigation projects), widespread waste, continued failure to implement adequate labour incentives for farm workers, ecological problems and increased fossilisation of the bosses in the late Brezhnev period. In response to this situation, a number of changes were introduced in Soviet agriculture as part of the *perestroika* programme. One of them was official support for new forms of organisation of agricultural labour. These new institutional forms ('family contract', 'individual contract', 'leasing contract' etc.) if actually implemented on a large scale seemed as if they might well be the beginning of a decollectivisation process. They were the practical reflection of the new developments in Marxist–Leninist agricultural theory noted above. They were also confirmations of the incorrectness of the traditional Marxist–Leninist arguments about the universal advantages of large-scale production in agriculture.

Summary

In the coercive model, which was applied in the USSR under Stalin, the resources for rapid industrialisation are obtained from agriculture by coercion. The application of this model did enable the state to increase sharply its inflow of basic wage goods and its stock of labour. It also was, and is, an important explanation of the high costs and low productivity of Soviet agriculture. From the standpoint of intersectoral flows, the increase in marketed output of basic wage goods was offset by the decline in the marketed output of livestock products and the increased flow of industrial goods (e.g. investment goods) to agriculture. The increase in investment in the USSR after 1928 required both labour and commodities. The increase in the labour force came mainly from agriculture and was fed on food obtained from agriculture. The increase in commodities came largely from industry and construction themselves.

In a speech of 1928 Stalin considered two sources of Soviet accumulation, the working class and the peasantry. The purpose of Soviet collectivisation was to finance industrialisation by levying a tribute on the peasantry. In the outcome a large share of the burden *did* fall on the peasantry. Agricultural output fell but marketed output of basic wage goods rose, so that many peasants starved. Simultaneously, however, real wages fell (largely because of the scarcity of food) and employment enormously increased so that the major part of the contribution to the increase in investment came from the working class.

The coercive model was gradually abandoned in the USSR and the other CMEA countries after Stalin's death, because of its adverse effect on output.

THE MAOIST MODEL

The model

The Maoist model has much in common with the coercive. The dominant role of the state, coercion, the powerlessness of the rural population, restrictions on household enterprise and tying the rural population to the soil, are all the same. Nevertheless, there are some important differences. First, whereas Soviet collectivisation was primarily aimed at collecting tribute, Chinese collectivisation was not. Secondly, in the Maoist model a major role in rural social transformation is played by the rural party organisations. Thirdly, in the Maoist model greater attention is paid to the utilisation of rural resources.

Because China embarked on collectivisation long after the USSR, it had the possibility of learning from the experiences of the USSR. In *On the ten major relationships* (1956) Mao referred to 'the prolonged failure of the Soviet Union to reach the highest pre-October level in grain output'. The conclusion he drew is that the Soviet stress on collecting tribute had hindered production. A successful collective agriculture, with rising production, required that the real income of the peasantry should grow steadily. In accordance with this line of analysis, in China net grain procurements, as a proportion of output, did not increase during collectivisation, in marked contrast with the situation in the USSR. This is shown in table 4.3. In the USSR, the net procurement ratio increased sharply during the collectivisation process. In China it did not. This gain (from the standpoint of the peasants) was abandoned after the formation of the communes, in

Table 4.3 *Collectivisation and grain extraction, USSR and China (millions of tonnes*)*

(1) Year	(2) Output	(3) Net procurements	(4) (3) as % of (2)
		USSR**	
1928	63–73	8.3	11.4–13.2
1929	62–72	10.2	14.2–16.5
1930	63–78	17.9	22.9–28.4
1931	51–67	18.8	28.1–36.9
1932	50–67	13.7	20.4–27.4
		CHINA***	
1953	167	35.9	21.5
1954	170	31.6	18.6
1955	184	36.2	19.7
1956	193	28.7	14.9
1957	195	33.9	17.4

* The absolute magnitude of the output figures for the USSR and China are not comparable.
** Collectivisation in the USSR began at the end of 1929 and embraced the majority of peasant households by the end of 1932.
Soviet output figures are given as a range rather than a single number because there is considerable uncertainty about the magnitude of Soviet grain output in these years.
*** Collectivisation in China took place mainly in 1955–7.
Sources: S. G. Wheatcroft, R. W. Davies & J. M. Cooper, 'Soviet industrialization reconsidered, *Economic History Review* (May 1986) p. 283; A. A. Barsov, *Balans stoimostnykh obmenov mezhdu gorodom i derevnei* (Moscow 1969) p. 103; *China trade and price statistics* (Beijing 1987) p. 58 for 1953–6, *Statistical Yearbook of China 1986* (Beijing 1986) p. 460 for 1957. Different figures are given in K. R. Walker, *Food grain procurement and consumption in China* (Cambridge 1984) p. 55.

the immediate aftermath of which (1959) the net procurement rate reached the very high level of 28 percent. This was a significant contribution to the 1960–2 famine. It was, however, an aberration, and throughout the 1960s and 1970s the net procurement ratio was no higher than prior to collectivisation. The level of taxes, the prices paid for state purchases and the prices charged for agricultural inputs, however, were fixed by the state in a way which squeezed rural living standards. Despite Mao's words, there was no steady increase in the real incomes of the peasantry under collectivisation. Hence in practice Maoist China failed to implement the sensible conclusion Mao had drawn from the Soviet experience.

Because it came to power after a long civil war in which its strength lay in rural areas, the Chinese Communist Party had very large numbers of rural cadres and a considerable knowledge of rural conditions when it achieved power. This was a complete contrast to

the situation in the USSR and had many important policy consequences. For example, whereas land reform in the USSR was a
mainly spontaneous process, in China it was organised and directed
by the party. Similarly, collectivisation in China did not have to be
primarily extractive because the strength of the rural party organisation enabled the Government to obtain quite a high rate of
marketed output even with private ownership, as can be seen from
table 4.3. In addition, whereas Soviet collectivisation relied heavily
upon direct coercion, the Chinese cadres generally succeeded in
organising collectivisation without employing direct coercion.

In traditional rural China there existed substantial surplus labour
during the farming off-season (November–February), unutilised
natural resources (e.g. limestone, rivers suitable for the generation of
hydro-electricity) and an acute shortage of modern inputs (e.g.
chemical fertilisers, farm machinery and electricity) for agriculture.
A major aspect of the Maoist model was an attempt to use fully the
available resources in the interests of agriculture. This took a number
of forms.

First, the use of off-season farm labour for labour-intensive rural
infrastructure activities. These included the construction of water
control and irrigation systems, land terracing, afforestation, road
building, the construction of schools, hospitals, other public buildings and housing. Since the labourers on these projects were usually
paid in work points[8] issued by their normal production teams, and
construction machinery was conspicuous by its absence, the cost to
the state was zero or very little. The advantage of this system is that
extra output is produced at zero or very small state opportunity cost.
The disadvantages are that arduous work is performed during time
which may well have considerable private opportunity costs for the
labourers (e.g. in terms of leisure or household activities), that it may
have an adverse effect on agricultural output (if some of the labour is
not really surplus or if the resulting reduction in food and cash
payments per work point has disincentive effects), and that the
output may be useless (like the Pyramids of Ancient Egypt) or
harmful (e.g. badly planned irrigation projects).

Secondly, the development of rural small-scale industries. Under
Mao rural small-scale industries meant industrial enterprises
administratively subordinated to counties, communes or brigades,
and not to higher level bodies. Being subordinate to a county usually
implied obtaining the bulk of inputs, and distributing the bulk of

---

[8] The 'work point' system is explained in chapter 7.

outputs, within the county. Rural small-scale industry was not necessarily rural (some of it was located in county towns) and was not always so small (some plants employed more than 500 people). Its essential characteristics were that it largely functioned outside the state planning and administrative system, that output per plant and per person was much lower than in the state sector, that it often made more use of indigenous technology than the state industrial sector with its large plants often using imported machinery, that it was often concerned with serving agriculture, that it mainly used local resources and that average employment per plant was less than in the state industrial sector. It is a sector which evolved sub-stantially over time and was heavily influenced by the course of political events. It began during the Great Leap Forward, was generally closed down in 1961 and 1962, and was revived again during and after the Great Proletarian Cultural Revolution. The main rural small-scale industries were energy (e.g. hydro-electricity and coal mining), iron and steel, chemical fertilisers, cement and farm machinery

Many of the rural small-scale industries set up at the time of the Great Leap Forward were very inefficient, producing poor quality products at high cost. During and after the Cultural Revolution they seem to have been more rational, using local resources to produce goods useful for agriculture. Small nitrogen fertiliser plants, for example, seem to have played a useful role in a country where food output, foreign exchange and engineering capability for large process plants were all serious constraints slowing down development.

The Maoist attempt to use all the resources available in rural areas in the interests of agriculture is in striking contrast to the coercive model. A feature of the Soviet manpower scene in the Stalin period, and to a lesser extent also in the 1950s and 1960s, was the existence and persistence of rural underemployment. The main cause of this was political. The Bolsheviks viewed the countryside as a source of tribute and of possible political enemies and neglected the welfare of the rural population. In Maoist China, on the other hand, rural infrastructure projects and a narrow range of rural small-scale industries were encouraged. (Private rural enterprise was, of course, severely restricted in the Maoist period, to an extent which fluc-tuated over time.)

A Maoist policy which had an adverse effect on efficient resource utilisation in the countryside was that of grain selfsufficiency. Each province, and each district, he argued, should be self-sufficient in grain. This policy led to the loss of the gains from specialisation and caused considerable waste and loss of potential income and consumption.

The outcome

During the 1950s, there was a rapid transformation of rural social relations in China. A large-scale land reform in 1950–2 (mostly in 1950 and 1951) was followed by the organisation of mutual aid teams, cooperatives (first elementary and then advanced) and finally communes (1958). The transition from peasant agriculture to fully socialist cooperatives (i.e. collectivisation) mainly took place in 1955–7. Collectivisation in China was much more successful than in the USSR in a number of important respects. First, there was no decline in grain output. Secondly, there was no dramatic decline in livestock numbers. For example, in the two years 1928–30, the number of pigs in the USSR fell by 47 percent and by 1932 had fallen still further. In China, on the other hand, the number of pigs fell by only 17 percent in 1954–6, and then increased in 1956–8. Thirdly, it required far fewer deaths as a proportion of the rural population. Fourthly, it was not accompanied by the death or deportation of the best farmers.[9] This greater success resulted from the non-extractive nature of the collectivisation, the greater strength of the party in the countryside and the possibility which China had (but which the USSR as the pioneer did not have) of learning from the experience of other countries. An important aspect of the latter point was that collectivisation was better prepared and planned in China than in the USSR, where basic issues such as the private plot were only worked out during and after the collectivisation process. Nevertheless, this gain relative to the Soviet experience was thrown away by the Great Leap Forward, which led to a sharp fall in crop output and livestock

---

[9] To some extent this comparison is too favourable to China. As far as the triumph of voluntarism is concerned, the Chinese analogy with the year of the breakthrough (1929) was not 1955–7 but the Great Leap Forward (1958). This, like its Soviet counterpart, did lead to a significant decline in output of crops and livestock numbers and deaths from starvation. As far as political violence in the countryside is concerned, the peak period in China appears to have been not collectivisation (1955–7) but land reform. According to one source (Moise 1983 pp. 142–3) the number of executions during the land reform and the campaigns that led up to it was probably in the range 1–1½ million. The total number arrested (most of whom seem to have been imprisoned) was probably more than double this. Furthermore, about half (?) as many persons as were formally arrested 'were put in the custody of the masses for surveillance and reform through labour' without being formally arrested. In addition, members of the families of those executed, and of the victims of other punishments, were discriminated against until the end of the 1970s.

Table 4.4 *Productivity of Chinese agricultural labour in grain output*

Year	Agricultural labour force (millions)	Grain output (million tonnes)	Grain output per labourer (kg/labourer/year)
1952	173.17	163.92	946.6
1957	193.10	195.05	1,010.1
1958	154.92	200.00	1,290.9
1959	162.73	170.00	1,044.7
1960	170.19	143.50	843.7
1962	212.78	160.00	752.0
1965	233.98	194.53	831.4
1970	278.14	239.96	862.7
1975	294.60	284.52	965.8
1976	294.48	286.31	972.3
1977	293.45	282.73	963.5
1978	294.26	304.77	1,035.7

Source: Statistical yearbook of China 1985 (Hong Kong & Beijing 1985) pp. 213 & 255; for 1958, 1959 & 1960, A. Watson, 'Agriculture looks for "shoes that fit"', *World Development* (August 1983).

numbers. The revolutionary euphoria of 1958–9 in certain party circles in China, like that of 1929–30 in the USSR (and also like that during the Civil War in the USSR and in the 1960s in Cuba), had a severe negative effect on output.

The main achievements of the 1950s were an immense increase in labour inputs (e.g. into irrigation works) and a substantial change in the distribution of income. Another important aspect was the increase in the share of the national income going to accumulation as a result of redirecting what was formerly property income derived from agriculture (Lippit 1975). Much of the increased labour input (e.g. into backyard steel furnaces and poorly planned irrigation projects) was wasted. The increase in agricultural output was modest. The combination of these factors ensured a sharp fall in real income per unit of labour input and this, together with the 1958–9 attempt to move towards distribution according to need, led to a sharp decline in labour incentives. This, together with the managerial diseconomies of scale in agriculture, was one of the causes of the three bad harvests 1959–61. Subsequently output rose, but so did population. Some figures on output and productivity are set out in table 4.4.

From table 4.4 it can clearly be seen that between 1960 and 1977 grain output per labourer remained below the level of the late 1950s.

In 1977, after two decades of collectivisation, grain output per labourer was less than it had been twenty years earlier. Collectivisation had failed entirely in one of its main aims, a steady and significant rise in agricultural labour productivity.

Grain is the basic foodstuff in China, and food accounts for a high proportion of consumption. The failure of grain output per capita to rise significantly and steadily under collectivisation therefore automatically had an adverse effect on consumption. China experienced a major famine between 1958 and 1962. Measured absolutely, by the number of victims, it seems to have been China's and the world's largest ever.[10] Estimates of the number of excess deaths in 1958–62 naturally depend on assumptions about the accuracy of official population statistics and about what the death rate would have been in the absence of a famine. Assuming that the population registration data should be adjusted in the light of the census and fertility survey data, Ashton, Hill, Piazza and Zeitz (1984) estimated that in the four year period mid 1958 to mid 1962 there were about 30 million excess deaths (of which about 20 million were between mid 1959 and mid 1961). They also estimated that the shortfall in births was even bigger, about 33 million. This makes a total population deficit in mid 1962 resulting from the famine of about 63 million, of which the shortfall in births is the larger component. This shortfall in births was followed by a births boom in 1962–5. Hence an estimate of the population deficit at the end of 1965 would be much lower than one of the population deficit in mid 1962 and would be sensitive to the precise counter-factual assumptions made about mortality and fertility in 1958–65. Even after the national recovery (1962) hunger and malnutrition persisted in the poorest provinces (notably in Guizhou, Gansu and Ningxia) even during normal years and affected other provinces at times of droughts, floods or political upheavals (e.g. Sichuan in 1976). Some data on food availability is set out in table 4.5.

It would appear, subject to data limitations, that throughout the Maoist period average food availability in China was no higher, and possibly lower than it had been in the 1930s. It was only in the early 1980s that average food availability rose sharply relative to the 1930s.

[10] Measured relatively, as a share of the national population affected, the Chinese famine of 1958–62 was much less serious than the Irish famine of the late 1840s. The population deficit resulting from the latter (excess deaths + shortfall in births, but excluding emigration) seems to have been in the range of 13–18 percent of the total population. Including emigration it was about 30 percent of the total population. Moreover, the Irish population never regained the pre-famine level. Relatively speaking, the Irish famine of 1846–50 was a much bigger disaster than the Chinese famine of 1958–62.

Table 4.5 *Per capita food availability in China (kcal)*

Years	Daily per capita food availability (kcal)		
	Total	Plant foods	Animal foods
1923–33	2,280	2,070	210
1933	2,130	1,940	190
1931–37	2,226	2,073	153
1957	2,075	1,962	113
1974	2,045	1,910	135
1977–78	2,130	1,995	105
1983	2,710	2,555	155

Note: Both the reliability of the data (for any particular year/s) and their comparability over time are imperfect.
Source: V. Smil, 'Food production and quality of diet in China', *Population and Development Review* vol. 12, no. 1 (March 1986) tables 2 and 5. I have excluded from table 4.5 the FAO data in Smil's table 2, since the FAO's data on animal food availability is clearly non-comparable with Smil's own calculations.

Data on average food availability is inadequate to answer the question of how extensive rural undernourishment is. That depends on the distribution of consumption and the calculation of needs. Data on both of these is imperfect, but using the available data, Smil (1986) has estimated that in 1983 about 90–100 million peasants were undoubtedly short of food and a further 100 million had a diet which probably fell short of the requirements for a healthy and vigorous existence in the Chinese countryside. In the Maoist period these figures would have been much larger.

From a peasant point of view, an important defect of collectivised agriculture was that it subjected them to the orders of cadres. The cadres were often arrogant, made arbitrary decisions, and were frequently corrupt. They were responsible not to the peasants but to their own superiors. This authoritarian system was unpopular and resented and it collapsed as soon as the political pressure for it from the centre weakened.

Chinese agriculture was decollectivised in 1979–84. The land tenure arrangements existing in the mid 1980s over most of the country in the collective sector could be characterised as a state tenancy system. The land was in public ownership and officially could not be bought or sold. It was rented out to households for periods of at least fifteen years. Provided they met their tenancy obligations (set out in a contract between each household and the state) the tenants were free in deciding what and how to produce.

Table 4.6 *Rate of growth of Chinese agricultural production (in % p.a.)*

	1973–8	1978–83
Gross value of agricultural output*	3.93	8.99
Grain production	2.28	4.08
Grain yield/sown ha	2.39	5.43
Grain output/head	0.89	2.75
Cotton production	−4.48	16.56
Cotton yield	3.94	10.31

* Constant prices.
Source: K. R. Walker, 'Chinese agriculture during the period of the readjustment, 1978–83', *China Quarterly* no. 100 (December 1984).

The hiring of labour was permitted. Leasehold rights were transferrable between households. Furthermore, households were free, on their own or in cooperatives or as companies with other households, to engage in a variety of agricultural, commercial and industrial operations. The production and marketing arrangements were a mixture of peasant farming (the households organised production themselves and consumed a large part of their own output) and smallholder farming (much of the production is for the market). Private plots too have been encouraged in the post-Mao period. By 1981 they accounted for more than 40 percent of peasant income.

As a result of decollectivisation, procurement price increases, increased specialisation and favourable weather, output and incomes in rural China developed very favourably after 1978. Some data on production is set out in table 4.6.

A striking testimony to the magnitude and significance of the progress in production in 1978–84 came in 1985. In that year it was announced that the state monopoly of the purchase of grain was abolished (although in practice the change was less radical than the announcement suggested). Production levels and procurement prices were such that the state had found its purchasing obligations a burden!

The land tenure pattern created by decollectivisation, with average household holdings of 0.6 hectares divided into 9.7 small pieces, was far from ideal. Hence further institutional changes are quite possible.

A very striking feature of the Chinese rural scene in the 1980s was the rapid growth of the rural non-agricultural sector. The number of township (formerly commune), village (formerly brigade), cooperative, individual and private, rural non-agricultural enterprises grew very quickly in numbers, output and employment. By 1985, the total number of enterprises was 12.2 million, with a labour force of 70 million, or 19 percent of the total rural labour force, a gross output of about 17 percent of national gross output and exports equal to about 5 percent of national exports. They were a development of the small-scale rural industries initiated in the Maoist period, but differed from them in a number of respects. These included, their wider range of activities, wide range of institutional forms, the position of their managers and their workers, their market position and the scope they offered for legal economic activity outside the state or collective sectors. Their growth reflected, *inter alia*, the rise after 1978 in rural incomes (which created their market), the partial restoration of pre-1949 patterns of rural economic life, and their encouragement by the authorities. The development of this sector made an important contribution to the goods and services available in rural areas and to the incomes of the rural population. It also played a positive role in preventing rural-urban differences in living standards and hence urbanisation getting completely out of control in a society in which the dramatic relaxation of rationing had made movement to the towns much easier.

Did Chinese collectivisation enable the net transfer of resources from agriculture to industry to be increased? According to a study based on the data available in the mid 1970s (Paine 1976a p. 285), 'although data problems preclude any firm conclusions about the absolute magnitude of the intersectoral resource transfer in any particular year, the direction of the transfer (i.e. a steady shift in *favour* of agriculture) during the first half of the 1950s is clear in *relative* terms from both the financial and real standpoints'. As far as the policies pursued since the end of the 1959–61 economic crisis are concerned (ibid. p. 295), 'Whether or not these policies merely reduced the extent of agriculture's net contribution to accumulation in the rest of the economy or turned it into a net deficit sector is not clear.' The question was reexamined by Lardy (1983). He argued that previous studies had underestimated the transfers from agriculture to industry because they ignored non-grain agricultural deliveries to the state, hidden inflation in the price of industrial products sold to agriculture and the tax element in agricultural deliveries to the state, and treated investments in urban water supply, transport and state farms as if they were investments in collective agriculture. When all these factors were accounted for, he estimated that the state *had* extracted considerable resources from collective agriculture. Nevertheless, Ishikawa's calculations, which are not disputed by Lardy, show an agricultural trade deficit for 1953 and 1956 and Lardy lacked the data to present analogous calculations for the 1960s and 1970s. Taking some of Lardy's points into account, Perkins and Yussuf (1984 chapter 2) estimated that the intersectoral financial flows were such that state industry had obtained substantial resources from agriculture, but that this source of finance had steadily *declined* in relative importance under collectivisation. According to Perkins and Yussuf, the main resource contribution of agriculture to accumulation came from its importance (and in the 1950s, 1960s and 1970s predominance) in exports. The differences between the various studies of this issue result from different definitions of the sectors (does 'agriculture' include only collective and private agriculture, or does it also include state farms, or rural non-agriculture?) different data and different methodologies. A careful study by Sheng (1986) found that at 1957 prices, there was an agricultural import surplus throughout the period 1952–83. She also found that with the exception of 1960–5, both farm exports and imports have increased over time, but in general the latter have increased more quickly than the former. Hence over time the import surplus has tended to grow. Sheng's conclusions are in line with Ishikawa's results for the 1950s and Barsov's findings for the USSR.

The reasons why collectivised agriculture is not effective in generating increasing net transfers of commodities to industry are three-fold. First, a predatory procurement policy has an adverse effect on output. Secondly, socialised agricultural production has a greater capital and materials intensity than private production. Thirdly, peasant and smallholder agriculture are efficient institutional forms under certain conditions.

A predatory procurement policy, often combined with attacks on rural-urban trading links, has an adverse effect on rural incomes, rural consumption and agricultural production. Hence it becomes a serious brake on economic development. This is why it was (gradually) abandoned in the USSR after 1953 and why the terms of trade of the Chinese farm sector were improved by 38 percent in 1977–81. Squeezing agriculture to produce 'surpluses' may simply impoverish the population and fail to benefit industry because of its adverse effects on urban food consumption (and thus on labour availability and productivity), the substantial investments and material inputs required by agriculture and the foreign exchange cost of agricultural imports. Agriculture and industry are not independent sectors but are interdependent. To suppose that agriculture produces 'surpluses', independent of the level of industrial inputs into agriculture and of the supply of industrial consumer goods for the agricultural population, which are available for appropriation in the interests of accumulation, is complete fantasy.

Socialised agriculture typically requires more investment per unit of output than private agriculture. Private farmers tend to substitute their own relatively abundant labour for purchased inputs. On the other hand, socialised farms, faced with the difficulties of disciplining and motivating labour, the allocation by the state of investment resources independent of prospective returns, a soft budget constraint, and a state which sees in investment the solution to all economic problems, tend to substitute material inputs and investment for labour. Similarly, private farmers tend to use to the maximum possible extent self-produced agricultural inputs whereas socialised farms with their large scale of operation and soft budget constraint tend to rely on externally purchased inputs of industrial or foreign origin. The relatively high materials intensity and investment intensity of socialised agriculture is well known from many Polish studies (Simatupang 1981). In Polish agriculture in 1975, the average value of fixed assets per fully employed person was four times greater in the socialised sector than in the private sector. Although gross output per hectare in the socialised sector was somewhat higher than in the private sector, net output was much lower. Similarly, in China between the mid 1960s and 1977 agriculture was technically modernised (improved seeds, electrification, water control, artificial fertilisers) but the economic returns resulting from this were disappointing. To suppose that agriculture can be expected to provide a huge net outflow of goods for an industrialisation programme, and that this is a major rationale for collectivisation, is a fallacy. The socialisation of agriculture Marxist-Leninist style, can be expected to lead to a greater materials and investment intensity of agriculture.

The efficiency of peasant and smallholder agriculture under certain conditions was explained above. It results from their tendency to apply labour till its marginal product is zero and the absence of economies of scale in many lines of agricultural production. The traditional Marxist-Leninist idea that efficient production and technical progress in agriculture always require large units is not true and is refuted by the experience of Western Europe. Naturally, smallholder agriculture is not efficient under all circumstances. Where there are significant economies of scale, where the land-labour ratio is high, or where the capital required for efficient production is not available to smallholders, smallholder production is not efficient. Nor is it viable under conditions of extreme price volatility. The genuine economies of scale that do exist in some branches of agriculture and related activities (e.g. marketing) do not require state control of the sector. They can perfectly well be captured by genuine cooperatives of the type existing in Denmark and in China after decollectivisation.

Summary

The coercive and Maoist models of the role of agriculture in socialist economic development have much in common. The main differences between them were that the latter did not emphasise tribute collection and did emphasise the role of the rural cadres and the need to mobilise fully all the resources available in rural areas in the interests of agriculture. The Maoist period in China saw a major famine and rates of growth of output and output/head which were modest by international standards. This lack of dynamism and the resulting low level of incomes and widespread poverty led to the abandonment of the model in 1979–84.

The technocratic model

From a purely production point of view, the problems of the coercive and Maoist models largely result from the poor labour incentives, the very limited decision-making autonomy of farm management, and the limitations on the private sector and on the non-agricultural activities of the farms. In the technocratic model, agriculture remains predominantly organised in state or collective farms, but a wage system analogous to that in state industry is introduced so as to provide labour incentives and labour discipline, the management of state and collective farms is given wide autonomy, and the private sector is encouraged as is the non-agricultural activity of farms. Elements of the technocratic model have been introduced throughout Eastern Europe in the 1970s and 1980s. In the mid 1980s, perhaps the country which came nearest to the model was Hungary.

In Hungary, peasant monetary incomes had already surpassed those of urban workers by 1966 and by 1971–2 they were about 10 percent greater. Social benefits of the workers remained greater, and their hours of work shorter, so that their total remuneration package per hour worked remained better than that of the peasants. Nevertheless, the existence of substantial wages for farm labour meant that rural labour could be mobilised and disciplined by farm management and hence that, unlike the situation in the early 1960s (and in the USSR in the 1970s and 1980s), it is not necessary to rely on students, workers from the towns, and the army, to bring in the harvest.

The autonomy of agricultural enterprises after 1968 (when the NEM was introduced) increased significantly compared with the nominal autonomy which collective farms enjoyed earlier. In 1957 compulsory deliveries from the farms to the state had been 'abolished' and agricultural procurement prices raised. The procurement 'recommendations' of local government bodies, however, based on breaking down state plan requirements for particular areas, tended to carry the force of orders. The introduction of the NEM definitely marked a great expansion of the real autonomy of farms.

Planning continues to have a significant impact on agricultural enterprises, but the planning mechanism under the NEM differs markedly from the old 'direct' plans. Enterprises are still obliged to submit annual plans. The Central Planning Office continues to use the balance method to reconcile supply and demand *ex ante*. The difference from the old system is that, to overcome projected imbalances, the Central Planning Office relies not on issuing instructions to the enterprises, but on altering prices, credit policies, subsidies and wage regulations so as to induce the enterprises to change their plans in a direction calculated to eliminate the anticipated imbalance. When revised measures of indirect control are being considered for agriculture, managers of some of the major agricultural enterprises are consulted. Agricultural enterprises may buy inputs from a variety of different sources, in quantities and types of their own choice.

It would, however, be a mistake to suppose that Hungarian agriculture has been left to market forces. Large subsidies, state determined prices, bank credit or other official aid needed for investments, and long-term contracts remain important instruments of government regulation of agriculture. Nevertheless, despite these limitations, Hungarian agricultural enterprises *do* have extensive freedom in decision making and use this to make the best of market opportunities.

An important feature of Hungarian agriculture is the symbiosis of collective and private farming. Side by side with the large-scale collective and state farming sectors is a flourishing private sector. There are about 800,000 private plots of members of collective farms and nearly 1,000,000 small auxiliary farms of non-agricultural or state farm employees. This private sector involves approximately half the national population. The relative contribution of the private sector to output fell sharply between 1960 and 1981 (from 55 percent to 31 percent) but remains significant. It is more important in the livestock sector than in the arable sector, but even in the latter it is very important for the production of fruit and vegetables. The collective and state farms provide facilities for the private sector and recognise its importance and permanence. It is officially recognised that the private sector makes good use of resources (e.g. the labour of pensioners and housewives, small buildings) which would otherwise not be available to the national economy and whose replacement by the state would be expensive.

A feature of the NEM was the rapid growth of the ancillary (e.g. industrial, construction, service) activities of farms. Collective farms in particular have shown great energy in exploiting market niches. By 1981, the ancillary activities of collective farms accounted for c.31 percent of their gross output (excluding the private plots).

The achievements of this system in Hungary are substantial. A wide range of good quality food products are available in that country and its per capita food production and consumption are high by international standards. It has also become a net food exporter. Nevertheless, it continues to face a number of problems, such as official attempts to restrict the scope of rural enterprise and rural incomes, the slow growth of combined input productivity, difficulties in obtaining access to remunerative export markets and the stratified nature of the labour force. There is substantial inequality between management and labour.

Summary

The technocratic model is marked by wage labour, extensive autonomy for individual farms, a symbiosis of individual and collective or state farming and encouragement for the non-agricultural activities of farms. It has had favourable effects on agricultural output, but continues to experience a wide variety of problems, political, technical, commercial and social.

HARVEST FLUCTUATIONS

The fact that in general throughout history and throughout the world, weather and natural disasters (e.g. droughts, floods) have been major influences on the volume of agricultural output is well known. Until recently, however, little attention was paid, either in the USSR or outside it, to the use of weather data to explain fluctuations in Soviet harvests since 1929. The reasons for this are quite simple. In the USSR, for many years, the influence of the environmental factors which help to determine agricultural outcomes were underestimated relative to the plan, whose possibilities for determining agricultural outcomes under socialism were grossly exaggerated. 'There are no fortresses which Bolsheviks cannot storm' was a well-known Stalinist slogan. Hence bad harvests were blamed not on the weather but on 'wreckers', 'kulak saboteurs', etc. Rather than admit that agriculture was not doing well and analysing the causes of this, the Soviet Government started publishing spurious output statistics (so-called biological yield) and relying on quacks (such as Lysenko). In the West, too, little attention was paid to the effects of the weather on Soviet harvests since this interpretation conflicted with propaganda needs. Since each poor harvest showed 'the failure of socialist agriculture', why bother about the effects of the weather?

In China, during the Maoist period, the three bad harvests of 1959–61 were officially blamed mainly on the weather. In the post-Mao period, they were predominantly blamed on the lack of incentives and policy errors. Similarly, in China in the 1980s, the good harvests of the decollectivisation period were officially ascribed to the reintroduction of incentives and successful policies, and the role of the weather was neglected.

Recently, considerable research has been done on the effect of the weather on harvest outcomes, both in the USSR and in China. This has thrown new light on a number of important historical issues. For example, in 1932–4 there was a famine in the USSR with extensive deaths. This is generally blamed on the lack of work incentives under collectivised agriculture, the predatory procurement system and Stalin's hostility to the Ukrainian peasants. Wheatcroft, Davies and Cooper (1986), however, have argued that 1931 and 1932 were years of freakishly low grain harvests which mainly resulted from freakish weather (droughts). Similarly, Kueh (1984) has argued that the freakishly low grain yields in China in 1960 and 1961 were primarily a result of bad weather (as the Maoists said at the time). Furthermore, the very good Chinese grain harvests of 1982 and 1983, which are often ascribed to decollectivisation, appear to be largely due to favourable weather (and the increase in procurement prices).

This does not mean that policy and institutions have no impact. For example, the main cause of the decline in Chinese grain output in 1959 seems to have been the decline in area sown. This resulted from a misconceived official policy. (This was the so-called 'three-three' system. It involved allocating a third of the arable land to crops, a third to horticulture and a third to fallow.) Similarly, in the USSR in the 1930s (Wheatcroft, Davies and Cooper 1986 p. 290), 'Ignorance by the authorities both of the agrotechnical consequences of pressure for short-term increases in the area sown to grain, and of the need for

careful crop rotation, undoubtedly had a harmful effect.' These
examples are illustrations of a general phenomenon which has been
established by Brada (1986) for Eastern Europe. Comparing private
with socialised agriculture, socialised agriculture has greater annual
fluctuations in crop output and this is mainly caused by fluctuations
in the area sown to crops. These fluctuations are caused by central
instructions. This illustrates the proposition argued earlier in this
chapter, that an important problem of socialised agriculture is that it
is vulnerable to the use of administrative methods by the authorities,
and that in agriculture the use of administrative methods often causes
inefficiencies.

Summary

Socialised arable production suffers from sharp year to year output
fluctuations. These result from the interaction of the environment,
economic policy and economic institutions. Year to year fluctuations in yield are primarily a result of weather fluctuations. Another
major influence on year to year fluctuations in output are fluctuations
in area sown, which are largely policy determined and destabilising
under socialised agriculture. Socialised agriculture is vulnerable to
destabilising policy interventions because it has an institutional
structure which gives the centre the possibility of interfering with day
to day farming decisions.

CONCLUSION

Marxists have traditionally considered that peasant or smallholder
farming is not a viable way of organising agriculture. Comparing
capitalist with socialist agriculture, Marxists traditionally argued
that the latter has four important advantages. First, it prevents rural
exploitation. Secondly, it allows the rational use of the available
labour and other resources. Thirdly, it facilitates a rapid increase in
the marketed output of agriculture. Fourthly, it helps transfer
resources for investment from agriculture to industry. The experience of collectivisation in various countries shows that it has a
number of problems, e.g. the absence of some of the postulated
economies of scale, labour incentives, the use of collective farms for
taxation, inequality, and the use of administrative methods. It also
shows that the third and fourth arguments for collectivisation are
erroneous. In addition, it shows that the first argument ignores the
enormous inequalities of power and lack of social control over

decisions taken, to which collectivisation normally leads. Furthermore, it shows that the second argument is sometimes true, but often false. The problems of collectivised agriculture led to decollectivisation in Yugoslavia (1950), partial decollectivisation in Poland (1956) and decollectivisation in China (1979–84). Elsewhere (for example in Hungary) they led to the development of the technocratic model, marked, *inter alia*, by a symbiosis of collective and private farming. They also led to changes in the USSR under Gorbachev which looked as if they might develop into decollectivisation. In addition to these institutional changes, under the impact of experience important developments have taken place in Marxist-Leninist agricultural theory. It has been explicitly recognised that under certain circumstances household production can be efficient in agriculture and that the factory model is often unsuitable in agriculture.

The practice of collectivisation in various countries and in various periods has differed very much. In the USSR, the coercive model of collectivist agriculture was successful in increasing the marketed output of basic wage goods, and the urban labour force. It also created, however, a quasi-feudal social system and a high-cost low-productivity agriculture. It was gradually abandoned after 1953 because of its adverse effect on output. In China, the Maoist model was abandoned in 1979–84 because of its failure to lead to a satisfactory rate of growth of output and incomes. In Hungary, the technocratic model has led to a satisfactory development of output and consumption, but suffers from political, technical, commercial and social problems.

The coercive model, the Maoist model and the technocratic model of collectivist agriculture are all unsuitable for a country aiming at a rapid rate of growth of agricultural output and equality. As far as collectivist agriculture in general is concerned, like private agriculture, it is compatible with a wide range of outcomes, favourable and unfavourable, depending on non-ownership factors.

Socialised arable production suffers from sharp year to year output fluctuations. These result from the interaction of the environment, economic policy and economic institutions.

SUGGESTIONS FOR FURTHER READING

GENERAL

J. Blum, *The end of the old order in rural Europe* (Princeton 1978).
B. Moore Jr., *Social origins of dictatorship and democracy* (Boston 1966).
A Bhaduri, 'On the formation of usurious interest rates in backward agriculture', *Cambridge Journal of Economics* vol. 1, no. 4 (December 1977).
M. Ellman, *Collectivisation, convergence and capitalism* (London & New York 1984) pp. 2–21.
S. Ishikawa, *Economic development in Asian perspective* (Tokyo 1967).
R. P. Sinha, *Food and poverty* (London 1976).
M. E. Bradley & M. G. Clark, 'Supervision and efficiency in socialized agriculture', *Soviet Studies* vol. XXIII, no. 3 (January 1972).
K. E. Wädekin, *Agrarian policies in Communist Europe* (Totowa NJ 1982).
J. Brada & K. Wädekin (eds.) *Socialist agriculture in transition* (Boulder Co. 1988).
R. K. Sah & J. E. Stiglitz, 'The economics of price scissors', *American Economic Review* vol. 74, no. 1 (March 1984).

MARXIST THEORY

A. Hussain & K. Tribe, *Marxism and the agrarian question* (London 1983).
A. Hussain & K. Tribe (eds.) *Paths of development in capitalist agriculture* (London 1984).
K. Wittfogel, 'Communist and non-Communist agrarian systems', in W. A. Douglas Jackson (ed.) *Agrarian policies and problems in Communist and non-Communist countries* (Seattle 1971).
M. Ellman, 'Agricultural productivity under socialism', *World Development* (September–October 1981).
V. N. Starodubrovskaya, 'Obobshchestvlenie proizvodstva i sblizhenie dvukh form sobstvennosti v sel'skom khozyaistve', chapter 7 of O. T. Bogomolov (ed.) *Agrarnye otnosheniya v stranakh sotsializma* (Moscow 1984).
Zhou Qiren & Du Ying, 'A study on specialized households', in Wang Guichen, Zhou Qiren *et al. Smashing the communal pot* (Beijing 1985).

USSR

Y. Taniuchi, 'A note on the Ural-Siberian method', *Soviet Studies* (October 1981).
M. Lewin, *The Making of the Soviet system* (New York 1985).

R. A. & Zh. A. Medvedev, *Khrushchev. The years in power* (Oxford 1977).
J. R. Millar, 'The prospects for Soviet agriculture', *Problems of communism* (May–June 1977).
K. E. Wädekin, *The private sector in Soviet agriculture* (Berkeley 1973).
B. Rumer, 'The "second" agriculture in the USSR', *Soviet Studies* (October 1981).
T. Gustafson, *Reform in Soviet politics* (Cambridge 1981) chapter 9.
M. Ellman, 'Soviet agricultural policy', *Economic and Political Weekly* (June 11 1988).

EASTERN EUROPE

East European economies: slow growth in the 1980s vol. 1 (Joint Economic Committee US Congress, Washington DC 1986) pp. 383–445.
N. Swain, *Collective farms which work?* (Cambridge 1985).
K. Hartford, 'Hungarian agriculture: A model for the socialist world?' *World Development* (January 1985).
C. Csaki, 'Economic management and organization of Hungarian agriculture', *Journal of Comparative Economics* vol. 7, no. 3 (September 1983).

CHINA

V. D. Lippit, *Land reform and economic development in China* (New York 1975).
N. R. Lardy, *Agriculture in China's modern economic development* (Cambridge 1983).
J. Sigurdson, *Rural industrialisation in China* (Cambridge Mass 1977).
'The American rural small-scale industry delegation', *Rural small-scale industry in the People's Republic of China* (Berkeley 1977).
J. E. Nickum, 'Labour accumulation in rural China and its role since the cultural revolution', *Cambridge Journal of Economics* vol. 2, no. 3 (September 1978).
B. Ashton, K. Hill, A. Piazza & R. Zeitz, 'Famine in China, 1958–61', *Population and Development Review* vol. 10, no. 4 (1984).
V. Smil, 'Food production and quality of diet in China', *Population and Development Review* vol. 12, no. 1 (March 1986).
K. R. Walker, *Food grain consumption and procurement in China* (Cambridge 1984).
E. B. Vermeer, *Water conservancy and irrigation in China* (Leiden 1977).
Luo Hanxian, *Economic change in rural China* (Beijing 1985).
CHINA Agriculture to the year 2000 (World Bank, Washington DC 1985).
P. Nolan. 'Decollectivisation of agriculture in China', *Cambridge Journal of Economics* (December 1983).
P. Nolan & S. Paine, 'Towards an appraisal of the impact of rural reform in China, 1978–85', *Cambridge Journal of Economics* (March 1986).
J. C. Oi, 'Peasant grain marketing and state procurement', *China Quarterly* no. 106 (June 1986).
'2nd stage rural reform' I, II & III, *Beijing Review* nos 19 & 22 (1987).

VIETNAM

E. E. Moise, *Land reform in China and Vietnam* (Chapel Hill NC 1983).
A. J. Fforde, *The agrarian question in North Vietnam* (NY forthcoming).

AFRICA

R. Dumont & M. F. Mottin, *L'Afrique Etranglée* (Paris 1980).
J. Hanlon, *Mozambique: the revolution under fire* (London 1984).
M. Wuyts, 'Money, planning and rural transformation in Mozambique', *Journal of Development Studies* vol. 22, no. 1 (October 1985).

HARVEST FLUCTUATIONS

Y. Y. Kueh, 'A weather index for analysing grain yield instability in China, 1952–81', *China Quarterly* no. 97 (March 1984).
Y. Y. Kueh, 'Weather cycles and agricultural instability in China', *Journal of Agricultural Economics* vol. XXXVII, no. 1 (January 1986).
J. C. Brada, 'The variability of crop production in private and socialized agriculture: Evidence from Eastern Europe', *Journal of Political Economy* vol. 94, no. 3, part 1 (June 1986).
R. V. Garcia (ed.) *Nature pleads not guilty* (Oxford 1981).

5

INVESTMENT PLANNING

Unfortunately, some of our departments still begin by taking a decision to build one or another plant, and only then begin a scientific analysis of their choice...

A. Babaev (*Pravda* 10–2–86)

Traditionally, for both neoclassical and Marxist economists the normative approach to investment planning was dominant. They analysed such planning problems as how to determine the choice of technique so as to maximise the rate of growth. They assumed that investment planning either was, or could be transformed into, a socially rational process for implementing social goals. The function of economists, according to this interpretation, is to work out methods and techniques (e.g. methods for selecting between investment projects) enabling this to be done. This approach, which is that of the Soviet school of optimal planners from Yushkov onwards, turns the economist into a technician, an applied welfare economist, into what Keynes once called a dentist.

In fact, however, investment planning has little in common with maximising the welfare obtained from scarce resources. It is only one part of the social relations between individuals and social groups in the course of which decisions are taken, all of which are imperfect and many of which produce results quite at variance with the intentions of the top economic and political leadership.

For a writer of the behavioural school on the other hand, this is well understood, and attention is focused on those features of the decision-making process mainly responsible for the irrational results. Bauer (1978) focused attention on the behavioural patterns generating investment cycles, for socialists a quite unexpected phenomenon in a planned economy. Kornai (1980) analysed such phenomena as investment hunger and investment tension. The behavioural analysis of state socialist economies, like that of capitalist economies, was a considerable scientific advance. It developed in Hungary in the

1970s. A more general analysis, which also rejected the traditional normative approach, but in addition provided an alternative theoretical framework, was that of the systems theorists. It developed in the USA in the 1970s (e.g. Montias 1976). In the work of the Hungarian economist Kornai, the behavioural and systems approaches were combined, the former providing the empirical material for the latter.

This chapter combines the normative, behavioural, Marxist, and systems approaches to investment planning. The Marxist problem of the relationship between accumulation and the relations of production is only briefly touched on in this chapter, but is also considered in chapters 4, 6 and 10.

THE SHARE OF INVESTMENT IN THE NATIONAL INCOME

The problem of deciding what proportion of the national income ought to be invested is of great practical importance and has generated a vast theoretical literature. Three different approaches will be considered here, the utility maximising, descriptive and growth maximising.

The utility maximising approach

In this approach the problem is to maximise a utility function subject to certain constraints. Graphically the situation is as depicted in figure 5.1. If net investment were zero, in the absence of technical progress, the situation would be as shown by consumption path (1), a constant rate of consumption. If a small amount of present consumption is sacrificed, then a consumption path such as (2), which grows steadily over time, is possible. Similarly, if more present consumption is sacrificed, then higher growth rates and ultimately higher levels of consumption, as on paths (3) and (4), are possible. The question is, which path should be chosen?

Either we consider a situation in which there is a finite time horizon, or one in which there is an infinite time horizon. In the first case, the solution is largely determined by the length of the time period and the valuation of the terminal capital stock. In the second case two possibilities have been considered.

The first is to reduce the infinite case to the finite case by introducing an horizon, consumption beyond which does not count. This has been done in two ways. One way was Ramsey's concept of 'Bliss', a hypothetical level of consumption which satiates all desires.

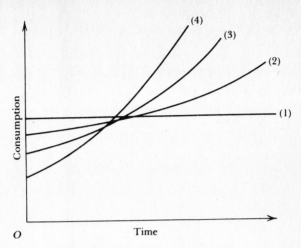

Figure 5.1 Feasible consumption paths

This assumption may have appealed to a Fellow of King's College, Cambridge, who had everything that man could reasonably want, but its general plausibility is open to question, to say the least. The other way is to introduce a discount rate to make infinite consumption streams comparable. The logic of pure time preference, *for an immortal society*, is doubtful. It is, however, a sound idea to introduce a discount rate on the assumptions that per capita consumption is rising over time and that the marginal social significance of consumption is inversely related to the level of per capita consumption. Its numerical determination, however, raises numerous difficult issues (*Guidelines* 1972 chapter 13).

The second is to introduce a preference ordering of all the feasible consumption streams between now and infinity. The main problem with this approach is how to determine the preference ordering. The chief attraction of those orderings which have been considered in the literature is their mathematical tractability. Furthermore, on the usual assumptions, the 'optimal' share of accumulation in the current national income is excessively high (because future consumption has not been discounted).

The main weakness of the utility maximising approach, however, is that the problem that it tackles is not the one which planners face. Economic policy is not decided by people who start off from a well defined preference ordering of all the feasible consumption streams

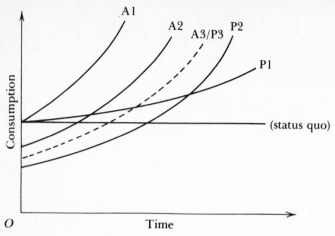

Figure 5.2 The convergence of aspirations and feasibilities

between now and infinity. This observation is the starting point for the descriptive approach.

The descriptive approach

The descriptive approach has been developed by the Hungarian economist Kornai (1970). It begins from the proposition that the plan formulation process as it actually takes place is primarily a process of interaction between the aspirations of the political authorities and the tentative plans which have been explored by the planners. Diagrammatically, this idea can be represented as in figure 5.2. A plan is necessary because the status quo, in which consumption remains steady over time, is regarded as unsatisfactory by the policy makers. Accordingly they instruct the planners to calculate a plan which ensures rising consumption over time. The planners come up with P_1, which enables consumption to rise over time without any sacrifice of present consumption. The policy makers were hoping, however, for a plan such as A_1, which, without any sacrifice in current consumption, would enable consumption to grow at a rapid rate. Hence they reject P_1 as inadequate. The planners, noting that their previous plan was rejected as insufficiently ambitious, go away and calculate plan P_2. This plan envisages a more rapid rate of growth than P_1, but at the cost of a substantial sacrifice in present consumption. P_2 is presented to the policy makers. They like it better than $P1$, but are still not satisfied by it. Under the influence of the planners' arguments about objective possibilities, the policy makers have reduced their aspirations. They now only aspire to $A2$, but even as this is much more ambitious than $P2$, and therefore they reject $P2$ as inadequate. In view of this the planners go away and compute a new plan, $P3$. On receiving and analysing $P3$, the policy makers reduce their aspirations further, to $A3$. An acceptable plan has been found $(A3/P3)$, which the policy makers accept and the planners regard as feasible, and which can now be promulgated.

The descriptive approach captures an essential feature of the socialist planning process, that plans are worked out by a process of interaction between the aspirations of the political leaders and the calculation by technicians of what is feasible. It does not, however, throw any light on the normative question of what the share of investment in the national income ought to be. For an attempt to answer this question we turn to the growth maximising approach.

The growth maximising approach

This argument has been developed by the Yugoslav economist Horvat (1958). It is based on three assumptions. First, that the objective of economic policy is to maximise the rate of growth. Secondly, that the marginal productivity of investment is a diminishing function of the share of investment in the national income. Thirdly, that the marginal productivity of investment reaches zero well before the share of investment in the national income reaches 50 percent, because an economy has a maximum absorptive capacity. 'The easiest way to use this concept is to conceive the economy as a giant productive capacity capable of being expanded at a certain *maximum* rate, also at a lower rate, but *not at a higher* rate. Any additional inputs (investment) would not produce *additions* to but *reductions* of output.' The idea is that, at a certain point, the technical and social problems caused by the reorganisation of production to accommodate the investment are such that the marginal product of the investment is zero.

Given these three assumptions, the problem of planning the optimal share of investment can be illustrated by figure 5.3. The diagram depicts a situation in which, when the share of investment is low, the return on marginal investment is high. As the share rises the return falls. When the absorptive capacity of the economy is reached, the maximum rational share of investment (A) is attained.

Accordingly, for an economy, the problem of finding the optimal

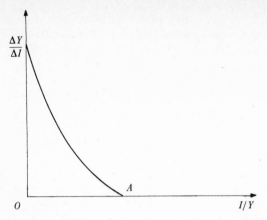

Figure 5.3 Absorptive capacity and the optimal rate of investment. $\Delta Y/\Delta I$ is the incremental output-investment ratio. I/Y is the share of investment in the national income.

share of investment resolves itself into the empirical question of finding out what the maximum absorptive capacity of that economy is. According to Horvat (1965 p. 575), his criterion 'produces a share of investment in national income of about 35 percent ... if recent experience and national income statistics may be trusted'.

Given the second and third assumptions made above, and assuming that A is known, the Horvat approach fits in well with the 'overtaking and surpassing' approach to economic policy discussed in chapter 1. It gives that share of investment which enables the gap to be eliminated in the shortest time. It can only be considered 'optimal', however, if the 'optimum' is defined as that share which enables the gap to be closed in the shortest time, rather than in a more conventional way.[1] A valuable feature of the Horvat approach is that it directs attention to the possibility of wasteful overinvestment (investment which is in excess of A). It seems that this situation has often occurred in the state socialist countries.

Another economist who stressed the dangers of overinvestment was Kalecki (1972a, 1986). He went beyond Horvat's macroeconomic argument and considered the structural bottlenecks that constrain the optimal rate of investment. He stressed the limits to

[1] That Horvat's 'optimal' share is not 'optimal' in the conventional welfare economics sense was shown by Sen (1961 pp. 485–6). Horvat's approach can be thought of as a variant of the utility maximisation approach in which a constraint (absorptive capacity) is introduced and the maximand is switched from a subjective one (utility) to an objective one (growth).

rational investment set by natural resource constraints, the availability of labour, the need for balance of payments equilibrium, the
construction period of new plants and the need not to sacrifice
present consumption unnecessarily.

This section has so far only considered the analytical issue of what
the optimal share of investment ought to be, while ignoring the
political issue of how to attain the desired level of investment. The
latter issue is particularly important and difficult. It was in the First
Five Year Plan (1928–32) that the USSR made the transition from
the kind of investment ratio characteristic of third world countries to
the much higher investment ratio characteristic of state socialist
countries. In 1928–32 there was a gigantic increase in investment in
the USSR, with the volume of investment more than quadrupling
and rising from 15 percent of the net material product in 1928 to 44
percent in 1932. The question of the sources of this enormous
increase in investment was examined in Ellman (1975).

From a Keynesian point of view, the sources of the increase in investment in
1928–32 were (a) the utilisation of previously wasted resources (e.g.
unemployed labour), (b) the increase in the urban labour force, (c) the
increase in the volume of basic wage goods marketed by agriculture, (d) the
fall in urban real wages, (e) imports (both of machines and skilled labour),
and (f) the increase in the output of industry and construction during the
First Five Year Plan. The two key mechanisms for obtaining the additional
investment resources were collectivisation (which made possible the increase
in the volume of basic wage goods marketed by agriculture and the increase
in the urban labour force) and the rapid inflation (which facilitated the fall in
urban real wages).

From a Marxist point of view, the origin of the huge increase in
accumulation during the First Five Year Plan was (a) an increase in absolute
surplus value resulting from the increase in the urban labour force (30%),
and (b) an increase in relative surplus value resulting from the fall in real
wages (101%), less (c) a decrease in unequal exchange with agriculture
(−31%). The four key mechanisms for obtaining the additional accumulation were: the transition of the unions from trade unionism to production
mindedness, the rapid growth of forced labour, the replacement of a market
relationship between agriculture and the industrial sphere by a coercive
relationship, and the increased differentiation between the elite and the
masses.

Detailed examination of the sources of the increase in accumulation
in China appear to be lacking. Lippit (1975) has drawn attention to
the role of land reform in enabling what was formerly property
income to be converted into investment resources.

In human societies there is often a discrepancy between *intentions*
and *outcomes*. Marxists expected that under socialism this divergence

would disappear, since mankind would consciously determine its own future. Nevertheless it has persisted, even under state socialism. For example, in the USSR the leadership has been repeatedly confronted by the unexpected outcomes of its own policies, from the economic crisis of 1931–3 to the stagnation of the late Brezhnev period. As a result of this discrepancy, it is necessary to study not only plan choices but also the processes governing plan outcomes. For example, given that the actual share of investment in the national income often differs from that which was planned, it is necessary to study both normative theories about what the share should be and the behavioural processes and properties of the economic environment that influence what it actually is.

A major factor determining it is the behaviour of the investors (e.g. ministries, enterprises, republics). This has been characterised by Kornai (1980) as *investment hunger*. This term describes a situation in which there is an almost unlimited desire by potential investors for additional investment resources, regardless of the likely economic return to them. Not facing the threat of bankruptcy but facing a situation in which the interests of their organisations and officials would only benefit from additional investment, they try by hook or by crook to obtain additional investment resources. For example, expected costs may be underestimated or the benefits to be expected may be overstated.

The share is also influenced by the economic environment. For example, the sharp fall in the share of investment in the national income throughout Eastern Europe in the early 1980s partly resulted from the sharp worsening of the credit rating of Eastern Europe, the deterioration of the international political climate, the second oil shock and the difficulty in finding remunerative export markets (this resulted from both environmental and system-related factors).

Summary

Three approaches to the choice of an optimal share of investment in the national income were considered, the utility maximising, descriptive and growth maximising. The first has given rise to a huge literature. Its weakest point is its basic assumption, that planning is concerned with maximising utility. The second provides a good description of the planning process, but offers no prescription. The third is a useful way of thinking about the problem for an economy aiming to maximise the rate of growth. It draws attention both to the inverse relationship between the share of investment in the national

Table 5.1 *Division of Soviet industrial production between consumer and producer goods (in %)*

(1) Year	(2) Producer goods	(3) Consumer goods
(1913	35.1	64.9)
1928	39.5	60.5
1940	61.2	38.8
1946	65.9	34.1
1950	68.8	31.2
1955	70.5	29.5
1960	72.5	27.5
1965	74.1	25.9
1970	73.4	26.6
1975	73.7	26.3
1980	73.8	26.2
1985	74.8	25.2

Note: Column (2) refers to what in Soviet planning and statistical practice is known as group A, and column (3) to group B. This division corresponds neither to the Marxist distinction between Departments 1 and 2, nor to the division between heavy and light industry.
Source: Soviet statistical handbooks.

income and the return on investment and to the possibility of wasteful overinvestment. Both theory and practice suggest that actually attaining a desired level of investment may involve changes in the relations of production. The actual share of investment results from the interaction of the central leaders trying to impose their priorities on the economic process, the other economic actors (ministries, republics or provinces, enterprises) striving to begin and then complete their pet projects, and the economic environment.

THE SECTORAL ALLOCATION OF INVESTMENT

An important feature of the early stage of socialist industrialisation has been the allocation of investment resources primarily to producer goods industries rather than consumer goods industries. In the USSR, where socialist planning has existed longest, the share of consumer goods in total industrial output fell almost continually from 1928 to 1966, and since then has fallen further. The data are set out in table 5.1.

In China, the share of heavy industry in total industrial production rose steadily in the First Five Year Plan (1952–7), rose very sharply in 1958–60 as a result of the GLF but then declined in the ensuing

Table 5.2 *Division of Chinese industrial production between light industry and heavy industry (in %)*

(1) Year	(2) Heavy industry	(3) Light industry
1952	35.6	64.4
1957	46.9	53.1
1960	66.7	33.3
1967	48.5	51.5
1970	56.6	43.4
1979	56.9	43.1
1981	48.6	51.4
1985	50.4	49.6

Source: *Statistical yearbook of China 1986* (Hong Kong & Beijing 1986) p. 225.

economic crisis. From its low of 1967–8 it rose again to a level in the late 1970s roughly equal to the 1958–9 level but then declined somewhat in the early 1980s. The level of the early 1980s was significantly below that of both 1958–60 and of 1970–9. It remained, however, above the level of 1957. Some data is set out in table 5.2.

For many years it was customary for Soviet economists to assert (*Political Economy* 1957 p. 721) that 'the law of priority growth of the production of the means of production ... is a necessary condition for ensuring the uninterrupted advance of socialist production'. This formulation is actually a paraphrase of the view expressed by Stalin in *Economic problems of socialism in the USSR* (1952) that, 'the national economy cannot be continuously expanded without giving primacy to the production of means of production'. As policy changed this position was abandoned, and replaced by the view (Dovgan' 1965) that the sharp increase in the share of producer goods output in total industrial output had been necessary during the early stages of socialist industrialisation, but that it is *not* a necessary condition of steady economic growth that the share of producer goods output in total industrial output rises indefinitely. The traditional Soviet doctrine was criticised in China before it was abandoned in the USSR. Already in *On the ten major relationships* (1956) Mao criticised the excessive emphasis on heavy industry at the expense of light industry and agriculture in the USSR and Eastern Europe. He suggested that China should learn from this experience and develop light industry and agriculture proportionately. Nevertheless, heavy industry was developed disproportionately in China in 1957–60 and

Table 5.3 *Share of consumer goods in industrial output in selected countries (in %)*

	1871	1901	1924	1946
Great Britain	52	41	40	31
France	65a	44b	35c	34d
Germany	n.a.	45e	37f 25g	– 23h
United States	44i	34j	32k	30l
Switzerland	62m	45n	38o	34p
Italy	n.a.	72q	53r 37s	–
Japan	n.a.	n.a.	59t	40u
USSR	–	– 67v	– 61w 39x –	29y

a 1861–65, *b* 1896, *c* 1921, *d* 1952, *e* 1895, *f* 1925, *g* 1936, *h* 1951, *i* 1880, *j* 1900, *k* 1927, *l* 1947, *m* 1882, *n* 1895, *o* 1923, *p* 1945, *q* 1896, *r* 1913, *s* 1928, *t* 1925, *u* 1950, *v* 1913, *w* 1928, *x* 1940, *y* 1955.
Source: Patel (1961).

1969–79 and this outcome came under much criticism in China after 1978.

Is there any economic justification for the proposition that the share of group A in total industrial production ought to rise during the early stages of socialist industrialisation, and if so, what is it? One line of argument is that the increase in the share of producer goods in total industrial output is a normal feature of economic growth regardless of the mode of production. Some figures which have been selected to support this view are set out in table 5.3.

Assuming that it is a fact that there is a general tendency for the share of producer goods in total industrial output to rise over time,[2] it is easy to explain it in terms of the nature of technical progress.

Economic development largely consists of the replacement of the production of commodities primarily with labour, with the assistance of a small quantity of intermediate goods and a very limited capital stock, by the production of commodities primarily by capital goods with the assistance of long chains of intermediate goods and limited labour. Comparing eighteenth-century cotton textile production with twentieth-century synthetic fibre production, the latter requires, in addition to the requirements of the former, construction of the factory, electricity to power, light and heat it, a heavy engineering industry to produce the capital equipment needed, and a chemical industry to produce the synthetic fibre. If, as a result of technical

---

[2] For a denial of the validity of this 'fact' see Wiles (1962 pp. 286–8).

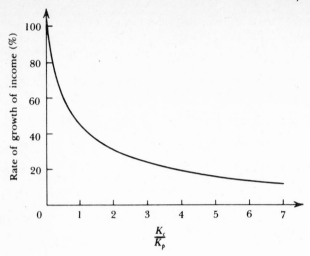

Figure 5.4 Feldman's first theorem
K_c is the capital stock in the consumer goods industry, K_p is the capital stock in the producer goods industry

progress, an increasing proportion of the gross output of consumer goods industries is accounted for by inputs of intermediate products, and a decreasing proportion of the gross output of consumer goods industries is accounted for by value added in the consumer goods industries, as in the above example, then over time the share of consumer goods output in total industrial output will fall. A similar result will occur if an increasing proportion of consumer demand is for products a low proportion of whose gross output consists of value added by consumer goods industries.

The first economist to focus attention on the relationship between the consumer goods and producer goods industries in a plan for rapid economic growth was the Soviet economist Feldman.[3] He derived two important results, one about the ratios of the capital stock in the two sectors, the other about the allocation of investment to the two sectors. The first result was that a high rate of growth requires that a high proportion of the capital stock be in the producer goods sector. This is illustrated in figure 5.4. Feldman's second theorem was that, along a steady growth path, investment should be allocated between the sectors in the same proportion as the capital stock. For example,

[3] Feldman's model was published in the USSR in 1928. For an English translation see Feldman (1964). For an analysis of the model by one of the founders of Western growth theory see Domar (1957).

Table 5.4 *Feldman's two theorems*

$\dfrac{K_p}{K_c}$	$\dfrac{\mathrm{d}Y}{\mathrm{d}t}$ (in % p.a.) (when $K/Y = 2.1$)	$\dfrac{\Delta K_p}{\Delta K_c + \Delta K_p}$
0.106	4.6	0.096
0.2	8.1	0.167
0.5	16.2	0.333
1.0	24.3	0.500

suppose that a 20 percent rate of growth of income requires a K_c/K_p of 3.7. Then to maintain growth at 20 percent p.a. requires that 3.7/4.7 of annual investment go to the consumer goods industries, and 1.0/4.7 of annual investment go to the producer goods industries.

The interrelationship of the two theorems is shown in table 5.4, in which Feldman explained how any desired growth rate, given the capital-output ratio, determined both the necessary sectoral composition of the capital stock and the sectoral allocation of investment.

Given the capital-output ratio, the higher the K_p/K_c ratio, i.e. the greater the proportion of the capital stock in the producer goods sector, and correspondingly the higher the $\Delta K_p/(\Delta K_c + \Delta K_p)$ ratio, i.e. the greater the proportion of new investment in the producer goods sector, the higher the rate of growth. With a capital-output ratio of 2.1, to raise the growth rate from 16.2 percent to 24.3 percent requires raising the proportion of the capital stock in the producer goods sector from 1/3 to 1/2, and the share of investment in the producer goods sector from 1/3 to 1/2.

The conclusion Feldman drew from his model was that the main task of the planning organisations was to regulate the capital – output ratios in the two sectors and the ratio of the capital stock in the producer goods sector to that in the consumer goods sector. For the former task, Feldman recommended rationalisation and multi-shift working, for the latter, investment in the producer goods sector.

Both at the time, and for some decades thereafter, Feldman's conclusion that to begin a process of rapid economic growth it is necessary to expand rapidly the capacity of the producer goods industries, seemed paradoxical. It was contrary to the traditional view that the 'proper' path of development was 'textiles first'. What was Feldman's proof, and is it valid?

Feldman's own argument was rather laborious, but the essence of

Table 5.5 *Consumption paths on various investment strategies*

Year	Initial investment in the consumer goods sector (strategy S)			Initial investment in the producer goods sector (strategy F)		
	Consumption	K_c	K_p	Consumption	K_c	K_p
1	500	1000	0	500	1000	0
2	550	1100	0	525	1050	100
3	550	1100	0	550	1100	100
4	550	1100	0	575	1150	100
5	550	1100	0	600	1200	100
6	550	1100	0	625	1250	100

the matter is very simple and can be explained by means of an arithmetical example. Consider a two sector (consumer goods and producer goods) economy with a capital–output ratio of 2 in each sector which has available 100 units of investment resources which can be invested either in the consumer goods sector or in the producer goods sector. The choice is represented in table 5.5.

If the initial investment is made in the consumer goods sector then there will be a once and for all consumption increment of 50. Consumption will rise from a level of 500 in year 1 to a level of 550 in year 2, and thereafter remain on a plateau. If, on the other hand, the initial investment is made in the producer goods sector, then there will be an annual increment of 50 to the capital stock in the consumer goods sector, which will ensure an annual consumption increment of 25. Consumption will rise by only 25 in year 2, but it will also rise by 25 in each subsequent year. When the initial investment is made in the producer goods sector there is an initial loss of possible consumption, but by year 3 consumption is equal on the two paths, and from year 4 onwards annual consumption is greater on strategy F than on strategy S, and the absolute difference increases annually. Given a long enough time horizon, strategy F is clearly superior.

The reason why investing in producer goods is advantageous in models of an economy divided into horizontal sectors, is very simple. An investment in the producer goods sector enables the capital equipment of the consumer goods sector to expand. This is not a flash in the pan. After each period of production in the producer goods sector, the capital stock in the consumer goods sector rises. This enables the output of consumer goods to rise. There is a steady rise in the output of consumer goods, the annual increment being the capital stock in the producer goods sector divided by the product of the two capital-output ratios. In the example, the capital stock in the producer goods sector is (from period 2 onwards) the initial investment of 100 units.

An investment in the consumer goods sector, on the other hand, merely results in a once and for all expansion of the productive capacity of that sector, and consequently a zero growth rate in the output of consumption goods (after the initial increase).

From this point of view, the crucial difference between an investment in the producer goods sector and in the consumer goods sector is as follows. The former produces a steady stream of capital goods for use in the consumer goods sector, each of which in turn produces a steady stream of consumption goods. The latter, however, merely produces a steady stream of consumption goods, the absolute level of this stream thereafter remaining unchanged.

The argument depends crucially on the assumptions that construction periods are the same in both sectors, machines are immortal and the sectoral capital-output ratios the same. If these assumptions are dropped, it is possible to assign values to the construction periods, lives of the capital goods and the sectoral capital-output ratios, that reverse the results. The argument also assumes that the supply of investment resources is independent of the allocation of investment, a long enough time horizon and a closed economy. Feldman's argument was developed in terms of a two sector model, but applies equally to a model of a closed economy divided into m ($m > 2$) horizontal sectors, provided that the other Feldman assumptions are made.

The main lesson to be learned from the Feldman model is that the capacity of the capital goods industry is one of the constraints limiting the rate of growth of an economy. There may well be other constraints, such as foreign exchange, urban real wages or marketed output of agriculture. Indeed, it is possible that one or more of these is/are the binding constraint/s and that the limited capacity of the producer goods sector is a non-binding constraint. Economic planning is largely concerned with the removal of constraints to rapid economic growth. Accordingly, in its early stages a prominent role is often played by the rapid development of the producer goods sector. This was also recognised by the Indian economist Mahalanobis (1953) at the start of Indian planning.

Feldman's division of an economy into two sectors is crude and scarely operational. A major advance in economic analysis since the publication of his paper has been the development of numerical

Table 5.6 *Industrial implications of different macro-economic growth rates (rates of growth in % p.a.)*

	Variants				
	1	2	3	4	5
Net material product	5.6	6.1	6.6	7.1	7.5
Consumption	6.7	6.8	6.9	7.0	7.0
Investment	2.5	4.1	5.7	7.3	8.7
Engineering and metal working	7.1	8.2	9.3	10.4	11.4
Light industry	6.3	6.6	6.8	7.0	7.2
Food industry	7.1	7.3	7.4	7.5	7.6

Source: Ellman (1973) pp. 70–1.

multi-sectoral models (Leontief 1966). One important use of these models is to study the relationship between the rate of growth of the national economic aggregates and the relative output of the various industries. In the usual input-output notation

$$X = (I - A)^{-1} Y$$

Assuming that A is given, X can be calculated for varying values of Y. Assuming that the variants of Y considered refer to some future year, this enables the changes in the relative output of the different industries in this final year resulting from various hypothetical national income aggregates, to be studied.

Such studies are now an integral part of the planning process in the state socialist countries. An example taken from Soviet experience with the elaboration of the 1966–70 Five Year Plan is set out in table 5.6. The table shows how the technological relationships between industries are such that, the higher the rate of growth of the national economy, the wider the divergence between the rate of growth of an industry such as engineering and an industry such as the food industry.

Summary

The technological structure of a closed economy is such that the higher the rate of national economic growth required, the higher the rate of growth of the output of industries such as engineering and the greater the share of investment that has to be allocated to them. In a closed economy where the capacity of these industries is an operative constraint, a major task of planning for raising the growth rate must be to direct investment resources towards expanding the capacity of these sectors. This proposition was first formulated in a 1928 paper by the Soviet economist Feldman and is now generally accepted.

INDUSTRY PLANNING

The state socialist countries investment plans are worked out for the country as a whole, and also for industries, ministries, departments, associations, enterprises, republics, economic regions and cities. An important level of investment planning is the industry. Industry investment planning is concerned with such problems as the choice of product, of plants to be expanded, of location of new plants, of technology to be used, and of sources of raw materials. To resolve these questions it is necessary to collect and process the necessary data.

Data collection

For a producer goods industry, part of the demand will be for given products, but there will in general be considerable substitutability between products. It will therefore be necessary to gather data on the relative costs and usefulness of different products. If this is not done properly, and the results acted on, then waste will result. For example, as Abouchar (1971) has pointed out, a major source of waste in the Soviet cement industry prior to the Second World War was the large number of grades produced and the failure to capture the gains from standardisation.

The possibility of expanding plants largely depends on the availability of space, labour, and raw materials, and the cost of transport of output to customers. Similarly, possible locations of new plants depend largely on the availability of raw materials and labour and on transport costs. An important difficulty at this stage is that in general the prices of producer goods and labour power in the state socialist countries are not equal to their national economic opportunity cost. It may therefore be necessary to mount a special investigation of costs, or use the shadow prices resulting from the investment plan of the appropriate industry. In an economy in which producer goods are rationed, it is not in general true that the prices at which transactions take place (*Guidelines* 1972 p. 62) 'may ... provide a good first step in the estimation [of social costs]'.

In a well-known aphorism, Lenin defined communism as 'Soviet power plus electrification', and the introduction into production of advanced technology has always played a major role in socialist planning. The first state socialist country, which under capitalism was notorious for its wooden ploughs, is now well known for its space programme. In the traditional Soviet type of organisation each industry has a Ministry which is responsible for adopting the latest ideas, incorporating them in its investment plan and imposing a unified technical policy on its industry. Complaints are frequent, however (see for example Bek 1971), that innovation is hindered by the monopoly position of the major R & D organisations. Examples of technical conservatism at the R & D stage in the USSR include the fact that alternatives to the home-grown SKB process for the manufacture of synthetic rubber were almost ignored, and that processes for the manufacture of alloy and quality steel other than electric-slag remelting receive inadequate attention (Amann 1977).

The possibilities for obtaining raw materials depend on known reserves, geological prospecting and foreign trade possibilities. The state socialist countries have devoted extensive efforts to geological prospecting, in which field they have a good record.

Data processing

The main method used at the present time in the CMEA countries for processing the data relating to possible investment plans into actual investment plans is mathematical programming. In the USSR, after extensive experience in this field, a Standard Methodology for doing such calculations was adopted by the Presidium of the Academy of Sciences ('Standard' 1978). The use of mathematical programming for calculating optimal investment plans is an example of the possibilities for efficient control of national economies which the scientific-technical revolution in the field of management and control of large systems is bringing about.

The Soviet Standard Methodology presents models for three standard problems. They are, a static multiproduct production problem with discrete variables, a multiproduct dynamic production problem with discrete variables, and a multiproduct static problem of the production-transport type with discrete variables. The former can be set out as follows:

Let $i = 1\ldots n$ be the finished goods or resources, $j = 1\ldots m$ be the production units, $r = 1\ldots R_j$ be the production technique in a unit, $a_{ij}{}^r$ be the output of good $1\ldots n'$ or input of resource $i = n' + 1\ldots n$, using technique r of production in unit j; $C_j{}^r$ are the costs of production using technique r in unit j; D_i is the given level of output of good i, $i = 1 \ldots n'$; P_i is the total use of resource i, $i = n' + 1 \ldots n$ allocated to the industry; Z_j^r is the unknown intensity of use of technique r at unit j.

The problem is to find values of the variables Z_j^r that minimise the objective function

$$\sum_{j=1}^{m} \sum_{r=1}^{R} C_j^r \, Z_j^r$$

i.e. minimise costs of production subject to

$$\sum_{j=1}^{m} \sum_{r=1}^{R_j} a_{ij}^r \, Z_j^r \geqslant D_i \quad , i = 1 \ldots n'$$

i.e. each output must be produced in at least the required quantities

$$\sum_{j=1}^{m} \sum_{r=1}^{R_j} a_{ij}^r \, Z_j^r \leqslant P_i \quad , n' + 1 \ldots n$$

i.e. the total use of resources cannot exceed the level allocated to the branch

$$\sum_{r=1}^{R_j} Z_j^r \leqslant 1, j = 1 \ldots m$$
$$Z_j^r = 0 \text{ or } 1, j = 1 \ldots m, r = 1 \ldots R_j$$

i.e. either a single technique of production for unit j is included in the plan or unit j is not included in the plan.

In order to illustrate the method, an example will be given which is taken from the Hungarian experience of the late 1950s in working out an investment plan for the cotton weaving industry for the 1961–5 Five Year Plan (Kornai 1967 chapter 5). The method of working out the plan can be presented schematically by looking at the decision problem, the constraints, the objective function and the results.

The decision problems to be resolved were:

(a) How should the output of fabrics be increased, by modernising the existing weaving mills or by building new ones?
(b) For part of the existing machinery, there were three possibilities. It could be operated in its existing form, modernised by way of

alterations or supplementary investments, or else scrapped. Which should be chosen?
(c) For the other part of the existing machinery, either it could be retained or scrapped. What should be done?
(d) If new machines were purchased, a choice has to be made between many types. Which type should be chosen, and how many of a particular type should be purchased?

The constraints consisted of the output plan for cloth, the investment fund, the hard currency quota, the building quota and the material balances for various kinds of yarn. The objective function was to meet the given plan at minimum cost.

The results provided answers to all the decision problems. An important feature of the results was the conclusion that it was much cheaper to increase production by modernising and expanding existing mills than by building new ones.

It would clearly be unsatisfactory to optimise the investment plan of each industry taken in isolation. If the calculations show that it is possible to reduce the inputs into a particular industry below those originally envisaged, then it is desirable to reduce planned outputs in other industries, or increase the planned output of the industry in question, or adopt some combination of these strategies. Accordingly, the experiments in working out optimal industry investment plans, begun in Hungary in the late 1950s, led to the construction of multi-level plans linking the optimal plans of the separate industries to each other and to the macro-economic plan variables. Multi-level planning of this type was first developed in Hungary, but has since spread to the other CMEA countries.

Problems of industry planning

The three chief problems of industry planning appear to be, the lack of the necessary data, technical conservatism, and departmentalism. Consider each in turn.

Soviet experience has shown (Ellman 1973 pp. 77 and 86–7) that the biggest obstacle to the compilation of useful optimal industry plans is the lack of the necessary data. In the section on the use of mathematical models in a book on improving planning written by some officials in the Soviet Gosplan it is stated that (Drogichinsky 1971 p. 184):

the information required for models, optimising the utilisation of resources, is not readily available, and it is necessary to gather it separately. It is this work which occupies at the present time not less than 80% of all the work involved in solving such problems, and for complicated problems – 90%.

At first sight this situation may arouse surprise, because for the working out of plans, it would seem, all the necessary information is available. For the efficient utilisation of models, however, for example for planning production, the nomenclature must be substantially wider than that confirmed in the plan. This results from the necessity to exclude the influence of possible assortment changes on the decision taken. The following examples may clarify this. In the national economic plan there are two figures for the production of leather shoes and children's shoes. The calculations underlying the plan are based on 7 aggregated groups of shoes and 4 small groups. For the problem which enables the maximum production of shoes subject to the structure of demand and the given resources to be calculated, shoes are divided into 257 types, and the full nomenclature of shoes and related items runs to about 36,000 items. The types are chosen in such a way that an alteration in the assortment inside each of them would have a much smaller influence on the plan than changes in the assortment between types.

The data required are not purely physical, but have to be made comparable by means of prices and a rate of interest. The prices and recoupment period used in many of the calculations were unsatisfactory in a number of respects. It was even necessary to devote extensive research to calculate the 'proper' figures to use for transport costs, the actual freight tariffs being of little significance from an efficiency point of view! All these difficulties are a result of the partial ignorance of the planners.

The technical conservatism of the major R & D organisations is often a serious problem. Some examples were given above. Its seriousness for the economy arises from the policy of concentration of initiatives.

Departmentalism refers to the fact that planning organisations often give greater weight to the interests of their own organisation than to the national economy as a whole. For example, Val'tukh (1977) and Bufetova and Golland (1977) estimated that in the USSR investment in the production of better *quality* steel would generally produce bigger returns to the national economy than the investment of the same resources in producing a greater *quantity* of steel. The ministry, however, ignores this possibility, since it is evaluated by quantity of output and the gains from greater quality accrue to the users. This is an example of the problems for the national economy created by the fact that decision makers form a coalition and not a team. The central planners, who are supposed to check the proposals of the branch ministries, often do not have enough knowledge of the problems of the users, interest in responding to them, or authority over the branch ministries, to do other than rubber stamp the suggestions of the producers.

Summary

A major type of investment planning is industry planning, carried out by the branch ministries. The main method used for this at the present time in the CMEA countries is mathematical programming. Considerable difficulties exist in the drawing up of rational industry plans, largely resulting from the partial ignorance of the planners and the fact that the decision makers form a coalition and not a team.

THE CHOICE OF TECHNIQUE

A feature of traditional Soviet planning is the emphasis on large modern plants, embodying the latest international technology, and often imported or scaled-up versions of foreign plants. Well-known early examples were the Stalingrad tractor plant and the Magnitogorsk iron and steel plant. Such plants can take full advantage of economies of scale. In addition, it is thought that their construction will be a quick way of reducing the technology gap and catching up with the most advanced countries. They also have the political advantage of creating proletarian islands in a peasant sea. As constructed in the USSR, these plants have often been labour-intensive variants of capital-intensive techniques. This means that for the auxiliary operations (such as materials handling), unlike the basic operations, labour-intensive methods have often been used in order to save scarce investment resources. This is discussed in chapter 6.

The adoption of this type of technology was not the result of precise calculations by economists as to the relative merit of this or that type of technology. Indeed, during the Stalin era (1929–53), the orthodox view in the USSR was that the function of economists was to provide ex-post rationalisations of government economic policy. In *Economic problems of socialism in the USSR* (1952) Stalin decisively rejected the view that the function of political economy

is to elaborate and develop a scientific theory of the productive forces in social production, a theory of the planning of economic development ... The rational organisation of the productive forces, economic planning, etc., are not problems of political economy but problems of the economic policy of the directing bodies. These are two different provinces, which must not be confused ... Political economy investigates the laws of development of men's

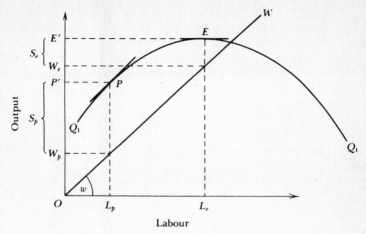

Figure 5.5 The choice of technique

relations of production. Economic policy draws practical conclusions from this, gives them concrete shape, and builds its day to day work on them. To foist upon political economy problems of economic policy is to kill it as a science.

As Yaroshenko, one of the participants in the discussion of the draft textbook of political economy to which Stalin was reacting, put it, in a passage quoted by Stalin: 'healthy discussion of the rational organisation of the productive forces in social production, scientific demonstration of the validity of such organisation' was replaced by 'scholastic disputes as to the role of particular categories of socialist political economy – value, commodity, money, credit, etc'.

Many years after the traditional Soviet policy was first implemented, it was rationalised by Dobb (1960 chapter 3) and Sen (1968). They argued that, in an economy where the share of investment is sub-optimal and all profits are reinvested and wages consumed, investment ought to take the form of capital-intensive projects (i.e. projects with a high capital-labour ratio) and *not* labour-intensive ones. The logic of this argument can be seen by looking at figure 5.5, which is taken from Sen.

Consider an economy with a given quantity of investment resources which can be combined with varying quantities of labour to produce output. Labour is assumed to have a zero social opportunity cost (because it is assumed that the country is characterised by large open or disguised unemployment). The production function is given by the curve Q_1Q_1. The wage rate is given by tan w and the wage bill by OW. Consider the choice between two techniques of production, P and E. P is the more capital-intensive technique and E the more labour-intensive technique. At P the marginal product of labour equals the wage rate and the surplus is maximised. At E the marginal product of labour equals zero and output is maximised. The criterion of maximum output and employment per unit of investment would indicate that E is the preferred technique. Consider, however, technique P. It has a lower output and employment than E, but the surplus of output over consumption (i.e. $S_p \equiv OP' - OW_p$) is greater than the surplus generated by E (i.e. $S_e \equiv OE' - OW_e$). If the share of investment in the national income is sub-optimal, then the additional surplus $(S_p - S_e)$ resulting from the adoption of technique P may be more valuable to the economy, because it permits an increase in the share of investment and the rate of growth, than the loss of consumption $(W_e - W_p)$ and employment $(L_e - L_p)$ that adopting technique P would cause. Hence technique P, and not E, is the desirable one. In general, developing countries should use 'conveyor belts' rather than 'wheelbarrows'.

Considered as a rationalisation of traditional Soviet policy, the Dobb–Sen argument is entirely irrelevant, since there is no reason to suppose that under traditional Soviet planning the share of investment has been sub-optimal or that the surplus generated by the construction of modern plants was a significant source of investment finance. Indeed, it seems likely that the share of investment has often been in excess of the absorptive capacity of the economy, and the new plants, with their long construction and running-in periods, production of producer goods and foreign exchange requirements, a significant source of inflationary pressure. The argument, ironically, has most relevance under capitalism as a defence of the social utility of the traditional family controlled business, that has no access to outside finance, squeezes real wages and reinvests all profits.

An important disadvantage of the traditional Soviet strategy is that it can lead to a substantial waste of resources and hence to lower living standards than are necessitated by the level of accumulation chosen. The waste arises from the fact that there may be material and human resources which have a zero opportunity cost from the standpoint of the national industrialisation programme but which could be used to provide useful goods and services. For example, a collective farm may be able to establish a workshop to produce toys out of local timber during the farming offseason. Such local initiatives, which were illegal in the USSR during the Stalin period, cost

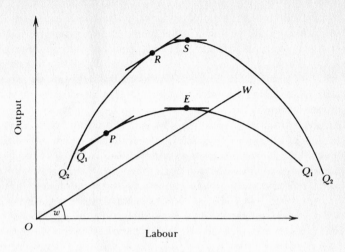

Figure 5.6 Technical progress and the Dobb-Sen criterion

society nothing and benefit the members of the collective farm. Accordingly, a feature of the reaction against the Stalinist model, both in Eastern Europe and China, has been a stress on the usefulness of capital-saving techniques and small enterprises. Indeed, in some countries where there are no significant economies of scale and private persons are able to obtain resources (e.g. their own labour or that of their families, or their own home) otherwise unavailable for social production, small-scale private enterprise is permitted (e.g. in running shops, restaurants, motor car repairs and housing repairs). Although this can be (and often is) criticised from the standpoint of utopian socialism, with its emphasis on moral factors rather than material ones, from a Marxist perspective it makes excellent sense. It contributes to the efficient utilisation of resources and hence to the attainment of a high level of labour productivity.

A well-known theoretical challenge to the traditional Soviet policy was delivered by the Polish economist Kalecki (1972a chapter 10). He emphasised that in the short run the adoption of the Dobb-Sen strategy would lead to a loss of employment and output. He objected to a policy that would delay the transition to full employment and waste potential output. He also suggested that in the long run technical progress considerably reduces the practical significance of the Dobb-Sen argument. The reason for this is that with technical progress the marginal product of labour corresponding to each level of the capital-output ratio will, in general, grow. This means that the optimum technique, on the surplus maximisation criterion, has a capital-labour ratio which falls over time. Hence, although there is a static case for the Dobb-Sen position, once dynamic factors are introduced, even on their choice criterion the policy implications are at variance with the traditional Soviet policy. This second argument is illustrated in figure 5.6.

The production function in period 1 is $Q_1 Q_1$, and in period 2, as a result of technical progress, $Q_2 Q_2$. Consider the choice between techniques E and P. P maximises the surplus, but provides less employment and output than technique E. In period 2 the same is true for R and S, but the difference in capital intensity is smaller and R is less capital-intensive than P. Hence the Dobb-Sen argument loses much of its practical significance when dynamic factors are introduced.

Kalecki's first argument is true and important. It was also argued by Joan Robinson (1977 p. 164). Kalecki's second argument is also valid, but it does not eliminate (although it does reduce) the advantages of the more capital-intensive technique at any moment in time. In addition, the trend in the capital-labour ratio suggested depends on an assumption about the nature of technical progress which is not the only possible one.

Another challenge to the traditional Soviet policy came from Maoist China. There a policy was adopted, generally known as 'walking on two legs', which stressed the need to adopt both investment-intensive and investment-saving techniques. This is discussed by Robinson (1977), Bagchi (1978), Xue Muqiao (1983 pp. 29–30) and Xu Dixin (1982b p. 28). The Maoist policy of using, where possible, capital-saving techniques led to the widespread development of both urban and rural small-scale industry. (The latter was discussed in chapter 4.) Despite the widespread existence of very important economies of scale, small-scale industry can have several important advantages. First and most important, it can produce goods that otherwise would not have been produced. This may have an important positive effect on output, labour morale and labour productivity. Secondly, it can produce output quickly, unlike large modern plants which may have long construction and running-in periods. Thirdly, the diseconomies of small enterprises may be compensated by the use of otherwise unutilised resources. Fourthly, it can provide employment. Fifthly, the training received by those working in small-scale industries may be a significant contribution to training the labour force required by a national industrialisation programme.

A big disadvantage of a policy of encouraging capital-saving techniques is that it may lead to the use of inferior techniques. (An inferior technique is one which, in terms of figure 5.5, is to the right of *E*. It has a lower output per unit of investment than other feasible techniques and hence its adoption slows down development.) This has happened both in China and in India.

A large-scale programme for the development of small-scale industries requires a very different style of economic management from that implicit in the traditional model. In the latter model, the job of medium- and low-level economic management is to carry out instructions from above. The use of local initiatives to improve the allocation of resources can be a criminal offence. In the former it is necessary to give local officials wide autonomy. This was recognised by Mao in *On the ten major relationships*.

At present scores of hands are reaching out to the localities, making things difficult for them. Once a ministry is set up, it wants to have a revolution and so it issues orders. Since the various ministries don't think it proper to issue them to the Party committees and people's councils at the provincial level, they establish direct contact with the relevant departments and bureaux in the provinces and municipalities and give them orders every day. These orders are all supposed to come from the central authorities, even though neither the Central Committee of the Party, nor the State Council, knows anything about them, and they put a great strain on the local authorities. There is such a flood of statistical forms that they become a scourge. This state of affairs must be changed.

This does seem to have happened. Ishikawa (1972 pp. 73–4) noted that in Maoist China

The Party leadership plays a crucial role in the establishment of the industrial enterprises under the direct control of the county governments. This leadership is exercised at present mainly to initiate local industries within the means of the local governments and by mobilising the co-operation of other local enterprises ... This type of leadership seems to be different from the behaviour observed in a highly centralised system of government where an official's behaviour is influenced by individualistic considerations of performance criteria or by the profit-loss calculation ... This kind of party leadership ... is a special [investment inducement] mechanism, which could not exist in the context of a Soviet-type bureau-cratic system and it is also an indispensable ingredient of the present system of organisation of county industry.

It is also an example of the use of indirect centralisation via the political process to local authorities.

Experience has shown that stress on small-scale production may lead to a number of problems. The output may be of low quality, produced at a high cost, and the pay of the workers very low. After 1978, there was much stress in China on the need for merging small-scale enterprises into specialised concerns that could benefit from economies of scale and technical progress. In some cases modern plants had been partially idle for lack of raw materials which were being used at small-scale plants with much higher costs. Nevertheless, small-scale production continued to flourish in China after 1978, as a result of the increased freedom given to state, collective and private enterprises, but with a greater attention to market needs, costs of production and technical progress. The policies of the post-Mao period also required an appropriate management model, one based on extensive autonomy for qualified enterprise management.

In the USSR, Stalin's theoretical legacy was criticised at the 20th Congress of the Soviet Communist Party (1956) and the way left open for Soviet economists to contribute to raising efficiency. The first area in which they achieved significant results was in the field of project evaluation. An official Method of project evaluation was published in 1960, and revised versions in 1964, 1966, 1969, and 1981. The following is a very abbreviated outline of the 1981 version.

In evaluating investment projects, a wide variety of factors have to be taken into account, e.g. the effect of the investment on labour productivity, capital productivity, consumption of current material inputs (e.g. metals and fuel), costs of production, environmental effects, technical progress, the location of economic activity, etc. Two indices which give useful synthetic information about economic efficiency (but which are not necessarily decisive in choosing between investment projects) are the coefficient of absolute economic effectiveness and the coefficient of relative economic effectiveness.

At the national level, the coefficient of absolute effectiveness is defined as the incremental output-capital ratio

$$E_P = \frac{\Delta Y}{I}$$

where E_p is the coefficient of absolute effectiveness of a particular project; ΔY is the increase in national income generated by the project, and I is the investment cost.

The value of E_p calculated in this way for a particular investment, has to be compared with E_a, the normative coefficient of absolute effectiveness, which is fixed for each Five Year Plan and varies between sectors. In the Eleventh Five Year Plan (1981–5) it was 0.16

in industry, 0.07 in agriculture, 0.05 in transport and communications, 0.22 in construction and 0.25 in trade. If

$$E_p > E_a$$

then the project is considered to be efficient.

For calculating the criterion of absolute effectiveness at the level of individual industries, net output is used in the numerator instead of national income. At the level of individual enterprises and associations, in particular when a firm's own money or bank loans are the source of finance, profit is used instead of national income.

The coefficient of relative effectiveness is used in the comparison of alternative ways of producing the same product. In the two products case

$$E = \frac{C_1 - C_2}{K_2 - K_1}$$

where E is the coefficient of relative effectiveness, C_i is the current cost of the ith variant, and K_i is the capital cost of the ith variant.

If $E > E_n$ where E_n is the officially established normative coefficient of relative economic efficiency, then the more capital intensive variant is economically justified. In the Eleventh Five Year Plan, E_n was in general 0.12, but exceptions were officially permitted in the range 0.08/0.10 − 0.20/0.25.

In the more than two variants case, they should be compared according to the formula

$$C_i + E_n K_i \to \text{minimum}$$

i.e. choose that variant which minimises the sum of current and capital costs.

After the 1960 Method was promulgated in the USSR very similar criteria were adopted throughout Eastern Europe. In Poland, Czechoslovakia and Hungary a transition was fairly quickly made from a recoupment-period type criterion to a present-value type criterion.

Since the promulgation of the first edition of the Soviet Method, official methods for project evaluation have been issued throughout the world, for example in the UK (*Investment* 1965), and by international organisations for developing countries (*Manual* 1968–69, *Guidelines* 1972). Perhaps the main lesson to be learned from the experience of the European state socialist countries is that the formulation of a rational criterion for deciding between investment projects is only part of the process of reducing waste in investment. One of the problems common to all these investment criteria is that they are concerned with the choice between given investment variants, and do not consider the generation of the variants between which choice has to be made. Important factors which influence the latter are foreign trade policies and the criteria used for evaluating the work of economic organisations. Poor decisions in these areas may lead to substantial waste despite the use of rational criteria to decide between given projects. For example, as pointed out in the previous section, organisations judged by the quantity of their output are unlikely to be very interested in proposals to increase quality at the expense of quantity, regardless of their national economic efficiency. Often no genuine use of rational criteria to choose between projects takes place at all. What actually happens is that the criteria are used to make an arbitrary choice look scientific. For example, a favoured project is advocated, and made to look attractive by a comparison, using the criterion, with a purely spurious alternative. If by some mischance the project advocated by some organisation fails to meet the official criterion, the costs are often underestimated or partly transferred to some other organisation (e.g. in the case of multipurpose projects such as hydro-power stations). In general, the choice of projects owes more to inter-organisation bargaining in an environment characterised by investment hunger than it does to a detached choice of a cost minimising variant. This situation is likely to persist as long as investment hunger persists.

A good example of the factors actually influencing investment decisions under state socialism is the notorious Baoshan steel plant near Shanghai. The site was apparently chosen because of the political influence of a high-ranking Shanghai party official. The location decision ignored the fact that because of the swampy nature of the site, necessitating large expenditures on the foundations, this was in fact the most expensive of the sites considered. Very expensive, dogged by cost overruns, involving major pollution problems, the project was kept alive for some time by a powerful steel lobby. Eventually, as a result of a national policy reversal in Beijing, the second phase was deferred for a time and those involved publicly criticised. Judging by its costs of production, it produced gold rather than steel.

The main function of project evaluation criteria in state socialist countries appears to be to provide an acceptable common language in which various bureaucratic agencies conduct their struggles. Agencies adopt projects on normal bureaucratic grounds and then

Table 5.7 *Construction periods and economic institutions (years)*

	Capitalist countries	Poland during the three year plan (^{a}) (1946–9)	Poland during the six year plan (^{b}) (1950–5)
Coal mine of 5,000 ton capacity per day	8 – 10^c	–	13 – 15
Electric thermal power station of 200–300 MW	c. 2^d	–	4 – 5
Quality steel mill of medium size	2 – 3^e	–	over 7
Canned meat factories, slaughter houses	–	0.75–1.0	3 – 4

^{a} The three year plan was a rehabilitation plan similar to those throughout Europe after the Second World War.
^{b} The six year plan was Poland's first Soviet-style plan.
^{c} UK and FRG.
^{d} Western Europe.
^{e} Western Europe. (A similar mill was built in pre Second World War Poland in two years).
Source: Zielinski (1973) p. 5.

try to get them adopted by higher agencies, or defend them against attack, by presenting efficiency calculations using the official methodology but relying on carefully selected data.

Another way of reducing waste is to cut the construction and running in periods for new plants. Ways of doing this include reducing the share of investment in the national income, improving the criteria for evaluating the work of construction organisations, and improving the supply of materials to construction sites. An example of the waste resulting from excessive construction periods is given in table 5.7. Excessive construction periods are one of the results of *investment tension* (Kornai 1980 chapter 9). This term describes the chronic shortage of investment goods that characterises state socialist economies.

Summary

The traditional Soviet view is that capital-intensive plants, embodying the latest international technology, and often imported or scaled up versions of foreign plants, should be built. This view was rationalised by Dobb and Sen. They argued that in an economy where the share of investment in the national income is sub-optimal, and profits are reinvested and wages consumed, techniques should be chosen so as to maximise the surplus. This argument is not relevant to the USSR and also probably not relevant to the other state socialist countries.

The traditional Soviet view was criticised in theory by Kalecki and in practice both in Eastern Europe and in China. Kalecki emphasised the loss of employment and output caused by following the traditional Soviet policy, and the diminished practical importance of the Dobb-Sen argument caused by technical progress. The Chinese developed the policy of 'walking on two legs', using both capital-intensive and capital-saving technologies. Emphasis on capital-saving techniques may lead to the adoption of wasteful inferior techniques. Widespread development of small-scale industry requires a different style of economic management from the traditional model.

In the USSR, efforts to reduce waste in technological choice have been of a technocratic kind, with the development of formal criteria for project evaluation. Their introduction, however, is only a part of the long and difficult struggle to reduce waste in investment planning.

INVESTMENT TENSION

The permanent shortage of investment services and goods (e.g. capacity of design and construction organisations, availability of engineers and workers, materials, machines and equipment) has important consequences. For one thing, it leads to long construction and running-in periods (see tables 2.1 and 5.7). Since the goods and services required to finish projects are being used elsewhere, each project takes longer to complete than it should. Hence, the waste of resources in uncompleted investment projects. For another example of this phenomenon see table 5.8. In addition, investment tension leads to diminished rates of technical progress, since by the time a project is completed the technology it embodies may be out of date. Both these factors reduce the efficiency of investment.

Periodic campaigns to reduce investment tension by concentrating resources on key projects and postponing the others, are normal under state socialism. They have no permanent effect, however, because of investment hunger. This is a deep-rooted phenomenon resulting partly from the ambitious plans of the party leadership and partly from the lack of financial discipline, which it is difficult to eradicate. In Hungary, for example, even the transition to the NEM was insufficient to end it.

Table 5.8 *Construction periods in Hungary and Japan*

HUNGARY: average construction time	1976	32.5 months
	1977	32.5 months
(the sample covers several industries)		
JAPAN: average construction time	1966	
wood industry		12 months
synthetics		16 months
pharmaceuticals		6 months
textiles		12 months
power stations		30 months

Source: J. Kornai, *Growth, shortage and efficiency* (Oxford 1982) p. 136.

INVESTMENT CYCLES

A characteristic feature of capitalism is its cyclical development. Marxists have traditionally considered this to be one of the inefficiencies of capitalism, one of the examples of the anarchy of production, which would not exist in a socialist economy. In this connection it is interesting to consider whether or not history has corroborated the Marxist view.

Experience has, in fact, shown that economic development under state socialism does not necessarily proceed smoothly. It is entirely possible, as has been shown by events in China, Poland, Cuba, Czechoslovakia and Yugoslavia, for output in one year to fall below that of the previous year. For example, according to official Chinese statistics, the Chinese national income fell by 18 percent in 1961 and a further 7 percent in 1962. Still more common have been substantial fluctuations in the rate of growth of investment. What explains these fluctuations? The attempt to answer this question has given rise to an extensive discussion.

Some authors suggest that, although there are fluctuations, these have political causes and should not be confused with economic cycles. For example, Wiles (1982) examined the data for Eastern Europe for 1950–80 and argued that the sharp fluctuations visible all had political causes. Furthermore, he argued, there are no cycles since no regular periodicity can be observed. On the other hand, Bauer (1978) has developed a theory which assumes that the investment fluctuations observed are cycles and explains them as resulting from the behavioural regularities generated by investment hunger and investment tension.

The Bauer model is as follows. It distinguishes four phases, run-up, rush, halt, and slowdown. In the run-up, as a result of investment hunger, more investment projects are begun than was foreseen in the Five Year Plan, so that the investment front is widened. In the rush phase, the increased number of projects started leads to an increased volume of investment outlays. Actual investment outlays exceed planned investment outlays and shortages of investment resources (e.g. capacity of the design and construction organisations, materials, machines and equipment) reemerge or grow. The share of investment in the national income rises, at the expense of either consumption or the balance of payments. Completion dates recede into the future.

The increased chaos on the investment front and consumption or balance of payments problems lead the planners to cut sharply their approval of new investment projects (halt). The planners attempt to deal with the situation by completing the projects already begun. This proves very difficult, however, because of the shortages of investment goods and services and the understatement of costs which now come to light.

The final phase is slowdown. In this phase the approval coefficient for new projects continues to fall and in addition the planned and actual outlays on investment are reduced. As a result, the share of investment in the national income falls, to the benefit of consumption or the balance of payments. Resources are concentrated on the completion of key projects and the volume of unfinished investment projects falls. Hence shortages are reduced. Conditions exist for a new run-up.

The Bauer model is interesting because of its economic explanation of the observed fluctuations and because of the key role it assigns to the behavioural regularities generated by the system in explaining these fluctuations. Analogous models have been found to explain developments in Czechoslovakia (Gerritse 1982) and the GDR (Boot 1984). Nevertheless, it is clear that in certain periods and in certain countries political factors have been of great importance. For example, the East European investment upswing of 1951–2 and the downswing of 1953–5 were results of the reaction of the Soviet leadership to the Korean War and the death of Stalin. Similarly, the Chinese investment booms of 1959 and 1978 were primarily a result of political decisions. Furthermore, the USSR appears not to fit into the Bauer theory, as he himself recognises. (In the USSR, official statistics show a fairly steady growth rate of investment outlays.) Even in the USSR, however, the approval coefficient fluctuates. Furthermore, the picture for that country may be distorted by misleading official statistics.

Both purely political and purely economic explanations are only partial, since they ignore the interaction of political, economic and environmental factors. More complex political-economic or systems-theoretical models might be able to explain more of the phenomena.

Summary

State socialism is not a sufficient condition for eliminating investment fluctuations. The state socialist countries have experienced sharp investment fluctuations. Some of them have been caused by political factors. Behaviourist models to explain cycles have been developed, based on forms of behaviour specific to the state socialist economic system. These models, or developments of them, have substantial explanatory power for a number of countries for normal periods.

IS INVESTMENT PLANNED?

The existence of a substantial gulf between investment activities and the plans which are supposed to regulate them, has been demonstrated both historically and theoretically. On the historical level, a number of case studies have demonstrated the difference between plan and outcome. An example is set out in table 5.9. The table depicts a situation in which the plans and actual outcomes for a top priority project for many years were widely divergent. The planners simply did not see how long it would take to build and bring into operation the Kuznetsk Combine. The 1931 plan for pig iron production was not reached until 1937. The 1938 plan was not fulfilled before the war.

Another historical example of the nature of Soviet investment planning, also drawn from the experience of the First Five Year Plan with high priority projects, concerns the Magnitogorsk metallurgical combine (Kirstein 1984). In January 1929, the USSR Council of Ministers approved the project, with a planned capacity of 650,000 tons and it was included in the First Five Year Plan. In the spring of 1929, construction began. Obtaining workers was not easy in view of the difficult living conditions (only tents or earth huts to live in, poor food, no electricity, etc.). Labour turnover was high. Construction materials were scarce, so that the construction site had to organise its own production of bricks and materials from local resources, thus losing economies of scale. In July 1929, planned capacity was raised

Table 5.9 *Plans and outcome for the Kuznetsk Combine*

Plan	Planned costs	Actual expenditures	Planned pig iron capacity	Actual pig iron production
	(million roubles)		(thousand tons)	
Goelro Plan (1920)	–	–	330	–
Project for the 1st FYP (1926)	79.7	0.1	First part 330 For 1935/6 660	–
Ural-Kutznetsk Project (1926)	–	–	820–1,070	–
First FYP (1928)	130	2.5	First part 160– 330	10.4
Project 1929	–	–	800	–
Plan for 1931	350	–	1,200	–
Plan for 1932	–	–	1,200	242.4
Second FYP (1934)	629.4	–	1,200	–
1933	–	429.0	–	–
1934	–	586.9	1,280	854.5
1935 Plan	762.0	717.0	1,200	–
1936 Plan	941.2	860.2	1,700	–
1937	–	–	–	1,471.3
1938 Plan	–	–	1,917	–
1939	–	–	–	1,453.7
1940	–	–	–	1,535.9

Source: R. W. Davies (ed.), *Soviet investment for planned industrialisation, 1929–1937: policy and practice* (Berkeley 1984) p. 71.

to 850,000 tons. In November it was raised to 1,100,000 tons. Subsequently, this was raised to 1,600,000 tons. Then in February 1930, the Politburo adopted a resolution calling for 2,000,000 tons capacity for Magnitogorsk, with an option to expand production to 4 million tons. The first two blast furnaces were to be put into operation earlier than previously planned, on 1 October 1931. This resolution necessitated a complete revision of planning for the entire project.

On the theoretical level, the behaviourists have stressed the importance of phenomena (such as investment cycles and investment tension) which have a marked impact on the investment process but are not planned by the centre. Nobody consciously plans for investment tension and investment cycles. In fact, they plan to overcome them. Nevertheless they persist, since they result from definite forms of behaviour generated by the given social relations and institutional conditions.

In view of these factors, the question arises, in what sense is investment (and indeed, economic development in general) planned?

An answer to this question has been provided by the systems school. They have pointed out that a planned economy is a complex system in which the plan is just one of the factors, along with the behaviour of the entities in the system and the economic environment, which determine the outcome. Hence it is only to be expected that the outcome will differ from the plan. The fact that the plan is not a completely insignificant input into the processes determining the outcome is shown by the fact that priority projects such as the Kuznetsk and Magnitogorsk combines generally do get built, even if many years after the planned date.

Summary

Investment is not planned in the sense that the outcome accords closely with the plan. Normally it does not. Investment is planned in the sense that the plans are an important input into the complex process which shapes the investment effort.

CONCLUSION

As far as the normative problem of the optimal share of investment is concerned, a useful way of thinking about the problem, for an economy aiming to maximise the rate of growth, is Horvat's growth-maximising approach. This fits in well with the 'overtaking and surpassing' approach to economic policy. A valuable feature of this approach is that it draws attention both to the inverse relationship between the share of investment and the return on investment and also to the possibility of wasteful overinvestment. As far as the actual share is concerned, the Marxist and systems approaches are both useful. The former draws attention to the influence of social factors, for example land reform. The latter stresses that outcomes are influenced not only by plans but also by behavioural regularities and the economic environment.

For many years in the CMEA countries it was orthodox that 'the law of the priority growth of the production of the means of production ... is a necessary condition for ensuring the uninterrupted advance of socialist production'. A theoretical basis for this view was provided by the Soviet economist Feldman in 1928. The key assumptions of his two-sector model are, a long time horizon, a closed economy, the independence of the allocation of investment and the supply of investment resources, equal construction periods in the two sectors, immortal machines and identical capital-output ratios in the two sectors. The main lesson to be learned from the Feldman model is that the capacity of the capital goods industry is one of the constraints limiting the rate of growth of an economy. In a closed economy where the capacity of this sector is a binding constraint, a major task of planning for raising the growth rate must be to direct investment resources towards expanding the capacity of this sector. The use of input-output enables the high growth industries to be pinpointed more precisely, while preserving the essence of Feldman's insight.

A major type of investment planning is industry planning, carried out by the branch ministries. The main method used for this at the present time in the CMEA countries is mathematical programming. Considerable difficulties exist in the drawing up of rational industry plans, largely resulting from the partial ignorance of the planners and the fact that the decision makers form a coalition and not a team.

The choice of techniques is an interesting and much discussed problem. The traditional Soviet view is that (labour-intensive variants of) capital-intensive plants, embodying the latest international technology, and often imported or scaled-up versions of foreign plants, should be built. This view was criticised in theory by Kalecki and in practice both in Eastern Europe and China. The Chinese developed a policy of 'walking on two legs', using both capital-intensive and capital-saving technologies. Emphasis on capital-saving techniques may lead to the adoption of wasteful inferior techniques. Widespread development of small-scale industry requires a different style of economic management from that in the traditional model. In the USSR, as in other parts of the world, efforts to reduce waste in technological choice have been of a technocratic type, with the development of formal criteria for project evaluation. Their introduction, however, is only a part of the long and difficult struggle to reduce waste in investment planning.

Investment tension is an endemic problem under state socialism. It results from the behaviour generated by the system and is a serious source of waste.

State socialism is not a sufficient condition for the elimination of economic fluctuations. In particular, investment fluctuations are common under state socialism.

Investment activities under state socialism are not planned in the sense that the outcome accords closely with the plan. Normally it does not. Investment is planned in the sense that the plans are an important input into the complex process which shapes the investment effort.

The state socialist countries normally have both a high share of investment in the national income and low returns on investment. The former is an important cause of the latter (because of diminishing marginal productivity of investment and investment tension).

Investment planning is not a socially rational process for achieving the efficient allocation of scarce investment resources. It is part of the relationship between individuals and groups in the course of which decisions are taken all of which are imperfect and many of which produce results quite at variance with the intentions of the leadership.

SUGGESTIONS FOR FURTHER READING

SHARE OF INVESTMENT

J. Kornai, 'A general descriptive model of planning processes', *Economics of planning* nos. 1–2 (1970).
B. Horvat, 'The optimum rate of investment reconsidered', *Economic Journal* (1965).
Xue Muquiao, *China's socialist economy* rev. edn (Beijing 1986) pp. 155–61.

SECTORAL ALLOCATION

R. W. Davies, 'Aspects of Soviet investment policy in the 1920s', C. H. Feinstein (ed.) *Socialism, capitalism and economic growth* (Cambridge 1967).
G. A. Feldman, 'On the theory of growth rates of national income', pp. 174–99 & 304–31 of N. Spulbur (ed.) *Foundations of Soviet strategy for economic growth* (Bloomington, Indiana, USA 1964).
E. Domar, 'A Soviet model of growth', E. Domar, *Essays in the theory of economic growth* (New York 1957).
M. H. Dobb, 'The question of "investment priority for heavy industry" ', M. H. Dobb *Papers on capitalism, development and planning* (London 1967).
D. Granick, *Soviet metal fabricating and economic development* (Madison, Milwaukee USA and London 1967).
K. N. Raj and A. K. Sen, 'Alternative patterns of growth under conditions of stagnant export earnings', *Oxford Economic Papers* (1961).
K. N. Raj, 'Role of the "machine-tools sector" in economic growth', C. H. Feinstein (ed.) *Socialism, capitalism and economic growth* (Cambridge 1967).
Ma Hong, *New strategy for China's economy* (Beijing 1983) chapter 2.

INDUSTRY PLANNING

J. Kornai, *Mathematical planning of structural decisions* (1st edn Amsterdam 1967, 2nd edn Amsterdam 1975).
Michael Ellman, *Planning problems in the USSR* (Cambridge 1973) pp. 75–90.
L. M. Goreux & A. S. Manne, *Multi-level planning* (Amsterdam 1973).
'Standard methodology for calculations to optimize the development and location of production in the long run', *Matekon* vol. XV, no. 1 (fall 1978).
L. V. Kantorovich, N. I. Cheshenko, Iu. M. Zorin & G. I. Shepelev, 'On the use of optimization methods in automated management systems for economic ministries', *Matekon* vol. XV, no. 4 (summer 1979).

CHOICE OF TECHNIQUE

A. K. Sen, *Choice of techniques* (3rd edn Oxford 1968).
A. Chilosi, 'The theory of a socialist economy of M. Kalecki', *Economics of Planning* no. 3 (1971).
Mao Tse-tung, *On the ten major relationships* (Peking 1977).
S. Ishikawa, 'A note on the choice of technology in China', *Journal of Development Studies*, vol. 9 (1972).
S. Wantanbe, 'Reflections on the current policies for promoting small enterprises and sub-contracting', *International Labour Review* (November 1974).
A. Bergson, *The economics of Soviet planning* (New Haven & London 1964) chapter 11.
D. M. Nuti, 'Large corporations and the reform of Polish industry', *Jahrbuch der Wirtschaft Osteuropas* vol. 7 (Munich 1977). Section 7 ('The selection of investment projects').
A. K. Bagchi, 'On the political economy of technological choice and development', *Cambridge Journal of Economics* vol. 2, no. 2 (June 1978).
J. Giffen, 'The allocation of investment in the Soviet Union', *Soviet Studies* vol. XXXII, no. 4 (October 1981).
J. Kornai, 'Appraisal of project appraisal', M. J. Boskin (ed.) *Economics and human welfare* (New York 1979).
T. Gustafson, *Reform in Soviet politics* (Cambridge 1981) chapter 4.
J. Robinson, 'Employment and the choice of technique', in K. S. Krishnaswamy, A. Mitra, I. G. Patel, K. N. Raj & M. N. Srivinas (eds.) *Society and change* (Bombay 1977). Reprinted in J. Robinson, *Collected Economic Papers* vol. V (Oxford 1979) chapter 22.

INVESTMENT TENSION

J. Kornai, *Economics of shortage* vol. A (Amsterdam 1980) chapter 9.
Xue Muquiao, *China's socialist economy* rev. edn (Beijing 1986) pp. 183–4.

INVESTMENT CYCLES

A. Eckstein, *China's economic development* (Ann Arbor 1975) chapter 11.
T. Bauer, 'Investment cycles in planned economies', *Acta Oeconomica* vol. 21, no. 3 (1978).
P. Wiles, 'Are there any Communist cycles?', *ACES Bulletin* vol. 24, no. 2 (Summer 1982).
R. Gerritse, *The realm of necessity* (Amsterdam 1982).
P. Boot, 'Industrial cycles in the German Democratic Republic and Professor Wiles' thesis', *ACES Bulletin* vol. XXVI, no. 1 (Spring 1984).
T. Bauer, 'Des cycles à la crise?', B. Chavance (ed.) *Regulation, cycles en crises dans les économies socialistes* (Paris 1987).

IS INVESTMENT PLANNED?

R. W. Davies (ed.) *Soviet investment for planned industrialisation, 1929–1937: Policy and practice* (Berkeley 1984).

E. Neuberger & W. J. Duffy, *Comparative economic systems: a decision-making approach* (Boston 1976) chapter 2.

6

PLANNING THE LABOUR FORCE

It shall be the duty and honour of every able-bodied citizen of the USSR to work, according to the principle 'he who does not work, neither shall he eat'.

Constitution of the USSR (1936)

Those in urban employment are in a way a privileged elite, into which many a peasant's child would wish to climb. They work and live in more secure and comfortable conditions than the agricultural population and in general receive much higher cash remuneration, as well as labour insurance and medical benefits; this applies more particularly to the regular workers in modern enterprises who are an elite within an elite.

Donnithorne (1967 p. 182)

OBJECTIVES

The main objective of labour planning in the state socialist countries is to facilitate the fulfilment and overfulfilment of the national economic plan by ensuring that the requisite types of labour are available in the right quantities and places and perform the necessary work. This involves, developing the abilities of the labour force, so as to produce the right types of labour, providing full employment so as to avoid waste of resources, ensuring a rational regional distribution of employment and ensuring the efficient utilisation of labour. Each of these objectives will be considered in turn.

Development of the abilities of the labour force

The technical re-education of a society involves not only the implantation of technical knowledge and skill but also a certain mental readjustment. This requires time. Consequently, certain dividends arising from the introduction of new techniques may be realized only after a long period, perhaps as much as the life of a generation. From this point of view the comparatively short time in which the Soviet Union managed to educate its technical cadres is impressive, and an encouraging example for those underdeveloped countries which stand today very much where the Soviet

Union did at the end of the 1920s. In this respect the Soviet 'model' of industrialization has proved a success and demands special and careful study.

Swianiewicz (1965 pp. 263–4)

In the Utilitarian tradition, the objective of economic activity is consumption. Productive labour is a disutility which is only engaged in until the diminishing marginal utility of earnings equals the marginal disutility of work. For a Marxist, on the other hand, productive labour is potentially an opportunity to take part in creative activity. A major aspect of the Marxist critique of capitalism is that it transforms the work process in such a way as to generate meaningless jobs and a stratified society. A classic modern exposition of this view is Braverman (1974). Accordingly a major objective of the Marxist movement is to transform the labour process so as to replace the narrowly specialised worker by an individual who has wide possibilities for creative labour. As Marx put it in *The German Ideology*:

in communist society, where nobody has one exclusive sphere of activity, but each can become accomplished in any branch he wishes, society regulates the general production, and thus makes it possible for me to do one thing today and another tomorrow, to hunt in the morning, fish in the afternoon, rear cattle in the evening, criticise after dinner, just as I have a mind, without ever becoming a hunter, fisherman, shepherd or critic.

It is in accordance with this tradition that the imaginary author of the lectures in Preobrazhensky's book *From NEP to socialism* (1922) is simultaneously a professor of history and a fitter in a railway workshop.

Utilitarianism treats man as the possessor of an insatiable appetite, greater satisfaction of which is an 'increase in welfare'. An alternative view is one which sees man not as a consumer of utilities but as a doer, a creator, an enjoyer of his (or her) human attributes. These attributes may be variously listed and assessed. They may be taken to include the capacity for rational understanding, for mastery of the whole of a socially necessary labour process, for moral judgement and action, for aesthetic creation or contemplation, for the emotional activities of friendship and love. Whatever the uniquely human attributes are taken to be, in this view their exertion and development are seen as ends in themselves and not simply as means of consumer satisfaction. This point has been elaborated by Macpherson (1973). Accordingly, a major objective of socialist planning in the field of labour is to develop the abilities of the labour force. This has important implications for policy in such areas as education, participation rates and hours of work.

Labour policies in the state socialist countries have developed under the influence both of the Marxist critique of capitalism and of the real historical problems confronting these societies. Hence they partly diverge from, and partly converge to, the path taken by the capitalist countries.

Long before human capital theories became fashionable in the West, Soviet economists had analysed the economic importance of education and training. In a well-known paper, Strumilin (1924) argued that expenditure on education was a very high yielding investment. Strumilin (1931 p. 598) estimated that for every rouble spent on schooling, the annual national income of the country would be increased by at least six roubles. The benefits to the economy of a literate and skilled workforce long ago became commonplace in the state socialist countries, which have very extensive education and training programmes. This is organised both in special institutions (e.g. schools, specialised institutes) and also on-the-job. Despite the stress on on-the-job training, formal education has not been neglected.

The Soviet Union provides nursery places for a higher proportion of the relevant age group than the USA. The general opinion of Soviet emigrants in the USA is that the quality of Soviet schools is above that of US schools (Birman 1983). The output of higher education (adjusted for institutional differences) is higher in the Soviet Union than in the USA. The quality of Soviet engineers, computer specialists and mathematicians compares well with the USA. A striking feature of formal education in state socialist countries has been that it has been concentrated on areas of importance to the national economy. This is a result of basing higher education on manpower planning rather than on, say, the Robbins principle of providing places in higher educational institutions on the basis of the preferences of schoolchildren.[1]

A problem of educational planning, Soviet style, is that lower-level teachers and administrators are under considerable pressure to pass all, or virtually all, the students in any year, so as to avoid underfulfilling the plan. This ensures that a proportion of those with diplomas are in fact not qualified for their supposed specialism. A

---

[1] Professor Lord Robbins was the chairman of an official committee which recommended this principle as the basis for higher educational planning in the UK. Hence the term 'Robbins principle'.

well-known literary example is given in *The first circle* (Solzhenitsyn 1970 pp. 38–9).

A feature of Soviet labour policy compared with the practice of capitalist countries at comparable stages of development has been the very limited reliance on child labour. As Eason (1963) has observed, of the population between 10 and 15, the proportion of the Soviet labour force fell from 59 percent in 1926 to 23 percent in 1939 and 12 percent in 1959. This decline mainly reflects the spread of schooling.

An important aspect of labour policy under state socialism has been urban participation rates much higher that those in capitalist countries at comparable stages of development. This largely results from the fact that a much higher proportion of women are employed. This partly reflects the Communist rejection of the bourgeois subjection of women, partly reflects the need for labour by the state and partly reflects the difficulty of keeping a family on one income. In addition to positive features, this emancipation of women has a number of negative features. For example, Soviet women, by and large, have to work much harder than men. This is partly because they do both paid employment and unpaid domestic labour. Partly it is because they do much of the heavy manual work. Furthermore, women in the USSR primarily hold the lower-level posts. For example, Soviet medicine is primarily a feminine profession but most of the senior positions in it are held by men. In addition, household chores are a heavier burden than in comparable capitalist countries because of lack of investment and low levels of employment in distribution and services such as laundries. In the hard years of Soviet industrialisation, 1929–50, Soviet women formed a particularly disadvantaged proletarian stratum.

Despite equal pay legislation, throughout the world employed women earn on average less than men. This is so in the advanced capitalist countries, in the third world, and also in the economically advanced central Europe state socialist countries. It is also so in the USSR. There are no official Soviet statistics of the relative earnings of men and women (because of the awkward picture they would show) but a variety of sample surveys have been taken and reported in the specialist Soviet literature (McAuley 1981 chapter 2). These all show earnings inequalities similar to those in Western Europe. Although women occupy a variety of interesting and satisfying jobs in the USSR, most Soviet women are engaged in unskilled work, low-level jobs and traditional 'feminine' occupations. Soviet women work primarily to earn enough to support a family (this is normally impossible on only one income) and their jobs are often monotonous and boring. As living standards under state socialism advance, there is a tendency to improve this situation by measures giving women more choice between paid employment and looking after their children (e.g. improved family allowances and extended maternity leave) and also by providing more part-time work so as to enable women to combine paid employment with domestic labour without having to accept the onerous double burden that full-time work enforces. The reeducation of men, although officially supported, is a slow process. In fact, Soviet women have to deal with an additional problem resulting from widespread heavy drinking by men. This often leads to domestic violence directed against women.

An important aspect of Soviet labour policy has been hours of work below those in capitalist countries at a similar level of economic development. The eight hour day, a classic objective of the labour movement, was decreed immediately after the Great October Socialist Revolution. In 1929 and 1930 the work week was reduced further to c. 41 hours a week. In 1940 the standard work week was increased to 48 hours (six 8 hour days). Under Krushchev the standard work week was reduced to c. 41 hours a week (although overtime also takes place). In addition a decree of 1967 announced a transition to a five-day week, and this was generally achieved by 1970. Furthermore, retirement age in the USSR is below that in many capitalist countries at 60 for men and 55 for women.

Similarly in China, retirement age in state enterprises is normally 60 for men and five years earlier for women. As far as hours of work in China are concerned, workers in the state sector of industry have, since 1956, been supposed normally to work 8 hours a day, 6 days a week. Longer hours are in fact often worked, especially towards the end of plan periods. At many periods workers have in addition been obliged to participate in political activities.

When comparing hours of work, and more generally the utilisation of time, between systems it is necessary to take account not only of hours worked in the state sector, but also of both system-related differences in time needed for everyday chores (e.g. shopping) and also hours worked by state employees in the non-state sector. Pryor (1977) has shown that there are significant differences between time devoted to shopping in the two systems, with extensive queues causing shopping time in state socialist countries, e.g. Poland, to be considerably greater than in comparable capitalist countries. Hungarian studies have shown that, in Hungary in the

1970s, about 17 percent of the total manhours available were spent in the informal sector (Kornai 1985 p. 103).

Workers in state socialist countries are often better off from the standpoint of social security (in old age or illness) than workers in capitalist countries at comparable stages of development, or than workers in the socially backward capitalist countries (e.g. the USA). In Eastern Europe this results from the existence of earnings-related old age pensions and sickness pay, free medical care and the absence of cyclical unemployment. In China it results partly from the same factors and partly from the fact that the rural population is organised in villages which provide basic security for their members.

Inter-system comparisons of industrial diseases, accidents and deaths is not possible because of lack of data for the USSR and China. For the USSR, the absence of data suggests a poor record. A US delegation that visited the Soviet coal-mining industry in 1972 made a special effort to find out about safety. Though unsuccessful in obtaining any data, the delegation deduced from discussions with Soviet officials that in underground mining Soviet fatalities per million tons mined are several times greater than the US figure. They also concluded that mine fires and explosions must be quite frequent. There is much discussion in the USSR of programmes for combating pneumoconiosis, but no information on its frequency. The US delegation could get no statistics on this matter either, but their impressions were that silicosis and black lung were quite prevalent and increasing (Campbell 1976 p. 257). The main reasons for the poor Soviet record in industrial safety are the priority given to production and the absence of independent trade unions.

A well-known feature of the labour process in the USSR compared, for example, with the USA, is its lower intensity, i.e. its slower pace and lower effort. From a capitalist, or consumer, point of view, this is a 'problem' of socialist planning. From a labourist point of view it is an advantage.

An important feature of employment in the traditional model is job security. The prospect of losing one's job because of the vagaries of the conjunctural situation, which is a permanent reality and major source of anxiety under capitalism, normally does not exist in the traditional model. By and large, all workers in the traditional model enjoy the kind of job security enjoyed by civil servants under capitalism. In the capitalist countries the expansion of state employment has substantially improved conditions of employment (e.g. job security, pensions, promotion prospects etc.). Similarly, the spread of state employment to the whole economy in the traditional model has led to the virtual universal spread of these favourable employment conditions.

Full employment

Marxists consider that unemployment is one of the wasteful and irrational features of capitalism. In addition it is socially unjust, falling disproportionally on manual workers, especially unskilled manual workers. Marxists consider that unemployment is not a peripheral feature of capitalism which can be prevented by Keynesian demand management policies, but an integral part of this mode of production. Marx explained in volume I of *Capital* that:

The greater the social wealth, the functioning capital, the extent and energy of its growth, and therefore, also the absolute mass of the pro- letariat and the productiveness of its labour, the greater is the industrial reserve army. The same causes which develop the expansive power of capital, develop also the labour-power at its disposal. The relative mass of the industrial reserve army increases therefore with the potential energy of wealth. But the greater this reserve army in proportion to the active labour-army, the greater is the mass of a consolidated surplus-population, whose misery is in inverse ratio to its torment of labour. The more extensive, finally, the lazarus-layers of the worker class, and the industrial reserve army, the greater is official pauperism. *This is the absolute general law* of capitalist accumulation.

Marxists consider that the maintenance of permanent full employ- ment is incompatible with the capitalist mode of production because full employment under capitalism will hinder accumulation by undermining labour discipline, generating inflation, threatening profits, and hindering the manning of new plants.

The experience of the state socialist countries shows that maintain- ing permanent full employment is no easy matter, even when there is state ownership of the means of production and national economic planning. The USSR in the 1920s, China in the 1950s and Vietnam in the 1970s and 1980s all experienced large-scale unemployment. The reason for this, was the large-scale influx of peasants into the towns. The rate of the influx was much in excess of the growth of jobs in the towns. Both the USSR and China dealt with the problem by the use of administrative measures. In the USSR from 1930 to the late 1970s the Soviet authorities prevented the excess rural popu- lation causing urban unemployment by administrative controls over the outflow of labour from the villages (depriving villagers of internal

Table 6.1 *Urban unemployment in China*

Year	Unemployment (millions)	Unemployment rate (as % of employed + unemployed)
1952	3.8	13.2
1957	2.0	5.9
1978	5.3	5.3
1982	3.8	3.2
1983	2.7	2.3
1984	2.4	1.9
1985	2.4	1.8

Source: Statistical yearbook of China 1986 (Hongkong & Beijing 1986) p. 104.

passports).[2] This reflected, and enhanced, the position of the rural population as second-class citizens. In China, urban unemployment resulting from the influx of peasants into the towns was a very serious problem in the 1950s. Some data are presented in table 6.1. The main method of dealing with it is by the household registration system (Whyte 1977) and 'sending down' or *xiaxiang and xiafang* (Bernstein 1977) people from the towns to the countryside. Household registration books are legally required of all residents in Chinese cities. An application to be registered in a city may be refused by the relevant officials and normally is in the case of arrivals from the countryside. Sending down means that people, generally recent arrivals, are rounded up and sent back to the countryside.[3] This has the great advantage of saving on urban food demands and hence on the marketed output of agriculture. Once the unemployed are back in their villages, the responsibility for feeding them rests primarily on themselves and their family. Sending down was also used, after the victory of state socialism in South Vietnam, Laos and Kampuchea, to reduce the unproductive urban populations in those countries. In Kampuchea it was used on a particularly large scale. The use of sending down has enabled China to avoid the bloated urban agglomerations and shanty towns that are common in third world countries. In China during the Maoist period sending down appears to have been fairly successful in reducing the urban unemployment from the high figures of the 1950s. By 1971 the authorities claimed that full employment had been reached. This 'success' was based on

[2] An internal passport is an identity document. Without one it is illegal to live in a town.

[3] This is analogous to the repatriation of immigrant workers from the industrialised West European countries when the demand for their labour fell.

the use of coercion to enforce sending down on school leavers. In 1978 the existence and importance of unemployment was again officially recognised. This resulted from the lesser reliance on coercion by the post-Mao leadership. After the 11th Congress, the widespread dissatisfaction with sending down by educated youth in China surfaced in *samizdat* publications, wallposters and demonstrations. Partly as a result of this, in 1979, the authorities announced that sending down would be supplemented by cooperatives. In other words the state would allow groups of youngsters for whom the state was unable to provide proper jobs to try and make a living as best they could, on their own initiative, in a legal urban informal sector. In the early 1980s, as table 6.1 shows, the state was successful in eliminating unemployment, but partly at the cost of low productivity in the state sector.

The USSR has experienced continuous urban full employment since 1930. (Rural underemployment in the USSR was discussed in chapter 4.) Urban full employment is also normal in the other state socialist countries. This elimination of urban unemployment results from the restricted role of the law of value[4] and direct control by the state of aggregate distribution.

The restricted role of the law of value has six aspects, rationality criteria, large investment programmes, the choice of techniques, the expansion of the quaternary sector,[5] the right to work and administrative control over the influx of rural labour.

In principle the appropriate *rationality criteria* for a capitalist firm and a socialist state differ. This is familiar from the literature on choice in techniques in less developed countries and on cost-benefit analysis. A capitalist firm is interested in its survival and profits. Costs borne by society as a whole are 'externalities'. A socialist state is concerned (or ought to be) with social costs and benefits. Hence it may be entirely rational for a socialist state, but not for a capitalist enterprise, to employ workers whose marginal product is below their wage. Just as it may be rational for a peasant household to react to an increase in the labour-land ratio by intensifying its methods of production so may it also be rational for a socialist state. For both, capitalist rationality which considers wages purely as a cost and profits as the only income generated by production, is irrelevant. As

[4] In this context the 'law of value' means atomistic decision making in an economy coordinated by the market mechanism.

[5] It is customary to divide economic activity into four sectors, primary, secondary, tertiary and quarternary. The first consists of agriculture and mining, the second of manufacturing industry, the third of marketed services and the fourth of non-marketed services.

Stalin (1927) long ago explained, 'the extraction of profit is neither an aim nor a motive of our socialist industry'.

What determines the behaviour of enterprises in an economy in which profit seeking has disappeared as a rationality criterion? According to the well-known and influential argument of Kornai, the main motivation of enterprise management under state socialism is *identification with their own job*. This means a wish to do the job in a way that will generate social approval. In a non-market economy without the risk of producing unsaleable products or of bankruptcy this implies a total demand by the enterprises for virtually unlimited material and labour inputs. This is because more inputs enable the output of each enterprise to grow and hence its apparent contribution to society to increase. This bureaucratic expansionism is a major factor in generating full, but not efficient, employment of the labour force.

The *large investment programmes* pursued over decades in all the state socialist countries are an important factor in raising employment in them. These investment programmes are pursued for national economic reasons and quite independently of the short-run profitability of particular plants. (This is why they can be considered an aspect of 'the restricted role of the law of value'.) The new plants have provided jobs for large numbers of workers. Rapid accumulation in order to catch up with and overtake the most advanced capitalist countries is an important feature of state socialism (although in the late 1970s and early 1980s when the rate of growth fell throughout Eastern Europe, investment was slashed to protect consumption). That this should play a major role in maintaining full employment is in complete accord with Keynesian theory. In the *General Theory* Keynes wrote that 'I conceive, therefore, that a somewhat comprehensive socialisation of investment will prove the only means of securing an approximation to full employment'. How large are the investment programmes under state socialism? Some data on this question is set out in table 6.2.

Although, as explained in the note, the data in table 6.2 are not directly comparable with that for the capitalist world, they are indicative of a substantial investment effort, maintained over decades.

The analytical and practical issues arising from these large investment programmes and the conditions necessary for their implementation, were considered in the previous chapter.

It is obvious that the *choice of techniques* to be embodied in the investment programmes plays a major role in determining the extent

Table 6.2 *Gross investment as a proportion of net material product (in %)*

Country	1970	1975	1980	1985
Bulgaria	29.2	32.5	24.9	24.1
China	32.9	33.9	31.5	33.7
Czechoslovakia	27.0	29.2	26.2	20.2
GDR	24.2	22.2	22.7	20.1
Hungary	23.5	24.7	19.6	10.0
Mongolia	32.7	38.1	36.3	40.3
Poland	25.1	34.1	18.4	26.0
USSR	29.5	26.6	23.9	26.5

Notes:
a) The figures in this table are analogous to, but different from, those for gross investment as a share of the national income of capitalist countries. The difference arises from a number of causes. For one thing, net material product and national income are different concepts. For another, the measured share of investment naturally depends on relative prices, relative wages and accounting conventions, some or all of which often differ significantly from those prevailing in the capitalist world.
b) The sharp fall in the share of gross investment in Hungary in the 1980s reflects the pro-consumer policy in that country. Given the virtual macroeconomic stagnation, the adverse shift in the terms of trade and the foreign debt burden, the planners protected consumption by slashing investment.
Source: Statisticheskii ezhegodnik stran – chlenov soveta ekonomicheskoi vzaimopomoshchi 1986 (Moscow 1986) p. 43; *Statistical yearbook of China 1986* (Hong Kong & Beijing 1986) p. 49.

to which they will contribute to raising employment. This is a particularly topical issue at a time when it is widely feared that technical progress in the capitalist world may take on a labour saving form so that investment programmes may simply reduce the volume of employment. As explained in the previous chapter, as far as the state socialist countries are concerned, the view of economists such as Kalecki (1972a) and Joan Robinson (1977) is that where choices exist a socialist state should make a different one from capitalist firms. Whereas one would expect a capitalist firm to maximise profits, a socialist state should aim at maximising employment and output.

In practice, the USSR has traditionally adopted what have come to be known as 'labour-intensive variants of capital-intensive techniques'. This means that investment has tended to take the form of the construction of large modern plants, often imported from the West or scaled up versions of Western plants, in which the basic production technology is highly mechanised but in which many auxiliary processes, e.g. materials handling, are not highly mechanised and are labour intensive. This dualism had the advantage

of combining modern technology with some saving of scarce investment resources.

From this point of view, an interesting development in China has
been the development of the rural non-agricultural sector. This was
discussed in chapter 4, where attention was drawn to the output,
employment and incomes it generates and its positive effect on
migration.

The theoretical arguments of Kalecki and Joan Robinson, and the
two practical examples which have just been given, indicate that the
technology embodied in new investment and hence the employment
effect associated with it, is not purely exogenous but has an important
policy component.

The fact that the employment effect of investment depends on the
volume of investment and the choice of techniques embodied in it, is
obvious from the analysis of any growth model. What the study of
state socialism adds to the analysis of growth models is the observation that, if entrepreneurs are unwilling to invest in sufficient volume
and in appropriate techniques, then the state can do the job.

The *expansion of the quarternary sector* has played an important role in
maintaining full employment in the state socialist countries. This
involves services such as education, medical care and scientific
research.

The effectiveness of the three policies discussed above can easily be
seen by looking at the data about the Soviet labour force set out in
table 6.3.

Four interesting conclusions can be drawn from the Soviet employment data. First, the USSR has been very successful in expanding
state employment. In the thirty four years 1951–85 state employment
increased by almost 200 percent. Secondly, there is an absence of
cyclical unemployment in the USSR. In every year of this period
employment was greater than in the previous year. Thirdly, there
were no signs in the USSR in 1951–85 of the much discussed
'de-industrialisation' which haunts some OECD countries. Industrial employment in the USSR steadily increased throughout this
period. Fourthly, employment in the quaternary sector (education
and culture, medical care and science) has increased both absolutely
and relatively. On the whole, the table is evidence of the success of the
three policies discussed above, i.e. large investment programmes,
suitable choice of technique and expansion of the quaternary sector.
In fact, at the present time, when the capitalist world is suffering from
an unemployment problem, the USSR and her allies in Eastern
Europe are suffering from a labour shortage.

Table 6.3 *State employment in the USSR (in millions)*

Year	Total[a]	Industry	Agri-[b] culture	Con- struction	Trans- port	Education & culture	Trade	Medical	Science
1951	40.4	15.3	3.4	3.3	4.1	3.3	3.4	2.1	0.7
1956	51.9	19.7	6.0	4.5	5.2	4.1	3.8	2.7	1.1
1961	65.9	23.8	7.5	6.5	6.5	5.2	5.0	3.7	2.0
1966	79.7	28.5	8.9	7.5	7.4	6.9	6.3	4.4	2.7
1971	92.8	32.0	9.5	9.5	8.2	8.3	7.8	5.2	3.3
1976	104.2	34.8	10.8	10.7	9.4	9.3	9.0	5.9	3.9
1981	114.0	37.2	11.8	11.3	10.5	10.6	9.8	6.3	4.5
1985	117.5	38.1	12.2	11.5	10.9	11.3	10.0	6.5	4.6

Notes:[a] The total is greater than the sum of the subheadings given since some sectors (e.g. forestry, communications) have been omitted.
[b] This column excludes non-state (i.e. collective farm) employment in agriculture. This (together with the policy of expanding the state sector of agriculture) explain why it grows over time.
Sources: Soviet statistical yearbooks.

The right to work is a traditional demand of the labour movement. This right is recognised in the state socialist countries and often enshrined in their constitutions. Workers cannot easily be dismissed, and workers without jobs can expect jobs to be found for them even if their marginal output in them is low or non-existent. This means that part of the 'employment' in the state socialist world corresponds to unemployment benefit in the advanced capitalist countries. That is, it is a means of ensuring an income rather than a means of ensuring output. According to Mikul'skii (1983 p. 243) the traditional estimate of the extent of superfluous industrial employment in the USSR is 15–20 per cent. This estimate, he suggests, is inaccurate and may be too low.

Administrative control over the influx of rural labour is very important in countries such as the USSR and China. It was discussed above.

Direct control by the state over aggregate distribution is a major feature of state socialism (Brus 1977) and of great importance. Whereas under capitalism important chunks of expenditure (investment, consumption, exports) are partly determined by exogenous factors, under state socialism these are all (more or less) under the control of the state. This has numerous important consequences. For example, whereas under capitalism an increase in savings may have the adverse effects discussed by Keynesian economics, under state socialism it simply means that retail prices can be lower than they would otherwise have been. As far as full employment policy is concerned, direct control by the state over aggregate distribution has three aspects. They are, the rational low-wage policy, the absence of the demand constraint, and direct control over the size of the labour force.

The '*rational low-wage policy*' (this is the traditional Chinese terminology) is an important part of the explanation of permanent full employment under state socialism. By a 'rational low-wage policy' is meant a deliberate policy of keeping down real wages per worker so as to spread the available wages fund over as many workers as possible and hence maximise employment and output. It is normal in the state socialist countries, especially in the early stages of industrialisation, for the rate of growth of real wages to be kept well below the rate of growth of labour productivity. This limits the demand for wage goods and contains urban-rural inequalities. Limiting the demand for wage goods enables a given marketed output of agriculture to provide employment for the maximum number of workers. In addition, it enables industry to increase the share of its output devoted to accumulation. Both these factors, *ceteris paribus*, contribute to raising the growth rate of employment and output. To operate a rational low-wage policy requires a government which pursues an economic policy with a long time horizon, and prevents active working class opposition (e.g. by ensuring that the trade unions function as transmission belts for government economic policy and by using sufficient repression). Examples of the rational low wage policy are, that in the USSR the level of real wages per worker did not permanently exceed the 1928 level till the mid 1950s,[6] and that in China real wages appear to have been lower in the mid 1970s than they were in 1957.

Under state socialism, a rational low-wage policy may encounter two problems. First, it may have an adverse effect on labour productivity. This seems to have happened, for example, in the USSR in the early 1930s and in China in 1958–77. Secondly, it may be impossible to implement because of working class opposition. This was an important factor in Poland in 1956–60 and in the early 1970s. The Polish Government in those periods had come to power largely as a result of working class opposition to the previous low growth of real wages and wished to appease the workers. Similarly, in China the wage increase of 1977 came after prolonged industrial unrest. These two problems are important and suggest that it is a mistake to imagine that independent trade unions are the only barrier to a rational low-wage policy.

[6] To a considerable extent, of course, this was caused not by the rational low wage policy but by the Great Patriotic War.

The *absence of the demand constraint* is an important factor explaining full employment under state socialism. The state can use its control over aggregate distribution to ensure that unemployment due to lack of effective demand does not exist. It can do this because the state monopoly of foreign trade, conservative monetary and fiscal policy, and state control of prices, prevent international developments causing unemployment or full employment causing runaway inflation. On the other hand, the state socialist countries do experience unemployment, or irrational use of labour, arising through lack of supplies. Examples are, the decline in employment in Chinese industry in the wake of the Great Leap Forward, and the permanent under-utilisation of labour in the traditional model resulting from the rationing of producer goods (see chapter 2). This illustrates the general proposition that a basic difference between capitalism and state socialism is that in the former growth is normally demand constrained and in the latter supply constrained. It is important to note that the elimination of the demand constraint is likely to have a dramatic effect on the working of all parts of the economy (Kornai 1971 chapter 19).

Direct control over the size of the labour force is another important factor explaining full employment under state socialism. This concerns the choice of the retirement age and the length of the educational period. Retirement age in the state socialist countries is low by international standards. In addition in all the state socialist countries education has been enormously increased and extended.

Regional employment

Keynesian regional policy is primarily concerned with the provision by the state of financial incentives to private industry. Socialist regional policy is primarily concerned with the direct provision by the state of the necessary investment.

Regional employment policy in socialist countries has both socio-political and economic aspects. First, it is an aspect of the Leninist nationalities policy. The latter is concerned, not with ensuring purely 'formal' political freedom for formerly subject nationalities but with their rapid social and economic development. Secondly, it is concerned with the efficient utilisation of natural resources. Hence, Soviet regional policy has combined large-scale industrial investment in densely populated formerly backward areas, such as Central Asia, with large-scale natural resource development in sparsely populated Siberia. The enormous expansion of urban employment opportunities in Soviet Central Asia during the period of Soviet power is a major achievement of Soviet power.

One would expect that in a market economy the labour force would have to adjust to the availability of jobs, but that in a socialist planned economy the supply of jobs would be adjusted to the availability of labour. In an empirical study Pryor (1973 pp. 290–7) corroborated this expectation. He found that regional differences in the proportion of the population engaged in mining and manufacturing showed an approximately equal tendency to diminish in the post Second World War period in the state socialist and capitalist countries, but that in the former this was associated with jobs moving to where people were, and in the latter with the reverse. There are problems with the data used for this exercise, but this is an interesting, if provisional, finding.

Socialist regional policy, however, has its limitations. For example, in the USSR in the late 1980s, emphasis was placed on the economic, rather than socio-political, aspects of regional policy. It was argued that the goals of the Leninist nationalities policy had been achieved and that therefore decisions on the location of economic activity should normally be considered from the perspective of the USSR as a whole (Bromlei 1987). This policy reflected the political ill-repute of the Brezhnevite Central Asian leadership under Gorbachev, the initial centralising nationalities policy of the Gorbachev leadership and its attention to costs and returns. The apparent abandonment of the aim of generating employment where the people are, is unlikely to be popular in the southern republics of the USSR with their rapidly growing populations. This will particularly be the case if it were to lead to pressure to migrate to labour shortage regions or to under-employment in rural Central Asia.

Rational utilisation of labour

The traditional model is generally good at attaining and maintaining full employment. It is much less good, however, at attaining the rational use of labour. It leads to a *volume* of employment that compares favourably with that under capitalism, but a level of *productivity* that compares adversely with that under capitalism. The systemic reasons for this are fourfold. First, the enterprises are primarily concerned with plan fulfilment and expansion and not with profit making. Hence incentives for cost reduction are weak. Additional workers are always useful. They make plan fulfilment easier. They form an insurance against plan increases or the diversion of part of the labour force to public duties (e.g. help with the harvest). Furthermore, by increasing the total wage bill they may have a favourable effect on the income of the management or of the enterprise. Secondly, under permanent full employment workers have a strong bargaining position. When enterprises are competing against each other for extra workers, the law and custom prevent management easily sacking unsatisfactory workers, and workers can easily find employment elsewhere, slack work is unlikely to be penalised. Thirdly, the adverse effect on labour incentives of low wages. Low real wages result in worker dissatisfaction and have an adverse effect on labour productivity. The link between satisfaction, or otherwise, with living standards and labour effort is expressed in popular jokes in all the state socialist countries. There is a familiar Russian saying, 'As long as the Government pretends that we live well, we will pretend that we work well', and a Polish saying, 'The Government pretends to pay us – we pretend to work.' Fourthly, the adverse effects of the absence of countervailing power. Lacking trade unions independent of the state and collective bargaining, normally lacking employment possibilities outside the state sector and some-times lacking the possibility of legally changing their jobs (e.g. China, USSR 1940–56) workers have little control over their work and are very vulnerable to arbitrary measures by the bosses. This naturally affects the quality of their work adversely.

The need to raise productivity gets continuous attention in the state socialist countries. The chief methods used to attain this goal are, investment and training, discipline, foreign trade, hardening the budget constraint and transforming the enterprises from economic and social organisations into purely economic organisations.

For efficiency, the socialist countries primarily rely on investment and training. This investment and training have largely taken the form of copying the technology and division of labour prevalent in the capitalist world. Labour productivity in the USSR has always been considerably below that of the most advanced capitalist countries. Hence great stress has always been placed in the USSR on utilising the progressive aspects of Western methods for raising labour productivity. In his well-known pamphlet *The immediate tasks of the Soviet Government* (1918), Lenin wrote that the Taylor system of scientific management

like all capitalist progress, is a combination of the refined brutality of bourgeois exploitation and a number of the greatest scientific achievements in the field of analysing mechanical motions during work, the elimination of superfluous and awkward motions, the elaboration of correct methods of work, the introduction of the best system of accounting and control etc. The Soviet Republic must at all costs adopt all that is valuable in the achievements of science and technology in this field. The possibility of building socialism depends exactly upon our success in combining Soviet power and Soviet organisation of administration with the up to date achievements of capitalism. We must organise in Russia the study and teaching of the Taylor system and systematically try it out and adapt it to our ends.

This attitude has persisted down to the present and explains the admiration Soviet officials, planners and economists have for the large Western corporations, which they regard as marvels of the scientific organisation of labour.[7] It also explains the concessions offered by the Soviet Government to Western firms in the 1920s, the import of technology by all the state socialist countries in the 1970s, the R&D cooperation agreements between Western firms and the USSR, the East–West industrial cooperation agreements and the East-West joint ventures. With the Western technology has come the Western organisation of labour within the strong independent worker organisations that exist in the West. M. Dido (1971), the Secretary of the CGIL, Italy's Communist Party dominated labour federation, has discussed this question with specific reference to the huge car plant built by Fiat at Tol'yatti in the USSR.

The entire project has been carried out on the basis of plans prepared and supervised by Fiat technicians ... not only the technical equipment but also the organisation of work is of the Fiat type ... it is impossible to distinguish the administrative organisation ... whether with regard to working conditions or the absolute priority given to productivity from that of the Turin plant ... At Tol'yatti ... they have adopted not only Western machines but also Western systems of organisation. To have a minimum of equilibrium, however, such a system presupposes at the very least the existence of a strong trade union force. But at the present moment such a force does not exist, either in the Soviet Union or in the other countries of Eastern Europe.

When asked what disturbed him most about the plant at Tol'yatti, Dido replied that it was hearing the Turin bosses say that 'the trade union demands are unjustified, since even the Soviet leaders pay no attention to them at Tol'yatti'.

It is no accident that the halting attempts to develop a new technology appropriate to a new, more human, organisation of labour, have taken place not in a state socialist country but in

---

[7] The standard Soviet phrase for the efficient utilisation of labour *(nauchnaya organizatsiya truda,* literally 'the scientific organisation of labour') is a literal translation of *l'organisation scientifique du travail,* the French term for Taylorism. In France the phrase *l'organisation rationelle du travail* was adopted when the reaction against Taylorism set in, but in the USSR the original term, which had Lenin's support, has been retained.

Social-Democratic Scandinavia. The USSR, and the countries which follow her, have *en principe* postponed any attempt to transform the organisation and division of labour till the higher stage of communism, and in practice postponed it till the Greek kalends.

The irony of the endorsement of Taylorism by a 'proletarian Government' which has 'abolished the exploitation of man by man' has not gone entirely unnoticed in the state socialist countries. In 1923–4 there took place in the USSR a very interesting debate on this subject (Bailes 1977). The Taylorist position was defended by the Central Labour Institute, founded in 1920, and its leader A. K. Gastev. It was criticised by 'The Moscow Group of Communists Actively interested in Scientific Management'. In traditional Marxist fashion the latter criticised Taylorism as having the 'aim of transforming the living person into an unreasoning and stupid instrument without any general qualifications or sufficient all-round development'. The views of the Moscow Group were criticised by the head of the trade unions and a number of prominent party figures. At a conference held in 1924 to resolve this dispute, the Central Labour Institute was victorious. Its assumptions and approach were recognised as standards for the whole national economy. The use of piecework as an incentive to greater productivity has remained an important feature of work in the CMEA countries. Disputes about piecework norms have been endemic, sometimes with explosive political consequences, as in Poznan in 1956. Perhaps the supreme triumph of Soviet Taylorism was the Stakhanov movement of the 1930s, which was a state organised rate-busting campaign on an unparalleled scale. One of its organisers was A. K. Gastev.

Some observers have suggested that steps towards a fundamental transformation of the labour process took place in China in 1966–76. According to Bettelheim, the transformations that occurred during the Cultural Revolution signified, *inter alia*, that a struggle was being waged to overcome the division between intellectual and manual labour. Similarly, a new type of technical progress was supposedly taking place in China during the GPCR (Bettelheim 1974b pp. 78–89). Richman (1969 pp. 258–9) confirmed that the division of labour in China in the 1960s was often less pronounced in Chinese than in 'normal' factories. He suggested, however, that this was simply a rational response to the extreme shortage of qualified specialists in a backward country. He also considered that it resulted in serious inefficiencies, for example, in some of the larger and more complex firms he visited. Richman (1969 pp. 325–6 and 252–3) also confirmed the great stress on technical progress resulting from innovations introduced by the workers themselves in China in the 1960s. He suggested, however, that the reason this was worthwhile was because of the low technical level of Chinese industry. In future, he argued, science-based innovations were likely to become more important. In addition, he considered that stress on the virtues of 'worker engineers' and 'peasant scientists' at the expense of scientific research and development had serious costs for China (non-utilisation of qualified people, waste of resources in irrational projects). The waste of time at endless political meetings has been stressed by a Soviet scientist who worked in China (Klochko 1964).[8] The main source of technical progress in Chinese industry, of course, is the import of technology from more advanced countries, in the First Five Year Plan from the USSR and in recent years from the leading capitalist countries. This technology, naturally, is associated with the capitalist division of labour. In 1977 China endorsed the Leninist view of Taylorism, and in 1980, the Chinese State Council decided to introduce piecework in all possible industrial and mining enterprises.

Low labour discipline is a permanent problem for the rulers of state socialist countries. From time to time they attempt to raise it by increased use of repression and criminal sanctions (as under Stalin) or discipline drives (as under Andropov and Gorbachev). These have some positive effects but are not permanent solutions. They deal with symptoms rather than causes.

Another common method for raising labour productivity is by the import of technology and collaboration with the multinationals.

An important reason for low labour productivity is the economic environment in which enterprises find themselves and the behaviour that this generates. In the traditional model, financial results and profits are basically not very important for enterprises. Even if officially profits are an important plan index, a loss-making enterprise can usually rely on its supervising ministry to improve its performance by subsidies, price increases, tax reductions, plan

---

[8] According to Klochko (1964 p. 80), 'The primary waste in the organisation of Chinese science was in the wasted time of the people engaged in scientific work, rather than in any failure to utilize a piece of equipment or in carelessness with books. Beautiful, well-equipped labs stood deserted for days on end; thousands of technical books in excellent libraries remained closed while potential readers were at meetings, making confessions, or tilling the soil. This poor country, which had invested immense sums of hard currency between 1955 and 1958 to construct libraries and laboratories, had failed to use these capital investments. Trained personnel were distracted from their duties, and even the equipment was allowed to deteriorate through lack of proper maintenance.'

alterations or other manoeuvres. Hence, compared to the situation of a capitalist enterprise, for whom bankruptcy is an ever present danger, socialist enterprises have a soft budget constraint. Financial results and efficiency indices are less important for them than plan fulfilment in physical terms and responsiveness to official campaigns. If they get into financial trouble it will normally be taken care of by accounting tricks of the supervisory or financial organisations. This situation is the reason why an important aspect of economic reform in the state socialist countries is attempts to harden the budget constraint. It is hoped in this way to motivate enterprises to overcome difficulties by raising efficiency rather than by appealing to superiors for subsidies and other assistance. For this reason, creating the possibility of socialist bankruptcy, and a few actual bankruptcies, in countries such as Hungary, China and the USSR in the 1980s, were intended as factors generating higher labour productivity. Making bankruptcy a normal economic phenomena, however, turned out to be very difficult in view of the paternalistic relationship between the owner of the means of production, i.e. the state, and the enterprises it owned and their employees. Enterprises in state socialist countries are not just economic units. Like large Japanese enterprises they function as mini-welfare states, providing housing, holidays, food and other benefits to their employees. Furthermore, attractive national welfare programmes are often absent (for example in the traditional model there is no right to unemployment benefit for the frictional – or other – unemployed). This makes dismissal of redundant workers exceptionally painful and is one of the factors hampering it and thus reducing labour productivity. Hence one aspect of economic reform is to nationalise welfare programmes and to reduce the social role of enterprises. It is hoped in this way to make labour mobility less costly to the individuals concerned. Hence unemployment benefits under certain conditions were introduced in Hungary, China and the USSR in the 1980s.

Full employment and the reform process

There has been much discussion of the relationship between full employment and the reform process. In Yugoslavia, the abandonment of the traditional model led to the reemergence of unemployment, which has remained a normal phenomenon and a serious social and economic problem in that country. In Vietnam, full employment was never attained, even with the traditional model. In the remaining state socialist countries, although the introduction

of unemployment has sometimes been explicitly advocated by economists and managers in order to raise labour discipline and labour
productivity, it has in fact not emerged, even in countries with many
years' experience of the reform process. The main reason for this
seems to be that the behaviour of the enterprises characteristic of the
traditional model has not been significantly changed by the first steps
of the reform process. Another reason is the continued recognition by
the authorities at all levels of the right to work. The fear of
unemployment has often been used by opponents of the reform
process and may have played some role in the cautious approach
generally taken by the authorities to economic reform. It is also an
important factor explaining the scepticism about, and hostility
towards, the reform process often displayed by the working class.
The wish to maintain full employment naturally limits the extent to
which it is possible to introduce strict financial discipline with
bankruptcy as a last resort (this is known as the 'full employment
constraint on economic reform'). The question of whether, and how,
during the reform process, it is possible to combine full employment
with the rational utilisation of labour is a central and controversial
issue for that process.

METHODS

The three chief methods of labour planning in the state socialist
countries are administrative, economic and moral.

Administrative methods

In the CMEA countries it is customary to distinguish between
'administrative' and 'economic' methods of plan implementation. By
'administrative' methods is meant instructions from the top of an
administrative hierarchy followed by obedience from below. It is the
pattern normal in all armies and civil bureaucracies. Administrative
methods are very extensively used in the state socialist countries. By
'economic' methods is meant the use of financial sticks and carrots.
This is the method normal in market economies.

During the Civil War the Bolsheviks relied heavily on administrative methods and their leaders and intellectuals developed the
ideology of reliance on administrative methods, building on the
foundations laid by Marx and Kautsky. As far as the founders of
Marxism-Leninism are concerned, it is well known that, according to
Marx and Engels, commodity production will cease under socialism

because society will organise social work directly, without the mediation of the market. It will deliberately allocate the available forces of production according to plan, in accordance with the needs of society. Does it follow from this that the system of organising production in a socialist economy demands a strict central allocation of means of production, labour and consumer goods in physical form? As Brus (1972 p. 19) has noted,

If we ignore their reluctance to scientifically describe the future socialist economy and draw conclusions from scattered incomplete statements, the answer would be 'yes'. At any rate in their work it is comparatively easy to find corroborating formulations and hard to find contradictory statements – for instance one's foreseeing the introduction of market forms. Moreover, from the point of view of ideology and its influence on practice, the ultimate important fact is what the socialist movement *understood* Marx to have said. And of this there is no doubt.

In the works of the late-nineteenth-century German Social Democrats the idea that a socialist economy is a natural, non-market, economy is clear, explicit and repeated.

In *The economics of the transition period* Bukharin explained that the transition from capitalism to socialism in the field of labour meant the liquidation of the labour market and its replacement by the allocation of labour by the state. The same thought was expressed by Trotsky in his well-known speech at the 9th Party Congress.

A well-known and much-discussed use of the administrative methods was the creation and utilisation in the USSR in 1930–57 of a network of forced labour institutions, the Gulag Archipelago. This partial reintroduction of serfdom was largely a result of the decision to adopt the coercive model of the role of agriculture in economic development (see chapter 4). Many of the first inhabitants of the camps were farmers deported from their villages at the time of collectivisation. From the point of view of numbers employed, agriculture in the USSR in the 1930s was by far the most important branch of the economy. Reliance on coercion in various construction and mining enterprises was simply a small generalisation, from a quantitative point of view, of the principle, reliance on coercion, on which the main branch of the economy was organised.

Herding labour into camps had the advantage of saving on costs per worker and reducing demand for scarce food, but against this must be set the costs of the guards, officials, punitive apparatus etc., as well as the low productivity of the labour. The use of forced labour camps was copied in China. In May 1951, during the repression of that period, Mao (1977b p. 55) pointed out that large numbers of prisoners under suspended death sentences formed a useful labour force 'which will be conducive to our national construction'. A widespread system of camps for 'reform through labour' and 'education through labour' was established in China, but information about its quantitative significance, evolution over time and economic efficiency, is very sparse. According to a former inmate of reform through labour camps, the Chinese camps are more efficient than the Soviet ones (Pasqualini 1975 p. 12). This may be so, but Pasqualini had no personal knowledge of Soviet camps on which to base the comparison, and in fact there seems to be no firm evidence on this issue.

A necessary condition for the use of coerced labour in the USSR and China was the absence of independent worker organisations.

Another example of the use of administrative methods in the USSR is the allocation of new graduates by the state for the first three years of their working lives. A further example of the use of administrative methods concerns the temporary residents of closed cities. According to Granick (1975 p. 68) 'it seems reasonable to estimate that something over 10% of Romania's total labour force in industry, mining and construction is subject to *de facto* job direction which is imposed upon temporary residents of closed cities'. In Bulgaria in the early 1970s there was a revived stress on administrative methods. A decree of 1972 and a supplementary decree of 1973 reintroduced virtual tying of workers to their place of work. It was forbidden to employ workers who had left their previous job voluntarily or who had been dismissed for disciplinary reasons. This revived emphasis on administrative methods was part of the reaction against economic reform in the CMEA countries in the early 1970s.

When the Chinese planned economy was established during the First Five Year Plan (1953–7) one of the things copied from the USSR was the use of economic methods to allocate the labour force. One of the features of the Maoist strategy of development adopted in China from 1958 onwards was the increased use of administrative methods of labour allocation. The three key institutions which replaced the labour market were the employment system, i.e. the system for allocating employees, the personnel system, i.e. the procedures governing personnel matters, and the household registration system, i.e. the regulations governing residence and ration entitlements. Under the employment system, a worker's first job was obtained neither by application to an enterprise nor as a result of choice by an enterprise. The worker was allocated to his/her first job via the assignment office of the school he/she left, or, less frequently, the assignment office of the area where he/she lived. A worker's first job normally became a lifelong career. According to the personnel system, an employee had no right to apply for another job without the permission of the enterprise where the employee was already working. Such permission was normally denied. Resignation without the approval of one's current employer was considered to be unacceptable. The personnel system was similar to that in the USSR in 1940–56 or in the large-firm sector of contemporary Japan. The household registration system, which was closely linked with the rationing system and corresponded to some extent to the registration and passport system in the USSR, hindered physical movement from place to place.

In the 1980s there was much discussion in China of the need, within the state sector, to expand the role of market relations with respect to the allocation of labour and reduce that of administrative methods. Concretely, this meant granting enterprises themselves a greater role in the hiring decision and giving them the right under certain conditions of firing unsatisfactory workers, and making greater use of fixed term employment contracts (which in principle come to an end after a fixed period) rather than indefinite contracts. In 1986 new national labour regulations were adopted allowing for enterprise choice in employment decisions, fixed-term contracts and unemployment benefits. Traditional patterns, however, remained deep-rooted, and within the state sector administrative methods remained of great importance.

It was intended that, after the adoption of these regulations, all new workers (but not cadres, managerial specialists or graduates) would be employed initially on fixed term contracts and the old style permanent employment arrangements would apply only to those workers already employed, workers who had successfully completed a fixed-term contract, or cadres etc. It is noticeable, however, that although the 1986 regulations were supposed to be part of an enlargement of market relations, they contained no explicit provision enabling a worker with a fixed term contract to resign for personal reasons (e.g. to take a better job elsewhere or because of dissatisfaction with his/her work situation). In this respect the pre-1986 situation according to which workers were in general not free to resign, seems to have remained basically unchanged. Naturally, much will depend on how the new regulations are interpreted.

One change in China that really was implemented and did have a big impact, was the dramatic relaxation of the rationing system after 1980. This, together with the expansion of the non-state sector, greatly facilitated the big increase in population mobility which took place in the 1980s.

An important administrative method for implementing the labour plan in all the state socialist countries is keeping files on workers so as to determine their fitness for particular jobs and material rewards. In the USSR, since 1938 each worker has had a labour book, an official document recording his name, age, education, trade, information about his work, transfers from one enterprise to another (with reasons) and details of encouragements and rewards. Enterprises are supposed to engage workers and employees (other than those entering employment for the first time) only on presentation of their labour books, which the enterprise then keeps till the worker is discharged. In addition, the party committees responsible for filling all important posts keep files on actual and possible holders of such posts, and the state security organs also keep personnel files which play an important role in appointments and dismissals. In the USSR there is a large apparatus of informers and spies collecting information about other people's views and behaviour for these files. The accumulation of information in the hands of the authorities naturally plays a major role in determining behaviour in a one-employer state.

In China, too, the records kept by the authorities play an important role. A major factor governing a cadre's career is his personal file. This is kept within his work unit and records all the important facts about his life including such things as his family and class origins, his technical qualifications, the quality of his work and his attitudes towards various political issues. When a cadre is considered for promotion, this file forms the basis for judgement. Naturally, everyone works hard to avoid getting a black mark on his record. During the Cultural Revolution these files became the centre of considerable debate. Political opponents used them to attack each other and the Red Guards were able to get a lot of confidential information from them about cadres. Several of the most intense local struggles concerned whether a cadre had been correctly labelled during the course of the movement or whether an earlier judgement should be reversed.

Economic methods

The use of economic methods, i.e. of pay, is very common in the state socialist countries. Material incentives play a very big role, for example, in Soviet (and Chinese) regional policy, where pay is much higher and where the number of years work required for a pension are much lower in inhospitable regions than in the main cities. Similarly, in the USSR and China, the relative pay of workers in the non-productive sector (e.g. distribution, education and medical care) has traditionally been low, so as to direct labour towards the productive sector.

Administrative and economic methods are often used in combination. A very important example is the system of national job evaluation in the state socialist countries. This is considered further in chapter 7 below. Similarly, in the CMEA countries, the quantitative planning of the demand for labour and of the output of various kinds of graduates, is normally combined with the planning of relative pay levels so as to attract the appropriate volume and quality of labour.

The ways in which the planners manipulate relative pay, and its effects, have been investigated by Hamermesh and Portes (1972). They examined Hungarian data for 1951–67. They found that the planners did raise the relative pay of workers in industries with the fastest rates of growth of output in order to attract labour to them. They also found that this policy was apparently ineffective, since the supply of labour did not appear very responsive to relative earnings. The main influences on the supply of labour appeared to be the outflow from agriculture and the availability of jobs. The conclusion reached by Hamermesh and Portes is that 'the planners were mistaken. They erred in believing that changes in wages of the magnitude they used would affect labour supply.' It is ironical that the mistake of the planners was to take seriously a traditional idea of neoclassical economics, the importance of relative pay in allocating labour.

The use of economic methods is naturally more important in countries where labour is permitted freely to change jobs, e.g. the USSR since 1956 and the smaller East European countries, than in countries with direction of labour, e.g. China in the Maoist period.

Moral methods

The use of moral incentives is very widespread in all state socialist countries. In all of them great efforts are devoted during the educational process to internalise the value of hard work for the good of society. The noticeboard with pictures of honoured workers who have worked particularly well, the brigades of communist labour who have pledged themselves to feats of socialist competition, the public meetings at which good workers sit on the platform, the distribution

of honours such as 'hero of socialist labour', are familiar features of
state socialist life.

So far as non-material incentives are concerned, many of the forms evolved in
the Soviet Union have also been used in China; and yet certain techniques
have been pushed to greater lengths by the CCP. For example, the
mechanism of 'criticism and self-criticism' has been generally employed to a
much greater extent than in the USSR. Generally it seems that the Chinese
have relied more on non-material incentives and persuasion than the
Russians. This reliance on non-material spurs was undoubtedly a factor of
great moment in the miscarriage of the Great Leap Forward
                                                    (Hoffman 1967 p. 119)

A problem with moral methods is that in fact they are often
administrative methods with a veneer of non-compulsion. For
example in the USSR today, the Communist Saturday, when
workers work on some Saturdays, supposedly voluntarily, to help in
the construction of communism, is actually simply a day's compulsory unpaid work.

How does worker morale and motivation in the state socialist
countries compare with that in capitalist countries? To answer this
question properly would require an international research programme involving fieldwork in many countries. Such research is
not possible in the USSR, China or most of the other state socialist
countries. Nevertheless, there is some knowledge in this area,
largely arising from the increase in East-West industrial cooperation agreements in the 1970s. A study of the experience of US firms
with industrial cooperation agreements with Poland and Romania
(Hayden 1976), reported that in these two countries (ibid. p. 108)
'worker morale and initiative [are] close to non-existent'. The
account of how the US capitalist corporation Clark Equipment
Company, as part of its technology transfer agreement with the
Polish concern Bumar Union for the manufacture of heavy-duty
planetary reduction axles, had to instill pride of achievement into
the indifferent Polish workers by appealing to their patriotism
(ibid. p. 49) is deeply ironical. If these accounts are typical, they
would seem to indicate that, at any rate in Poland and Romania,
worker motivation and morale and pride in work under state
socialism compare unfavourably with that normal under
capitalism.

It seems that, in general, workers in the state socialist countries
continue to regard themselves as wage workers rather than as
co-owners of the means of production. Hence there continue to exist
such phenomena as worker attempts to limit the work content of a

day's labour power,[9] e.g. conflict over piecework norms. These phenomena are startling and unexpected from a Marxist-Leninist point of view. What explains them? There appear to be four chief factors.

First, the adverse effect of state socialism on personal consumption (see chapter 8 below). As the Chinese economist Xue Muqiao (1981 p. 52) has observed, 'If the leaders of the state and enterprises do not concern themselves with the livelihood of the workers and fail to improve it steadily as production grows, the workers will not concern themselves with the interests of the enterprises and the state, but treat them with the mentality of wage labourers.'

Secondly, the lack of control by workers over their working lives. This does not arise from the malevolence of this or that official, but has a definite theoretical explanation. Experience has shown that state (or cooperative) ownership, by itself, is not sufficient to transform the relations of production. As the Soviet sociologist Arutiunian (1973 pp. 109–10) has noted with special reference to Soviet collective farms, though the argument is perfectly general,

it is necessary to face the essence of the phenomenon of *collectivisation of property*. It is not a once and for all affair. Rather, it *is a long process*. From the legal or, more precisely, the political act of collectivisation to actual collectivisation there is a whole period, perhaps even epoch, of historical development that only begins with the immediate act of collectivisation. The revolution in our country eliminated the order under which property was separated from work and created the conditions for their unification. But such a unification is possible only through a long evolution and a series of intermediate socio-economic forms. The criterion for the unification of the means of production and labour power, materialised and living labour, is the degree of the realisation by the producer himself of the functions of management or, in other words, of the disposition of collectivised property ... Empirical studies, however, show that in practice this mechanism [i.e. the formal constitution of a collective farm] by itself does not ensure sufficiently effective participation of each person in the disposition of property.

This important thesis and the general conclusion to be drawn from it, are considered further in chapter 10. Here it is necessary to note that acceptance of this thesis undermines any expectation of a higher work morale under state socialism than under capitalism. Furthermore, given that new relations of production have not been fully established, the old means of defending worker interests retain much of their usefulness. Workers under state socialism, however, lack the independent worker organisations normal under capitalism, and

[9] This is what Taylor called 'soldiering' and what is known in UK management terminology as 'restrictive practices'.

from this point of view their position is worse than under capitalism. As A. Hegedus, a former Hungarian Prime Minister, has noted (Hegedus 1976a p. 88), during the Stalin period:

The principal function of the trade unions became to bring about the realisation of state plans. Work competition, managed from above and largely manipulated, became their principal contribution to the fulfilment of production plans; their management of this competition, together with the support they gave to the fixing of norms, alienated the working masses from the trade unions and, it may be said, robbed the latter completely of their character as a movement.

This situation has largely persisted down to the present time.[10]

Thirdly, the huge and all-pervading gulf between the words and slogans of the authorities and economic, social and political reality. An example was given above, the Communist Saturday. A compulsory day's unpaid work is treated in the media as if the whole labour force is selflessly working for the common good.

Fourthly, the difficulty of making individual gains by individual effort in the white sector (i.e. the legal state sector). The state socialist countries have full employment and job security, a relatively egalitarian income distribution, wage differentials that do not depend very much on the economic performance of enterprises, and an economic system in which it is not legitimate work but other factors (access to closed distribution, black earnings or political decisions) which are decisive for generating real income differences. In the CMEA countries, as in the capitalist world, prolonged overfulfilment of piecework norms is likely to lead, not to prolonged high earnings, but to an upward revision of the norms. Hence it is not surprising that individual effort in the white sector is conspicuous by its absence. Many observers have suggested that individual effort is typically greater in Yugoslav factories than in the CMEA factories. Granick (1975 pp. 426–77) has suggested that the reason for this is the strong relationship between the success of individual enterprises and the incomes of their workforces, under the Yugoslav system of self-management.

It would seem that the Marxist project of overcoming alienation, of overcoming a situation in which the worker is not interested in his/her work (which forms only a small part of the whole production process and over which he/she has no control) and its outcome (the use values that are created) but only in the wage that he/she receives,

[10] An independent trade union movement did emerge in Poland in 1980–1 but it was crushed by the riot police and the army.

	Previous period			Planning period		
	Total of which			Total of which		
		urban	rural		urban	rural
1. Labour resources (including natural increase)						
of which:						
population of working age (excluding invalids)						
workers of pension age or 15 or less.						
2. Distribution of labour resources						
(a) By type of occupation:						
(1) occupied in the social economy						
(2) full-time students of 16 and above						
(3) household and private gardening						
(b) By branch of the national economy:						
(1) working in the material production sector (by industry)						
(2) working in the non-productive sectors (by sector)						
(c) By social group (workers and employees, collective farmers, cooperative craftsmen, artisans, families of workers, employees and collective farmers occupied in housework and private gardening)						

Figure 6.1 A planning labour balance

has made no progress under state socialism. As under capitalism, Taylorism dominates the labour process. On the other hand, there are a number of respects in which the situation is worse than under capitalism. There are no independent trade unions, the link between the wage and the use values created is even more tenuous than under capitalism because of the dictatorship over needs, and workers are partly alienated from their wages because of the difficulty of buying with them the things they want (due to shortages and the non-market nature of the economy).

INSTRUMENTS

The basic method of planning the rational utilisation of labour is the balance
method.   Litvyakov (1969 p. 166)

The main instrument of labour planning used in the socialist
countries is the labour balance. A labour balance is simply a material
balance which deals with labour. In the USSR a whole series of
labour balances are regularly drawn up, both statistical (concerned
with the past) and planning (concerned with various future periods),
for the country as a whole and for its subdivisions (e.g. republics and
smaller regions). A planning labour balance can be set out schematically as in figure 6.1.

The chief task of the labour balance is to coordinate available
labour resources with the requirements for labour. The available
labour resources are calculated from statistical and demographic
data, account being taken of any special factors (e.g. the increased
provision of nursery facilities for children). The required distribution
of labour resources is calculated from statistical data and the planned
levels of output and labour productivity. Shortages of labour, in
general or in specific categories, give rise to policies (e.g. increase in
training, import of foreign machinery, acceleration of mechanisation)
designed to overcome them. The labour balance is only a part of the
balance of the national economy, and its various sections should be
harmonised with the other parts of that balance. For example, the
plan for technical progress affects labour productivity and labour
requirements in various industries.

Some economists, in particular Keynesians, may be surprised at
the emphasis placed in socialist manpower planning on supply side
factors. The reason for this is that in the state socialist countries an
adequate demand for labour can generally be assumed, and the
principal task of manpower planners is to satisfy this demand with
respect to quantity, quality and location. It is the supply side, rather
than the demand side, that chiefly constrains the growth of the state
socialist countries.

Labour coefficients

A relatively new instrument of labour planning in the state socialist
countries is the labour coefficient. It is now possible to calculate the
direct and indirect labour embodied in each unit of particular
outputs. This is particularly interesting for Marxists because it gives

empirical content to the Marxist concept of the socially necessary labour embodied in a commodity, or the value of that commodity.

An analytical expression for the calculation of full labour inputs was first given by Dmitriev (1898). The first calculation of the analogous concept of full commodity inputs was by Leontief. Leontief's empirical and conceptual work is now regularly employed in the state socialist countries for the compilation of input-output tables in labour units and the calculation of direct and full labour input coefficients.

The first such table was compiled by the Soviet Central Statistical Administration for 1959 and published in 1962. It showed, in terms of labour, the interindustrial flows, the formation of the final bill of goods, the formation of national product and the costs incurred in the non-productive sphere. This calculation corresponds to the Dmitriev-Leontief full labour coefficients. It showed, for example, that out of 97 million man years expended in the national economy in 1959, about 50 million were ultimately devoted to the production of consumer goods, 30 million to capital formation, exports and other items, and 17 million to the non-productive sphere. Subsequently the Soviet Central Statistical Administration compiled a similar table for 1966. Although input-output tables in labour terms are regularly compiled in the USSR, and full labour coefficients have been much discussed and also calculated, it would appear that they have not become an important instrument of labour planning, being confined to various kinds of analytical calculations.

CONCLUSION

Labour planning in the state socialist countries is concerned with facilitating the fulfilment and overfulfilment of the national economic plan by ensuring that the requisite types of labour are available in the right quantities and places and perform the necessary work. This involves developing the abilities of the labour force so as to produce the right types of labour, providing full employment so as to avoid waste of resources, ensuring a rational regional distribution of employment and ensuring the efficient utilisation of labour. The main methods used, separately and in combination, are administrative, economic and moral. The main instrument is the labour balance.

In general, the position of workers in state socialism with respect to opportunities for improving qualifications, work intensity, social security, hours of work, security of employment and availability of employment, compares favourably with that in comparable capitalist countries. In some cases, the position of workers does not compare favourably with that in comparable capitalist countries. Notable examples are the Gulag Archipelago and 'reform through labour' and 'education through labour' camps, sent down people, Soviet collective farmers for much of their history and those in political disfavour. The effect of state socialism on industrial safety is impossible to assess fully in the absence of data. For the USSR, the absence of data suggests a poor record. State ownership of the means of production and national economic planning are not sufficient to eliminate unemployment. Urban full employment has been established and maintained in the chief state socialist countries partly by administrative methods, the passport system in the USSR and the household registration system and sending down in China.

No progress has been made under state socialism towards a new, more human, organisation of the labour process. The state socialist countries copy the capitalist organisation of labour without the countervailing power exercised by worker organisations in the West. The fragmentary evidence available about labour morale suggests that, at any rate in Poland and Romania, it compares unfavourably with that normal under capitalism. The absence of independent worker organisations has adverse effects, not only on labour morale, but also on industrial safety and the use of coerced labour.

SUGGESTIONS FOR FURTHER READING

GENERAL

J. Mouly, 'Employment: a concept in need of renovation', *International Labour Review* vol. 116, no. 1 (July–August 1977).
J. Kornai, *Economics of shortage* vol. A (Amsterdam 1980) chapter 11.
H. Scott, *Does socialism liberate women?* (Boston 1974).
R. Selucky, *Marxism, socialism, freedom* (London 1979) chapter 2.
J. Timar, 'Problems of full employment', *Acta Oeconomica* vol. 31 (1983).
H. A. Zimon, 'Regional inequalities in Poland: 1960–1975', *Economic Geography* vol. 55 (1979).

USSR

M. McAuley, *Settling labour disputes in Soviet Russia* (Oxford 1969).
P. Wiles, 'Soviet unemployment on US definitions', *Soviet Studies* vol. 23 (April 1972).
Planning of manpower in the Soviet Union (Moscow 1975).
K. E. Bailes, 'Alexei Gastev and the Soviet controversy over Taylorism', *Soviet Studies* (July 1977).
A. McAuley, *Women's work and wages in the Soviet Union* (London 1981).
D. Lane (ed.) *Labour and employment in the USSR* (Brighton 1986).

CHINA

C. Howe, *Employment and economic growth in urban China, 1949–1957* (Cambridge 1971).
C. Howe, 'Labour organisation and incentives in industry, before and after the Cultural Revolution', S. Schram (ed.) *Authority, participation and cultural change in China* (Cambridge 1973).
C. Hoffman, *The Chinese worker* (Albany 1974).
D. Davin, *Women-work: Women and the party in revolutionary China* (Oxford 1976).
A. G. Walder, *Communist neo-traditionalism – work and authority in Chinese industry* (Berkeley 1986).
A. G. Walder, 'Wage reform and the web of factory interests', *China Quarterly* 109 (March 1987).
M. Korzec, 'New labour laws in the People's Republic of China', *Comparative Economic Studies* vol. XXX, no. 2 (Summer 1988).

CUBA

C. Mesa-Lago, *The labour sector and socialist distribution in Cuba* (New York 1968).
A. C. Jiménez, 'Worker incentives in Cuba', *World Development* (January 1987).

POLAND

'Agreement between the Government commission and the Inter-Factory Strike Committee concluded on 31 August at the Gdansk Shipyard' ('The Gdansk Agreement'), numerous translations, e.g. K. Ruane, *The Polish challenge* (London 1982) Appendix A.
'The Programme of Solidarity', numerous translations, e.g. *Labour Focus on Eastern Europe* vol. 5, nos. 1–2.
B. Simatupang, 'Economic crisis and full employment: The Polish case', *Journal of Communist Studies* (September 1988).

HUNGARY

J. Timar, *Planning the labour force in Hungary* (New York 1966).
P. Galasi & G. Sziraczki (eds.) *Labour market and second economy in Hungary* (New York 1985).

7

PLANNING INCOMES

Distribution is a method, an instrument, a means, for increasing production.

Lenin (1921)

The actual distribution of income in any country at any time depends on the balance of class forces, the institutional arrangements and indeed the whole history of the country. It is not likely to reflect any uniform principle. Before approaching actual data, however, it is useful to consider alternative principles of income distribution so as to illuminate the actual data and policy debates of various countries. Two well-known, and conflicting, principles of income distribution are those of need, and of desert. The first principle is that income should be distributed in accordance with need, so that, for example, the highest incomes should go to cripples and those with many dependants and the lowest to healthy people with no dependants. The second principle is that income should be distributed in accordance with the contribution that has been made to society so that, for example, the highest incomes go to inventors, prospectors, engineers, coal miners and farmers, and the lowest to the blind, children and the idle.

The Marxist view of distribution under socialism is that the ultimate aim of the socialist movement is to create a society in which distribution is on the basis of need, but that in the years immediately after the revolution it will be still necessary to base distribution on work performed, i.e. on desert.

This thesis has remained orthodox in all the socialist countries but has been interpreted in very different ways at different times and in different countries. In the USSR it was used in the 1930s to justify an attack on egalitarianism and a widening of differentials. From the mid 1950s it was used to support a new approach to wages and wage differentials. In this latter period the socialist distribution principle was interpreted as requiring equal pay for equal work and this was used to justify greater equalisation of incomes, the rationalisation of wage scales within industries and plants, the use of comparison and job evaluation to a much greater extent than in the capitalist world, and a reduction in urban-rural differentials. The intention to rationalise wage scales was often not realised, however, due to labour shortages. Under Gorbachev, renewed attention was given to the need to increase differentials and relate pay closer to productivity. The communist principle of distribution according to need is supposed to be realised by the transfer payments and free public services. In China, where the bulk of the population is engaged in agriculture, Marxist-Leninist ideas on income distribution have been used both to justify the Maoist policy of organising agricultural production on a collective basis and also the subsequent policy of organising it on a household basis.

The emphasis placed on distribution according to need was an important feature of Chinese agriculture in the Maoist period. For approximately the first three and a half decades of their existence, the incomes of Soviet collective farmers derived from their private plots and the number of labour days they worked for the collective farms. Both of these are examples of distribution according to desert (subject to tribute exacted by the state and differences in natural conditions). In China, when communes were first organised (1958), distribution within them was on the basis of need. Communal mess halls were organised and communal meals provided for all, free of charge, regardless of work done. This system of free supply was much praised in the Chinese media in 1958 as an example of communist distribution. It appears, however, to have had an adverse effect on work incentives and hence to have been one of the factors contributing to the crisis of 1959–61. 'Why should we work hard if we will eat anyway?' seems to have been a widespread thought. Hence completely free supply was soon abandoned.

Partial distribution on the basis of need, however, was revived during and after the Cultural Revolution. In the early 1970s it typically worked as follows. The basic accounting unit was the team. (A team was a group of households, on average about 30–5, which was the basic collective unit of production and distribution in rural China. It was a sub-unit of a brigade, which itself was a sub-unit of a commune. It was intended to combine incentives to produce – the members were neighbours and often relatives as well – with the advantages of collectivist agriculture.) Out of its gross output the first claimant was the state, which received a tax in kind, often about 6 percent of gross output. The second claimant was the reserve fund. Into this say 20 percent of gross output would be paid to cover grain reserves, seed and other working capital, investment and welfare (e.g. sickness and old age benefits and burial expenses). The balance was split into approximately equal portions (the ratio between the two portions differing in different areas) and distributed (in kind and cash) in two different ways. The first was equally distributed among the members of the team as that member's grain ration. The second was divided among the members of the team in accordance with the number of work points earned. Team members also had the income from their private plots and also remittances from relatives (e.g. sons working in industry) where applicable.

This system had two important things in common with the Soviet one from collectivisation up to 1966 (when something akin to a wage system was introduced into Soviet collective farms). First, peasant incomes were a residual item of the farm accounts and not a prior charge like the wages of workers in state industry. The income of the farmers varied directly with their output. In this respect their position was like that of primary producers in the capitalist world. Unlike the latter, however, they did not suffer from violently fluctuating prices. Secondly, payment for work done took the form of labour days or work points which depended on work performed and the value of which was not known until long after the event. It had one special feature, however, a greater stress on distribution according to need (i.e. the grain ration and the welfare benefits). The Maoist system required two special inputs, numerous rural cadres and extensive political education campaigns aimed at replacing the old family-centred psychology by a new collectively oriented one. As pointed out in chapter 4 its effect on output and income levels was unfavourable. This system of partial distribution on a basis of need had an adverse effect on work incentives and hence on output and average incomes. The need to increase labour incentives, raise output and reduce poverty were important reasons for the decollectivisation of Chinese agriculture in 1979–83.

SOCIALIST INCOMES POLICY

Marxists consider that the decentralised system of income determination that exists under capitalism is just another aspect of the anarchy of production that must be replaced under socialism by a planned and centralised system. The state socialist countries normally operate what in Western terminology would be called permanent incomes policies. Important aspects of these policies are, price control, the planning of foreign trade, the elimination of large property incomes, compulsory arbitration, national job evaluation, uniform regional net advantages, the production mindedness of trade unions, full employment, a proletarian government and a non-permissive approach to breaches of labour discipline.

Price control is a basic part of incomes planning in state socialist countries. By keeping prices under control a major source of pressure for wage increases is removed. In some periods, the state socialist countries have been quite successful in controlling prices. For example, between the mid 1950s and the mid 1970s the European CMEA countries, and in 1963–75 China, managed to maintain more or less stable prices. In other periods, rapid inflations have been experienced. The difficulties which spiralling prices cause for incomes policy are clearly shown by Soviet experience in 1928–40. In that period the USSR experienced a massive inflation, with state retail prices rising tenfold (Holzman 1960). A major reason for this was the huge rise in food prices which forced up wages. Similarly, the huge Polish inflation of the early 1980s made it impossible to implement a successful incomes policy.

The planning of foreign trade has the advantage of insulating the economy somewhat from shocks originating on the world market. Both sudden sharp price fluctuations and sudden falls in effective demand can be avoided by planning foreign trade on a medium-term basis. This enables the planners to avoid either sudden money wage increases (in response to an increase in prices) or sudden real wage cuts (in response to a sudden deterioration in the terms of trade). This naturally facilitates the planned development of incomes.

Marxists have always laid great stress on the absence of the distinction between property owners and proletarians as a necessary condition of a harmonious society. Inequalities of wealth (e.g. housing, money, consumer durables) are substantial under state socialism. They result from income inequalities, inheritance, abuse of official positions, the non-state sector, political stability and economic growth. Nevertheless, an important difference between the state socialist and capitalist worlds is the absence in the former of the small minority of individuals with huge holdings of the means of production that plays such an important role in the latter. In the USSR, for example, there is some property income, e.g. interest on savings bank deposits and some rent, and widespread corruption, but conspicuous consumption is limited, and the luxuries enjoyed by top officials, although substantial, do not compare favourably with those of Western millionaires and are less visible. The dysfunctional effect of conspicuous consumption, often deriving from property income, in securing worker agreement to incomes policy, is well known. 'Why should we make sacrifices when at Ascot people are living off champagne and caviare?' is a familiar remark.

In any system labour disputes are bound to occur. In the West these are resolved by collective bargaining, with the strike and unemployment being the chief weapons in the hands of the parties. The Soviet system of compulsory arbitration (McAuley, M. 1969) provides a method of settling factory level disputes without interrupting production or wasting resources.

Experience with incomes policy in various countries shows that the conscious determination of relative incomes is very difficult. The Soviet system for dealing with this is that of national job evaluation (Handy 1971). This is a system whereby, in principle, all jobs and all workers are graded, the jobs by function and the workers by skill. The wages actually received by any worker, above the minimum wage, depend on his occupation and grade, the grade of the job, the work norms, the level of output (if on piecework) or the length of time worked (if on a time system), and the receipt of bonuses and regional coefficients (if any). The underlying idea is to replace the determination of relative incomes by market forces, by their determination in a rational, objective fashion, and to stimulate the raising of the qualification of the labour force, production and productivity. Nevertheless, the 'scientific', 'objective' nature of the resulting income distribution is something of a myth, and national job evaluation has not succeeded in establishing a satisfactory relationship between the wages of similar workers in the same plant and in different plants and industries. This seems to result from market pressures, the drive by the authorities to raise labour productivity, the existence of priority sectors and the labour shortages generated by the traditional model. National job evaluation arose, in large part, as a reaction against the fragmented ministerial wage system that existed in the USSR during the Stalin period.

As far as income relativities are concerned, Adam Smith and his successors stress the allocative function of wages and the need for differentials so as to equalise the net advantages of all occupations. Keynes and his successors stress the availability of jobs and the segmented nature of the labour market and argue that differentials are largely historic and arbitrary. The experience of the state socialist countries suggests that the Keynesian doctrine is largely correct as far as relative occupational earnings are concerned, and the classical doctrine is largely correct as far as relative geographical earnings are concerned. Manpower planning, both current and in the field of education, can control the number of people qualified in particular specialisms. This can ensure that there are sufficient people with the requisite qualifications for any category of employment. Although changes in relative earnings may affect the relative attraction of careers as perceived by schoolchildren and their parents, the gestation period is very long. Hence relative earnings can be changed significantly without in the short run much affecting quantitative labour availability. (It may well affect, however, the quality of work performed in the relatively poorly paid occupations. In labour intensive services such as education and medicine this can have serious adverse effects.) On the regional plane, however, things are very different. In the USSR, the higher earnings to be obtained in the towns would have caused such a mass movement from the villages if free movement of labour had existed, that administrative measures had to be used for decades to prevent this. Similarly, in China the use of administrative methods to prevent an excessive influx of labour to the towns is a permanent feature of the economy. Furthermore, administrative measures have to be used in all the state socialist countries to control emigration. In the USSR the desirability of certain cities (e.g. Moscow) is not offset by lower earnings so that administrative measures have to be used to control access to them. Similarly, in the USSR the inhospitability of many regions (such as the Far North and Far East) has required very substantial regional coefficients for them to recruit and hold labour. In addition, an unplanned migration of labour has taken place to certain areas (such as the North Caucasus, Transcaucasia and Central Asia) where uniform national wage scales failed to reflect the advantages of abundant sunshine, fruit and vegetables. The need to equalise regional net advantages is naturally more important in a continental country, such as the USA, Canada, the USSR or India, than in a small country.

West European trade unions, like the Social Democratic movement in general, are primarily concerned with distribution. They seek to raise labour's share in the output of capitalism, to protect workers from changes in work organisation that would have an adverse effect on them, and to increase state expenditure on free or subsidised public services (e.g. education, medical care, housing). Trade unions in state socialist countries also seek to advance the interests of their members both during plan compilation and plan implementation. For example, in 1970 in the GDR a discussion was going on about changes in relative earnings in different sectors of the economy. The trade unions accepted that there should be larger wage increases in high priority than in low priority industries, but they objected to stagnation of earnings for any group and insisted on the principle that no group should ever suffer a reduction in earnings. At one point, the draft plan of one ministry called for a stagnation of earnings for some worker groups and an actual reduction for a few. Its trade union thereupon engaged in a struggle to have these tentative decisions reversed (Granick 1975 p. 168). Similarly, during plan implementation, the trade unions seek to protect their members in factory or shop level disputes and represent their interests. That they do actually play a positive role in protecting their members is shown for example, rather ironically, by the fact that in China when they were dissolved during the Cultural Revolution the reason given was that they supported and protected their members, the permanent workers, who were a privileged elite compared to the temporary workers and peasants. Nevertheless, they are primarily organs of the state concerned with increasing production. (The need for resistance to changes in work organisation is of course much less for workers in the state socialist countries than in most capitalist countries because of the much greater degree of job security which the former enjoy.) Their main function is to stimulate the increases in productivity that, given the distribution of the national income, are the only source of increasing real wages. The transition of Soviet trade unions from trade unionism to production mindedness was part of a revolution from above which took place in the USSR in 1928–34.

Full employment is an important aspect of incomes policy in all state socialist countries. Full employment (which can always be ensured by a government prepared to reduce sufficiently the current real income of those who would anyway be employed) is a traditional objective of the labour movement and its attainment removes a major obstacle to labour cooperation in the reorganisation of production.

The proletarian character of the governments of the state socialist countries is an important aspect of their incomes policy. This proletarian character is self proclaimed, reflected in some real policies (e.g. full employment and security of employment) and also in the personal backgrounds of many of the top leaders. In the UK, the non-proletarian character of the Conservative Party is the main reason why, for that party, incomes policy is not a feasible policy (as Heath discovered and Thatcher accepted).

The ultimate sanction in any society is repression. In the UK, at

the present time, the control of shoplifting, the Irish Republican
Army, the heroin trade and other types of activity deemed anti-social
is in the hands of the police and the army. Similarly, in the state
socialist countries strikes are in general dealt with by the arrest of
'ringleaders' and 'agitators', as Polish experience in 1976 and 1981
once more indicated.

Of the conditions listed above, which are necessary and which are
sufficient for the maintenance of a permanent incomes policy? This is
difficult to judge. Experience up till now suggests the conjecture that
all the conditions taken together are sufficient, and that four of them,
price control, full employment, a proletarian government and a
non-permissive approach to breaches of labour discipline, are
necessary.

INTER-SYSTEM COMPARISONS

International comparisons of the distribution of income are very
difficult both because of the poor quality of the data and because of
the existence of numerous different measures of income distribution
which can be used for comparative purposes. Nevertheless, there has
been some work in this area, notably by Pryor, Vortmann, Wiles and
Morrison.

Pryor (1973 chapter 3) found that, comparing Western countries
with East European countries, three variables played a statistically
significant role in explaining the pre-tax distribution of non-agricultural labour incomes. They were, level of development, size of
population, and economic system. The degree of inequality declined
as the level of development rose, increased as the population rose,
and was less for Eastern than for Western countries. The effect of
property incomes was to increase the advantage (from an egalitarian
point of view) of the East European countries.

Similarly, a comparison of the GDR and the FRG (Vortmann 1979
pp. 209–210) showed that throughout the period 1960–74 the distribution of the net incomes of employee households was more equal in
the GDR than in the FRG. (It also showed that the average income
per household in the FRG was significantly above that of the GDR
and that this difference rose significantly in 1960–75, and that the
income of pensioner households relative to that of employee households was significantly lower in the GDR than in the FRG.)

Wiles considered the effects of taxation and used a different
measure of income distribution. His findings are summarised in
table 7.1.

Table 7.1 *Ratios of income per head in selected countries (ratio of top 5 percent to bottom 5 percent)*

	Before tax	After tax
UK (1953–4)	5.7	5.0
UK (1969)	5.9	5.0
USA (1968)	13.3	12.7
Italy (1969)	11.2	–
Hungary (1967)	4.2	4.0
Czechoslovakia (1965)	4.5	4.3
Bulgaria (1963–5)	3.8	–
USSR (1966)	6.0	5.7
Sweden	–	3.0
Denmark	–	6.0
Canada	–	12.0

Source: Wiles (1974a) pp. 48 and xiv.

From the data in the table the following points emerge. First, the three most unequal countries (USA, Canada, Italy) are all capitalist. Secondly, the most equal country (Sweden) is also capitalist. Thirdly, two capitalist countries (Sweden and the UK) are more equal than the USSR. Fourthly, the state socialist countries are more equal than one would expect on the basis of the international relationship between level of development and size of population, and inequality. Accordingly, two conclusions may be drawn from the Wiles data. First, state socialism is neither a necessary nor a sufficient condition for a more equal distribution of income than any capitalist country. It is not necessary, because Sweden does without it. It is not sufficient, because even with it the USSR is more unequal than Sweden or the UK. Secondly, in making international comparisons, state socialism is one of the factors associated with greater income equality. This corroborates Pryor's findings. It is important to note that these conclusions depend on the period studied, the countries selected, the quality of the data, and the measure of income distribution used.

The data on Soviet income distribution were reexamined by McAuley (1977). He reached three interesting and important conclusions. First, that Wiles had overestimated inequality in the USSR. In fact, according to McAuley, income inequality in the USSR in the late 1960s was about the same as that calculated by Wiles for Hungary and Czechoslovakia. Secondly, in the late 1960s more than

Table 7.2 *Elite occupational groups in the USSR in 1970*[a]

	Thousands	%
Party officials	95	38
State, Komsomol and trade union officials	60	24
The intelligentsia[b]	43	17
Enterprise managers	22	9
The military, police, diplomatic service	30	12
Total	250	100

[a] Persons earning 450 roubles a month or more and having access to substantial non-cash benefits. (Average wages in the USSR in 1970 were 122 roubles per month.)
[b] I.e. academicians, heads of higher educational institutions, institutes, faculties and laboratories; head doctors; senior legal officials; editors and senior journalists; leaders in arts and artistic bureaucracy.
Source: Matthews (1975) p. 13.

two fifths of the Soviet population were still living in poverty.[1] Thirdly, that since 1956 the USSR had experienced a major reduction in inequality. This had already been noted by Wiles (1974a p. 25), who had observed that 'the statistical record since Stalin is a very good one indeed. I doubt if any other country can show a more rapid and sweeping progress towards equality.' A very significant factor in this reduction in inequality has been the repeated increases in the minimum wage.

It is important to note that the income distribution statistics analysed by Wiles and McAuley concern normal money income only and exclude both top money incomes and non-money incomes such as imputed rent from owner-occupied dwellings, the subsidy element in state rents and free medical and educational services. Since there are systematic differences between the value of the subsidy element in state rents and free educational and medical services, between social groups, measurement of money incomes only might give a distorted picture of the distribution of real income. For example, in the USSR, there are very great differences between the quality of medical care available in Russian villages and that provided in the special facilities available to top party and state officials, members of the Academy of Sciences and the Union of Writers, officers in the armed forces and state security organs, foreigners and other elite groups. Whereas in

[1] 'Poverty', of course, is a relative and culture-bound concept. In the United States, for example, half a million families below the 'poverty' line own two or more cars. The measure of 'poverty' used by McAuley is a Soviet one, developed by Soviet specialists for Soviet conditions.

Table 7.3 *Distribution [a] of income [b] in selected capitalist and socialist countries*

Country	D_1	D_2	D_3	D_4	D_5	D_6	D_7	D_8	D_9	D_{10}	D_{10}/D_1	Relative income of deciles 1, 2, 3 & 4 [c]	Gini coefficient	Theil coefficient
Hungary (1977)	4.3	6.0	7.0	7.7	8.5	9.3	10.2	11.4	13.1	22.5	5.2	0.62	0.244	0.102
Poland (1975)	3.2	5.2	6.2	7.0	8.0	8.6	9.9	11.2	13.7	27.0	8.4	0.54	0.308	0.167
USSR (1973)	3.2	5.3	6.2	6.9	8.0	8.6	9.8	11.1	13.7	27.2	8.5	0.54	0.309	0.169
Czechoslovakia (1973)	5.0	6.2	7.1	7.8	8.6	9.4	10.2	11.4	12.8	21.5	4.3	0.65	0.224	0.086
United Kingdom (1975)	4.4	5.5	6.7	7.3	8.5	9.4	10.6	12.3	14.6	20.7	4.7	0.60	0.249	0.097
Sweden (1970)	4.3	5.7	6.4	7.4	8.5	9.5	10.5	12.3	14.8	20.5	4.8	0.60	0.250	0.099
Canada (1969)	2.7	4.6	6.0	7.0	8.0	10.0	11.8	13.0	14.0	22.9	8.5	0.51	0.299	0.146
USA (1970)	2.6	3.6	5.7	6.1	8.0	9.0	11.0	13.0	15.2	25.8	9.9	0.45	0.342	0.192

Notes: [a] Unit: individuals ranked according to per capita income.
[b] Income concept: secondary income distribution account being taken of non-monetary income of elite.
[c] Relative to mean income in the country concerned.

Source: Morrison (1984) p. 133.

the West the labour movement regards the free provision of medical services as a means of equalising real incomes, it is entirely possible that in the USSR, where the facilities are financed out of indirect taxation and differentially provided, charging the user for medical services on the basis of costs would increase equality. A similar situation exists with respect to housing. As the Hungarian sociologist Szelenyi (1972) noted in a classic study of the sociology of housing distribution in Hungary, 'Rent subsidies thus turned into wage supplements increasing the differences between low and high incomes ... the administrative system of housing distribution proved to be dysfunctional, that is it led to a result which differed from its declared aim.'

The existence of important real income differences not reflected in the published data used by Wiles and McAuley does not mean that there is no information available on these differences. In an important paper, Matthews (1975) investigated the question of whether there existed in the USSR an elite with real incomes much above the rest of the population. His investigation is summed up in table 7.2.

Table 7.2 shows an elite group of 0.2 percent of the employed population, with real incomes much above the average. Matthews' paper is only an initial investigation of this important subject. It has been taken further in his (1978). Further information on this matter can be found in Voslensky (1984 chapter 5).

The need to take account of top people's privileges in calculating income distributions for socialist countries was the starting point for the interesting paper of Morrison (1984). He adjusted the standard income distribution data for Eastern Europe to allow for the additional emoluments of the elite. His chief results are set out in table 7.3.

The following conclusions can be drawn from the Morrison data:

(1) A socialist country, Czechoslovakia, is the most egalitarian of all the countries considered.
(2) The most unequal country (the USA) is a capitalist country.
(3) As far as the share of the top 10 percent of incomes in total income is concerned, the most unequal countries of all are two socialist ones, the USSR and Poland.
(4) The position of the worst off parts of the population (the bottom 10 percent or the bottom 40 percent) relative to the national mean is generally better in the socialist countries than in the capitalist ones.
(5) The position of the middle class (individuals or households in

deciles 7 and 8) is worse off in socialist countries than in capitalist ones. This difference is still more marked if the ninth decile is included in this group.

(6) Because of the relatively favourable position of deciles 1 to 4, the relatively unfavourable position of deciles 7–9 and the favourable position of the tenth decile in the socialist countries, there is less inequality than in capitalist countries when only deciles 1 to 9 are taken into account but as much inequality as in capitalist countries for all incomes above the median.

Conclusions (1) and (5) help explain why the Czechoslovak liberalisation movement of 1968 was associated with anti-egalitarian sentiments. Conclusion (3) helps explain why the Polish renewal movement of 1980/1 was associated with widespread exposure of corruption and high living by the former leadership. Conclusions (3) and (4) taken together are part of the explanation for the stability of the USSR.

Morrison's work is useful but not the last word on the subject. His data on the income distributions are out of date and his list of countries not exhaustive.

The distribution of income and wealth in the two systems differs also in ways that cannot be seen from comparisons of the overall personal income distribution. A characteristic feature of capitalism is that it produces a small number of very rich people with large amounts of legitimate capital. The absence of this group under socialism is a major difference between the systems. (There are millionaires under state socialism, chiefly corrupt officials and second economy operators, but their wealth is usually not legitimate, not in the form of means of production, and liable to confiscation with a change in the political situation.) The relative incomes of different occupational groups often differs sharply between the systems. For example, whereas in the capitalist world the free professionals are traditionally high earners, in the USSR medical doctors (except for senior medical administrators) are traditionally a low-paid group. On the other hand, some groups of Soviet manual workers, e.g. coal miners and dockers, are rather well paid, with incomes in excess of most university graduates. The relative position of tenants and owner-occupiers also differs. Whereas in the capitalist world, the latter are generally better off than the former, in the socialist world the situation is reversed. For example, in the USSR the majority of houses in private ownership are traditional style houses without running water and central heating. The high income groups live predominantly in modern flats with good facilities and low rents which are the property of the state.

Inter-system differences in inequality have been examined not only by economists but also by sociologists, a well-known study being Lane (1982). He concluded (ibid. p. 159) that although there were important differences in inequality between the systems (e.g. the absence of ownership classes under state socialism) nevertheless inequality was important in both systems. Under state socialism,

in a relational sense, there is inequality of control over wealth, inequality of political power, and in a distributional sense, there is inequality of income and inequality of status. The origins of such social stratification lie in the bureaucratic nature of political power, in the role structure created by the division of labour sanctioned by the educational system and perpetuated by the family. Such structural features give rise to a hierarchy in which some groups of men (and few women) have power, prestige and privilege while others lack them. Politically, and not without internal conflict, the privileged acquire the means to help maintain and justify ideologically their advantage.

In China, as in the USSR, a large proportion of the population have very low incomes. In addition, in both countries there are substantial inequalities, between high officials and others, between town and country, between regions and between genders. Nevertheless, comparing China with other third world countries, the World Bank has argued (*China* 1985 p. 29) that China has average living standards (as measured for example by life expectancy) that are very high for a third world country, has virtually abolished the constant fear of destitution that haunts a significant fraction of the population in other third world countries, has a level of rural inequality that is low by the standards of South Asian countries and an egalitarian distribution of urban incomes. The most positive feature of China's income distribution, according to this World Bank study, is that the relative position of the worst off sections of society is much better than under capitalism. This is what one would expect on the basis of Morrison's findings for Eastern Europe. It should be noted that these achievements have required massive use of administrative methods. For example, urban inequality would be much higher if free movement of population to the towns were permitted. No doubt inequality in Calcutta or Mexico City could be reduced by deporting the poor to the countryside but would this represent a social improvement? China's striking achievements in the field of average living standards relative to average per capita GNP are considered further in chapter 8. Although inequality in China is low by the standards of many other third world countries it is not insignificant.

An interesting example of the importance of income differences in China prior to the Cultural Revolution is provided by the schools. At this time only a small minority of the relevant age group went to secondary schools due to a shortage of facilities. In the early 1960s the authorities pursued a policy of concentrating resources on a minority of successful schools. The idea was to ensure that sufficient qualified people would be produced to meet the needs of the national economy. The privileged position of the pupils at these schools was pronounced. Schooling was not free. Tuition fees were not high, on average they were about 5 or 6 yuan a year, at a time when average wages were about 50 yuan a month. Nevertheless, they were not insignificant, particularly if there were several children in a family, bearing in mind that textbooks and stationery also had to be paid for, and that there was an opportunity cost of secondary schooling in terms of wages forgone. Furthermore, the better schools tended to charge more. In 1966 Watson (1975 p. 127) visited a boarding kindergarten in Zhengzhou which charged 13.50 yuan per month for each child, and one in Beijing which charged 25 yuan. In important cities, a number of the well-endowed schools took children almost exclusively from the families of leading cadres. A well-known example was the Number 2 Primary School in Beijing where many of China's leaders sent their children and grandchildren. The existence of these selective facilities, the substantial charges they made, and the fact that only a small minority received any secondary education, were all aspects of massive inequality by West European standards. In the post Mao period, as part of the policy of recreating shattered academic standards, the state once more consciously pursued a policy of concentrating resources on a limited number of key schools. This recreated a situation in which there were major differences in life chances between those who did, and those who did not, attend the key schools.

Similarly, unequal access to medical care, both as regards payment and quality, has been a permanent feature of Chinese society since 1949 (and also one of the issues in the GPCR). Only party and state cadres and insured workers have had free medical care. These two groups appear to have amounted to less than 25 percent of the urban population throughout. The remainder of the urban population has had to pay for curative care or do without. The quality of care has varied substantially, with that available to top cadres being higher than that to temporary workers. Prior to the GPCR (and probably also today) each large hospital had several single rooms, furnished with sofas and chairs and very comfortable, for cadres of rank 13 upwards. (Since 1956 the Chinese bureaucracy has been graded into 30 ranks, with 30 the lowest and 1 the highest. Rank 13 approximately corresponds to the secretary of a county party committee.) In the rural areas, medical care has generally been scanty, of low quality, and had to be paid for. During the GLF free medical care was introduced into the rural areas, but this programme disintegrated in the economic stringency that followed. In the GPCR local rural medical insurance was generally introduced, with small payments for use to discourage waste, and large numbers of paramedical personnel ('barefoot doctors') trained. Both programmes appear to have continued to the present. Although the People's Republic has been unable in the first four decades of its existence to meet its founders' goal of free high quality care for all, it has greatly increased standards for all as measured by mortality and morbidity statistics, and greatly improved the access to, and quality of care available to, the poor and middle rural inhabitants. Life expectancy in China (sixty-eight years in 1981) is outstandingly high for a low-income country.

In the 1970s it became fashionable, especially in World Bank circles, to argue that economic growth that did not benefit the rural poor was quite unacceptable. Great efforts should be made, it was argued, to alleviate rural poverty by combining economic growth with an equitable distribution of income. This doctrine appears to have been implemented in the Chinese countryside from the establishment of the People's Republic onwards. A reasonable rate of economic growth has been combined with a relatively equal distribution of income. If the World Bank data are reliable, it would seem that income distribution in rural China, in the whole period since land reform, has been significantly more equal than in much of the rest of Asia. How has this been achieved?

The main factor is obviously the abolition of private ownership of land, which eliminated the distinction between landlords and landless labourers. Another factor is the emphasis on distribution according to need (e.g. the grain ration to which each household was entitled, low-cost basic services such as medical care and education, and welfare benefits for the needy). The price policy pursued, which has been consciously pro-poor, with low prices for basic necessities and high prices for luxuries, has also been a factor. For example, in China the state prices of food grains and cotton textiles have been much lower, relative to the price of bicycles, than in India.

It is most important to note that what has been achieved in the state socialist world is not equality, but inequalities which partly differ from but partly resemble those under capitalism. To establish and maintain these differences has required very substantial inequalities of power. This illustrates the general proposition that money income and wealth are much less important factors in social stratification in the state socialist countries than in the capitalist world, because of the overwhelming importance of the state in the former. In the USSR, the millionaire Ostap Bender was unable to do anything with his wealth. The state security officer Erchov, on the other hand, was able to get the woman he wanted without any trouble, even though she was someone else's wife. He simply instructed the couple to divorce and her to marry him.[2]

Similarly, China is a country where the entire society has been transformed by a continuous process of social change from above. The mass of the population has been subordinated to the cadres, and cadres at each level to their superiors. Being a cadre has often been a thankless task. Nevertheless, the great inequalities of power between cadres, and between cadres and the masses, have always been present. Without them it would have been impossible to carry out the social transformation which has in fact taken place. As one work point recorder put it during the Socialist Education Movement (Chen 1969 p. 218), 'The handle of the sword is always in the hands of the cadre. We are powerless.' As was pointed out in chapter 4, an example of these inequalities of power, and of their importance, is provided by the Great Leap Forward. This forced the mass of the population to perform greatly increased work, much of it wasted, and was a major factor causing the deaths from malnutrition and starvation which took place in 1959–61.

Sen (1983) has pointed out that, comparing China and India, China combines a much better performance with respect to malnutrition, life expectancy and general destitution in normal years, with a much worse record with respect to famines. India has not experienced a famine since independence. China, on the other hand, experienced a major famine in 1959–61. The reason why famine has proved possible in China but not in India is that India, unlike China, has functioning democratic institutions. In China in 1960, just as in Ireland in the 1840s, the dying had no political influence and there were no political forces (opposition parties, independent

---

[2] Ostap Bender is the central character in Ilf and Petrov's famous novel *The golden calf*. By devious means he eventually becomes a millionaire, but the only thing he is able to do with his money is to travel on trains. All other goods are available on allocation only. State security officer Erchov is one of the characters in V. Serge's novel *The case of Comrade Tulayev*.

media) which could prevent the authorities covering up the situation.

Some writers have claimed (e.g. Alder-Karlsson 1976) that state socialism is superior to capitalism in the provision of essentials. This claim is very one sided bearing in mind the repeated failures of the USSR in the Lenin-Stalin period, of China in 1959–61, of Kampuchea under Pol Pot, and of African countries of socialist orientation such as Ethiopia and Mozambique in the 1980s to provide all the population with the most basic essential of all, sufficient food to prevent starvation.

In Maoist China, inequality was primarily a political, rather than economic, phenomenon. Whereas in capitalist countries differences in ownership of the means of production are very important for social stratification, under state socialism the entire population is propertyless but a bureaucratic stratum controls the means of production. Hence, for example, whereas in India the landless agricultural labourers are a particularly oppressed social stratum, in Maoist China it was those with the wrong class origins, victims of repression such as camp inmates, victims of disastrous policies (such as the GLF) and sent down educated youths, whose lives were blighted.

An important feature of Maoist China was the development of a caste system based on the class (or politics) of a person's father (or grandfather). There were five red castes, workers, poor and middle peasants, soldiers, cadres, and relatives of revolutionary martyrs, and eight black castes, landlords, rich peasants, counter-revolutionaries, bad elements, Rightists, renegades, enemy agents and capitalist-roaders. In 1966–76 intellectuals belonged to the ninth black category, the 'stinking ninth'. Those born into a black category were discriminated against from birth and the person's spouse, family and children were similarly affected. Lee (1978 p. 39) gives a graphic illustration of the importance of caste lines in Maoist China.

A friend of ours stayed at a farm in northern Guangdong for six years. He met a man by the name of Chan there. This young man was by nature taciturn and clumsy, and smiles and talks little. He was conveniently classified as 'backward' for his father was a schoolteacher, an intellectual. His parents were struggled against and denounced in the Cultural Revolution. But he remained quiet, kind, solitary and 'backward'. And he developed secret sentiments towards a girl in the herding brigade. When he could contain himself no longer, he wrote a fiery letter of love to this girl. The girl was a 'poor peasant' and therefore of impeccable family history. She was startled and scared and immediately showed the letter to her brigade (all girls). All the farm marvelled at his recklessness. A man of his position daring to touch the daughter of a poor peasant family! The local party branch secretary saw fit to warn him in person, this was a gross violation indeed.

An intellectual (i.e. the son of a school teacher) aspired to marry a poor peasant (i.e. the daughter of a poor peasant)! Obviously an unacceptable breach of the caste system.

Categorisation by class origins made some sense during the civil war and subsequent radical social changes (e.g. land reform). Furthermore, it is very striking that the groups benefiting from positive discrimination in Maoist China were those suffering from discrimination in old China and in the capitalist world. Such a reversal of the traditions of millenia was an understandable feature of a revolutionary society. Nevertheless, as a permanent, hereditary, caste system, it was profoundly unsatisfactory. It came under strong attack after the downfall of the 'Gang of Four'. In 1978–9 official attention in China switched from class struggle to economic modernisation. It was declared that most of China's bad origin persons had remoulded themselves. Though their class-origin labels remained in dossiers, the Central Committee directed that their 'hats' – their official stigmata – be permanently removed. Within a short time, the structure of discrimination based on class labels had simply disappeared. It had been replaced by stratification based on income and wealth. As one villager put it in a 1982 interview (Watson 1984 p. 141) 'It's not class origin which counts any more; what counts now is making money.'

Categorisation by the class position of one's parents is quite normal under state socialism, especially in the first few decades of the new society. It can have major effects on one's job, marriage, housing and overall life chances.

INCOME DISTRIBUTION AND ECONOMIC REFORM

Economic reform involves a greater monetisation of the economy and a greater role for stratification by income relative to stratification by political criteria. Hereditary castes and the allocation of consumer goods by administrative methods decline in importance. A significant example of the importance of the difference between a traditional and reformed economic mechanism concerns housing (Bauer 1983b). In the USSR most new housing is state or cooperative and new private housing is of minor importance. State housing is provided to the occupants very cheaply. In Hungary, on the other hand, most new housing is private, and very expensive. As a result of this difference, money incomes in Hungary are soaked up by housing whereas in the USSR they are spent on other goods. This is an important factor explaining the widespread shortages of consumer goods in the USSR and the need in that country to mobilise millions of students and other town dwellers every year to bring in the harvest. Whereas in Hungary money is a powerful motivating force because it can be used to buy a wide range of everyday consumer goods and is essential to pay for housing, in the USSR it is rivalled by administrative methods for everyday consumer goods and virtually replaced by administrative methods for housing. Hence the motivating power of money is much less.

Does the greater importance of money mean growing inequality? Economic reform in socialist countries (Czechoslovakia 1968, Hungary from 1968, China from 1979, the USSR in 1965 and the second half of the 1980s) is frequently associated with anti-egalitarian rhetoric. Investigations of what has actually happened, however, show that this rhetoric can give a misleading impression. Important empirical studies are Flakierski (1979, 1981 and 1986), Adam and Nosal (1982) and *China* (1985).

These show that:

(a) economic reform is often associated with a *reduction* in inequality between the urban and rural populations,
(b) economic reform is often associated with an increase in earnings inequalities,
(c) earnings inequalities and per capita income differentials are determined by different factors and may move in different directions,
(d) an increase in inequality can take place within the framework of a traditional economic mechanism, and
(e) economic reform tends to increase the importance of money, relative to political position, as a stratifying factor.

Both in Hungary and in China, rural incomes prior to the reform were below those in urban areas. In both countries, economic reform was associated with a major increase in rural incomes, both absolutely and relative to urban incomes. For example, whereas in 1966, prior to the NEM, median incomes of state employees in Hungarian agriculture were only 92 percent of those in the state sector as a whole, by 1974, six years after the NEM had been introduced they had risen to 100 percent. Similarly, the per capita income of members of peasant households rose from 98 percent of that of workers in 1967 to 107 percent in 1973.

The introduction of the NEM was associated with an increase in the relative earnings of senior managers. In 1968 their earnings were on the average 2.9 times higher than those of wage earners whereas in

1971 they were 3.2 times higher. This resulted from a conscious policy of linking managerial earnings to economic outcomes so as to improve economic performance. In 1973–8, as part of the retreat from the reform which characterised the mid 1970s, these differentials narrowed.

Per capita income differentials are determined by earnings differentials, transfer payments (e.g. child benefits and old age pensions) and the ratio between earners and dependants per household. In state socialist countries, earnings differentials make a relatively small contribution to per capita income differentials. Hence by increasing transfer payments it is possible at the same time to aim at increasing earnings differentials and reducing per capita income differentials. This was the official policy in Hungary in the 1970s. In the mid 1970s it was more successful in the latter aim than the former, at any rate in the state sector.

Poland in the 1970s is a good example of how an increase in inequality can be associated with maintenance of the traditional economic mechanism. During the 1970s earnings inequalities in Poland increased considerably. At the same time, the relative political stability of the Gierek era combined with increased trade with the West, permitted substantial wealth accumulation by the elite. These factors contributed powerfully to the proletarian upheaval of 1980.

Economic reform implies an increased monetisation of the economy and a reduced role for political decisions in the determination of consumption. Hence the determinants of inequality are altered, as pointed out above with special reference to Chinese agriculture. This can cause considerable resentment amongst beneficiaries of the traditional economic mechanism. For example, in Hungary in 1974, as part of the retreat from the NEM, hunting, which is a high status activity, was restricted to senior officials of at least the rank of deputy minister. The idea that persons such as doctors or presidents of agricultural cooperatives who had simply earned large sums of money, should aspire to the same status giving leisure activities as high party and state officials was regarded as an unacceptable breach of the hierarchical order of society. This was analogous to the sumptuary laws of mediaeval Western Europe and an example of the importance of pre-capitalist practices under state socialism.

Why does inequality persist under state socialism? There seem to be four main reasons, the division of labour, the family, the sexual division of roles and the role of the state in state socialism. The division of labour has persisted, so that, for example, some people are high officials and others are agricultural labourers. The family has persisted, so that, for example, some children come from intelligentsia families and have the advantages that go with this in settled societies, while others come from worker or peasant families. The sexual division of roles ensures that most top jobs are in the hands of men, while many of the most arduous jobs are undertaken by women. The dominant role of the state in state socialism has ensured that those holding high official positions have attractive and well-paid jobs while others, especially those in political disfavour, have dreary, poorly paid jobs, no jobs at all or die from repression or starvation.

CONCLUSION

The Marxist view of incomes planning under socialism is that on the morrow of the revolution it is necessary to eliminate parasitical incomes and base distribution on work performed, but that the ultimate objective of the socialist movement in this field is distribution according to need. Experience shows that distribution according to need can have an adverse effect on output. All the state socialist countries operate what in Western terminology would be called permanent incomes policies. The experience of the state socialist countries suggests that the following are sufficient conditions for a permanent incomes policy: price control, the planning of foreign trade, the elimination of large property incomes, compulsory arbitration, national job evaluation, uniform regional net advantages, the production mindedness of trade unions, full employment, a proletarian government, and a non-permissive approach to breaches of labour discipline.

Satisfactory comparisons between the distribution of incomes under state socialism and capitalism are not yet possible, owing to the poor quality of the available data. Nevertheless, it is clear that the distribution of income under state socialism and capitalism differs in complex ways that cannot accurately be summarised as more or less inequality. Furthermore, income distribution and inequality are related under state socialism and capitalism in different ways. In the latter money income and wealth ownership are the major factors determining differences in consumption, life chances and social stratification. In the former, position in the political hierarchy, income in kind and membership of a favoured (or unfavoured) caste are of greater importance.

The available empirical evidence about the distribution of income in the USSR is very poor. The most striking changes in the Soviet income distribution over time are the very big increases in inequality in the first two Five Year Plans (1928–37) and the very big reduction in inequality since the 20th Party Congress (1956). As far as China is concerned, the widespread impression of an extremely equal society appears to be quite wrong from the viewpoint of Social Democratic Western Europe, but correct from the viewpoint of countries such as Mexico. The main feature of China's income distribution is the lesser importance in normal years of the extreme destitution which is the lot of a significant proportion of the population in those third world countries which have retained private ownership of the means of production. The main dynamic characteristic of China's social stratification is the development of a caste system based on the class (or politics) of a person's father (or grandfather) in the Maoist period, followed by the revived importance of stratification by income and wealth after 1978.

Economic reform is normally associated with a reduction in income differences between the rural and urban populations, an increase in earnings inequalities in the state sector and an increased monetisation of the economy. The transition to the traditional model (as in the USSR 1928–37) or the maintenance of it (as in Poland in the 1970s) may also be associated with increased earnings inequalities.

The main reasons for the persistence of inequality under state socialism appear to be the division of labour, the family, the sexual division of roles and the role of the state in state socialism.

SUGGESTIONS FOR FURTHER READING

P. Wiles, *Distribution of income: East and West* (Amsterdam 1974).

A. Bergson, 'Income inequality under Soviet socialism', *Journal of Economic Literature* vol. XXII, no. 3 (September 1984).

D. Lane, *The end of social inequality?* (London 1982).

F. Parkin, *Class, Inequality and Political Order* (London 1971).

W. Brus, 'Income distribution and economic reforms in Poland', *Il Politico* vol. XXXIX, no. 1 (1974).

M. Matthews, *Privilege in the Soviet Union* (London 1978).

C. Howe, *Wage patterns and wage policy in modern China 1919–1972* (Cambridge 1973).

A. McAuley, *Economic welfare in the Soviet Union* (London 1979).

E. B. Vermeer, 'Social Welfare provisions and the limits of inequality in contemporary China', *Asian Survey* vol. 19, no. 9 (1979).

E. B. Vermeer, 'Income differentials in rural China', *China Quarterly* 89 (March 1982).

J. Unger, 'The class system in rural China: a case study', J. L. Watson (ed.) *Class and social Stratification in post-revolution China* (Cambridge 1984).

M. Korzec & M. K. Whyte, 'Reading notes: The Chinese wage system', *China Quarterly* 86 (June 1981).

M. Ellman, 'Income distribution in the USSR', chapter VII of M. Ellman, *Collectivisation, convergence and capitalism* (London 1984).

H. Flakierski, *Economic reform and income distribution* (New York 1986).

M. Matthews, *Poverty in the Soviet Union* (Cambridge 1986).

B. Askanas & F. Levcik, 'The dispersal of wages in the CMEA countries', in S. F. Frowen (ed.) *Controlling industrial economies* (London 1983).

8

PLANNING CONSUMPTION

INTRODUCTION

Consumption planning is concerned with planning the production of consumer goods and services, and with ensuring the consistency of these plans with those for income and expenditure. The main instrument used for harmonising planned incomes with planned expenditures is the balance of money incomes and expenditures of the population.

In order for the latter to balance, it is necessary that wages issued in those sectors of the economy not producing wage goods (investment, social consumption, defence) be soaked up by direct or indirect taxation or by savings (Dobb 1960 p. 91). If only indirect taxation is used, then the average mark-up (p) of retail prices over costs should be determined by the formula

$$ p = \frac{W_{sc} + W_i + W_d}{W_{pc}} $$

where W_{sc} is the wage bill in social consumption,
$\quad W_i$ is the wage bill in the investment industries,
$\quad W_d$ is the wage bill in defence, and
$\quad W_{pc}$ is the wage bill in the industries producing goods for personal consumption.

For example, if one third of wages are issued in social consumption, investment and the defence sector, and two thirds in the personal consumption sector, then in the absence of savings and direct taxation the average mark-up should be 50 percent. Two corollaries of this proposition are as follows. First, the higher the ratio of the wage bill in the non-personal consumption sectors to the wage bill in the personal consumption sector, the higher the mark-up must be. Secondly, in a socialist economy the effect of an increase in savings is that it permits the equilibrium price level to be lower than it

Table 8.1 *Personal consumption plan for China for 1981–5*

Product	Initial level 1980	Plan 1985	Outcome
NON-DURABLES (consumption p.a.)			
Grain (kg/person)	214.0	222.0	254.0
Edible vegetable oil (kg/person)	2.3	3.3	5.1
Cloth (metres^2/person)	10.0	11.0	11.7
Sugar (kg/person)	3.9	5.0	5.6
DURABLES (stock in hands of population per hundred persons at year end)			
Bicycles	9.7	18.7	21.4
Sewing machines	4.7	9.0	9.4
Watches	12.9	26.2	34.5
Radios	12.1	22.8	23.1
TVs	0.9	3.4	6.7

Sources: The Sixth Five-Year Plan of the People's Republic of China for economic and social development (1981–1985) (Beijing 1984); *Statistical yearbook of China 1986* (Beijing & Hong Kong 1986) pp. 596 & 598.

otherwise would be. If the equation is violated this will result either in excess stocks (if the mark-up is too high) or in shortages and queues (if the mark-up is too low).

In calculating the volume of particular goods and services required, the planners use two main methods. One is forecasts of consumer behaviour, based on extrapolation, expenditure patterns of higher income groups, income and price elasticities of demand and consumer behaviour in the more advanced countries. The other method is that of plan norms. The first method attempts to foresee consumer demands, the latter to shape it.

An example of a consumption plan is the one for China for 1981–5. Its key indices are set out in table 8.1.

The substantial discrepancy between the plan and the outcome is yet another illustration of the fact that the plans often do not determine the course of economic development under state socialism. The planners failed to foresee the size of the increase in consumption which took place.

Consumption in the state socialist countries has not been planned in a uniform way throughout the whole period of their existence. On the contrary, consumption planning has depended very much on the stage of economic development they have reached, the economic policies pursued and the planning techniques used. In some periods in some countries it has been neglected, and in other periods and other countries much attention has been paid to it.

A major innovation in Soviet planning in the 1970s was the compilation not just of industry and republic or regional plans but also of comprehensive programmes aimed at the solution of major national economic problems. A comprehensive programme is primarily a plan for the achievement of a certain objective which requires resources from several industries, has a major impact on the structure of the economy and may extend over a period of more than five years. An important advantage of the programme approach to planning is that it focuses on the results to be achieved rather than on marginal adjustments to the initial situation. Another advantage of comprehensive programmes arises from the fact that the achievement of a particular goal in one sector can have a major impact on many other sectors of the economy. This must be taken into account if disproportions are to be avoided.

In the USSR in the 1980s, several of these comprehensive programmes related to consumption. For example, a Food Programme was adopted in 1982. This was a programme aimed at coordinating the work of agriculture itself, the sectors which provide it with inputs such as agricultural engineering and agricultural chemicals, and the sectors which transport, process and distribute its products. It embraced irrigation, land drainage and other land improvement schemes, the pay of agricultural workers and the provision of social facilities in the villages, procurement prices and the debts of farms, and a variety of other agro-industrial questions. The Food Programme derived its importance and urgency primarily from the deteriorating availability of food in the USSR in the late 1970s, which led to the widespread introduction of food rationing in 1981. The bad harvests of 1979–85, the need to spend huge sums of foreign exchange on grain and meat imports, the use by the USA of the food weapon, the impact of food shortages in Poland, and the poor availability of meat and dairy products in much of the USSR in the late 1970s and early 1980s made the Food Programme of great political and economic importance. It turned out that much of the activity included in the Food Programme (e.g. irrigation of the black earth region, the use of heavy tractors, large-scale cattle complexes) was very wasteful and some of it hampered the development of agriculture. In the late 1980s the attention of Soviet agricultural policymakers switched to radically different policies (see chapter 4).

Another comprehensive programme in the field of consumption was the 'Comprehensive programme for the development of con-

Table 8.2 *USSR daily nutritional norms*

Age, sex and labour category	Calorific requirement (in kilocalories)	Intake of nutritional substances (in grams)		
		Proteins	Fats	Carbohydrates
Children to 1 year	800	25	25	113
Children 3–6 years	1,900	65	69	241
Youths 15–17 years	3,300	113	99	467
Working-age adults				
Group 1 (mental labour, e.g. students and office workers)				
Men	3,000	102	97	410
Women	2,700	92	87	369
Group 2 (light manual labour)				
Men	3,500	102	113	478
Women	3,200	109	103	437
Group 3 (heavy physical labour)				
Men	4,000	137	129	546
Women	3,600	123	116	492
Group 4 (very heavy physical labour)				
Men	4,500	146	145	615
Non-working pensioners	2,500	85	74	351

sumer goods and services' adopted under Gorbachev. Its effectiveness in raising living standards remains to be seen.

PLANNING BY NORMS[1]

A consumption norm is simply the quantity of a particular good or service required per head of the population. Although the method of norms is an alternative to the price mechanism for the determination of output, it is in fact quite widely used in Western countries. It is used in areas where distribution on the basis of purchasing power has been replaced by distribution on the basis of need. Examples are, the provision of housing, hospitals, schools and parks. Calculations of the desirable number of rooms, hospital beds and school places per person are a familiar tool of planning in welfare states. The use of

[1] The material in this section is taken from Weitzman (1974).

Table 8.3 *Actual and normative food consumption in the USSR and actual food consumption in selected countries (kgs/head/year)*

Food categories	USSR			EEC[b] 1984-/5 actual	USA 1982 actual	China 1985 actual
	Norm	1985 actual[a]	1985 as % of norm			
Bread (in terms of flour)	110	133	121	85[c]	96[d]	254[e]
Potatoes	97	104	107	75	52	
Vegetables & melons	146	102	70	110	91	n.a.
Fruits & berries	113	46	41	90	59	n.a.
Sugar	40	42	105	34	34	6
Vegetable oil & margarine	9	9.7	108	18	25	5
Meat & meat products	82	61	75	90	107	17
Fish & fish products	18[f]	17.7[f]	98	15	6	5
Eggs	16[g]	14[g]	88	14	15[g]	5

Notes: [a] Soviet consumption figures are not fully comparable with those for OECD countries. The Soviet figures give too favourable a picture of Soviet reality. For a discussion of relative food consumption in the USSR and USA see I. Birman, *Ekonomika nedostach* (New York 1983) pp. 251–91.
[b] 10 members.
[c] Total cereals in terms of flour.
[d] 'Grains'.
[e] 'Grain'.
[f] Live weight.
[g] Converted from numbers of eggs at the rate of 18 eggs = 1 kg.
Sources: The Soviet norms are derived from *Potrebnosti, dokhody, potreblenie* (Moscow 1979) p. 61; actual Soviet consumption is taken from *Narodnoe khozyaistvo SSSR v 1985g* (Moscow 1986) p. 445; US consumption comes from *Statistical abstract of the United States 1984* (Washington DC 1983) p. 129; the data for the EEC from *Agriculture statistical yearbook 1986* (Luxemburg 1986); and for China from *Statistical yearbook of China 1986* p. 596.

norms in consumption planning is illustrated in tables 8.2 and 8.3. Table 8.2 shows nutritional norms and table 8.3 the relationship between them and actual food consumption in the USSR and selected capitalist countries. This type of data clearly provides important information for the planning of agriculture, the food-processing industry and foreign trade.

Tables 8.2 and 8.3 illustrate two important facts about the method of norms. First, where there is an objective, scientific basis for the

Table 8.4 *USSR rational wardrobe and 1962 US Heller budget clothing stocks (no. of pieces/head)*

	USSR		USA			
	rational wardrobe		Heller budget I[a]		Heller budget II[b]	
	Men	Women	Men	Women	Men	Women
Coats	2.6	2.6	1	2	1	3
Raincoats	0.4	0.4	1	1	1	1
Jackets and sweaters	2.0	3.0	2	1	4	2
Suits	5.0	2.0	2	1	4	2
Trousers	2.0	n.a.	2	2	2	4
Dresses	–	15.0	–	9	–	13
Socks and hosiery (prs)	9.0	9.0	11	10	13	10
Leather shoes (prs)	7.0	10.0	3	5	5	8

[a] Family of a wage earner.
[b] Family of a white-collar worker (professional or executive).

norms, as in nutritional science, then the norms provide valuable information for the planners. Secondly, that the possibility of *substitution* between products causes serious difficulties for the norm method.[2] This is shown most clearly by table 8.4.

Why is it 'rational' for Soviet men to have 7 pairs of shoes? Why not 4 or 12? Why is it 'rational' for Soviet women to have 15 dresses? Why not more, or less? Perhaps women prefer fewer dresses and more trousers? It is clear that these clothing stock norms have little basis and are largely arbitrary. What is the 'rational' number of cars per person? In view of its limitations, the norm method of consumption planning came in for criticism in the USSR in the late 1980s (e.g. Rimashevskaya 1987).

What happens when the quantity of a particular good or service which the public actually wishes to buy differs from the 'rational' quantity provided by the planners in accordance with the norms? One possibility is to change the norms. For example, experience in the USSR in the 1960s showed that the norms for the purchase of consumer durables (televisions, refrigerators, washing machines, cars etc.) were too low and they were raised (Buzlyakov 1969 p. 172). Another possibility is to advertise the goods so as to boost sales.

[2] Even in the field of nutrition, the substitutability of many foods from a nutritive ingredients point of view, casts considerable doubt on the 'scientific' basis of the norms.

Table 8.5 *Polish consumption structure in 1967 (in %)*

	Total	From personal incomes	From social funds
Food	40.0	44.5	14.2
Drink	9.3	10.6	–
Tobacco	3.1	3.5	–
Clothes and shoes	13.6	15.5	–
Fuel and power	2.3	2.7	–
Housing	7.3	7.7	4.1
Hygiene and health	7.7	3.3	40.1
Culture, sport and tourism	9.8	5.4	41.5
Transport and communications	4.5	5.1	–
Other	1.5	1.7	0.1
Total	100.0	100.0	100.0

Source: Nuti (1971).

Hanson (1974) noted that in the early 1970s in the USSR and Poland there was an increasing tendency to use advertising to boost sales of those consumer goods for which buyers' markets existed. Another possibility is to alter prices to bring demand into line with supply. In the traditional model, however, only limited use is made of price changes (e.g. for seasonal fruits) and emphasis is placed on quantity changes in bringing supply and demand into equilibrium.

The use of price changes in the attempt to bring about equilibrium in the consumer goods market has several times (1970, 1976, 1980) generated spectacular political explosions in Poland. Although often blamed on the 'failure of the workers to understand the need for equilibrium' it seems that their real cause is the 'failure of the authorities to realise the conditions necessary for equilibrium'. The December 1970 decision by the Polish Government to raise food prices substantially, which led to riots in the working-class towns of north Poland and to the fall of Gomulka, had been preceded by an interesting economic discussion (Mieczkowski 1975 pp. 154–71, Nuti 1971). The discussion was initiated by J. Pajestka, the Vice-President of the Polish Planning Commission. He argued that the expenditure pattern of Polish consumers was being distorted by an irrational price system. Some relevant data is set out in tables 8.5 and 8.6.

The tables show that in 1967 more than half of the personal expenditure of Polish consumers went on food and drink. Pajestka suggested that this high share of food expenditure was partly a result

Table 8.6 *Social cost–retail price ratios (Poland in 1970)*

1. Food	1.288	
1.1. Meat and poultry		1.732
1.2. Fish		1.287
1.3. Fat		1.288
1.4. Sugar		0.867
1.5. Fruit and vegetables		0.864
2. Clothes and shoes	0.726	
2.1. Fabrics		0.817
2.2. Ready to wear		0.677
2.3. Shoes		0.673
3. Durable goods	0.748	
3.1. Means of transport		0.808
3.2. Electrical goods		0.732
4. Chemical manufactures	0.710	
5. Paper products	0.791	
6. Transport services	1.391	

Source: Nuti (1971).

of selling food too cheaply. Given the relative social costs of producing the different commodity groups (see table 8.6), he argued, it
would be more efficient to consume less food and more durables. The
argument is illustrated in figure 8.1.

Consider an economy which can produce either food or durables or
some combination of the two as given by the transformation line TT'.
If market prices equal this rate of transformation, consumption
would be P. Consumers would be on the indifference curve II'. If
actual prices underprice food relative to durables, then the actual
consumption point is A. A is a market disequilibrium point and is on
a lower indifference curve than P. Hence welfare maximisation
requires that consumers be confronted by the rational price TT'
rather than the cheap food price SS'.

This argument sounds plausible, but in fact rests on a number of
erroneous assumptions. First, it assumes that the relative price of
food in Poland was low. In fact, if a wide range of goods and services
is considered and account taken of the limited availability of many
non-food goods and services in Poland, by international standards it
was high. Secondly, it assumes that raising the relative price of food
reduces its consumption. Under Polish circumstances it normally
does not, since the government is forced to provide compensating
income increases which enable people to attempt to purchase at least
as much food as before. Thirdly, it fails to understand the role of
disequilibrium relative prices in generating apparent shortages of

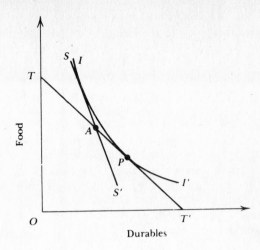

Figure 8.1 Changing relative prices to improve welfare

food products. The Polish economist Podkaminer (1982) has argued that throughout the period 1965–78 the disequilibrium in the consumer goods market could have been cured by *cutting* the price of food provided that the price of durables (e.g. housing) and services had been raised sharply. According to his analysis, the fundamental cause of disequilibrium on the Polish consumer goods market in the last 20–5 years has not been the low price of food but the low price of durables (e.g. housing) and services and their limited availability. Unable to spend their incomes on housing (which was either unobtainable or very cheap) or on other durables (which were often unavailable) or on leisure or cultural activities (which were either very cheap or unavailable) the population spent its money on food. This generated entirely artificial food 'shortages' (by international standards Polish food consumption was quite high).

Perhaps the most dramatic support for the Podkaminer thesis were the 'surprising' consequences of the huge food price increases imposed by the military regime in 1982. In February 1982, shortly after martial law had been declared, a price reform quadrupled the prices of virtually all foodstuffs (with the exception of bread and cereals, which had undergone similar treatment several months earlier), alcohol and tobacco. This reform naturally necessitated compensating wage and pension increases (otherwise much of the population would have died of poverty). This 'compensating' (in fact more than compensating) increase in income touched off an acute shortage of all non-food products the prices of which were now ridiculously cheap. The excess incomes resulting from the lack of availability of durables and their low prices in the state sector, were spent on food and in the second economy, generating new food shortages and intensified rationing and hectic activity in the second economy. Of the restoration of equilibrium in the consumer goods market there was no sign. This 'surprising' result was generated on one level, by a lack of understanding of the importance of substitutability between goods and the results of disequilibrium relative prices. On another level it was generated by the Bonapartist character of the Jaruzelski regime and its support for the peasantry at the expense of the urban working class and urban intellectuals. Furthermore, it is obvious that an alternative policy of dramatically increasing rents and the prices (and availability) of a wide range of durables and services would also have been unpopular, in particular with social groups on whom the authorities depended. (As pointed out in the previous chapter, cheap housing particularly benefits those holding senior posts in the bureaucratic apparatus. Similarly, holding the prices of cars at disequilibrium levels generates big benefits for those fortunate enough to be allocated a car.) In the late 1980s the Soviet authorities announced their intention in due course to drastically alter (i.e. increase) their retail prices. It will be interesting to see whether they have learned the lessons of Polish experience or whether they repeat the same mistakes.

Summary

The method of norms is the main method of consumption planning used in the state socialist countries. Its main weaknesses are the arbitrary nature of the norms and the phenomenon of substitutability. The norms can be implemented, *inter alia*, by quantity and price adjustments. The former is the main method used in the traditional model. Unwise use of the latter can trigger off dramatic political protests and fail to establish equilibrium in the consumer goods market.

SUPPLY AND DEMAND

In the USSR the growth of consumption (purchasing power) of the masses continually outstrips the growth of production and pushes it ahead, but under capitalism, on the other hand, the growth of consumption (purchasing power) of the masses never catches up with the growth of production and continually lags behind it, which condemns production to crises ... [In the USSR] the growth of the domestic market will advance beyond the growth of industry and push it forward towards continuous expansion.

J. Stalin (1955b pp. 300 and 332)

A characteristic feature of consumption in the state socialist countries is the existence of shortages and queues. This has marked the entire history of the USSR since its creation. The intensity of shortages varies over time and between countries. For example, in the USSR, the 1950s were a period of declining shortages, whereas the 1970s were a period of increasing shortages. Similarly in Poland there was a drastic worsening of shortages in the late 1970s, culminating in the crisis of 1981, after which the situation improved. What explains the shortages? This is a controversial question to which a variety of answers have been offered.

The macro-economic explanation is that the shortages and queues are symptoms of suppressed inflation. The volume of purchasing power in the hands of the public is in excess of the volume of consumer goods and services available, given the prices fixed by the state. In the 1920s shortages and queues were officially explained in the USSR as resulting from a 'goods famine'. This phrase suggested that the shortages and queues were a result of physical factors (low output and productivity) akin to the results of a bad harvest. This notion was criticised by a number of Soviet economists. In articles published in 1925 and 1926 Shanin and Novozhilov argued, in effect, that the shortages resulted from violation of the macro-economic equilibrium equation on page 233 above. The incomes being generated in the economy were in excess of the market value of consumer goods output. Looking at the matter from a static point of view, Novozhilov argued that the solution was to raise prices so as to restore equilibrium. Looking at the matter from a dynamic point of view, Shanin argued for a rapid expansion of the output of consumer goods and for only a small allocation of investment resources to producer goods. These ideas were decisively rejected by the party, which launched instead a rapid expansion of employment in, and output of, producer goods industries. This naturally exacerbated the situation. Rationing of all producer goods and many consumer goods, together with restricted access retail trade, had to be introduced to keep the situation under control.

Thirty-three years later, Novozhilov (1959 pp. 199–200) reverted to his earlier theme. He argued that the underpricing of goods leads to the expenditure of 'time and effort on the search for scarce goods and standing in queues. At the same time unproductive and even

criminal actions (speculation in scarce goods, under the counter sales
by assistants of the scarce goods etc.) become a source of unjustified
enrichment.'

The views of Novozhilov and other Soviet economists who share
his position on this issue, remained unorthodox up till the late 1980s.
The idea of the price mechanism as the most efficient way of allocating scarce goods between consumers, was repeatedly rejected by the
authorities. They argued that the way to overcome shortages was not
to raise prices but to expand output. For example, in a meeting with
Moscow workers in January 1983 (*Pravda* 1 February 1983) Andropov raised the question of how to overcome shortages. 'It is possible,
of course, to raise prices. This solution, however, in general does not
suit us ... What remains? ... It is necessary to produce more goods so
that the shops will not be empty.' The classic exposition of the traditional Marxist–Leninist point of view is contained in a speech by
Stalin at the 16th Party Congress (1930), an extract from which is
quoted at the head of this section. In that speech he contrasted the
relationship between demand and supply under capitalism and
under socialism. Capitalism is characterised by overproduction and
lack of demand (unemployed labour and machinery; schemes to keep
goods off the market by destruction, reductions in output or eliminating competition). Under socialism, on the other hand, demand runs
ahead of production and provides a stimulus to it. Instead of raising
prices to reestablish equilibrium, he advocated cutting prices so as to
increase real wages (as was done in 1948–54).

The view that the macro-economic situation in the USSR is
marked by permanent suppressed inflation focuses on the state sector
and ignores the second economy. Grossman (1977) pointed out that
'the very presence of a large second economy, and particularly of a
black market, in a sense does away with repressed inflation, despite a
fairly rigid control of official retail prices. In the second economy,
prices tend to be high enough to eliminate any overall "monetary
overhang" (that is, excess of purchasing power over the total supply
of goods and services at effective prices) and to forestall a repressed
inflationary situation in relation to the controlled and noncontrolled
sectors taken together.' This argument has been developed further by
Nuti (1986a).

In a well-known and influential series of papers, Portes has also
disputed the macro-economic explanation, but on different grounds.
He applied disequilibrium macro-economics to the available data
and concluded that for some countries (e.g. Czechoslovakia, GDR,
Hungary and Poland) for some periods (e.g. the mid 1950s to the mid

1970s) there is no evidence of permanent macro-economic disequilibrium. According to this line of reasoning, shortages and queues are not as universal as is often supposed and where they do exist may well be symptoms not of macro-economic disequilibrium but of micro-economic disequilibrium. Podkaminer (1988) however, found significant macro-economic disequilibrium in Poland in 1975–86. An interesting and important conclusion of the research of Portes was that macro-economic disequilibrium may be a greater problem for economies experiencing the reform process than for economies with the traditional model. Portes and Santorum (1987) applied the Portes analysis to China in 1955–83. They concluded that there were periods of macro-economic excess demand in China under the traditional model, notably in 1956–8, 1960 and 1976. Nevertheless, under the traditional model there was often a situation of macro-economic equilibrium or macro-economic excess supply. On the other hand, once reforms were embarked upon, macro-economic excess demand became a chronic problem, marking the whole period 1980–3. This was one of the reasons why the reform process in China was far from being a smooth, one way, process (see chapter 3).

The micro-economic explanation is that the state socialist countries suffer from disequilibrium *relative* prices. It is entirely possible for the macro-economic balance equation on p. 233 to be met, but for the prices of individual goods to differ substantially from the equilibrium levels. Indeed, one might expect this normally to be the case in the traditional model, since in it the planners frequently combine planned balancing of the incomes and expenditures of the population, with a policy of stable prices. The micro-economic explanation has the advantage over the macro-economic one of explaining the existence side by side both of shortages and excess stocks.

For adherents to the macro-economic and micro-economic explanations, the way to overcome the shortages is to adjust prices. Experience has shown, however, that just increasing prices may be ineffective in overcoming the shortages. For example in Poland in the 1980s there was a rapid increase in state retail prices. According to official data (which is unlikely to have been exaggerated) they doubled in 1982, rose by 20 percent in 1983, 14 percent in both 1984 and 1985, 18 percent in 1986 and 25 percent in 1987. Nevertheless, shortages remained widespread and equilibrium in the state retail sector was not reestablished. It is quite possible, however, that the failure to reestablish equilibrium was caused not by the inappropriateness of price adjustments but by the incompetence of the authorities. If Podkaminer is right, overcoming the disequilibrium on the consumer goods market required a big increase in the relative price (or availability) of non-food products, such as housing rents, durables and services. Since this did not take place, the shortages remained. Alternative explanations are considered below.

From a Marshallian point of view, the permanent existence in countries with the traditional model of shortages, queues and 'scarce goods' (i.e. goods that people want and which are produced but which are unavailable at a particular place at a particular time) and the replacement of shopping by 'obtaining with difficulty',[3] are a result of eliminating both the short-run and long-run equilibrating mechanisms which exist under capitalism. In the short run, it is appropriate to balance supply and demand by adjusting prices, in the long run by adjusting quantities. Both these feedback mechanisms, however, have been eliminated (or severely restricted) in the traditional model. Short-run price flexibility does not exist since prices are determined by state organs and often stable for prolonged periods. In addition, long-run adjustment of quantities in accordance with consumer demand only exists in an attenuated form, since the output of consumer goods industries is determined by planners in accordance with bureaucratic procedures. Hence to bring supply and demand into balance requires some other mechanism, e.g. queues, shortages or informal or formal rationing. From a Marshallian perspective, the way to overcome the shortages is to reintroduce the two mechanisms, i.e. flexible prices and the determination of quantities in accordance with consumer demand, the absence of which causes the shortages. The attempt to do this is an important part of the reform process.

The distributive explanation concentrates on factors specific to the distribution sector. For example, as was pointed out in chapter 6, the CMEA countries deliberately keep down the proportion of the labour force engaged in distribution and this is a major factor in explaining why shopping there takes longer than in comparable capitalist countries. Similarly, they also reduce investment in distribution. Research in Poland (Turcan 1977) suggests that the system of responsibility for missing goods is also very important. In the 1940s regulations were introduced in Poland making those employed in distribution personally responsible for losses, however incurred. The system is changing, but the most common arrangement when Turcan did his research was that staff were responsible for losses due to dishonesty and for losses exceeding 1 percent of the stock value. In these circumstances the staff must pay for the losses incurred. If a

---

[3] The word *dostat'* (literally 'to obtain with difficulty') is often used to describe buying goods in the USSR.

member of staff steals and though convicted is unable to pay, it is the responsibility of the remainder of the staff to pay for the losses, i.e. there is a common responsibility for looking after state property in shops.

Given this system of personal responsibility, stocktaking and checking the receipt of goods are matters of considerable concern to those employed. According to Ministry of Finance regulations there must be at least one stocktaking every year, but, if any sales assistant leaves the shop, a member of the remaining staff has the right to insist that a stocktaking be carried out. In view of this, the unexpected closure of shops, the lack of interest in selling, keeping customers away from products, queues for baskets in supermarkets etc. all become explicable. The sales assistant's job is partly that of a store detective or security guard. The staff are at least as interested in preventing theft as in selling.

Turcan's research is extremely suggestive. Whether or not the same system exists in the other CMEA countries is not known to the author. It may well do so. Obviously factors internal to distribution (low levels of employment and investment, the system of responsibility for preventing loss) are an important factor explaining shopping difficulties in the CMEA countries.

The social explanation is that increasing the relative prices of the scarcest goods is impossible because this would lead to riots and strikes. Experience in the USSR in 1962 and in Poland in 1970/1, 1976 and 1980 certainly suggests that large state price increases for basic food products are likely to produce an explosive political situation. Many workers evidently prefer shortages and queues, or rationing, to the free availability of goods that only those with money can afford. For example, one of the 21 demands of the August 1980 Gdansk strike committee was the introduction of meat rationing (as an alternative to price rises). Hence Poland rationed sugar in 1976 and the USSR in the 1970s and 1980s had enormous food subsidies combined with meatless days and poor availability of food in many areas. The situation is exacerbated by the policy of leaving prices stable for years, so that the necessary readjustments are very large. On the other hand, in some countries (e.g. Hungary and China) significant increases in food prices have proved feasible without explosive public opposition.

The behavioural explanation concerns the patterns of behaviour that characterise the state socialist countries, their causes and consequences. For example, according to Kornai (1980, 1985) the fundamental cause of shortages is the soft budget constraint that faces firms in the state socialist countries. The term 'soft budget constraint' refers to a type of behaviour within a particular social relationship. Firms with a soft budget constraint are not constrained by their financial situation. If they run into financial difficulties, their superiors will always bail them out. This results from the fact that they are state enterprises for whom the central bodies are responsible. Hence in place of economic considerations the dominant factors which determine the behaviour of enterprises are bureaucratic factors. This enables them to give free rein to typical bureaucratic objectives such as the desire to expand. The soft budget constraint thus implies a virtually unlimited demand for all products and this is the underlying cause of the shortages that so plague consumers. The only way of overcoming the shortages, according to this line of reasoning, is a radical economic reform (e.g. expansion of the private sector, end of directive planning, real self-financing, allowing the possibility of bankruptcies, etc.) which introduces hard budget constraints for the enterprises.

Adherents of the behavioural explanation argue that adherents of the macro-economic and micro-economic explanations are wrong to attach so much importance to the need for raising prices to overcome shortages, since raising prices may not overcome the shortages. This results from a combination of factors. First, many consumer goods are acquired not only by private consumers but also by state enterprises (e.g. foreign trade enterprises) and these are not price sensitive. Secondly, a significant proportion of consumer goods and services are distributed free (education, medical care) or at nominal prices (e.g. housing in many countries) and introducing market pricing for them would raise major social issues. Thirdly, in many cases the supply curve has a 'perverse' shape and can be char- acterised as a 'shortage preserving supply curve'. The shortage preserving supply curve is illustrated in figure 8.2.

Figure 8.2 shows a situation in which there is a normal shortage (e.g. a waiting period of 4 years for a car), which cannot be reduced by increasing prices because of the behaviour of the planners. When the price is increased, demand falls but so does supply, because the planners respond to the reduction in demand by reducing production or cutting imports or increasing exports. They aim to preserve the normal level of shortage in this market. This behaviour results from the planners' idea of what is normal and acceptable, the fact that decision making is not guided by profit maximisation, and the general environment of shortages which means that there are always attractive alternative uses for consumer goods (e.g. exporting them so as to earn scarce foreign exchange).

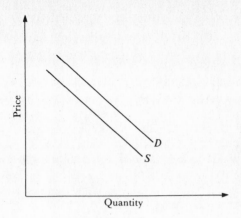

Figure 8.2 A shortage preserving supply curve

It seems likely that all the explanations have been important as causes of shortages and queues in the state socialist countries, the balance between the different explanations varying over time and between countries and products. The debate between adherents of the various explanations has been important in clarifying and deepening understanding of this important issue.

The inability of the state economy to meet all consumer needs has given rise to extensive economic activity in all the state socialist countries outside the state sector (see chapter 2). At some periods the authorities have vigorously attempted to suppress this kind of activity, and at others have tolerated it. When economic reform was first discussed (e.g. Poland in the 1950s, USSR in the 1960s) attention was usually focused on the state industrial sector and the need to make it less wasteful and more responsive to the needs of customers. Experience has shown, however, that this is very difficult. It has also shown, however, that small-scale non-state enterprises can respond quickly to requirements. They have the great merits of producing goods and services that people want, of providing incomes and employment, and of not requiring state subsidies. Furthermore, the private sector can play a useful role in reducing disequilibrium in the state sector. It can do this in two ways. First, by increasing the cash required by the population for transactions purposes. Secondly, taxes on the legal private sector can ensure that the output of this sector exceeds the net incomes generated by it and hence that it lessens the demand for consumer goods and services in the state sector. Accordingly an important feature of the reform process has been the relaxation of the restrictions on the small-scale non-state sector. For example, an important aspect of the deepening of economic reform in Hungary in the 1980s and of economic reform in China and Poland in the 1980s was the official encouragement of the small-scale non-state sector. Similarly, in 1986 the USSR adopted a radical law legalising individual economic activity. This was intended to legalise and encourage small-scale private service and production activities (e.g. repairs to cars and other consumer durables, the building and repair of housing, private lessons, private small-scale medical services, the making of clothes, shoes, furniture etc.). Similarly, from 1987 small cooperatives, e.g. for running restaurants, doing repairs and producing consumer goods, were encouraged in Soviet official documents.

Official encouragement for small-scale private service and production activities results from the fact that experience has shown that the state sector is unable to meet fully the demand for consumer goods and services. This is unexpected from the standpoint of traditional Marxism–Leninism. The fact that policies taking account of this fact have been implemented in a number of countries, including the most important, shows that the governments of state socialist countries are capable of learning from experience. It also shows that Marxism–Leninism is not a dogma which prevents rational decision making, but a flexible body of doctrine which can adapt itself to new developments.

The existence of a private sector in a predominantly state controlled economy can give rise to social and economic problems (e.g. it undermines the relative position of senior officials, may undermine work morale in the state sector, and may generate popular jealousy of its high incomes) which may lead to official campaigns against the sector. They may also lead to bureaucratic obstacles to the existence and development of the sector. These difficulties may prevent it developing into a productive, stable and fully accepted sector of the economy.

Another way of reducing shortages and queues in the state sector is that of monetary reform. Examples are the USSR in 1947, Poland in 1950, Romania and Bulgaria in 1952 and Vietnam in 1985. In a monetary reform most of the money held by the public, both cash and bank deposits, is confiscated (normally by ending the validity of the old money, unfavourable rates of exchange of old money for new, and/or converting part of the old money into non-negotiable long-term bonds). The aim is to reduce disequilibrium in the state retail sector (and often also to punish speculators). Monetary reform is normally quite effective in reducing disequilibrium in the state sector. For monetary reform to be successful requires that, measured in new money, after the reform the supply and demand for consumer goods should balance. If money wages in the new money are much in excess of the availability of goods and there is a significant free market (e.g. for food products) then instead of eliminating shortages and queues, rapid inflation will be generated. This happened in Vietnam in 1985/6 and seems to have resulted from combining the monetary reform with a transition to the payment to state employees of money wages rather than entitlements to heavily subsidised rationed commodities. This resulted in a big imbalance between the flow of money incomes and the flow of products, especially food products on the free market, and hence in rapid inflation.

An alternative to economic or monetary reform as a way of dealing with shortages is rationing. Formal rationing (as opposed to short-ages and queues, informal rationing by place of work distribution or limits on the quantity of particular products that may be sold to each person, or rationing by the price mechanism), has been extensively used in the state socialist countries. In the USSR there was rationing in the Civil War, in 1928–35, and during the Great Patriotic War. In China all major consumer goods were rationed from the early 1950s until 1980. After 1980 rationing of many products was gradually relaxed or abolished completely, but remained in force for grain and vegetable oil and was reintroduced for pork in December 1987. In Poland the rationing of some foodstuffs was introduced in 1976 and intensified in the early 1980s. In Cuba and Vietnam rationing is extensive and has lasted many years. Formal rationing has a number of advantages compared with the free market allocation of consumer goods. First, it enables commodities to be allocated on an egalitarian basis. Secondly, it facilitates control over population movement. For example, in Maoist China rural people could not freely migrate to cities and look for jobs. They had first to apply for permission and receive a ration book usable in the relevant city. (This has remained true, but as the number of rationed commodities has fallen, and as supplies on the free market have grown, this has become much less important.) Thirdly, it enables goods to be allocated in accordance with paternalistic criteria. For example, whereas distribution via the market may lead to children going without milk as parents spend their earnings on alcohol or tobacco, rationing can attempt to prevent this. Fourthly, it enables goods to be allocated on the needs principle, rather than on the desert principle. Fifthly, it enables discrimination to be made between deserving groups of the population who receive rations (e.g. officials and manual workers) and undeserving ones (e.g. white-collar workers, intellectuals or enemies of the people) who are left to starve.[4]

It also has a number of problems. First, extensive use of rationing undermines material incentives. This may have an adverse effect on labour productivity. Secondly, the accompanying development of a black market is both inefficient and has a demoralising effect. Thirdly, in general a person who receives rations is worse off with rations than with an equivalent quantity of money. The reason is that the relative quantities in which the person receives the various rationed goods is likely to differ from the relative quantities in which he/she would have bought the commodities. Unless the rations are only for a small number of very basic goods, or there are stringent punitive sanctions against this, this disadvantage of rations relative to universal purpose coupons (i.e. money) is likely to manifest itself in a formal or informal market in which rations for different commodities are exchanged against each other or for money. Fourthly, it separates consumption from the productive contribution people make to society and makes consumption partly dependent on connections, personal contacts, friendship etc. in the political and bureaucratic hierarchies. This undermines production and increases the role of political and bureaucratic factors in social life.

The balance between the advantages and disadvantages of formal rationing depends on the concrete circumstances of particular countries at particular times.

It is not necessary to introduce formal rationing in order to replace flexible prices and quantities, by administrative methods, in equilibrating supply and demand. A 1970s Soviet book on consumer demand (Levin and Yarkin 1976 pp. 284–9) considers a number of other administrative methods for regulating demand. They include, limiting the number of units sold per customer, only selling goods against preliminary orders, which may take a long time to be fulfilled (for example some types of refrigerators, suites of furniture and carpets), and distributing particularly scarce goods (e.g. cars) via employers rather than via the retail system. The fact that such methods were discussed in a book published in 1976 indicates that in the USSR in the mid 1970s the general availability of all goods in all

---

[4] In 1948 Zhdanov (then a leading member of the Soviet Politburo) told Djilas how his (Zhdanov's) criticism of the writer Zoshchenko had been taken in Leningrad. The local authorities simply took away Zoshchenko's ration coupons and did not give them back till after Moscow's magnanimous intervention (Djilas 1961 p. 150).

Table 8.7 *Pressure and suction compared*[a]

Area	Pressure	Suction
Output	In the short run brakes the increase in volume.	In the short run stimulates the increase in volume.
Inputs	Partial idleness of resources. Free combination of inputs.	Tight utilisation of resources. Forced substitution of inputs.
Technical progress	Stimulates introduction of revolutionary new products.	Does not stimulate introduction of revolutionary new products.
Quality	Stimulates improvements of quality and a high level of quality.	Does not stimulate improvements of quality or a high level of quality.
Competition	Sellers compete for buyers. Even the monopolist behaves 'like a competitor'.	Buyers compete for sellers. Even when there is a multiplicity of producers each producer behaves 'like a monopolist'.
Adaptation	Producers adapt to consumers in the short run. Producers attempt to establish product differentiation, brand loyalty and mould consumers.	Consumers adapt to producers in the short run. Sharp price adjustments needed occasionally.
Uncertainty	Burden of uncertainty carried by the seller.	Burden of uncertainty carried by the buyer.
Selection	Selection is made by buyer.	Selection is made by seller or central administrative organ.
	Generally progressive selection criteria.	Generally indifferent or counterproductive selection criteria.
Information flow	Generally the seller informs the buyer.	Generally the buyer seeks to obtain information about buying possibilities.
Social consequences	Generally unequal income distribution. Leads to demands for full employment. Efforts to deceive consumers. Waste of resources on advertising and marketing.	Generally equal income distribution. Leads to demands for economic reform. Creation of a market for elite where pressure rules. Creation of a black market where goods can be obtained – at a price.

[a] 'Pressure' and 'suction' correspond to a buyers' market and a sellers' market respectively.
Source: Adapted from Kornai (1971) p. 302.

places was still only a dream for the distant future. In the late 1970s and 1980s shortages in the USSR worsened and place of work distribution and local rationing grew in importance.

Rationing may exist not only for consumer goods but also for producer goods. The replacement of competition and flexible prices and quantities by rationing, as the allocation mechanism for producer goods, is an important feature of the traditional model. What effects on the economy are there of eliminating competition between firms, allocating producer goods via a rationing system and balancing supply and demand for consumer goods by increasing supply and maintaining prices stable (or even, if possible, reducing them)? The standard analysis of this question is by Kornai (1971 part III). His argument is summed up in table 8.7.

Looking at table 8.7 it is easy to see why capitalism is normally characterised by pressure. It brings rapid technical progress and benefits the upper income groups (as consumers). The costs (unemployment, insecurity of employment, inequality) primarily fall on the working class. It is equally clear why war-time capitalist economies move over to suction. It increases the volume of output; mobilises hitherto wasted inputs; and facilitates social peace by offering the workers full employment, security of employment, and greater equality. One can also see why the orthodox Marxist–Leninist view is that suction is preferable to pressure. It raises output in the short run, eliminates unemployment and insecurity of employment, and its adverse effects on consumption do not affect the elite because of the existence of special shops, sanatoria and hotels for the elite, where pressure rules. These special facilities also play a useful role in rewarding conformity.[5] The ill effects of suction on consumption are a major reason for the dissatisfaction with the traditional model by wide strata of the population in the state socialist countries. This is easy to understand once one appreciates that shortages and queues have major economic and social costs. These cover such things as the loss of leisure from standing in queues, the deterioration in social relationships (theft from the state, general disregard for the law, widespread dissemination of the petty trader mentality) and the loss of income resulting from the inability to spend money on desired goods or services at state prices. An attempt to measure the latter has been made by Collier (1985). He investigated the following question. How much income would a GDR family of four in 1977 have been prepared to give up if in return it could have been assured that the

---

[5] They also generate substantial popular dissatisfaction. One of the 21 demands of the August 1980 Gdansk strike committee was their abolition.

actual availability of goods in the GDR, at GDR prices, in the new lower money income situation would have been the same as in the FRG? In other words, what was the cost to the average GDR family of the fact that desired goods are often not available at state prices? He assumed that tastes in the two Germanies were the same, so that the typical GDR consumer, if faced by FRG prices and availabilities, would buy the same commodities as those actually bought by a typical FRG consumer with an equal real income. He estimated that the answer was 13 percent. This was a measure of the cost to consumers of forced substitution (i.e. the purchase of goods other than those actually wanted because the wanted goods were not available), transaction costs (e.g. bribes) resulting from shortages, the difference between state and second economy prices and extra savings held only because desired goods were unavailable at state prices. On the other hand it takes no account of the additional income which some people gain from the shortages. This is both monetary (e.g. bribes, second economy earnings) and in kind (e.g. the benefits to officials from the use of the housing and cars which they have been allocated at low prices). The additional income accrues to two groups of people, high officials by virtue of their position, and spivs (like Ostap Bender) by virtue of their trading ability and widespread contacts. It should be noted that the availability of goods in the GDR in 1977 compared quite well with that normal in the state socialist world.

Pressure in an economy divided into classes is accompanied by envy and class struggle. Suction, on the other hand, can give rise to widespread low morale and demoralisation.[6]

Kornai's argument stresses the advantage of competition, free entry and flexible prices and quantities, in a buyer's market, for stimulating technical progress and high quality. This corroborates the arguments of Schumpeter and J. M. Clark that the great merit of the competitive market economy is not that stressed by neoclassical economics, of driving prices down to costs and costs to a minimum.

---

[6] One phenomenon which accentuates popular dissatisfaction and demoralisation in state socialist countries is the existence of special shops where scarce, high quality and luxury goods can be obtained – for convertible currency only. This system, which was initiated in the USSR in the early 1930s, creates a privileged stratum with access to attractive consumer goods inaccessible to the mass of the population. The latter are naturally resentful. It is no accident that one of the 21 demands of the August 1980 Gdansk strike committee was the closing of these shops.

From the point of view of the authorities, sales in these shops are exports. Exports are necessary to pay for imports of machinery and grain and to service debt. Popular dissatisfaction and demoralisation, on the other hand, are so endemic that a little more seems to the authorities of little significance.

Rather it is the stimulus it provides to new goods and technical progress.

THE EFFECT ON CONSUMPTION OF THE TRANSITION FROM CAPITALISM TO STATE SOCIALISM

Judging by historical experience, the transition from capitalism to state socialism might be expected to have both positive and negative effects on consumption. On the negative side the following would seem to be the most important.

First, the costs of revolution (Bukharin 1920 chapter 6, Sakharov 1969, Ponchaud 1978). Revolutions result from internal and external political conflicts which have a major cost in terms of lives lost, physical destruction and loss of working time. This will reduce living standards.[7] In addition, the new regime may have to devote considerable resources (which might otherwise have been consumed) to repressing its internal enemies and/or fighting, or preparing to fight, its external enemies.

Secondly, there is the loss of the output of small-scale private enterprise. The suppression of artisans, small workshops, petty trade and small-scale private services can have a serious adverse effect on popular welfare.

Thirdly, once the state is transformed into the main engine of economic development, mistakes in economic policy can have a major – sometimes catastrophic – effect on consumption. Such mistakes are quite common.

Fourthly, the high share of investment in the national income of state socialist countries has an opportunity cost in terms of consumption forgone. Huberman and Sweezy (1969 p. 107) noted that this 'goes far to explain the extreme austerity of life in Cuba today, so much commented on by all visitors to the island'.[8]

Fifthly, the establishment of a shortage economy will lead to widespread queues, shortages and popular dissatisfaction.

On the positive side the following effects would seem to be the most important.

First, there are the gains to the poor from the distribution among

[7] Wiles (1974a p. 104) has noted that 'nothing harms the poor so much as a failed revolution, for that gives us the costs without the benefits ... I would put the odds against a revolutionary attempt, taken at random from human history, at three to one. This is a much more serious conservative argument than the futurity discount or the costs of a successful revolution.'

[8] Another factor causing the extreme austerity of Cuba in the late 1960s was the Maoist-Guervarist economic model.

them of the confiscated stocks of consumer goods of the rich (e.g. housing).

Secondly, to the extent that the level of production is not adversely affected, it is possible to redistribute the income which formerly accrued to the rich.

Thirdly, employment can be increased sharply.

Fourthly, security of employment can be introduced.

Fifthly, education and medical services can be extended to wider strata of the population and rapidly expanded.

Do the pluses outweigh the minuses, or vice versa? According to Huberman and Sweezy (1969 p. 108), writing about Cuba, but whose argument is perfectly general, the pluses clearly outweigh the minuses.

we must emphasise that Cuban austerity is not like that in the under-developed countries of the 'free world'. In the latter the burden of austerity is borne by the workers, peasants, unemployed, etc., whose incomes are extremely low or non-existent and who usually make up from 75 to 90 percent of the population. The middle strata live in relative comfort and the ruling oligarchies in outrageous luxury. The shops are full only because the price-income system keeps the vast majority from buying what is in them. To the superficial observer there appear to be no shortages; to most of the people there are nothing but shortages. How right was the Cuban boy who said to Yose Yglesias: 'If everyone in Mexico could afford to buy a pair of shoes, how many do you think would be left in the stores?'

The point is that in Cuba everyone *can* afford to buy a pair of shoes, and there are never any left in the stores. And the same goes for nearly all other consumer goods. The explanation is twofold: First, the minimum wage in Cuba is 85 pesos a month and a large percentage of workers get two or three times as much. Moreover, there is a labour shortage so that every able-bodied person can get a job and many families have two or more wage-earners. Second, average rents are very low, education and health and some other services are free, and rationed goods are cheap. The result is a large volume of 'free' purchasing power chasing after a very limited supply of goods. In these circumstances, the shortages which are hidden in other countries rise to the surface for all to see. What's more, they affect the entire population including the top management and the middle strata who would be comfortably off in other countries. In other words, *everyone* feels the shortages, and this sometimes gives the impression that they are a lot worse off than they really are.

For the truth is that the shortages which all Cubans have to bear are not nearly as bad as those which afflict the great majority of Latin Americans.

This verdict, however, is simply a repetition of the traditional Marxist–Leninist view point. To throw more light on the situation it is useful to calculate a synthetic social indicator, standardised for differences in economic development. This permits a simple numer-

Table 8.8 *Social indicators of the state socialist countries (ranks of indicators)*

Country (1)	Per capita GNP in		Life expec- tancy (4)	Stu- dents (5)	Health service (6)	Basic welfare (7)	Difference	
	1968 (2)	1970 (3)					D_1 (8=2−7)	D_2 (9=3−7)
GDR	15	12	6	36	3	15.0	0.0	−3.0
Czecho- slovakia	19	16	19	22	5	15.3	3.7	0.7
USSR	22	20	26	5	1	10.7	11.3	9.3
Hungary	23	23	27	37	9	24.3	−1.3	−1.3
Poland	26	24	23	21	23	22.3	3.7	1.7
Romania	28	31	32	26	26	28.0	0.0	3.0
Bulgaria	29	33	15	18	11	14.7	14.3	18.3
Albania	40	39	37	20	34	30.3	9.7	8.7
Cuba	43	41	35	46	35	38.7	4.3	2.3
Average	27.2	26.6	24.4	25.7	16.3	22.1	5.1	4.3

Source: Horvat (1974) p. 32.

ical comparison between welfare levels in the two systems. An attempt to do this has been made by the Yugoslav economist Horvat, whose work is reproduced in table 8.8.

The table was constructed in the following way. The sixty most developed countries for which there are statistics were ranked by various criteria. All the state socialist countries among them are listed in the above table. Column 5 ranks the number of tertiary students per ten thousand of the population. Column 6 is the arithmetic average of the rank of hospital beds per ten thousand of the population and the rank of physicians per ten thousand of the population. Column 7 is the average of columns 4, 5 and 6. Columns 8 and 9 give the differences, for each country and for the whole group of countries, between the ranking by GNP and that by basic welfare. For example, a figure of +5.0 in D_2 indicates that a country in 1970 had achieved a basic welfare level five places ahead of the world average for a country with its GNP per capita. Conversely a figure of −5.0 in D_2 indicates that a country in 1970 had only achieved a basic welfare level five places behind the world average for a country with its GNP per capita.

The table shows clearly that, using Horvat's method, both in 1968 and 1970 the state socialist countries had achieved significantly higher levels of basic welfare than the world average for countries with their GNP per capita.

Horvat's paper is interesting as a pioneering attempt to calculate standardised inter-system social indicators. It is also, as is natural with a pioneering work, rather crude. For example, its health service indicators are *partial* measures of *input*. They ignore some inputs, such as medicines and medical supplies, and fail to measure output, i.e. the good health of the population. For example, no hospital beds and one doctor in a country where oral contraceptives are available, may be at least as useful from a health point of view as twenty hospital beds used for abortions and ten doctors engaged in abortions and form filling. As a matter of fact, the Soviet death rate rose significantly in the Brezhnev period. The infant mortality rate and virtually all the age-specific death rates also rose in the Brezhnev period. Table 8.8 shows that in 1970 Soviet life expectancy was six places behind the world average for a country with its GNP per capita, while its Horvat health service index was nineteen places ahead. This simply indicates that measuring the *output* of a health service by the *inputs* it uses, is wrong. Furthermore, a number of important social indicators (e.g. those relating to housing) are omitted. In addition, the Horvat calculations are vulnerable to Seer's (1976) criticism of the UN's SSDS (System of Social and Demographic Statistics): it assumes that governments are benign. No attention, for example, is paid to statistics of the proportion of the population in detention. Although none of the state socialist countries publishes data on this awkward issue, it is well known that the number of detainees per thousand of the population is much higher in the USSR than in many capitalist countries.[9] Hence Horvat's calculations must be considered as a useful pioneering work in the calculation of standardised inter-system social indicators, but one to whose conclusions little significance can be attached.

A more recent attempt to estimate the effect of socialism on social indicators is Burkett (1985). He took an average of indicators of literacy, infant mortality and life expectancy at age 1 (the so-called PQLI or physical quality of life index) for 116 countries of whom 10 are socialist. He regressed a number of variables against this index and found that socialism had a significant position effect on the PQLI of a country, the size of which declined as average incomes increased and increased as the national homogeneity of the population declined. Burkett's paper is more sophisticated methodologically

---

[9] According to Shtromas (1977) the number of detainees in the USSR is about 2.5–3 million, i.e. 1–1.2 percent of the population. According to Medvedev (1979) it is 1.5–2 million, i.e. 0.6–0.8 percent of the population.

than that of Horvat, but as in the case of Horvat's study its conclusions must be approached with caution, for the following reasons.

The data, both that underlying the PQLI and that for GDP per capita, are far from perfect. Burkett considers the possibility of *random* errors in the PQLI data but not that of *systemic* errors. These are quite likely as a result of the important principle of partymindedness in economic statistics in state socialist countries (see chapter 2). Economic and social statistics in the state socialist countries are calculated and published in such a way as to create a favourable picture of the activities of the government. For example, Burkett uses the Soviet official infant mortality figure of 28 per thousand live births for 1974. This ignores, however, the fact that the USSR uses a definition of 'live birth' different from that of most other countries. Hence the internationally comparable figure for 'infant mortality' for the USSR for 1974 is not 28 but 32. It is very odd in an analysis which aims to throw light on systemic differences in PQLI not to examine the underlying data for systemic errors.

Furthermore, the choice of components for the PQLI index is arbitrary and throws only limited light on economic welfare. A number of indices not irrelevant to inter-system comparisons are omitted, e.g. the proportion of the population in detention, the proportion of informers in the population, the proportion of the national income devoted to the military and internal security sectors, the average length of time taken by a young person to acquire an independent dwelling, the proportion of the population who have died from famine in the twentieth century, the average time taken to do the family shopping per week ... Inclusion of these indices might well be not without consequences for the results of inter-system comparisons.

In addition, the Burkett calculations only refer to one point in time (the early 1970s). To draw inferences about the effect on welfare of economic systems in general (not just for a short period) would require a number of different observations.

An important merit of the various calculations of standardised inter-system social indicators that have been done up till now is that they draw attention to the achievements of the state socialist countries in the provision of public goods (e.g. education, public health) particularly relative to low-income capitalist countries.

COMMODITY NUMBER ONE

An important feature of personal consumption in the USSR (and Poland) is the role of alcohol. Alcohol consumption per head of the population is *not* exceptionally high in the USSR. It is in fact lower than in a number of capitalist countries (e.g. France). What is important about the Soviet case are:

(a) the share of strong drink (i.e. vodka) in total alcohol consumption (in Western Europe wine and beer are much more important). In the 1970s, spirit consumption per head in the USSR was probably higher than in any country in the world,
(b) the amount of drunkenness (this partly results from (a) and partly from the way alcohol is consumed),
(c) the share of alcohol in personal consumption,
(d) the income of the state budget generated by alcohol,
(e) the adverse effects of alcohol on labour productivity, and
(f) the suitability of alcohol for the traditional model.

Alcohol consumption per head in the USSR in the 1960s and 1970s was less than in countries such as France and Italy. The level of 'hard' drink consumption (i.e. vodka, whisky, gin etc.) per capita, however, was probably the highest in the world. The share of hard drink in total alcohol consumption was not uniquely high in the USSR (Poland and Japan had similar shares). What was unique about the Soviet case was the combination of a fairly high level of per capita consumption of alcohol with a high share of hard drink in total alcohol consumption. An important development in the USSR in the Khrushchev-Brezhnev period was the significant decline in the share of hard drink consumption in total alcohol consumption (from 85 percent in 1955 to 59 percent in 1979). This reflected the growing production and import of wine in this period. Data on Soviet consumption of alcohol is set out in table 8.9.

The table brings out clearly the substantial (but relatively declining) importance of illegal distilling, the substantial overall growth of alcohol consumption in the Khrushchev-Brezhnev period and the rapid growth in that period in consumption of weak drink (e.g. wine).

Drunkenness is a serious social problem in the USSR, resulting in numerous accidental deaths (e.g. car crashes), widespread diseases, domestic violence and marriage breakups, and adversely affecting life expectancy. The drunks lying around on the streets were long a familiar sight of Soviet cities. The USSR has a widespread network of sobering up stations where drunks are taken and left to sober up.

Table 8.9 *Consumption of pure alcohol in the USSR per person of 15 years old and over*

| Year | State-produced (or imported) beverages | | Samogon[a] | Total[b] | |
	All beverages	Strong beverages		All beverages	Strong beverages
1955	4.39	3.34	2.87	7.26	6.21
1960	5.52	3.90	2.93	8.45	6.83
1965	7.02	4.69	3.19	10.21	7.88
1970	9.54	5.35	3.33	12.87	8.68
1975	11.31	5.57	3.27	14.58	8.84
1979	11.94	5.71	3.30	15.24	9.01

Notes: [a] Illegally distilled vodka (analogous to moonshine in the USA).
[b] Excluding homemade wine and beer and stolen industrial alcohol.
Source: V. G. Treml, *Alcohol in the USSR* (Durham, NC 1982) p. 68.

According to Dudochkin (1981 p. 136) in the late 1970s in the USSR 12–15 percent of the adult population of the USSR ended up in sobering up stations annually.

The large share of household incomes spent on alcohol was a serious social problem in Tsarist Russia (Segal 1967 p. 226). It has remained one in the USSR. According to Treml (1982 p. 77) in the late 1970s and early 1980s about 15–20 percent of personal disposable incomes in the USSR were spent on alcohol. This was a very high proportion by international standards.

Alcohol sales bring in a very large income for the state budget. According to one estimate (Treml 1982 p. 32) taxes and profits from the production and sale of alcohol in 1982 were about 13 percent of the income of the state budget. Fiscal considerations are a major reason for the widespread use of alcohol in Tsarist Russia and the USSR. In 1913, taxes on spirits were a major source of state revenue and equalled about 5½ percent of the national income. Prohibition was introduced during the First World War but abolished in the early 1920s largely for fiscal reasons. (The official sale of vodka at the prewar strength, i.e. 40 percent, was resumed in 1925.) Stalin explained clearly the position of the party on the vodka question at the 14th Party Congress (1925). He stated that the need to rely on the revenue from vodka was disagreeable but essential, since it provided substantial funds for investment (about 10 percent of the income of the state budget derived from vodka in 1927).

The adverse effect of alcohol on labour productivity is notorious and a major cause of the Gorbachev anti-alcohol campaign. The 1914–15 cessation of the sale of vodka in Russia is often credited with increasing industrial labour productivity by at least 7 percent and Gorbachev hoped to achieve analogous results.

Alcohol as a consumption good fits in very well with the traditional model. It is easy to produce, very profitable for the state, does not require any after-sales service and performs the important ideological function of bringing some pleasure to the people and blotting out everyday problems, difficulties and frustrations.

In view of the economic and social problems it generates, the alcohol trade is periodically subjected to anti-alcohol campaigns in the USSR. In 1958/9 there was one such campaign, and in the early 1970s another. The Gorbachev campaign of the mid 1980s was particularly vigorous and far-reaching. Russian governments have been organising anti-drink campaigns since the seventeenth century but vodka has scarcely been eliminated. Alcohol abuse is no more likely to be abolished in the USSR than in the leading capitalist countries, where it is also a serious social problem and a useful source of revenue for the government.

CONCLUSION

The form which consumption planning has taken has varied very much over time and between countries depending on the concrete circumstances. A major method has been that of norms. This is a useful method, but has two weaknesses. These are, the arbitrary nature of many of the norms and the phenomenon of substitutability. The norms can be implemented by quantity and price adjustments. The former is the main method used in the traditional model. Price adjustments may be politically sensitive. They may also fail to establish equilibrium in the consumer goods market.

Shortages and queues are common under state socialism. Their intensity and their main causes vary over time and between countries. Important causes are, macro-economic disequilibrium in the state sector, disequilibrium relative prices, the (partial) elimination of the two feedback mechanisms which exist under capitalism, the behaviour of the planners and the organisation of the distribution sector. Shortages and queues have important consequences for the distribution of real income. Senior officials benefit from privileged access and spivs from their connections. They have considerable costs for the mass of the population and are a major reason for popular dissatisfaction with the traditional model.

One result of the inability of the official economy to satisfy all consumer needs is the existence of a large and flourishing second economy.

One way of tackling shortages and dealing with the second economy is that of economic reform. This has favourable effects on the availability of consumer goods and services but itself may give rise to social and economic problems. Other ways of dealing with shortages are monetary reform and rationing.

The general existence of seller's market conditions has an important effect not only on consumer satisfaction and real incomes but also on a wide range of economic phenomena, such as employment, job security, technical progress and information flows.

Experience has shown that the transition from capitalism to state socialism has both negative and positive effects on consumption. The calculation of standardised inter-system social indicators has not yet made much progress. Hence it is not yet possible to make well-based assertions about comparative welfare levels in the two systems. Work done up till now suggests that socialist countries have a relative advantage in the field of public goods, in particular in low-income countries, and capitalist ones in the field of private goods.

An important consumption good in the USSR is alcohol, which is produced in both the state and the private sector. Its sale has been encouraged by the state in some periods (for fiscal and ideological reasons) and restricted in other periods (because of its adverse effects on labour productivity).

SUGGESTIONS FOR FURTHER READING

P. Hanson, *The consumer in the Soviet economy* (London 1968).

P. Hanson, 'Acquisitive dissent', *New Society* (29 October 1970). This article is reprinted in P. Barker (ed.) *One for sorrow, Two for Joy: Ten years of New Society* (London 1972).

Economic aspects of life in the USSR (Brussels 1975)

B. Mieckowski, *Personal and social consumption in Eastern Europe* (New York 1975).

O. Sik, *The bureaucratic economy* (New York 1972) chapter 3.

A. Hegedus & M. Markus, 'The choice of alternatives and values in long range planning of distribution and consumption', A. Hegedus *et al.*, *The humanisation of socialism* (London 1976).

R. Huenemann, 'Urban rationing in Communist China', *China Quarterly* no. 26 (April–June 1966).

C. Howe, *China's economy* (London 1978) chapter 6.

A. Krasikov, 'Commodity number one', Part 1, R. Medvedev (ed.) *Samizdat Register I* (London 1977).

A. Krasikov, 'Commodity number one' Part 2, R. Medvedev (ed.) *Samizdat Register II* (London 1981).

V. Treml, *Alcohol in the USSR: A statistical study* (Durham NC 1982).

D. M. Nuti, 'Hidden and repressed inflation in Soviet-type economies', *Contributions to Political Economy* vol. 5 (March 1986).

China: Agriculture to the year 2000 (World Bank, Washington DC 1985) pp. 13–27.

I. L. Collier, *Connections, effective purchasing power and real product in the German Democratic Republic* (Berlin 1985) chapters I & II. A revised version of chapter II was published in *The Review of Economics and Statistics* vol. LXVIII, no. 1 (February 1986).

V. Tanzi (ed.) *The underground economy in the United States and abroad* (Lexington 1982).

A. Aslund, *Private enterprise in Eastern Europe* (London & New York 1985).

C. Davis & W. Charemza (eds.) *Modelling of disequilibrium and shortage in centrally planned economies* (London 1988).

L. Podkaminer, 'Estimates of the disequilibria in Poland's consumer markets, 1965–1978', *The Review of Economics and Statistics* vol. LXIV, no. 3 (August 1982).

L. Podkaminer, 'Persistent disequilibrium in Poland's consumer markets: some hypothetical explanations', *Comparative Economic Studies* vol. XXVIII, no. 3 (Fall 1986).

L. Podkaminer, 'On Polish disequilibrium once again', *Soviet Studies* vol. XXXIX, no. 3 (July 1987).

L. Podkaminer, 'Disequilibrium in Poland's consumer markets', *Journal of Comparative Economics* vol. 12, no. 1 (March 1988).

9

PLANNING INTERNATIONAL TRADE

If the free traders cannot understand how one country can get rich at the expense of another, we should not be surprised since they themselves are also not prepared to understand how, within a single country, one class can get rich at the expense of another class.

K. Marx, *The poverty of philosophy*

A proletarian state's foreign trade organisation in capitalist encirclement must serve two basic goals: (a) to facilitate as much as possible and to stimulate the development of the productive forces of the country, and (b) to defend the socialist economy under construction from economic attack by the capitalist countries. The whole difficulty of the problem of foreign trade organisation lies in the fact that a proletarian state cannot for a single minute lose sight of both these goals and, depending on the foreign situation and the needs of domestic socialist construction, must choose the appropriate forms of foreign trade organisation. It is absolutely indisputable that the slightest breach in the foreign trade monopoly would bring with it an increase in capitalist pressure on our socialist forms of economy and the inevitable widening of this breach would lead to a subjugation of our entire national economy to the more technologically developed economy of the capitalist countries, i.e. to the downfall of socialist construction. On the other hand, the preservation of the pace of development of the national economy necessary for building socialism requires a certain development and modification of the existing forms of carrying out the foreign trade monopoly.

Extract from the resolution 'On Foreign Trade' of the Central Committee of the Russian Communist Party (bolsheviks) of 5 October 1925

THE CRITIQUE OF THE CAPITALIST INTERNATIONAL DIVISION OF LABOUR

The Marxist-Leninist analysis of international trade is analogous to the Marxist-Leninist analysis of the labour market. Where liberal economists see fair exchange and mutual benefit, Marxist-Leninists see unequal exchange and exploitation. Standard expositions of the traditional Marxist-Leninist perspective can be found in Lenin's *Imperialism*, Sau (1978) and Carchedi (1986). From an analytical

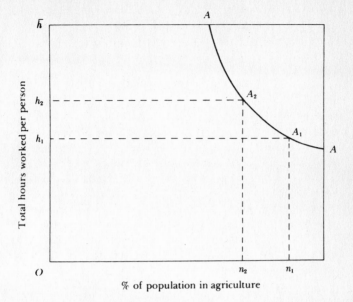

Figure 9.1 The pre-capitalist economy

point of view, it is clear that each school focuses on a different aspect of reality. The former concentrates on allocative efficiency and the latter on the dynamics of inequality. From an empirical point of view, the real issue is what proportion of actual historical experience is explained by each of the models. A neat illustration of the view of capitalist international trade which underlies much second and third world trade practice has been provided by Hymer and Resnick (1971) and is reproduced below.

Consider the standard problem of the gains from trade. To make the question more specific, we will analyse the Mercantilist era (*c.* fifteenth-nineteenth centuries). The situation in the pre-capitalist countries with which Portugal, Spain, the Netherlands, England and France traded is assumed to be as depicted in figure 9.1.

AA is an isoquant which is determined by the production function

$$\bar{d} = f\,(a, h, n) \tag{1}$$

where $\bar{d}$ is food produced (and consumed) per head,

a is output per man hour in agriculture,

h is hours worked per man in agriculture, and

n is the % of the population in agriculture.

Assume that $\bar{d}$ is given (for example by subsistence or custom) and a is given (by technology). The variables are h and n. Hence, comparing equilibrium positions, a lower n implies a higher h, and vice versa.

Consider the point A_1, assumed to represent the situation in pre-colonial Africa. The proportion of the population engaged in agriculture (n_1) is very high, and the hours of agricultural work of these people (h_1) are modest. Much time is availabe $(\bar{h} - h_1)$, after satisfying food requirements, for the production of rural household goods, for ceremonies and for leisure. The proportion of the population engaged in non-agriculture, $100 - n_1$, e.g. the ruler and his family, the aristocrats, soldiers, urban servants, clerks, urban traders and artisans (i.e. those termed non-productive by the physiocrats), is small.

Consider the point A_2, assumed to represent the situation in pre-colonial Asia. The non-agricultural proportion of the population $(100 - n_2)$ is larger than at A_1, and hence the hours worked in agriculture per agriculturist (h_2) is larger than at A_1, in order to provide food for the larger non-agricultural population.

Compare the welfare of the agricultural population (the great bulk of the total population) at A_1 and A_2. At both, food consumption per head is the same, but at A_2 hours of work in agriculture are higher than at A_1 because of the necessity of feeding the larger non-agricultural population. Except in the special case in which the agricultural population receives substantial benefits from the non-agricultural populations (e.g. irrigation systems which raise productivity in agriculture, or consumer goods) it seems reasonable to suggest that the welfare of the masses was higher at A_1 than at A_2.

Introduce (Mercantilist) trade into the model. In the African case the state grew. A military group that succeeded in monopolising coercive power in a given area could establish law and order for traders and levy taxes. The strength of the state could also be used to enslave part of the population and use it for export, either directly (as slaves) or indirectly (as slave-produced commodities such as gold). It was thus possible to appropriate a surplus through exploitation of labour as well as through the taxation of trade. As far as welfare is concerned, there were three significant effects. First, the state grew. Secondly, a proportion of the population was enslaved. Thirdly, there was an inflow of manufactured goods (e.g. whisky and guns). The first and third benefited the elite. The first and second were losses for the masses.

In the Asian case the state shrank. The indigenous 'oriental despotisms' were shattered. This was a clear gain to the local agricultural population. This gain was reduced, or eliminated altogether, however, in those areas where the Mercantilist traders levied significant taxes which fell, directly or indirectly, on the agricultural population.

In the Latin American case, contact with the Mercantilists led to the complete collapse of the local societies. Almost all the inhabitants of Mexico and Peru (and North America) were killed.

The gains and losses from Mercantilist trade are summarised in equation (2) below.

$$
\text{Gains from trade} \ (\equiv A) = \begin{bmatrix} \text{Gains to elites in Europe} \\ + \\ \text{Gains (or losses) to majority in Europe} \\ + \\ \text{Gains to elites in underdeveloped countries} \\ - \\ \text{Losses of exploited} \\ - \\ \text{Deadweight loss} \end{bmatrix} \quad (2)
$$

The question is, what is the sign of A? It is difficult to disagree with Hymer and Resnick's (1971 p. 482) view that, 'It is hard to imagine any reasonable set of calculations that would show that the value of the increase in world income during the sixteenth, seventeenth and eighteenth centuries could offset the tremendous costs associated with the murder and enslavement of Africans and Americans.'[1]

It is precisely to prevent the losses to the backward countries that, in the Marxist-Leninist view, unrestricted trade between advanced capitalist countries and backward countries brings, while obtaining the benefits of international trade, that state socialist countries create a state monopoly of foreign trade. The advantages of the state monopoly of foreign trade are fivefold. First, it enables the country concerned to use scarce foreign currency in the way that most facilitates rapid development (by cutting out imports of inessential goods and maximising imports of machinery). Secondly, it protects domestic industry. Thirdly, it insulates the economy from the law of value (e.g. it prevents capitalist recessions causing domestic

---

[1] The reasons why different conclusions follow in liberal models is because the latter treat the population as homogenous (rather than divided into classes), assume that welfare depends on marketed goods only, and assume that marketed output has two components, size and distribution, and that only the former is relevant for ascertaining 'efficiency'.

unemployment). Fourthly, it allows the country to use its monopoly power (as a seller) or monopsony power (as a buyer). Fifthly, it restricts capitalist influence over the development of the economy to a minimum. The problems of the state monopoly of foreign trade are threefold, strategic, technical and political. First, because state control of the economy tends to have an adverse effect on exports (see below), it may harm productivity and economic growth. Secondly, because the planners lack sufficient information and time to process it, they may make inefficient trading choices. Thirdly, the possibility of private individuals obtaining commodities they want from abroad (e.g. travel, books) or selling abroad commodities that they have produced (e.g. books, songs or wheat) is reduced.

Summary

The characteristic feature of socialist foreign trade is the state monopoly. This is based on a theory of trade between advanced and backward countries which stresses the losses which unrestricted commercial intercourse can bring the latter. State control of foreign trade has both advantages and problems.

THE SOCIALIST INTERNATIONAL DIVISION OF LABOUR

The disintegration of the single, all-embracing world market must be regarded as the most important economic sequel of the Second World War ... China and other, European, people's democracies broke away from the capitalist system, and, together with the Soviet Union, formed a united and powerful socialist camp confronting the camp of capitalism. The economic consequence of the existence of two opposition camps was that the single all-embracing world market disintegrated, so that we now have two parallel world markets, also confronting one another.

J. Stalin, *Economic problems of socialism in the USSR* (1952)

In this section five different models of socialist international trade will be considered. They are, the socialism in one country model, the socialist imperialism model, the international planning model, the socialist multilateralism model, and the economic integration model. Each model roughly corresponds to the actual historical experience of certain countries at certain times.

Socialism in one country

This model approximately corresponds to the experience of the USSR before 1945 and of China in 1960–78. In it the country concerned uses the state monopoly of foreign trade to ensure that scarce foreign exchange is used primarily to import machinery and thus accelerate economic growth. The country cuts itself off from the international labour and capital markets. The internal price level is insulated from world prices by the monopoly, the maximum possible volume of imports is acquired and the choice between possible imports is governed primarily by technological and political factors. Imports are paid for (apart from credits) by selling on the world market sufficient exports to generate the requisite foreign exchange, almost independently of domestic costs and profitability. The country regards the acquisition of technically advanced imports as the main object of foreign trade. In this it is unlike capitalist countries, which regard exports as the main desideratum in international trade. This is simply another example, analogous to those already encountered in chapters 6 and 8, of the general phenomenon that economic growth in the state socialist world is normally supply constrained. In the capitalist world, on the other hand, it is normally demand constrained.

One problem with this model is that it ignores the contradiction between the international nature of the productive forces and the nation state. This is less serious for huge countries such as the USSR and China, but it is very serious for smaller countries. Nevertheless, even for the USSR and China it has turned out to be a serious problem. In the USSR in 1986, as part of Gorbachev's campaign to raise the growth rate and in the wake of a sharp deterioration in the Soviet terms of trade, a decentralisation of the authority to make foreign trade decisions, a willingness to embark on joint ventures with firms from capitalist countries and an interest in participating in the work of GATT, were announced. These were cautious steps in the direction of reintegration into the world market. In China, as part of the post-1978 economic reform, major steps reintegrating the economy into the world market were undertaken. These included, a substantial delegation of powers to initiate foreign trade transactions, a great increase in foreign trade, foreign borrowing, joint ventures, the creation of special economic zones, the opening up of much of the country to foreign investment and the export of labour. Additional problems with the model are that the level and static efficiency of both imports and exports are often inadequate and also the country is unable to gain the dynamic growth and efficiency enhancing effects of an expanding and competitive export sector.

Socialist imperialism

At the end of the Second World War Soviet troops occupied much of Eastern and Central Europe, China and Korea. The USSR used the dominant political position which she acquired in this way to benefit herself economically and to impose her ideas on economic organisation on some of her neighbours. She removed machinery from East Germany, Hungary and Romania.[2] She reoriented trade towards herself,[3] and established companies with joint Soviet-local ownership and Soviet management in East Germany, China, Bulgaria, Hungary, Romania, Yugoslavia and Czechoslovakia which partly produced goods for the USSR.[4] She imposed an oppressive and inefficient agricultural system, a high share of investment and defence in the national income, and an economic model which

[2] 'Stalin showed himself a vastly more efficient extractor and recipient of direct tribute in 1945–52 than France and Britain in 1919–31. Indeed, since Mercantilism there has been nothing like it. The very notion that there was some difficulty in absorbing tribute would have seemed utterly astonishing to him: an example of the "internal contradictions of capitalism" too comical to be true. His own problems, although they were grave and caused terrible waste, affected only his procurement machinery. Once he had reformed that, reparations paid off handsomely' (Wiles 1968 p. 488).

[3] She is also widely believed to have manipulated the terms of trade in her own favour. Firm evidence for this is sparse. The best known example is Polish coal, of which the USSR bought *c*. 50,000,000 tons in 1946–53 at very low prices. This, however, was part of a deal made in 1945, whereby Poland received all German assets in Poland plus a share of the reparations due to be received by the USSR from Germany. In 1956, the USSR cancelled Poland's outstanding debt to the USSR ($626 million) in compensation for the losses Poland had incurred through selling her coal very cheaply.

[4] According to the Yugoslav Ministry of Foreign Affairs (*White book* 1951 pp. 37–8), in the Yugoslav case, as far as these companies were concerned, 'The formal parity (in ownership between the USSR and Yugoslavia) ... was only a screen to conceal direct exploitation and appropriation of profits by the utilisation of Yugolavia's natural resources and of the values created by the labour of the Yugoslav working people ... The two following examples are sufficient to reveal the way these companies were operated to the detriment of Yugoslavia. The JUSPAD (Yugoslav-Soviet Danube Shipping Stock Company) transported Soviet cargo at the price of 12–18 para for one kilometer-ton, while the price was 42 para for Yugoslav cargo. The JUSTA (Yugoslav-Soviet Stock Company for Civil Air Transport) took over complete control of civil air navigation in Yugoslavia even refusing to give the Yugoslav state air transport authorities the data needed for their control work. The operation of these mixed companies at the expense of the Yugoslav economy is but a pale picture of the degree of exploitation that would have resulted from the establishment of a number of mixed manufacturing companies, which the Soviet Government had been proposing to Yugoslavia. In such companies undoubtedly, the exploiting tendencies would have been much greater.'

disregarded personal consumption, throughout Eastern Europe. Soviet behaviour towards her dependants in this period was much less favourable to them than US behaviour towards her dependants.[5]

The main burden of socialist imperialism fell on what was first of all the Soviet occupation zone of Germany and then became the German Democratic Republic. According to one source (Marer 1974), in 1945–60 Soviet Zone/GDR net transfers to the USSR were about 19 milliard current US dollars.[6] This huge sum represented between a fifth and a third of Soviet Zone/GDR GNP in 1946–53 and exceeded the total flow of Marshall Aid to all Western Europe. According to an estimate quoted in the same source, Soviet Zone transfers were about 3 percent of Soviet national income in 1950 and higher percentages in the immediate post-war years. The burden on the Soviet Zone/GDR was greater than the gain to the USSR because of the inefficient dismantling of machinery.

Economic relations between the USSR and Eastern Europe (especially the Soviet Zone of Germany) in this period, were analogous to those between the Soviet Government and Soviet collective farms under Stalin. In both cases coercion was used to collect tribute. In both cases the Soviet Government collected a substantial revenue in this way. In both cases, however, there was a substantial cost in terms of low rates of growth of labour productivity, high costs of production and poor development of quality and technical progress, and a sullen resentful attitude by the labour force. Because the collective farmers are geographically isolated, in their case the latter never led to any very strong resistance. In the foreign trade case, however, because of the existence of nation states and compact groups of workers in industrial cities, it led to the break with Yugoslavia in 1948, the demonstrations by the German workers in 1953 and the Polish workers in 1956.

In 1953–6 the USSR radically changed her policies. The legitimacy of varying roads to socialism was recognised. The Soviet shares of the mixed companies were returned to the host countries and reparations were ended. (The removal of machinery had already

[5] At the end of the Second World War, during which the USSR had liberated all Eastern Europe from the Nazis, her economic situation was extremely grave. Much of her manpower had been killed in the war and her richest industrial and agricultural areas devastated. The United States, on the other hand, suffered relatively few casualties and greatly expanded her output during the war. In addition, the Marshall plan brought the United States major political and economic gains.

[6] Other estimates are still higher. One plausible estimate is 65 milliard 1938 marks, which equals *c*. 26 milliard 1938 US dollars.

ended in 1946.)[7] The prices at which CMEA has traded since the early 1950s have persistently been more favourable for the exporters of finished products than for the exporters of raw materials. As a result the USSR, which mainly exports raw materials and imports machinery, has generally had worse terms of trade inside CMEA than those that prevailed on the world market (Marer 1972). In addition, the USSR extended (mainly by way of trade) substantial economic assistance towards China, notably by providing the designs, machinery and many of the specialists for the construction of the majority of the modern industrial plants, the building of which constituted the core of the Chinese First Five Year Plan (1953–7). These economic policy changes were part of the general attempt to replace coercion by cooperation in the relationship between the Soviet Government and its subjects which characterised 1953–6. (Another example is Soviet agricultural policy.) Similarly, during the 1960s and 1970s the USSR provided Cuba with designs, machinery and specialists for industrialisation, substantial credits, and rela-tively. attractive export markets. In addition, in the 1970s and 1980s the USSR has provided economic assistance to Vietnam.

By the mid 1970s, CMEA had become something of an economic burden for the USSR. It required the USSR to supply valuable raw materials such as oil to allies on terms less favourable than those prevailing on the capitalist world market. In addition, assistance to countries such as Cuba and Vietnam was costly. A big difference between the pattern normal in the capitalist world and that in the CMEA between a dominant power and the dependent states it trades with, is the 'colonial' character of Soviet trade with Eastern Europe. The USSR mainly exports raw materials (e.g. oil and gas) to Eastern Europe and predominantly imports machines and equipment from them. The 'colonial' pattern of trade, combined with the higher living standards in countries such as the GDR, Czechoslovakia and Hungary than those in the USSR, clearly demonstrate that the USSR does *not* behave relative to her dependents in a classical imperialist way. By the late 1970s, perhaps the main economic gainers from the CMEA were its less developed members, such as Bulgaria, Cuba and Vietnam. These gained guaranteed export markets, stable supplies of

[7] It was very inefficient. In Germany, the Soviet organisations concerned often 'failed to pack, label or despatch properly. Very many priceless assets were simply destroyed or lost. Meanwhile, the ministries quarrelled vehemently over who should have what, and the military government found it impossible to set any upper limit to dismantling. Hence a party arose within the military government and the Ministry of Foreign Trade … that favoured the better organised and less destructive process of taking reparations out of current production' (Wiles 1968 p. 488).

Table 9.1 *CMEA population of members at the end of 1986 (millions)*

Member	Population
Bulgaria	9.0
Cuba	10.2
Czechoslovakia	15.6
GDR	16.6
Hungary	10.6
Mongolia	2.0
Poland	37.6
Romania	22.9
USSR	281.7
Vietnam	61.7

Source: Statistischeskii ezhegodnik stran chlenov soveta ekonomicheskoi vzaimopomoshchi 1987 (Moscow 1987) p. 7.

raw materials and the possibility of reexporting for hard currency raw materials imported from the USSR.

Nevertheless, relations between the state socialist countries have continued to be characterised not only by cooperation but also by conflict. The deterioration in Sino-Soviet relations after 1958 led to the withdrawal of Soviet specialists in 1960 and a rapid decline in mutual trade, similar to the decline in trade which followed the Soviet-Yugoslav dispute in 1948. Within CMEA the USSR has always occupied a dominant position. CMEA was established on the initiative of the USSR. Its headquarters are in the capital of the USSR. Its policies are largely determined by the USSR. This is inevitable in view of the enormous disproportion in population and output between the USSR and the other members (see table 9.1).

Table 9.1 shows that a single country, the USSR, accounts for about 60 percent of the entire population of CMEA. In this respect, CMEA is an organisation similar to the Zollverein. It is an economic organisation entirely dominated by one member, in the latter case Prussia, in the former the USSR. This has aroused considerable dissatisfaction in some of the other members. From the early 1960s the Romanians repeatedly counterposed national independence and national development to CMEA integration, which they regarded as an expression of Soviet national interests and a threat to their rapid industrialisation and national sovereignty. Many people in the more advanced CMEA countries consider that the structure of foreign trade and production which CMEA has imposed on them are not in their own best interests. In 1965, E. Apel, the Chairman of the GDR planning commission, committed suicide, after prolonged trade negotiations with the USSR, allegedly in protest against the planned trade agreements between the GDR and USSR for 1966–70. In 1968 it was widely asserted in Czechoslovakia, that concentration on the import of Soviet raw materials, their processing and the export of the finished products to the USSR, was not in the best interests of Czechoslovakia. The country would be better off, it was often said, producing producer and consumer goods for export to Western Europe and for domestic use. This would have a beneficial effect on the technical level of production and on home consumption. Similarly, the large defence effort imposed on the East European countries by the USSR is a serious burden for them.

Furthermore, the substantial aid which the USSR has given to the less developed members of the CMEA has itself given rise to conflicts. These have been of two types. First, the USSR has pressed, and the East European countries have resisted, the idea that more aid be given by the East Europeans. Secondly, in the mid 1980s the USSR became very concerned about the low efficiency with which its aid was being used. Whereas Vietnam accepted this criticism and engaged in self-criticism, Cuban officials were less self-critical and stressed the costs for Cuba of the hostile environment (US economic warfare).

Not only is the CMEA dominated by a single member, but its members also differ sharply between themselves in the level of development and the relative importance of trade with different blocs. This creates acute conflicts of interest. For example, whereas for Cuba 'overcoming the legacy of unequal exchange' (i.e. securing favourable prices for its sugar exports) is of great importance, for Czechoslovakia and the GDR low prices for raw material imports from the third world are advantageous. Whereas Bulgaria and Czechoslovakia have great need of the Soviet market, to which their exports are largely oriented, for Hungary access to the West European market is of great importance. These conflicts of interest make the formulation and implementation of agreed policies difficult.

Some data on the direction of trade of the CMEA members is set out in table 9.2.

This table illustrates, the declining share of intra CMEA trade in total trade in 1970–83, the growing importance of trade with the advanced capitalist countries, and the very wide dispersion between members in the share of trade with CMEA and in share of trade with the advanced capitalist countries.

Table 9.2 *Foreign trade of CMEA members by trade bloc in 1970 and 1983 (in %)*[a]

Country \ destination \ origin	CMEA countries		Developed capitalist countries	
	1970	1983	1970	1983
CMEA as a whole	60.8	58.6	23.7	26
of which				
Bulgaria	74.4	77.1	17.0	12.1
Hungary	62.4	49.6	24.8	33.3
Vietnam	–	79.2[b]	–	13.8
GDR	67.3	62.5	25.9	29.4
Cuba	–	83.1	–	9.4
Mongolia	–	97.2	–	1.2
Poland	63.1	68.5	27.1	21.6
Romania	49.3	47.7	35.8	23.8
USSR	55.6	51.2	21.2	30.1
Czechoslovakia	64.2	71.9	22.4	16.6

Notes: [a] The exchange rates used to aggregate the trade flows probably lead to an exaggeration of the share of CMEA trade in total trade.
[b] 1982.
Source: O. T. Bogomolov, *Strany sotsialisma v mezhdunarodnom razdelenii truda* 2nd edn (Moscow 1986) p. 292.

International planning

In the 1950s CMEA made the transition from the socialist imperialism model to the socialism in one country model, modified by bilateral trade. Each country planned its own development, its plans including a substantial and growing volume of bilateral trade with its CMEA partners. This, however, was insufficient to overcome the contradiction between the international nature of the productive forces and the nation state. The members of CMEA, with their existing institutions, were unable to capture all the gains that might have been available from specialisation and economies of scale. The rapid development of economic integration in the capitalist world, particularly in Western Europe, made them increasingly aware of this. In 1960 the Polish leader Gomulka observed of the relations between CMEA members, 'There is no cooperation whatsoever in the important sector of investment: everyone peels his own turnip – and loses by it.'

Accordingly, in 1962, Khrushchev suggested that CMEA should establish 'a unified planning organ, empowered to compile common plans and to decide organisational matters'. Marxists consider that within any nation the efficient allocation of resources requires national planning, as explained in chapter 1. Similarly, Khrushchev argued in 1962, the efficient allocation of resources within CMEA requires supranational, CMEA-wide, planning. This planning, it was suggested, should concern itself primarily with investment.

Nevertheless, CMEA was not transformed into a supranational planning organisation, for two reasons. First, Romania, as a less developed country, objected on classical Listian[8] grounds to supra-national investment planning based on current comparative costs. Secondly, in the early 1960s, it became increasingly realised within CMEA that there was a contradiction between seeking to raise efficiency and striving to increase still further the role of central planning. It was precisely at this time that there was widespread discussion of how, given the development of the productive forces and the techniques of planning, planning was hindering efficiency. Hence the focus of discussion within CMEA on measures to improve its *modus operandi* switched from strengthening the planning element to strengthening market relations.

Socialist multilateralism

According to standard Western theory, bilateralism in international trade is bound to lead to waste. It either constrains the volume of trade to the export potential of the country with the lesser export potential, or forces the country with a greater export potential to accept goods which it does not want very much. This argument has been applied to CMEA by van Brabant (1973, 1974) and Ausch (1972). Ausch's analysis is set out in figures 9.2, 9.3 and 9.4. In figure 9.2, the arrows indicate the direction of trade and the number of the volume. For example, A imports 40 units from B and exports 80 units to B. Trade is multilateral and each country is in balance of trade equilibrium. Total trade volume is 240. Under conditions of bilater-alism with the export constraint operative, trade will take place as in figure 9.3. Total trade volume is 120. Welfare is substantially less than in the multilateral case. In figure 9.4, h indicates hard commodi-ties, i.e. goods that are really wanted, and s soft ones, i.e. goods that are not much wanted. In a situation of bilateralism with soft com-modities, the volume of trade is 360. This is more than in the multi-lateral case, but one third of the trade consists of the import of soft

---

[8] List was a nineteenth-century German economist. He argued that free trade is only in the interest of the advanced countries and that backward countries require protection if they are to industrialise.

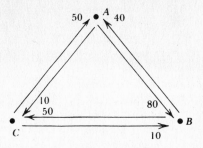

Figure 9.2 Multilateral trade

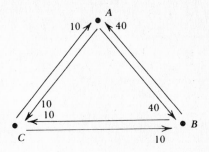

Figure 9.3 Bilateralism with the export constraint operative

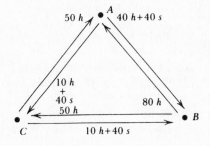

Figure 9.4 Bilateralism with soft commodities

commodities. Hence welfare may well be less than in the multilateral case. The softness of much of the trade taking place may be confirmed by the activities of capitalist import-export firms, re-exporting the soft goods and supplying hard ones in exchange, thus introducing elements of *de facto* multilateralism. Figure 9.4 also illustrates how the traditional model can generate a discrepancy between output levels and welfare levels.

The merits of multilateralism have been recognised in CMEA circles since the mid 1950s. In 1957 and 1963 agreements were reached between the members on multilateral clearing. The 1963 agreement created a special organ for this purpose, the Bank for International Economic Cooperation, accounts with which are kept in transferable roubles. (The transferable rouble is an inconvertible unit of account used for CMEA trade. It is basically just a new name for the 'clearing rouble', the unit of account for the bilateral trade between the USSR and other socialist countries, used from 1950. The new name signified a recognition in principle of the desirability of moving towards multilateralism and convertibility.) In the agreement setting up this bank it is stated that 'within one year from the foundation of the Bank ... the Board will study ways of introducing into the scope of its operations transacted in transferable roubles, the possibility of a conversion into gold or freely convertible currencies'. Nevertheless, currencies remained inconvertible and trade bilateral throughout the first four decades of the CMEA's history. Each member of CMEA strove for strictly balanced bilateral trade with each of her CMEA partners and for each calendar year.[9] Why is this?

The fundamental reason concerns the internal economic institutions of the USSR. Bilateralism in foreign trade is simply one specific example of the traditional model in action.

In the bilateral case, trade is carried on in accordance with instructions. Prices, which are important for accounting and aggregation, are barely relevant for allocative purposes. In the multilateral case, the volume and composition of trade is largely determined by relative prices. The price system of the traditional model, however, is most unsuitable for allocative purposes. For one thing, internal and external prices are separated. This means that an enterprise cannot realistically compare domestic and foreign prices with a view to making trade decisions. For another, the price a country obtains for its exports varies very much between its export markets. An example is set out in table 9.3.

---

[9] Strictly speaking, the trade is not even fully bilateral, since the members seek to balance their trade in hard and soft goods taken separately. A major part of CMEA discussions and trade negotiations consists of each country trying to export soft goods and simultaneously increasing the hardness of its imports. (In CMEA practice, 'hard' goods are those which rank high in the preferences of planners, e.g. because they can easily be sold on the capitalist world market for hard, i.e. convertible, currency, or are particularly short domestically. 'Soft' goods are those which have no hard currency market or to which the planners attach little importance. In the 1970s, examples of hard goods were oil and other raw materials, and of soft goods food and products of light industry.)

Table 9.3 *Price differences in Hungary's exports to CMEA countries in the mid 1960s*

Major commodity groups	Number of commodities exported to two or more countries	Number of commodities showing price differences exceeding 25 per cent (differences in per cent)								Total
		25–34	35–44	45–54	55–69	70–9	80–9	90–9	100 and over	
Machinery and equipment	608	42	25	10	21	11	2	8	20	139
Fuels and other materials (including metals)	52	3	8	3	6	2	–	–	3	25
Chemical products (including rubber)	18	1	–	1	1	–	–	–	1	5
Construction materials	10	–	–	–	–	–	–	–	–	–
Agricultural raw materials (excluding those used for food)	16	–	1	–	2	–	–	–	2	5
Live animals	–	–	–	–	–	–	–	–	–	–
Raw products for the food industry	2	–	–	–	–	–	–	–	–	–
Finished food products	66	5	5	3	6	3	1	1	3	27
Industrial consumer goods	248	20	11	13	13	7	6	6	16	92
Total	1,020	71	50	30	49	24	9	15	45	293

Source: Ausch (1972) p. 80

As can be seen from table 9.3, for many exports to CMEA countries, the same commodity can vary in price by more than 100 percent depending on which country it is sold to. In addition, the relative prices of primary and processed goods differ inside CMEA and on the world market. Furthermore, the CMEA countries operate a multiple exchange rate system.

Given all these price discrepancies, only administrative control over trade can preserve the present volume and structure of trade. The transition to multilateralism in foreign trade would require a reform of the price system so as to enable it to replace many of the administrative procedures which currently determine the volume and direction of foreign trade. Hence, foreign trade remained bilateral and currencies inconvertible while the USSR adhered to the traditional model. In the late 1980s, the need for convertibility and multilateralism received renewed attention in CMEA circles. This resulted from *perestroika*, the USSR's creditor position within the CMEA and the success of EEC integration. As a first step towards convertibility, a limited commodity convertibility of the transferable rouble into Soviet goods was planned for 1989. The subsequent introduction of a convertible transferable rouble (to replace the dollar for hard currency trade between CMEA members) seemed possible. These developments demonstrated the importance of the internal Soviet model, the interests of the USSR and the competition of the two systems for the CMEA.

Economic integration

The gains from adding to our mutual economic possibilities [within CMEA] are not measured, of course, only by purely commercial accounting.

L. I. Brezhnev (speech at the 26th Party Congress, 1981)

The abandonment in the late 1960s in Czechoslovakia and the USSR of a reform of the traditional model both internally and within CMEA, led to the emergence of a new model of CMEA cooperation, that of economic integration. This was clearly embodied in the 'Comprehensive programme for the deepening and improvement of collaboration and the development of socialist economic integration of the CMEA countries' adopted in Bucharest in 1971. The objective of economic integration is to maximise the gains from economies of scale, specialisation and participation in the international division of labour. Economic integration takes such forms as trade, industrial cooperation, movement of labour, technical and scientific cooperation, energy integration, the financing of investment, the creation

Table 9.4 *Growth of CMEA trade (milliards of current US dollars)*

Year	Total exports by CMEA countries	Of which exports by CMEA countries to their CMEA partners	Exports to other CMEA countries as percentage of total exports[a]
1948[b]	3.2	1.4	44
1950	4.2	2.5	60
1955	8.0	4.8	60
1960	13.2	8.1	61
1965	20.0	12.5	62
1970	30.9	19.3	62
1975[c]	77.4	44.4	57
1980	156.1	77.2	49
1983	174.6	87.7	50

[a] Because of price differences between intra-CMEA trade and world market trade, for most of the period these figures exaggerate the share of intra-trade in total trade. The differences between the data in this table and in table 9.2 probably result from the use of different exchange rates to aggregate the trade flows.
[b] CMEA was founded in 1949.
[c] Cuba, which joined the CMEA in 1972, and Vietnam which joined in 1978, are excluded throughout.
Sources: Kaser (1967) p. 144 (for 1948–65 inc); UN *Yearbooks of international trade statistics* (for 1979–83).

and operation of socialist common enterprises, and plan coordination.

A major aspect of CMEA integration is the coordination of the trade plans of the member states. This has facilitated a substantial increase in trade.[10] Some data are set out in table 9.4. In the 33 years 1950–83 the exports of CMEA rose 42 times (in current prices). It is interesting to observe that the share of their exports to each other in their total exports, which fluctuated around 60 percent in 1950–72, fell sharply in the period in which the integration model was supposedly being implemented. About 60 percent in the year the

[10] Some trade is discouraged by the plans. Foreign trade plans naturally tend to consist of the trade that took place in some base year, adjusted upwards by some percentage. Hence if a country wants to sell goods, e.g. the results of a good harvest for one year only, and does not wish to enter into a commitment to supply increasing quantities of them indefinitely, it will strive either not to sell them within CMEA or to exclude them from the basis and sell them on a one-off 'outside the plan' framework. For example, in the 1970s, Hungary sold the USSR agricultural products, and bought from the USSR industrial raw materials, settlement being in US dollars. This trade took place outside the framework of the five year Hungarian-Soviet foreign trade plan so that it should not be included in the basis.

comprehensive programme was adopted, it had fallen to about 50 percent a decade later. Major factors explaining this were the increase in world energy prices that enabled the USSR to increase greatly the income from its oil and gas sales to the capitalist world and the Soviet policy of using this windfall income to finance imports of grain and machinery. This illustrates the general thesis that plans are only one of the factors influencing economic outcomes, the environment and policy being others and often more important in determining the outcome.

Integration is concerned not just with trade but primarily with the structure of production. The members of CMEA try to coordinate their medium- and long-term planning to cut out duplication of production and gain the maximum benefits from economies of scale and specialisation. This coordination takes various forms.

One is the specialisation of production of particular products in one country, with all CMEA providing a market, e.g. buses in Hungary. In this way the producer can hope to gain the maximum economies of scale and consumers the possibility of using their resources more efficiently elsewhere. This has not been very success-ful. The main problem has been the predominance of finished products in cooperation projects and inadequate specialisation in the production of components. This situation, which compares unfavourably with that in Western Europe, appears to be an example, on the international level, of the adverse effects on an economy of the rationing of producer goods (see chapter 2 above).

Another is the supply of labour by one member to another. By the mid 1970s there were probably about 150,000 workers from CMEA countries working in other CMEA countries. A large share of the foreign workers are employed in the GDR, where the labour shortage is most acute. There are also foreign workers elsewhere. The pro-vision of labour is one of the ways countries such as Bulgaria and Vietnam meet their obligations. The movement of labour between CMEA countries (and from countries such as Yugoslavia to CMEA countries) is hindered by currency inconvertibility. Intra-CMEA movement of labour is distinguished from South-West labour move-ment by its small scale; its organised, inter-governmental character; and the fact that foreign workers do not seem to be employed mainly in unskilled poorly paid jobs.

Another area of integration is the joint research and development programme. An example is the joint R & D programme carried out (under an agreement signed in 1972) in the field of numerically controlled machine tools. Scientific and technical cooperation between CMEA members has a long history prior to the emergence of joint R & D programmes. For many years a major form of scientific and technical cooperation took was the free provision of scientific and technical documents, i.e. designs for new machines, products and processes. This was attractive to the less developed CMEA members, but unattractive to the more advanced members. In 1985 the CMEA adopted long-term joint research programmes in electronics, automation, nuclear energy, raw materials and biotechnology (see below).

A well-known and very tangible example of integration is the 5,500 km Druzhba oil pipeline which carries Soviet oil to Hungary, Poland, GDR and Czechoslovakia. Another is the 2,750 km Soyuz gas pipeline from Orenburg in the USSR to Eastern Europe. Hungary, GDR, Poland, Czechoslovakia and Bulgaria all helped to build it (as did West Germany which supplied pipes and France which supplied technical training) and received gas deliveries from 1979 onwards in exchange. In addition, the Mir united electric power grid allows members to lend or borrow electricity during peak periods and also to export (or import) electricity. The reliability of the joint electricity supply system, however, is imperfect. When there have been acute regional power shortages (as in the winter of 1984/5) some members have used more electricity than they were entitled to, at the expense of other members. Nevertheless, integration in the energy area (largely the import of Soviet oil and natural gas by the other CMEA members) has been one of the major activities of CMEA. It provides the smaller CMEA countries with an essential raw material, and the USSR with a means of paying for imports from Eastern Europe and a potent political lever. Despite this, East European imports of OPEC crude rose sharply in the 1970s. In determining export markets for oil and gas, the USSR has to balance its hard currency requirements against CMEA integration.

This latter fact illustrates the general proposition that the continued inconvertibility of the CMEA currencies is a serious problem for CMEA. It tends to ensure that the best quality goods go to the capitalist world and that it is only goods of lesser quality, or top quality goods in smaller quantities than are required, that go to other CMEA countries. This is simply an expression of one of the oldest propositions in economics, Gresham's Law, applied to barter trade. In effect, within CMEA two types of goods (and the corresponding forms of money) circulate, bad or soft goods and good or hard goods. As Gresham's Law leads one to expect, bad drives out good, so that it is difficult to obtain from a CMEA partner as much as one wants of goods that are hard. CMEA trade expands, but so do the frustrations of its members, who are unable within CMEA to obtain in sufficient quantities the goods they most want, due to institutional limitations.

Since 1971, CMEA has had a bank, the International Investment Bank, which extends credits for investments, i.e. project loans. (The IIB is analogous to the EEC's European Investment Bank (EIB) or the World Bank (IBRD).) Also in the financial field, the members of CMEA were committed by the comprehensive programme to study, in 1976–9, the possibility and procedures for establishing single rates of exchange between their currencies. The plan was to make a decision on this matter in 1980. Nothing happened in this area in 1980, due to the unwillingness at that time of the USSR to abandon the traditional model.

In addition, within CMEA there are socialist common enterprises ('socialist multinationals'). An early example was Haldex, the Polish-Hungarian concern for processing coal dumps. Other examples are Interatomenergo, the huge organisation created in 1973 to develop and construct nuclear power stations for all CMEA, and the cotton mill 'Friendship', jointly owned by the GDR and Poland and founded in 1972. Most of the socialist common enterprises have a bilateral character. As a result of the growth and usefulness of socialist common enterprises, CMEA adopted in 1976 the 'Uniform principles for the creation and functioning of international economic organisations'. This document was intended to provide a legal framework for the socialist common enterprises. It put forward two main principles. First, that the activities of socialist common enterprises should be governed strictly by economic criteria. Secondly that each socialist common enterprise should be governed by the economic and financial regulations of the country where its headquarters are. The absence of single exchange rates and uniform prices are big problems for these joint enterprises. According to Zubkov (1979 p. 59) while these problems are not resolved, in every case special coefficients have to be used to convert costs into the national currencies of the participating countries. In one case, it was necessary to use 14 main coefficients and 30 auxiliary coefficients for this purpose. It is obvious that such a multiplicity of coefficients introduce the possibility of arbitrary decisions, conflicts of national interests and manipulation.

An important aspect of CMEA integration is plan coordination. During the 1970s, the members of CMEA devoted increasing efforts to coordinating their medium- and long-term plans, and these plans formed the basis for their long-term trade agreements. Two other important aspects of plan coordination are the CMEA comprehensive programmes and the joint investment projects.

CMEA comprehensive programmes are an innovation of the late 1970s which are an application on the international level of the programme approach already applied internally (see chapter 8 for a brief discussion of consumption programmes). In July 1976, the 30th session of CMEA, meeting in Berlin, agreed to discuss five comprehensive programmes to be implemented in a ten to fifteen year period. Three were adopted in 1978 and two in 1979. In 1985 the 41st session of CMEA adopted a comprehensive programme of scientific and technical progress up to the year 2000. This was a joint research and development programme for five key areas of technical progress. They were electronics, automation, nuclear energy, new materials and biotechnology.

Examples of the joint investment projects are the Kiyembayev asbestos project in the Urals, the Ust' Ilim cellulose plant in Eastern Siberia and a nickel-cobalt mine in Cuba. The countries supplying the investment resources receive in return some of the output when the project is functioning. These joint investment projects have given rise to considerable conflicts. The smaller East European countries have striven to limit their contributions to them, the USSR to increase them. Another problem is the calculation of costs and national contributions for projects undertaken by countries with relative prices which differ between countries and from those on the world market and with multiple exchange rates. Because of all these problems, the actual volume of joint investments (7 billion transferable roubles in 1976–80 and 2 billion transferable roubles in 1981–5) has been considerably below the planned volume (9 billion transferable roubles in 1976–80 and 4.5 billion in 1981–5). This shows that the same economic mechanism which generates excess investment internally limits investment cooperation internationally. On the whole, it seems most appropriate to interpret these joint investments as a combination of a price rise for the exporters with a hardening of the structure of counter-deliveries received by them (Csaba 1985). They result, basically, from inconvertibility and bilateralism, which simultaneously partially demonetise international trade and generate goods of various degrees of hardness and softness.

The CMEA integration programme has failed to provide an attractive alternative to the world market for the CMEA members. When world commodity prices (especially oil) were rising, Soviet exports of these products were attractive to the importing countries. For the Soviet Union, however, the hard currency to be earned on the world market was more attractive than the products to be obtained from the CMEA partners. When oil prices declined (in the late 1980s) the inability of the USSR to expand the quantities of primary products exported set limits to the size of the Soviet market for the other CMEA countries and hampered their export industries. The CMEA was unable to provide the hard currency necessary to meet hard currency debt commitments, to provide a dynamic market, or to provide the stimulus to quality and world standards provided by the fierce competiton on the world market.

In addition, the integration process has been an important factor strengthening Soviet control over the economies of her junior partners. For example, the development of joint research and development programmes with Soviet lead organisations, and institutes and firms in other CMEA countries playing a subordinate role, weakens the role of national governments and strengthens the grip of the USSR on economic activities in the CMEA countries. This results from the dominant position of the USSR within CMEA. As Abonyi and Sylvain (1977) put it, in a useful survey of the political economy of this process, CMEA integration 'deepens Soviet penetration by structuring the behaviour of dependent ... elites'.

The integration process has also led to great efforts in the USSR to determine, and apply, reliable methods for determining the efficiency of foreign trade. There is a considerable literature on the optimisation of foreign trade (Shagalov 1973, 'Optimization' 1965). There is also, however, a very substantial gulf between the scientific literature and the real problems of, and methods used in, foreign trade planning. In the USSR, a temporary official method for calculating foreign trade efficiency was issued in 1967. The integration programme led to its being supplemented in 1973 by another temporary method, that for determining the efficiency of specialisation and cooperation within CMEA. These temporary methods were subsequently replaced by the official *Method for determining the efficiency of the foreign economic contacts of the USSR*. The Soviet use of efficiency criteria for foreign trade followed, with a lag, that of her East European allies. By the early 1980s, however, the USSR still had not learned the main lesson from the East European discussion of efficiency criteria in foreign trade that had begun in Hungary 30 years earlier. This is that the development of formal criteria for assessing the efficiency of foreign trade is not a major contribution to improving the role of foreign trade in the economy. There are two reasons for this. First, as in the case of the investment criteria considered in chapter 5, the foreign trade criteria do not actually play much role in foreign trade decisions. Secondly, the importance that used to be attached to them reflected the illusion that, given the right techniques, the planners would make efficient foreign trade decisions. The partial ignorance of the planners, and the complexity of the decision-making process, however, make this unlikely. Experience has shown that a more fruitful way to ensure that foreign trade plays an active role in the economy and that exports develop dynamically, is to devolve foreign trade decisions to the enterprises and create an economic mechanism in which they are encouraged to, and rewarded by, exporting.

The achievements of the economic integration model have turned out to be limited and inadequate. It has been hindered by institutional problems (bilateralism and inconvertibility), political problems (the desire of the CMEA members to preserve their national individuality) and the attractiveness of trade with the West. A decade after the integration model was adopted, the proportion of intra-CMEA trade had fallen significantly, single exchange rates had not been adopted, a significant and growing proportion of intra-CMEA trade was in US dollars, the CMEA was an increasing burden for the USSR and the adverse shift in the terms of trade of the oil importing countries a serious burden for them. A decade and a half after the model was adopted, dissatisfaction with its results was widespread throughout the CMEA and received vocal expression, in particular, in the speeches of Soviet politicians and the writings of Hungarian economists.

THE TRADITIONAL MODEL AND HARD CURRENCY EXPORT PROMOTION

A classic issue in the study of socialist planning is its effect on the share of foreign trade in the national income. Pryor (1963) concluded that in 1955, the trade of each CMEA country was below its 'potential' level by 50 percent or more. 'Potential' level was defined as the internationally normal relationship between foreign trade and factors such as per capita national income, per capita industrial production and population. Pryor (1968) reached similar results for 1958 and 1962. Hewett (1976) reached similar conclusions for 1970. He found that (ibid. p. 8) 'typical eastern foreign trade is, ceteris paribus, much lower than typical western trade ... '.

What explains this? Obviously Western economic warfare is one factor (Adler-Karlsson 1968, Rode and Jacobsen 1985). The US attempts to prevent the export of high-tech goods to the USSR, the imposition of US economic sanctions on the USSR and Poland, the activities of COCOM (the Paris based organisation of the NATO countries, less Iceland, plus Japan, which strives to prevent the export of strategically sensitive goods to the USSR) and the US economic blockades of Cuba and Vietnam, are all well known. Another factor is the CMEA itself, which to some extent functions as a 'trade-destroying customs union' (Holzman 1985). Trade creation occurs when the lowering of trade barriers between partners leads to the importer obtaining by trade goods that previously were produced domestically at higher cost. Trade diversion refers to the increase in trade between partners at the expense of third nations which, although the cheapest producers, lose their markets because of discriminatory measures. Trade destruction takes place when, as a result of a customs union or analogous institutions (e.g. the CMEA), a country produces at home goods that are available at a lower price in third countries not members of the group and/or the fall in income resulting from membership of the group leads to a fall in imports. Holzman argues that the CMEA can be analysed as a trade-destroying customs union because its members are poorly suited to trade with each other and membership is associated with barriers to trade with non-members.

Another factor is the traditional model which has an anti-export bias. An exposition of some aspects of this factor has been given by the Polish economist Winiecki (1986) partly building on Holzman (1974 pp. 102–3). Winiecki's argument can be presented as follows.

In the traditional economic mechanism there are widespread shortages (see chapters 5 and 8) and the economy is supply constrained rather than demand constrained. The planners are interested in generating exports to pay for imports, but at the same time because of the shortages they wish to keep the physical volume of exports as small as possible, compatible with generating the foreign exchange needed to pay for imports. As a result, unlike the situation in a market economy, under socialist planning the export supply curve has the shape of a rectangular hyperbola (this means that the foreign exchange earned by exporting remains constant regardless of the price per unit received, since the planners offset price falls by quantity increases, and vice versa). This is illustrated in figure 9.5.

If the planners anticipate an increase in the price of an exported good, they will then plan a smaller export volume, i.e. a point on the left part of S_{pe} so as to free resources for domestic utilisation. If they

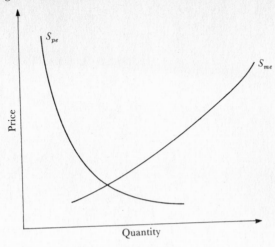

Figure 9.5 Exports and the economic mechanism
Note: S_{pe} is the supply curve of exports in a planned economy
      S_{me} is the supply curve of exports in a market economy

anticipate a price fall, they will choose a point on the lower part of S_{pe} so as to generate the necessary foreign exchange. The costs of export production are not taken into account at all. In a market economy, however, the supply curve normally slopes up to the right. This reflects the profit seeking behaviour of business firms. It may be assumed that the planners behaviour is identical *ex ante* and *ex post*. This means that a price increase in the plan implementation period will also cause a decline in the volume of exports and a price decrease will cause an increase.

This negative price elasticity of supply of exports is a major obstacle to the development of specialisation in the export of manufactures. The behaviour of the planners (a response to the general shortage situation) discourages the export of high price goods and encourages instead the export of low price ones.

Another aspect of the adverse effects of planners behaviour on exports concerns import demand, as is illustrated graphically in figure 9.6.

The figure illustrates a situation in which virtually all imports into the planned economy are complementary imports, i.e. goods which are necessary for production, either directly as intermediate or capital goods required for production or indirectly as food products

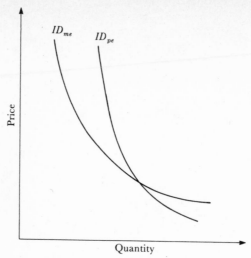

Figure 9.6 Imports and the economic mechanism
Note: ID_{me} is the demand curve of imports in a market economy
   ID_{pe} is the demand curve of imports in a planned economy

necessary to maintain labour productivity. It is assumed, however, that in the market economy foreign trade is larger and that therefore in addition to complementary imports there is a substantial volume of competitive imports, i.e. imports which compete with domestic production. This gives rise to the two different import demand curves shown in the figure. In the planned economy, the demand for imports is not very sensitive to a steep increase in their price. The reason is that since they are necessary inputs into production it is vital to import them. On the other hand, in a market economy as import prices rise hitherto uncompetitive domestic suppliers are able to increase their output. Hence, as import prices rise, instead of increasing domestic production as in a market economy, the planners have to throw on to the foreign market increasing volumes of whatever will sell. Both the product mix and volume of these additional exports will vary from time to time depending on domestic availabilities and foreign market possibilities. This too restricts the development of a specialised manufacturing sector.

Naturally, the combination of a negative price elasticity of supply of exports with a very low price elasticity of demand for imports is likely to generate permanent balance of payments problems. It also undermines the effectiveness of devaluation as an instrument to overcome balance of payments difficulties.

It is therefore entirely understandable that in Poland's negotiations with the IMF for loans in the late 1980s, a central role was
played by the IMF requirement that Poland introduce institutional
changes to reduce the control by the planners over foreign trade and
expand that of the enterprises. Only in this way, the IMF argued,
could Poland lay a reliable basis for an expansion of its hard currency
exports.

It would be a mistake to exaggerate the role of 'perverse' price
effects in limiting exports under traditional central planning.
Another important factor is the poor marketing of exports. For
example Brada (1973a, 1973b) found that CMEA trade with the
West was characterised by substantial inefficiencies. These largely
reflected the poor marketing of exports.[11]

'Perverse' price effects and poor marketing should not be considered as competing explanations of the poor export performance of
countries with the traditional model. They are both reflections of the
same underlying phenomenon, an economic mechanism characterised by widespread shortages. These both generate 'perverse'
behaviour by economic actors and lead to a downplaying of the
importance of marketing which under shortage conditions is of only
secondary importance.

CONCLUSION

Given suitable institutions, the capitalist international division of
labour normally leads to an enormous expansion of trade and rapid
economic growth. It also leads to enormous income inequalities and
substantial inefficiency (e.g. the waste of resources during periodic
recessions). The state socialist countries have attempted to create a
socialist form of cooperation which would capture the advantages,
while avoiding the problems, of the capitalist international division of
labour.

Up till now, however, the state socialist countries have been unable
to create a rival, socialist, international division of labour which is
clearly more equitable and efficient than the capitalist one. The
socialism in one country model worked for the USSR before 1945 and
for China in 1960–78, but is not a model for a group of countries. The
socialist imperialism model came into existence in unique circum-

---

[11] Brada's calculations led to two other interesting conclusions. First, bilateralism did
not seem to be an important source of inefficiency. Secondly, the introduction of the
NEM in Hungary appeared to lead to a *deterioration* in the efficiency of Hungary's trade
with the West.

stances which have largely passed away. The international planning model foundered on the conflict between static comparative costs and the industrialisation of formerly backward countries, national rivalries and the imperfect socialisation of the productive forces. The socialist multilateralism model could not be implemented while the USSR adhered to the traditional model internally. It may once more become relevant in the 1990s as a by-product of the internal Soviet economic reform. The economic integration model, currently being implemented by CMEA, suffers from a number of limitations. It is a grouping round a hegemonic power which is unable to include a country – China – which is state socialist but not a dependant of the USSR. Hence, it lacks appeal to countries jealous of their national independence. Its inability up till now to introduce multilateralism and convertibility has restricted trade and technical progress. Dissatisfaction with the model by member states is widespread.

The traditional model has an adverse effect on the share of hard currency exports in the national income. An important reason for this is the general shortage situation, which generates 'perverse' behaviour by the planners and leads to an underestimation of the importance of marketing.

The problem of establishing an international economic order which combines equity, efficiency and growth remains to be resolved.

SUGGESTIONS FOR FURTHER READING

THEORY

V. I. Lenin, *IMPERIALISM, the latest stage of capitalism* (numerous editions, first published in Russian in Petrograd in 1917).

M. Manoilesco, *The theory of protectionism and of international trade* (London 1931).

A. G. Frank, *Capitalism and underdevelopment in Latin America* (2nd edn New York & London 1969).

S. Amin, *Accumulation on a world scale* (New York & London 1974).

R. Sau, *Unequal exchange, imperialism and underdevelopment* (Calcutta 1978).

J. Spraos, *Inequalising trade?* (Oxford 1983).

I. Steedman, *Trade among growing economies* (Cambridge 1979).

J. Wilczynski, 'The theory of comparative costs and centrally planned economies', *Economic Journal* (March 1965).

A. Boltho, *Foreign trade criteria in socialist economies* (Cambridge 1971).

F. Holzman, *Foreign trade under central planning* (Cambridge, Mass 1974).

Shu-yun Ma, 'Recent changes in China's pure trade theory', *China Quarterly* 106 (June 1986).

G. Carchedi, 'Comparative advantages, capital accumulation and socialism', *Economy and Society* vol. 15, no. 4 (November 1986).

GROWTH STRATEGY

M. Dohan, 'Foreign trade and Soviet investment strategy for planned industrialization 1928–1938', R. W. Davies (ed.) *Soviet investment for planned industrialization, 1929–1937* (Berkeley 1984).

S. Gomulka & J. Sylestrowicz, 'Import led growth; theory and estimation', *On the measurement of factor productivities: theoretical problems and empirical results* (eds.) F. L. Altmann, O. Kyn & H. J. Wagener (Göttingen-Zürich 1976).

P. Hanson, 'The end of import-led growth?', *Journal of Comparative Economics* (June 1982).

'Eastern imports of machinery and equipment, 1960–1985', *Economic Bulletin for Europe* vol. 38, no. 4 (December 1986).

J. Winiecki, 'Central planning and export orientation', *Eastern European Economics* vol. XXIV, no. 4 (Summer 1986).

Teng Weizao, 'Socialist modernisation and the pattern of foreign trade', Xu Dixin *et al.*, *China's search for economic growth* (Beijing 1982).

USSR

M. R. Dohan, 'The economic origins of Soviet autarky 1927/28–1934', *Slavic Review* (December 1976).

M. R. Dohan & E. Hewett, *Two studies in Soviet terms of trade 1918–1970* (Bloomington, Indiana 1973).

V. P. Gruzinov, *The USSR's management of foreign trade* (New York 1979).

I. Birman, 'A note on Soviet foreign trade gains', *Soviet Studies* (October 1986).

CMEA

C. Adler-Karlsson, *Western economic warfare 1947–1967* (Stockholm 1968).

R. Rode & H.-D. Jacobsen (eds.) *Economic warfare or detente* (Boulder & London 1985).

F. D. Holzman, 'Comecon: A "trade destroying" customs union?' *Journal of Comparative Economics* vol. 9, no. 4 (December 1985).

S. Ausch, *Theory and practice of CMEA cooperation* (Budapest 1972).

E. A. Hewett, *Foreign trade prices in the Council for Mutual Economic Assistance* (Cambridge 1974).

A. Abonyi & I. Sylvain, 'CMEA integration and policy options for Eastern Europe: A development strategy for dependent states', *Journal of Common Market Studies* vol. XVI, no. 2 (1977).

J. M. van Brabant, *Adjustment, structural change and economic efficiency* (Cambridge 1987).

A. Bergson, 'The geometry of Comecon trade', *European Economic Review* (1980) (see also A. Bergson, 'The geometry of Comecon trade: A note', *European Economic Review* (1981)).

K. Pésci, *The future of socialist economic integration* (New York 1981).

F. D. Holzman, 'The significance of Soviet subsidies to Eastern Europe', *Comparative Economic Studies* vol. XXXVIII, no. 1 (Spring 1986).

L. Csaba, 'Joint investments and mutual advantages in the CMEA – Retrospection and Prognosis', *Soviet Studies* vol. XXVII, no. 2 (April 1985).

'Exports of manufactures from Eastern Europe and the Soviet Union to the developed market economies, 1965–1981', *Economic Bulletin for Europe* vol. 35, no. 4 (December 1983).

EASTERN EUROPE

J. Brada, 'The allocative efficiency of centrally planned foreign trade: a programming approach to the Czech case', *European Economic Review* no. 4 (1973).

J. Brada, 'The microallocative impact of the Hungarian economic reform of 1968: some evidence from the export sector', *Economics of Planning* nos. 1–2 (1973).

J. P. Sartre, 'Czechoslovakia: the socialism that came in from the cold', J. P. Sartre, *Between existentialism and Marxism* (New York 1974) pp. 84–117.

East European Economies: slow growth in the 1980s vol. 2, part I (JEC US Congress, Washington DC 1986).

P. Boot, 'East-West trade and industrial policy: the case of the German Democratic Republic', *Soviet Studies* vol. XXXIX, no. 4 (October, 1987).

J. Vanous, 'Macroeconomic adjustment in Eastern Europe in 1981–83', and B. Balassa & L. Tyson, 'Policy responses to external shocks in Hungary and Yugoslavia', both in *East European Economies: Slow growth in the 1980s* vol. 1, section A (JEC US Congress, Washington DC 1986).

CHINA

Chinese Economic Studies vol. XVI, nos. 3 & 8 (Spring 1983 & Summer 1983).

Fang Shen, 'On the issue of utilizing foreign capital', *Chinese Economic Studies* vol. XVIII, no. 4 (Summer 1985).

China's economy looks towards the year 2000 vol. 2, section VIII (JEC US Congress Washington DC 1986).

CHINA Long-term development issues and options (Baltimore & London 1985, for the World Bank) chapter 6.

10

RESULTS OF SOCIALIST PLANNING

The data on the East European societies show several disproportions and contradictions in economic, social and cultural growth. Basic among them is the contradiction between the growing economic and cultural sophistication of the population and the authoritarian structure of power relations. Even the private farmers in Poland are largely dependent on the state, not to speak of the rest of the population, which is employed in state-owned enterprises, offices and institutions.

A. Matejko (1974 p. xvii)

Experience shows that, in China as in some other socialist countries, the traditional system of planning cannot give full scope to the superiority of the socialist system and is even inferior to the practices in some developed capitalist countries in certain respects, such as in technological development and in suiting production to market demand.

Xue Muqiao (1981 pp. 169–70)

The consequences of state ownership and management of the economy can conveniently be considered under the two headings considered in the first chapter, the creation of a rational mode of production and catching up with the advanced countries.

A RATIONAL MODE OF PRODUCTION?

A major issue raised by the historical experience of socialist planning is whether or not the state socialist countries have established a new, more advanced, mode of production. In order to examine this question, seven criteria will be used. They all derive from the Marxist critique of capitalism and are, efficiency, the labour process, the division of labour, democracy and the state, distribution, the social ownership of the means of production and economic planning.

Efficiency

An early researcher in this field was the US economist Bergson (1968, 1978). He compared the level of productivity in the USSR and the USA, the level of productivity in the USSR and a number of OECD countries, and the rates of growth of productivity in the CMEA and OECD countries. From his comparison of the level of productivity in the USSR and USA, Bergson (1978 p. 90) concluded that it was much higher in the USA but that it was not possible to draw conclusions from this about the relative efficiency of the *systems*. This was because of the fact that the USSR and USA differ not just with respect to the system but also with respect to other variables, e.g. history and culture. Comparisons of levels of productivity between the USSR and a number of OECD countries led to the conclusion (Bergson 1978 p. 111) that socialism is far 'from the chaotic system critics once held it would be and from the potent mechanism that proponents have often envisaged. At least the Soviet variant of socialism seems neither colossally wasteful nor extraordinarily efficient but well within the extremes that are so familiar in polemics on socialist economies. The Soviet system, however, appears to be undistinguished by Western standards.' His comparison of the rates of growth of productivity in the CMEA and OECD led to the conclusion (Bergson 1978 p. 216) that 'the familiar claim as to the superiority of socialism over capitalism in that sphere [i.e. growth] appears to have little basis. On the contrary, the latter system may be advantageous.' Bergson's work was useful because he advanced beyond political assertions to empirical economic-statistical calculations, he devoted great efforts to trying to ensure the comparability of the data from the two systems, and because of the cautious and tentative character of his conclusions. Bergson also defined two concepts which played a considerable role in subsequent discussion, 'static efficiency' and 'dynamic efficiency'. By the former he understood output per unit of input at a given time. By the latter he understood the rate of growth of output per unit of input.

Bergson's work has a number of limitations, reflecting both his theoretical position and the data available to him. First, he realised (1978 pp. 100–7, 199–202) that productivity depends partly on the level of development, but his efforts to allow for this were very rough and ready. More sophisticated attempts have been made and are considered below. Secondly, he noted (1978 p. 98) that in capitalist countries there is often unemployment and that this should be taken into account when measuring inter-system differences in efficiency. He himself, however, paid little attention to this in his calculations and conclusions. Furthermore, his analysis, in accordance with standard Western theory, assumes that the resources available in a country are given and independent of the system and that the system effects only the efficiency with which the given resources are used. This is incorrect as has been noted by several authors (Hanson 1971, Gregory 1981, Ellman 1983). Traditional central planning is a system which is able to channel into employment and capital formation resources which other economic systems might leave unutilised. The higher participation rate normal in socialist than in capitalist countries was pointed out in chapter 6. An example of the significance of this for systems efficiency is considered below. The high levels of investment normal in socialist countries was pointed out in chapter 5. Another example of this mobilising aspect of economic systems concerns war and preparations for war. War is of decisive importance in the competition between the two systems, the present frontiers between which are mainly the result of armed struggles of one kind or another. Which system is more efficient at resource mobilisation for war? The case of the Second World War has been examined by Harrison (1988). He examined the mobilisation of resources by Germany, USSR, USA and UK in the Second World War. The available statistics suggest that the intensity of resource mobilisation for war purposes by the USSR compared favourably with that of the other belligerent countries. Given the very adverse environment in which the Soviet war economy existed (a shortage economy, very low living standards even before the war, large parts of the country occupied by the enemy) the performance of the USSR in mobilising the economy for total war was very impressive. Furthermore, in the post Second World War period the USSR has been quite successful in holding its own in the military competition with the USA and with NATO despite the fact that its national income has always been much less than that of the USA and very much less than that of NATO.

Thirdly, he took no account of externalities, although he realised their importance (p. 188). Some account of them is taken below. Fourthly, although recognising (p. 55) that the output of goods in the two systems may be of different qualities, no serious attempt to allow for this was made. Below indirect methods to allow for this are considered. Fifthly, no account was taken of the experience of the Asian socialist countries, due to data limitations. Below some atten-

Table 10.1 *Average growth rates in the EEC and CMEA (in % p.a.)*

Years	National income		Industrial production	
	CMEA	EEC	CMEA	EEC
1961–5	6.1	4.7	8.3	5.3
1966–70	7.3	4.5	8.4	4.8
1971–4	6.6	3.6	8.1	3.4
1975	6.4	−2.5	8.5	−7.6
1976	5.5	4.2	10.2	6.2

Sources: Kudrov (1976) p. 21, Kudrov (1977) p. 29.

tion will be paid to China, considered as an important example of the socialist system. Sixthly, he assumed that all output (at any rate in the USA) contributes to welfare, in accordance with the principle of 'consumers' sovereignty'. As pointed out below, this is not in general true.

The leading Soviet specialist on the relative efficiency of the two systems is V. M. Kudrov (1972, 1973, 1976, 1977). In his 1972 paper (p. 7) he argued that, as far as growth is concerned, the socialist countries had decisively established their superiority. 'In the course of economic competition, socialism as a world system has proved its decisive superiority over capitalism with respect to the rate of growth.' This conclusion was based on data of the type set out in table 10.1

As far as the level of efficiency was concerned, Kudrov argued that with respect to a number of indices (the proportion of the population employed, the early peaceful utilisation of atomic energy, the early development of supersonic passenger airlines), the USSR was ahead of the USA. Nevertheless, he recognised that in general the USA was still more efficient than the USSR (as Bergson had argued). Kudrov, however, argued that this gap was being narrowed and that in due course the USSR would establish the superiority of socialism in the field of efficiency as it had already done in the field of economic growth. In 1950–75 the growth rate of the Soviet economy substantially exceeded that of the US economy and hence the gap between the two countries was substantially reduced (see table 10.2). Kudrov (1976 p. 22) concluded that this 'superiority of the USSR in growth rates is the basis for the successful solution of the task of winning in the competition with capitalism with respect to the

Table 10.2 *A dynamic comparison of the Soviet and US economies (USSR as % of USA)*

	1950	1957	1965	1975
National income	31	50	59	>66
Industrial output	30	47	62	>80
Agricultural output	55	70	c. 75	85
Labour productivity				
in industry	30–40	40–50	40–50	>55
in agriculture	20	20–25	20–25	20–25
Output in physical units				
oil	14	28	63	120
steel	30	49	75	128
mineral fertilisers	31	42	69	125
cement	26	58	111	188

Source: Kudrov (1976) p. 22.

volume of production and its technical level'. Kudrov noted, however, that the USSR was less efficient than the USA in the utilisation of many raw materials and intermediate products. Other writers have found that CMEA countries generally have a lower efficiency in the use of raw materials and intermediate products than OECD countries (Drabek 1981, 1988, Gomulka & Rostowski 1988). Kudrov also noted (1977 p. 34) that what might be termed the consumption efficiency of the USSR was less than that of the USA in the sense that the production of one unit of consumption in the USSR required the production of more non-consumption (e.g. intermediate goods such as steel) than in the USA. This had also been pointed out by Bergson (1978 pp. 66–7) who had observed that by 1970, measuring in dollars, the Soviet volume of non-consumption (government administration, defence, gross investment) exceeded that of the USA whereas its volume of consumption was less than half of that of the USA.

Kudrov's conclusion about the superiority of socialism with respect to the rate of growth cannot be considered a valid inference from data of the type set out in table 10.1. The reason for this is that the statistics for the EEC and CMEA are non-comparable. The EEC statistics use the SNA method and the CMEA statistics the MPS method. Furthermore, the publication of statistics in the state socialist countries is guided by the principle of partymindedness (see chapter 2). In addition, CMEA statistics are coloured by 'the propaganda of success'.[1] A more technical reason for the non-comparability of the statistics is the use of methods for measuring 'real' growth in the CMEA countries that do not take adequate account of rising prices. These questions have been extensively discussed (Vainshtein 1969, Becker 1972, Cohen 1972, Ellman and Simatupang 1982, Khanin 1984). Some years ago the Hungarian economist Brody (1980 p. 196) asked, 'What happened to the national income [of Hungary] in 1974? At current prices it showed an increase of 4.7 per cent, while at comparable prices the growth became already 7 per cent ("Statistical Yearbook 1974", Budapest, 1975, pp. 73–4). Instead of "deflation", "inflation" of the index occurred. What was the real growth? In my opinion it was at most 1–2 per cent in 1974. And this would have been good to know at that time.' In other words, according to a well-known Hungarian economist, an official growth rate figure for Hungary of 7 percent corresponded to a realistic figure of only 1–2 percent!

In connection with Kudrov's extrapolation from the higher growth of the USSR than the USA in 1950–75 (this was probably a real, not purely statistical, phenomenon), it should be noted that in the late 1970s the USSR was hit by an unexpected and unplanned decline in growth rates. According to the official Soviet statistical handbooks (which significantly overstate the relative position of the USSR) Soviet national income, which reached 67 percent of the US level in 1975, remained at about that level in 1976–85. This was very disturbing for the USSR since it meant that the USSR was stagnating relative to the USA at a much lower level of per capita income. According to an unofficial Soviet estimate (Selyunin and Khanin 1987) the true situation was even more depressing than that shown in official statistics. In reality, they argued, Soviet national income per capita was almost stagnant in 1976–80 and fell slightly in 1981–5. This implies that Soviet national income fell relative to that of the USA in 1976–85. Not enough evidence is yet available to evaluate the reliability of this estimate. It is quite clear, however, that in the past twenty years the level of productivity in Soviet agriculture has fallen significantly relative to that in US agriculture. According to Kostakov (1987), the director of the USSR Gosplan's economic research

[1] This is a Polish phrase of the 1970s. It refers to the then official Polish practice of extravagant praise of achievements and projecting temporary successes into the future; combined with the maintenance of silence or the dissemination of falsehoods, about current problems and difficulties and possible future problems.

institute, whereas labour productivity in Soviet agriculture was about 20–25 percent of that in the USA in 1966–70, it had fallen to about 20 percent in 1976–80 and to less than 20 percent in 1981–5. The USSR's poor growth performance in the late 1970s and early 1980s was an important reason why in the late 1980s it reembarked on the reform process (see chapter 3).

Both Bergson and Kudrov assumed that all final output should be considered as a contribution to welfare. In fact, however, this is not the case. Both systems produce a large volume of products, e.g. weapons, alcohol, tobacco, heroin and cocaine, that have adverse effects on human welfare. Partly the output of these products is determined by domestic factors and hence their relative volume may be compared to elucidate the role of systemic factors. Partly their production is related to the competition between the two systems. (The fact that the performance of the two systems is related, makes separating out a purely domestic systemic influence more difficult.) Distinguishing between goods and bads has a large objective element (e.g. based on medical findings) but clearly also has a significant subjective element.

As Bergson pointed out, it is difficult to draw conclusions about 'the system' from comparisons of the USSR and USA because of the existence of very important non-system differences between the two countries. To draw conclusions about 'the system' it is desirable both to make comparisons between pairs of countries that really are alike in all respects except 'the system', and to take a large number of countries and look at the impact of system on performance. Both these methods have been widely used. As far as pairs of countries are concerned, there are two that come close to the requirement of being similar in all respects save the system, the Republic of Korea and the Democratic People's Republic of Korea, and the Federal German Republic (FRG) and the German Democratic Republic (GDR). A number of authors have tried to measure the relative efficiency of these pairs of countries. Both data problems and the quality of the work done up till now are such that at the moment studies of the relative efficiency of the two German states (Gregory and Leptin 1977, Sturm 1977, Wilkens 1981, Collier 1985) seem to be more reliable and useful than those of the two Korean states.

The work cited shows that in the post-war period the *level* of productivity in the FRG has consistently been above that in the GDR. In Bergsonian terminology one can say that the static efficiency of the FRG has been greater than that of the GDR throughout the post-war period. What explains this? Is it a result of the system or is it a result of exogenous factors (e.g. differential war-time destruction and differing policies by the occupying countries)? Gregory and Leptin incline to the first answer, and the author to the second. The gap appears to have arisen in the years 1944–50 and can hardly be considered independently of the military and political events of those years (e.g. the economic relations between the USSR and the Soviet Zone, as discussed in the previous chapter).

The cause of the significant difference in productivity levels between the two German states has been examined by Sturm (1977). He concluded that the main cause of the difference was nothing to do with the system. It was an environmental factor, namely that the GDR is much smaller than the FRG and is therefore much less able to take advantage of economies of scale. The lesser economies of scale open to the GDR, according to Sturm, are enough on their own to explain the entire observed difference in productivity between the two countries. This argument, however, is unconvincing. Small capitalist countries (such as Sweden) are able to gain substantial economies of scale by specialising and operating on a world scale.

As far as comparisons of the *growth* of productivity are concerned, these are sensitive to the period considered, the treatment of unemployment and female non-employment, and the data used. In 1950–8 the rate of growth of aggregate labour productivity (Gregory and Leptin 1977 p. 529) was 1/3 greater in the GDR than in the FRG. On the other hand, in the period 1960–73 the rates of growth of industrial labour productivity, overall labour productivity and total factor productivity were virtually equal in the two countries (Gregory and Leptin 1977 table 1). The biggest difference between the data for the two countries for this period is the greater dispersion of the series for the FRG resulting from the greater instability of a capitalist economy. This corroborates the argument of Kudrov (1976 p. 17) that an important feature of socialism is its greater stability. Extending the comparison forward to include the recession of 1974–5 produces the result that, using the data of Wilkens (1981 p. 106) it appears that labour productivity per *inhabitant* grew faster in the GDR than in the FRG in 1967–76, but per *economically active person* it grew slower in the GDR than in the FRG. (Output growth remained more stable in 1967–76 in the GDR than in the FRG.) This can be interpreted to mean that the inferior performance in dynamic efficiency by the GDR was offset by an increase in the activity rate, i.e. an increase in the burden of work extracted from the population. Alternatively, it can be interpreted to mean that the FRG has an inefficient economic system which wastes much of its potential labour force and deprives many people of the opportunity to participate in paid work.

The data for GDR GDP have been reexamined by Collier (1985). He argued that Wilkens' method produced too high figures for GDR GDP and that the increase in the relative position of the GDR shown by the Wilkens' data was a statistical illusion. Whereas, according to Wilkens, per capita GDR GDP rose from 78 percent of the FRG level in 1967 to 83 percent in 1976, according to Collier it was only about 70 percent of the FRG level in both 1975 and 1980.

Accordingly, it can be seen that as far as Bergsonian dynamic efficiency is concerned, the conclusions drawn from comparisons of the two German states depend heavily on the years considered, the data used, and the treatment of differences in the participation rate. The main impact of the system on the dynamic efficiency of the two countries appears to be not on its level but on its dispersion, on its fluctuations around a more or less common level of dynamic efficiency. Capitalism appears as the more unstable system. As far as Bergsonian static efficiency is concerned, comparison of the two German states draws attention to the difficulty of disentangling system and environmental effects on efficiency. Bergsonian static efficiency has consistently been higher in the Federal Republic than in the Democratic Republic, but the relationship between this fact and the relative efficiency of the two *systems* remains debatable.

When trying to draw conclusions about the efficiency of the system from relative growth rate statistics, it is necessary to take account of other factors which influence growth rates, e.g. levels of development. Bergson made a rough attempt to allow for this. A more sophisticated attempt has been made by Gomulka. His results are set out in figure 10.1.

Figure 10.1 shows the rate of growth of labour productivity plotted against a proxy for the level of development of the economy (the independent factor determining the rate of growth according to the Gomulka growth theory). The international mainstream falls within the upper and lower dotted lines. The upper dotted line shows the approximate upper rate of growth of labour productivity statistically recorded for various given levels of labour productivity. The lower dotted line shows the approximate minimum rate of growth of labour productivity statistically recorded for various levels of labour productivity. The dynamically efficient countries can be defined as those near, on, or outside, the upper dotted line. The dynamically inefficient countries likewise can be defined as those near, on, or below, the lower dotted line. It can be seen that the most dynamically efficient

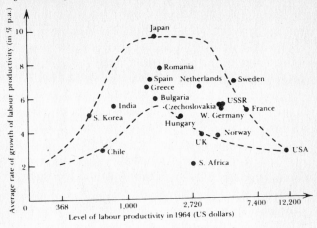

Figure 10.1 International dynamic efficiency 1958–68
Source: Gomulka (1971) p. 73

countries in this period (South Korea, Japan, Sweden, France) are all capitalist. Similarly, the least dynamically efficient countries (South Africa, Chile, UK) are all capitalist. The European state socialist countries are all in the mainstream of international economic development, with some (e.g. Romania) doing better than others (e.g. Hungary).

Gomulka's analysis is interesting in showing both the theory impregnated nature of international comparisons of dynamic efficiency and also that variations between countries with the same system may be greater than variations between the systems.

The Gomulka analysis of dynamic efficiency has been applied to China by Dirksen (1983) and the result of doing this is set out in figure 10.2.

From figure 10.2 it can be seen that China's performance in the Maoist period with respect to industrial labour productivity was a poor one. It was in the international mainstream, but right at the bottom of it. Hence the Chinese decision to embark on the reform process is entirely understandable.

Not only was the Chinese performance with respect to labour productivity in the Maoist period poor, but the performance with respect to capital productivity seems to have been worse. The figures given by the World Bank (*China* 1985 table 7.1) show a capital productivity in 1982 below that of 1952! This would seem to exaggerate the problem since it takes no account of depreciation and hence artificially raises the figures for capital stock (and consequently

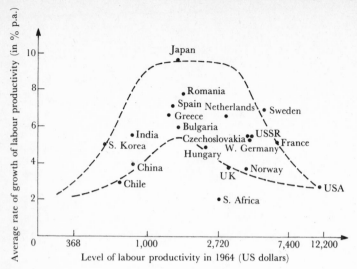

Figure 10.2 Dynamic efficiency in China in 1952–78

Source: Dirksen (1983) p. 384. I have taken his higher variant for industrial employment, because it corresponds to current official figures, and data for the rate of growth of industrial labour productivity in 1951–78 from *Statistical Yearbook of China 1985* (Hong Kong & Beiging 1986) p. 382. The entire period 1952–78 is considered since taking the same years as for the other countries (1958–68) would produce a misleading impression for China since this period included a major economic crisis which had a servere adverse effect on labour productivity.

artificially lowers the figures for capital productivity). Nevertheless, the revised capital stock estimates of Chen et al (*China Quarterly* no. 114) also suggest that capital productivity in Chinese industry declined in 1952–78.

Abouchar (1979 pp. 19–20) has argued that economies with the traditional socialist planning model have definite advantages over capitalist economies when it comes to executive ability, i.e. the ability to implement centrally decided policies such as space flight or the construction of the Baikal-Amur railway. This point of view is shared by Deng Xiaoping (1987 p. 15). He has argued that, 'the greatest advantage of the socialist system is that when the central leadership makes a decision it is promptly implemented without interference from any other quarters ... We don't have to go through a lot of repetitive discussion and consultation, with one branch of the government holding up another and decisions being made but not carried out. From this point of view our system is very efficient.'

In this connection, the following should be noted. First, the leadership often has difficulty in implementing its policies. What actually happens may differ substantially from the goals of the leadership. This was explained in chapter 5 in connection with the investment process. Secondly, the policies which are implemented by the 'efficient' process of avoiding 'repetitive discussion and consultation' may turn out to be very harmful, as Deng Xiaoping would certainly agree for China for 1966–76. Thirdly, in some cases it is quite true. Hence, even in capitalist economies, many activities, e.g. armies and large firms, are organised on a hierarchical rather than a liberal democratic or market basis. The relative advantages of hierarchical, discussion and market methods of resource allocation is a special subject with its own literature (e.g. Williamson 1975, Doel 1979). Each method has specific advantages and disadvantages.

It is well known that there is only a limited relationship between national income statistics and human welfare, because of the importance of distribution, pollution and the varying consumption efficiency of different systems. Distribution was discussed in chapter 7 and will be considered further below. As far as consumption is concerned, attempts to measure the effects of the system on economic welfare were made in chapter 8. It was concluded that it was difficult to draw unambiguous conclusions from the work that has been done up till now, but that there are tentative reasons to believe that capitalism has a favourable effect on the quantity, quality and availability of private goods and state socialism on public goods, particularly in low income countries.

Although there are numerous studies of pollution problems in individual countries, good studies of comparative pollution levels are rare. One such study is Slama (1986). He investigated the effect of the system on sulphur dioxide emissions (the cause of 'acid rain'). He concluded that the production of each billion dollars of GNP resulted in the emission of 7,000–8,000 tonnes of sulphur dioxide in the West, but more than three times this amount, i.e. about 26,000–27,000 tonnes in the socialist countries (European CMEA members + Yugoslavia). This was largely a result of the greater energy intensity of production in the socialist countries than in the capitalist countries. This in turn partly reflected different structures of production (e.g. a greater share of energy-intensive heavy industry in the socialist countries). It also partly reflected a worse energy efficiency in each line of production in the socialist countries. It was also in part a reflection of the worse (from a pollution point of view) structure of fuel use in the socialist countries, where the pollution-intensive brown coal is more extensively used. While this study on its own is inadequate to compare overall pollution levels between systems, it does suggest that as far as sulphur dioxide emissions are concerned, socialism is the less efficient system.

A significant test of the performance of an economic system is its achievements on the arena of the world market. Is it a dynamic system whose products are conquering the world market, or is it a backward system under permanent threat from the cheaper and better products available on the world market? Performance on the world market can be considered as a partial and limited proxy for the relative quality of the output of the tradeable goods sector of the systems. An interesting study of the performance of manufactures from Eastern Europe and the USSR on the capitalist market in 1965–81 has been undertaken by the United Nation's Economic Commission for Europe (ECE 1983). This found that the share of the Western market for manufactured goods held by the USSR and Eastern Europe (c. 2 percent) was small with no long-term tendency to rise and that it completely lacked the dynamism of the share held by the newly industrialised countries (NICs). On the whole it would seem that the export performance of the USSR and Eastern Europe in this period was poor. The capitalist countries, however, show a very wide dispersion in performance, some (Japan, the NICs) being very dynamic, and others (such as much of Latin America and Africa) being very poor performers.

Conclusions

(1) Comparisons of the level of productivity between the USSR and the USA, and between the GDR and the FRG both show that the level of productivity is higher in the capitalist country. Nevertheless, the relevance of this for analysis of the effect of 'the system' is debatable.
(2) Comparisons of the rate of growth between the systems do not show any general advantage for socialism. Comparisons between the CMEA and the EEC which purport to do this are based on inaccurate data. Comparison of the USSR and USA between 1950 and 1975 does show an advantage for the USSR, but this disappeared in 1976–85. The dynamic efficiency of China in the Maoist period was poor.
(3) The systems can affect not just the level of a variable such as the rate of growth but also its dispersion. Comparison of the rates of growth of the FRG and the GDR suggest that capitalism is the more unstable system.

(4) The system can affect not only the efficiency with which given resources are used, but also the volume of resources available to use. The socialist system is an efficient system for resource mobilisation, normally achieving high participation rates and high investment rates. It is also effective in mobilising resources for war and war preparations. Whether the higher participation rate normal under socialism should be considered a sign of higher efficiency (because it shows a more efficient use of resources) or of lower efficiency (because it shows that the amount of labour exacted from the members of society is higher) is a matter for debate. So are the implications for human welfare of the effectiveness of the socialist system in mobilising resources for war and war preparations. Furthermore, the effectiveness of the socialist system in mobilising resources for investment is one of the causes of the relatively low efficiency with which investment resources are used (see chapter 5).

(5) Differences between countries with the same system may be much greater than differences between systems. This is shown both by the application of the Gomulka model to international growth experience in 1958–68 and by the contrasting performance on the world market of Japan and the NICs on the one hand, and much of Latin America and Africa on the other.

(6) Both systems have substantial inefficiencies in the sense of devoting massive resources to the production of outputs with a negative effect on welfare.

(7) Socialism seems to be the less efficient system with respect to the use of raw materials and intermediate products.

(8) Inter-system comparisons of consumption suggest that capitalism is superior with respect to private goods and that socialism has an advantage with respect to public goods, particularly in low-income countries.

(9) There are a number of different methods of decision making, each with characteristic advantages and disadvantages.

(10) As far as pollution is concerned, the tentative conclusion from the limited studies done up till now is that it is quite possible that socialism is the less efficient (i.e. more polluting) system.

(11) The conclusions which can be drawn from the actual experience of the competition between the two systems are more complex and have more nuances than would be expected on the basis of simple-minded *a priori* expectations, either liberal or Marxist.

The labour process

As far as the labour process is concerned, the only notable differences between the state socialist countries and the advanced capitalist countries are twofold. First, that in the former the organisation of work typically copies, with a lag, that in the latter. Secondly, the pace of work is typically slower in the former than in the latter. In general, it seems reasonable to say that the state socialist countries have made no progress whatsoever towards organising the labour process so as to end the division between the scientist and the process worker. This is scarcely surprising, both in view of the Bolshevik attitude to Taylorism (see chapter 6 above) and in view of Marx's own thesis that a society in which the labour process has been fundamentally transformed would be one in which technical progress had eliminated dreary, repetitive, work. Such a state of affairs has not yet been reached in even the most advanced countries.

As far as labour conditions are concerned, it was pointed out in chapter 6 that there are a large number of important differences between the state socialist and capitalist countries. The state socialist countries normally provide full employment, security of employment, and social security, sometimes make significant use of coerced labour, lack independent trade unions and probably have a poor record in industrial safety.

The division of labour

As far as the technical division of labour is concerned, the Soviet model is to follow the capitalist countries in increasing the division of labour, in subdividing even more finely the labour process between an ever increasing variety of specialists. As far as the division of society into rulers and ruled is concerned, no progress has been made here either. During the revolutionary period itself, and during subsequent occasional dramatic upheavals, e.g. the mass promotion of the pushed up ones in the USSR in the 1930s,[2] numerous individuals have changed their position in society. Nevertheless, this has nowhere prevented the crystallisation of a privileged ruling stratum and the division of society into rulers and ruled.

[2] The 'pushed up ones' (*vydvizhentsy*) were people from working class or peasant backgrounds who, despite their lack of conventional academic qualifications, received an accelerated higher education in c. 1928–34 and were 'pushed up' into responsible positions. They took over the jobs of the liquidated Old Bolsheviks in 1937–38 and formed the social basis of the Stalinist regime. A typical pushed up one was Khrushchev.

Is this a result of the malevolence of the party leadership, the political institutions of state socialism, the technical backwardness of the countries concerned, or the inevitable result of the development of modern technology? This question was long ago considered by Gramsci, who posed the question, 'Does one start from the premise of a perpetual division of the human race [into rulers and ruled], or does one believe that this is only a historical fact answering to certain conditions?' He argued (Gramsci 1957 pp. 143–4) that 'this division is a product of the [technical] division of labour, that it is a technical fact'. This view, that even under socialism there is a technical need for the division of society into rulers and ruled, is orthodox in all the state socialist countries. Hence, the traditional view is that the Marxist aspiration to overcome this must be postponed to the higher stage of communism. Priority is given to the development of the forces of production. This priority, under Soviet political conditions of the late 1920s, led to the adoption of the coercive model in agriculture, and more generally of quasi-feudal relations of production throughout the economy. In the classic analysis of Brus (1975) this system is described as the 'etatist model' and its political aspect as 'totalitarian dictatorship'. Relative to capitalism, these developments were retrogressive and a major step backwards.

In Yugoslavia, on the other hand, the Soviet-Yugoslav split led, from 1950 onwards, to the development of a new variant of state socialism. Its evolution was briefly surveyed in chapter 3. In this chapter, however, we are concerned less with Yugoslavia herself than with the 'Yugoslav model'. From this standpoint the crucial question is, does the Yugoslav model exhibit new relations of production that are clearly superior to those of capitalism?

Two conclusions can be drawn about the Yugoslav model. First, that self-management has important advantages relative both to capitalism and to statist socialism. It reduces inequality within work units, and gives their members greater control over their working lives. This, of course, is not a Yugoslav discovery, but is the reason for the widespread development of producer cooperatives throughout the world, a well-known example being the Israeli kibbutz. A group of sociologists who compared industrial plants in five countries, kibbutz plants in Israel, self-managed factories in Yugoslavia, and capitalist plants in Austria, Italy and the United States, came to the conclusion that (Tannenbaum 1974 pp. 225–6),

Radically different organisational forms are possible and viable. An organisation in which policy is decided by top personnel is quite workable, and so is one in which policy is decided by the membership as a whole. Factories in which workers receive remuneration equal to that of managers can function effectively, just as can factories with substantial differences in reward between those at the top and those at the bottom. But the success of a system, however success may be defined, depends on 'conditions', and ultimately on the definition of success itself; and the preference that we as observers may feel for one system or another will depend on our own values. For those of us who place great value on equality, the kibbutz system, and perhaps the Yugoslav, is the model of success. The American model looks better to those who value individual achievement.

Secondly, as Brus (1975 p. 95) has noted, self-management, at any rate in the form adopted by Yugoslavia, can easily go beyond the 'limits defined by the economic and social rationality of central planning, by the growing need in the modern world for the internalisation of external costs and benefits, by the requirements of maintaining the supremacy of the point of view of the "system" as a whole over that of "sub-systems" '. If one considers the Yugoslav experience from the standpoint of such criteria as inflation, unemployment, foreign debt, the distribution of income, regional policy and the allocation of investment, it is difficult to disagree with Brus.

In China during the Maoist period there was also criticism of the alleged technical need for the division of society into rulers and ruled. The Maoist stress on the need, here and now and not in the distant future, to develop new, socialist, relations of production, led to three major innovations. They were, the obligation of all managerial personnel to perform manual labour, the elected revolutionary committee which was responsible for executive management in Chinese factories, and the possibility of criticising officials.

To interpret these phenomena as signs that new, socialist, relations of production were being created in China in 1966–76, however, simply confuses ideology with reality. Take, for example, the Maoist policy of sending educated young people into the countryside to work on the land. In the Maoist press one could read that this was a 'brilliant policy for building the new socialist countryside, an important measure for narrowing and eliminating the differences between mental and manual labour'. In other words, the official interpretation of this policy was that it was a step towards the Marxist goal of overcoming the division of labour and was a move towards socialism or communism. In fact, however, it was simply the compulsory allocation of the labour (and persons) of educated youngsters, resulting from the inability of the authorities to generate enough urban jobs to employ the growing labour force, the ban on urban private enterprise and the fact that discontented youngsters were less of a political threat in the countryside than as urban unemployed.

In the USSR, the reduction in the role of coercion in the decades after 1953 was a major step forward. Under Gorbachev, it came to be officially accepted in the USSR that the relations of production characteristic of the traditional economic mechanism were hampering the development of the forces of production. Acceleration of growth, it was proclaimed, would require social changes. The meaning and implementation of this thesis were controversial and difficult issues in the USSR in the late 1980s.

Democracy and the state

In chapter 1 it was suggested that there are theoretical and historical reasons for distinguishing between two types of democracy, liberal democracy and totalitarian democracy. Both make the value judgement that social choices ought to be determined by the wishes of all members of society, and in this sense both are 'democratic'. Liberal democracy assumes, however, that individual choices are both unconcerned with, and independent of, the choices of other individuals. Totalitarian democracy, on the other hand, assumes that the decision-making process normally corresponds to the 'Prisoners' Dilemma' situation. How do the two groups of countries, to which these two categories are intended to relate, compare, from a political point of view?

The traditional Marxist-Leninist view is that the state socialist countries are more democratic than capitalist ones. Under capitalism, although the people appear to choose the rulers, in fact the rulers are chosen by, and represent the interests of, a small group of monopoly capitalists. Although formal freedom exists, the workers are unable to take advantage of it because they lack the possibility of turning their formal freedom into real freedom. Everyone is free to own newspapers, but in fact they are owned by, and used to disseminate the views of, a tiny group of millionaires. The votes cast at elections simply reflect the views and interests of the capitalists, which are pumped into the population by the media and the whole indoctrination system (schools, churches, advertising, television etc.). In state socialist countries, on the other hand, power is exercised by leaders who are responsible to the population through the state electoral system and inner party democracy. In addition, the workers have not formal freedom but real freedom, since meeting places and means of communication are at the disposal of workers' organisations and the state provides employment, social security and free educational and medical services for all.

Experience has shown that this thesis does contain important elements of the truth. In capitalist countries the means of communication are often owned by tiny cliques, the state socialist countries do generally provide full employment, social security and free or cheap educational and medical services. But, it also excludes important elements of the truth. It ignores the possibilities open to the labour movement for using liberal democracy to advance both working-class interests and the interests of individual members of the working class. It also ignores the fact that the quality of the services provided (e.g. medical care) may be poor. Furthermore, experience has shown that the political freedoms offered by liberal democracy (the right to free movement of people and ideas, absence of censorship, independent social organisations, an independent judiciary and the right to strike) are of great benefit to all sections of society. In chapter 6, the negative effects of the absence of independent worker organisations in the state socialist countries, on industrial accidents and diseases, on labour morale and on the use of coerced labour, were briefly surveyed.

It is because of this important lesson of experience, that in 1964, Togliatti, the leader of the Italian Communist Party, a party with mass working-class support in an advanced capitalist country, clearly stated in his so-called Testament that, in assessing the political system in the state socialist countries, 'The problem attracting most attention, both in the USSR and in the other socialist countries is, however, the problem of overcoming the regime of restriction and suppression of democratic and personal freedoms.' Similarly, in China at the end of 1974 three young revolutionaries posted on the walls of a busy street in Guangzhou what came to be known as the Li Yizhe manifesto. This urged that the human rights and civic freedoms, which in the past, though guaranteed by the 1954 constitution, were constantly violated (arbitrary arrests, torture, executions for political crimes), should be reaffirmed and effectively enforced. Most important of all, it argued, is the freedom of opinion. Without free criticism from the people there can be no true political life, no participation of the masses, no socialist democracy. Up till now, no state socialist country has provided political freedom, although its absence is much less extreme now than in 1952. The progress in liberalisation that has been made throughout Eastern Europe since 1952, is a striking demonstration of the capacity of state socialism for self-renewal.[3]

[3] Since 1953 much progress in this area has been made throughout Eastern Europe. In the USSR, substantial steps forward are the reestablishment of a partial labour market

Considered from the standpoint of classical Marxism, it makes most sense to regard the state socialist countries as countries in which the Communist Party has substituted itself for the national bourgeoisie as the main engine of economic development. Hence its intolerance of independent social and political organisations, and its own internal organisation (the determination of policy by a small group of leaders or a single leader) takes on a decisive weight in the overall characterisation of these societies. It is characteristic of ruling Communist Parties that supreme power is concentrated in a single pair of hands for decades (e.g. USSR 1929–53, China 1949–76), in violation of all democratic principles but in a way familiar in the Roman Empire or Oriental Despotisms.

It is because of the use that these dictators have made of their power, that the crucial issue for Marxism-Leninism today concerns the development of the political system. As Hegedus (1970 p. 30) has put it, 'the fundamental problem of Marxism today concerns the position to be taken regarding the theoretical or practical alternatives within the political structure, the power structure, the state – or closer to reality – the administration of society. This problem can be avoided for a while as a so-called delicate question but social reality requires an answer more and more urgently.' This fundamental question has been posed theoretically by Hegedus (1976a), Carillo (1977) and Miliband (1977), and practically by Dubcek and Hu Yaobang, and remains the fundamental problem of the further development of state socialism. This fundamental problem has two aspects. The first concerns the evolution of the role of the party leadership within the party ('inner party democracy'). The second concerns the role of the state in state socialist society.

As far as the first is concerned, the general position throughout the international Communist movement remains as established by Lenin. That is, the leader has enormous power, remains in power till death and cannot be removed by the membership. Organisation of party members round political positions at variance with the leadership is banned, and has been since the resolution on fractions adopted at the 10th Congress of the Russian Communist Party in

(i.e. closing the camps, permitting workers to change their jobs freely but not permitting firms to fire workers, and issuing passports to villagers), the toleration of individuals such as Sakharov, the ending of jamming some radio stations broadcasting to the USSR, and allowing political opponents and a substantial proportion of one ethnic minority to leave the country. In some state socialist countries, e.g. Poland, the censorship has been quite liberal for many years. Further more, some state socialist countries, e.g. Hungary, allow substantial travel to capitalist countries by their citizens.

1921. Indeed in some countries (e.g. North Korea) the political system seems to be evolving in the direction of a hereditary personal dictatorship. The nearest the state socialist countries have moved to a Schumpeterian conception of democracy (rotation of elites) is in Poland, where in 1956, in 1970 and in 1980 the leadership changed in response to popular pressure. 'Democracy by riot and strike', like the 'collective bargaining by riot' which existed in late eighteenth- and early nineteenth-century Britain, is undoubtedly relatively progressive. While progressive relative to autocracy, however, it is scarcely a regular process for rotation of elites in response to popular wishes. In the USSR, the dismissal of Khrushchev (1964) and the partial tolerance of some unofficial political demonstrations (1987) were significant developments which expanded the oligarchic and democratic elements of Soviet political life. How the relative importance of the autocratic, oligarchic and democratic elements in the Soviet political system will evolve, remains to be seen.

As far as the second is concerned, perhaps the most important difference between the role of the state in capitalism and in state socialism concerns the existence of organisations independent of the state apparatus. As a Hungarian writer has put it (Rakovski 1977 p. 89),

In capitalism in general, a considerable part of social practice and social interests is hived off from the totality of multifunctional institutions and constitutes itself as a group of specialised and formally autonomous organisations.

This formal autonomy does not exclude a real dependence. It is hard to resist the temptation to consider these formal relations as nothing more than a mystification of the real relations. However, there is a basic difference between societies in which some at least of the specialised institutions are formally independent from the others, and those in which everything is subordinated to a single administrative hierarchy. It is this institutional difference which separates capitalist societies from soviet societies.

It is important to note that this institutional difference is now less extreme than it once was. In Poland, one significant and recognised independent social organisation – the Catholic Church – has existed since 1956. In the USSR, an important aspect of Gorbachev's *perestroika* was the grudging tolerance extended to independent social organisations (both non-political and political). Nevertheless, the very limited possibilities open to independent social organisations remained characteristic of state socialism and a major difference with capitalism, even at the end of the 1980s. It is difficult to regard the subordination of (almost) the whole of society to a single administrative hierarchy as a characteristic of a higher type of social organisation than liberal democratic capitalism.

Experience so far has shown that Trotsky's argument, referred to in chapter 1, is correct in that there are indeed circumstances in which 'the democratic tasks of backward bourgeois nations in our epoch lead to the dictatorship of the proletariat'. It is possible to establish dictatorships in backward countries that create a proletariat and solve problems (such as industrialisation and the build up of defence capacity) that other regimes may be unable to resolve. Experience has also shown, however, that it is not true that under these circumstances 'the road to democracy leads through the dictatorship of the proletariat'. The dictatorship appears to be a road leading to industrialisation, the rapid development of military power and permanent dictatorship. As far as the responsibility of the governors to the governed is concerned, and this is an important aspect of democracy, the dictatorship has not led to it anywhere.[4] The Indian people had an opportunity of passing judgement on Mrs Gandhi, but no such opportunity was available to the Chinese people during Mao's rule. Mao's own attitude to democracy was clearly explained in 1973 when he told the visiting French leader Pompidou that (Benton 1977 p. 102), 'Napoleon's methods were best – he dissolved all the parliaments and nominated those he wanted to rule.' This autocratic, pre-democratic, attitude is normal, but not universal, throughout the state socialist world. In Brecht's well-known words, the attitude of some of the governments of the state socialist countries to popular dissatisfaction is that 'if the government has lost the confidence of the people it is necessary to dissolve the people and elect a new one', an attitude illustrated once more by events in Kampuchea in 1975–6. In Poland and Hungary, on the other hand, the governments are much more responsive to popular feelings. For example, in Poland agriculture is still mainly in private hands.

It would seem that the state socialist countries apply a decision-making procedure appropriate to one particular situation (the Prisoners' Dilemma) to a wide variety of situations. What is common to all the situations is the authoritarian character of the decision-making process. What is characteristic of only one of them (the Prisoners' Dilemma) is that this leads to a result more favourable for the individuals concerned than the one they themselves would have chosen. Only in this one case is there a sense in which the outcome

[4] In the countries of peripheral socialism, the dictatorship has not led to industrialisation either.

can be considered democratic. The unwarranted extension of a decision-making process entirely justified in a special case, results in general and permanent authoritarianism. This authoritarianism is often more extreme than in traditional authoritarian regimes, since it is often part of a violent and revolutionary transformation of the entire society.

Distribution

As far as the distribution of income is concerned, it was argued in chapter 7 that the available evidence is inadequate to make satisfactory comparisons between state socialism and capitalism, largely because of the poor quality of the available data. Nevertheless, it is clear that the distribution of income under state socialism and capitalism differ in complex ways that cannot accurately be summarised as more or less inequality. Furthermore, income distribution and inequality are related under state socialism and capitalism in different ways. In the latter, money income and wealth ownership are the major factors determining differences in consumption, life chances and social stratification. In the former, position in the political hierarchy, income in kind and membership of a favoured (or unfavoured) caste are of greater importance. Countries with state ownership of the means of production naturally do not have the small minority of individuals with huge holdings of the means of production normal under capitalism.

The market for consumer goods and services in the state socialist countries is often marked by a situation of rationing, suction or shortage. This reduces real incomes, can generate widespread popular dissatisfaction and is one of the factors causing countries to embark on the reform process.

As far as the distribution of power is concerned, it would seem that the combination of a permanent dictatorship with the absence of independent social organisations leads to inequalities of power much greater than in liberal democratic capitalist countries. The inequality was enormous between those who organised, and those whose lives were transformed by, collectivisation and the Gulag Archipelago in the USSR; land reform, collectivisation, the Great Leap Forward and the Great Proletarian Cultural Revolution in China; and sending down the entire urban population in Kampuchea. On the other hand, in both capitalist and state socialist countries, the long-run tendency appears to be for inequalities of power to diminish. Capitalism no longer sports the slave-worked plantations of the eighteenth and nineteenth centuries, nor the great differences between the masters and servants of the early factories. In the state socialist world, Stalin was officially criticised at the 20th and 22nd Congresses and Mao Zedong in the 1981 'Resolution on certain questions in the history of our party since the founding of the People's Republic of China'.

The social ownership of the means of production

An important phenomenon distinguishing all the state socialist countries from the capitalist ones is the state ownership of all, or virtually all, of the means of production. Is this sufficient for a higher mode of production? The traditional Marxist-Leninist answer is positive, but, in addition to the points made above about the political differences between capitalism and state socialism, the following points are relevant.

What happens when the means of production are nationalised in an economy which is too backward for the emancipation of the proletariat? This question was long ago considered by the founder of the Russian Marxist movement, G. V. Plekhanov. Writing in the 1880s and polemicising against the Narodnik view that it would be possible to organise a socialist revolution in Russia in the near future, he argued that this was absurd. Russia, he wrote in *Socialism and the political struggle* (1883), lacked the necessary conditions for this. These conditions were both objective (huge development of the productive forces, need for full socialisation for further economic development, working class as bulk of the population) and subjective (general acceptance of socialist ideas). Were revolutionary socialists to take power under these conditions and attempt to establish socialism, they 'would have to seek salvation in the ideals of "patriarchal and authoritarian communism"', introducing into these ideals only the change that a socialist caste would manage national production instead of the Peruvian Children of the Sun [i.e. the Incas] and their officials.' Such a regime would be unable to attain the goals of the socialist movement.

This view was general in the Russian Marxist movement, and was endorsed two decades later by Lenin. In *Two tactics of Social democracy in the democratic revolution* (1905), he argued against

the absurd, semi-anarchist view that the maximum programme, the conquest of power for a socialist revolution, can be achieved immediately. The present degree of economic development in Russia – an objective condition – and the degree of class consciousness and organisation of the broad masses of the proletariat – a subjective condition indissolubly linked with the objective condition – make the immediate, complete emancipation of the working class impossible. Only the most ignorant people can ignore the bourgeois character of the present democratic revolution. Only the most naive optimists can forget how little as yet the masses of the workers are informed of the aims of socialism and of the methods of achieving it. And we are all convinced that the emancipation of the workers can only be brought about by the workers themselves; a socialist revolution is out of the question unless the masses become class-conscious, organised, trained and educated by open class struggle against the entire bourgeoisie. In answer to the anarchist objections that we are delaying the socialist revolution, we shall say: we are not delaying it, but we are taking the first steps in its direction, using the only means that are possible along the only right path, namely the path of a democratic republic. Whoever wants to approach socialism by any other path than that of political democracy will inevitably arrive at absurd and reactionary conclusions both economic and political.

It can be seen that the classical Marxist attitude to premature attempts to build socialism is not that this will lead to a higher mode of production, but that it can only lead to a 'partriarchal and authoritarian communism' with a socialist caste substituting itself for the Incas, i.e. what Lenin termed 'absurd and reactionary conclusions both economic and political'.

Despite this classical Marxist position, the means of production have in fact been nationalised in countries which, from a classical Marxist perspective, lack the possibilities of constructing a socialist society. How should one evaluate the social relations resulting from this? This question was considered by Lange (1962 p. 12), who argued that state ownership might experience either anarcho-syndicalist degeneration or bureaucratic degeneration. Anarcho-syndicalist degeneration (as in Yugoslavia) turns state ownership into group ownership. This emphasises one half of the socialist objective (use by society) at the expense of the other (use for society). Bureaucratic degeneration (as in the USSR) turns state ownership into bureaucratic control. This emphasises use for society at the expense of use by society. This argument was developed by Brus (1975), who argued that the socialisation of the means of production is a *process* which begins with nationalisation and continues with democratisation.[5] By this criterion none of the state socialist countries have yet achieved the social ownership of the means of production because they have not yet established democracy. Hence, it

[5] Similarly, the Soviet sociologist Arutiunian, whose argument about socialisation as a process was quoted in chapter 6, concluded that (Arutiunian 1973 p. 114), 'The social task of the day comes down to the need for further democratisation of the functions involved in the disposition of property.'

follows that the state socialist countries are not characterised by a higher mode of production than the capitalist ones (because they have not established the social ownership of the means of production). As the East German writer Bahro (1978 p. 11) has argued,

The abolition of private property in the means of production has in no way meant their immediate transformation into the property of the people. Rather, the whole society stands property-less against its state machine. The monopoly of disposal over the apparatus of production, over the lion's share of the surplus product, over the proportions of the reproduction process, over distribution and consumption, has led to a bureaucratic mechanism with the tendency to kill off or privatize any subjective initiative.

The distinction between state ownership and social ownership, and the identification of the former under certain conditions with bureaucratisation of the economy, were very radical arguments when they were first propounded. After some years went by, however, they became conventional arguments for *perestroika*. For example, at a conference organised by the Soviet Academy of Sciences in Moscow in April 1987 (*Pravda* 18 April 1987), A. N. Yakovlev, a CC Secretary, stated that, 'In practice, the dogmatic absolutisation of state ownership turned in fact into the primacy of arbitrary administrative decision-making [*administrirovanie*], increasing the scope for omnipotent bureaucratisation.'

The reaction to this situation has taken the form of the reform process. Experience in the 1970s and 1980s with the reform process showed that state ownership of the means of production was an important factor hindering the introduction of real market relations (see chapter 3). Enterprises whose managers were appointed from above, whose activities were assessed in accordance with official plans and campaigns, and which could rely on their superiors to care for them regardless of their efficiency (e.g. by altering their plan or financial regulators) remained more influenced by bureaucratic rationality than by economic rationality. The idea underlying much traditional thinking about market socialism, that state owned enterprises could be made to behave as if they were market oriented by laying down simple rules for them to follow (e.g. profit maximisation or marginal cost pricing) was shown to be an illusion. This gave rise to an international discussion about how to make enterprises follow market principles. Attempts were made to weaken the bureaucratic elements in their behaviour by giving some authority over appointments to their work force (China, Hungary, USSR) and also by enlarging the sphere of non-state activities, such as individual and cooperative sectors (China, Hungary, USSR) and joint stock companies (China). These measures were official recognition of the fact that state ownership can have an adverse effect on efficiency. They were also attempts to establish ownership forms that would achieve efficiency.

Economic planning

All the state socialist countries have national economic plans. Is this sufficient to characterise them as forming part of a higher mode of production? The traditional Marxist-Leninist answer is positive, providing there is also social ownership of the means of production. It is necessary to bear in mind, however, that the reason for this positive answer is the theory according to which

(a) a planned economy is bound to be more efficient than an anarchic one,

(b) planning and the market are two mutually exclusive categories, so that an economy can be either planned or market but not both,

(c) a country with a national economic plan is a planned economy, and

(d) planning is exclusively aimed at the realisation of the plan targets.

As far as (a) is concerned, seventy years after the October Revolution is it possible to consider this theory as an empirical proposition. This was done above. It was concluded that there was no convincing evidence for it.

As far as (b) is concerned, experience has shown that it is simply not true. At the present time a wide variety of countries both socialist and capitalist (e.g. France, Japan, Netherlands, Mexico) have plans. What distinguishes the state socialist countries is not that they have plans, but that in them a high share of resources is allocated by administrative or bureaucratic methods and that this is defended as necessary for economic planning. Furthermore, none of the state socialist countries has a complete absence of market relations. This is because when attempts have been made to eliminate market relations in the state socialist countries (the USSR in 1918–20 and 1930, China in 1958–9 and 1966–76, Cuba in the 1960s, Kampuchea in the late 1970s) the results have always been adverse and it has always been necessary to reintroduce some market relations.

As far as (c) is concerned, it was pointed out earlier in this book that the plan is simply one of the factors, and often not a very important one, in determining economic outcomes in countries which have one.

As far as (d) is concerned, this overlooks an important aspect of actually existing planning, to which attention was drawn in chapter 2. This is not so much to bring about the purported objectives of the plan but to function as a rationality *ritual* in the anthropological or sociological sense. As a ritual it has two aspects, giving significance to human life and legitimising the ruling group. It does the first by conveying the illusion that the chaos we see around us is in fact part of a rational order. It does the second by ascribing to the priests (planners, economists and other technicians) and rulers they serve, the function of bringing order out of chaos, of leading society to the Glittering Future.

Conclusions

(1) The CMEA countries do not differ fundamentally from the capitalist countries with respect to the rationality of the economic system, the labour process, the division of labour, and the social ownership of the means of production. In both groups of countries, most of the population is forced to engage in dreary labour in an inefficient, stratified, unequal society in which the means of production are not in social ownership.

(2) As far as the Marxist goal of overcoming the division of labour is concerned, the normal situation under state socialism is one in which the main aim of economic policy is to develop the forces of production. This gives rise to numerous issues which are discussed in this book. The aim of transforming the relations of production is usually relegated to the higher stage of communism. In some circumstances (Russia in 1918–20, China 1966–76, Cuba 1966–70) priority is given to developing the relations of production, or policies are pursued which are rationalised in these terms. Such policies have always been abandoned under pressure from the need for rapid economic development, opposition from their victims and popular desires for less coercion and more consumption. Sometimes (e.g. China under Deng Xiaoping) changes in the relations of production are introduced because they are thought to be necessary for the development of the forces of production. In the USSR, the quasi-feudal system introduced by the adoption of the coercive model in agriculture was retrogressive and marked a step backwards relative to capitalism. The abandonment of this model in the decades after 1953, and the associated liberalisation in other fields, were major

steps forward for the USSR. In the 1980s the USSR combined some
areas in which its economic system was more advanced than that of
the capitalist world (full employment and security of employment)
with areas in which its economic system was more backward than
that of the capitalist world (a shortage or suction economy and the
absence of independent trade unions). The advantages and disadvantages were closely related.

(3) The state socialist and capitalist countries differ with respect to
the distribution of income, the distribution of wealth and the distribution of power. These differences are important, difficult to reduce
to the question of more or less inequality and vary over time. The
market for consumer goods and services in the state socialist countries is often marked by a situation of shortage or rationing. This
reduces real incomes, can generate widespread popular dissatisfaction, and is an important reason for embarking on the reform
process.

(4) The most significant political differences between the state socialist and capitalist countries are threefold. First, the former lack any
regular process for rotation of elites in response to popular wishes.
Secondly, in the former (almost) the whole of society is subordinated
to a single administrative hierarchy. Thirdly, all the former but only
some of the latter, lack the traditional liberal political freedoms. In
these three important respects, state socialism is a *lower* form of
socio-economic organisation than liberal democratic capitalism.

(5) Experience has shown that the classical Marxist attitude to
revolutions by socialists in backward countries was partially correct.
Such revolutions have all led to what Plekhanov termed a 'patriarchal and authoritarian communism' with a socialist caste substituting itself for the Incas, i.e. what Lenin termed 'absurd and
reactionary conclusions both economic and political'. Although the
Parvus-Trotsky-Lenin theory of permanent revolution was correct in
stressing the possibility of making revolutions in backward countries
in the name of socialism, it was wrong, at any rate up till now, in
supposing that the outcome would be democracy, understood as
responsible government. The classical Marxist attitude was,
however, also partially incorrect, because it ignored the possibility of
such revolutions leading to rapid industrialisation. This is considered
below under 'catching up with the advanced countries'.

(6) Self-management exists only in producer cooperatives in capitalist countries and in Yugoslavia. While it has important advantages, it
does not eliminate the need for national economic planning and, in its
Yugoslav form, its macro-economic results are poor.

(7) All the state socialist countries have state ownership of the means of production. However, the premature introduction of state ownership can have very negative effects, state ownership of the means of production is not necessarily social ownership and state ownership can hinder efficiency.

(8) All the state socialist countries have national economic planning. All attempts to establish purely non-market economies, however, have led to adverse effects and had to be withdrawn. All existing state socialist economies (like some capitalist ones) have *both* planning *and* the market. As far as the relative efficiency of the capitalist and state socialist mixtures of planning and the market are concerned, this question was considered on pp. 299–311 above. It was concluded (conclusion (11), p. 311 above), *inter alia*, that 'The conclusions which can be drawn from the actual experience of the competition between the two systems are more complex and have more nuances than would be expected on the basis of simple-minded *a priori* expectations, either liberal or Marxist.'

(9) The traditional model of socialist planning is of an economy almost entirely administered and controlled by the state which develops in accordance with the plan. Experience has shown that efficient implementation of this model is not feasible. It is not feasible because the planners inevitably suffer from partial ignorance and inadequate techniques for data processing and society is complex. Hence the environment, policy and the interests of the various social groups involved are also of great importance in determining outcomes. The attempt to implement the traditional model is wasteful because it prevents firms and individuals responding to individual and social needs. As a result, some years after the traditional model was introduced, countries with it have generally embarked on the reform process. During this process private and/or cooperative sectors have reemerged and the role of indirect methods of plan implementation (e.g. prices and other financial regulators) has increased. The fact that 'socialist planning', in the original sense of a rational economy which replaced market relationships by direct calculation and direct product exchange, has nowhere been established, reflects not the malevolence of this or that social group, nor the backwardness of the countries concerned, but the theoretical inadequacy of the traditional conception.

(10) An important aspect of planning as it actually functions throughout the world is not to bring about its purported objectives but to serve as a rationality ritual.

CATCHING UP WITH THE ADVANCED COUNTRIES

The other major issue raised by the historical experience of the state socialist countries is their success, or otherwise, in catching up with, and overtaking, the most advanced capitalist countries.

It can be seen from table 10.2 that the USSR has made substantial progress in overtaking and surpassing the United States. It already exceeds it in the production of a number of basic industrial commodities (e.g. oil, steel and fertilisers) and in 1950–75 its national income rose sharply relative to that of the United States. Similarly, whereas in 1941–5 the Soviet war with Germany, not the strongest capitalist country, was very even and nearly resulted in a German victory, at the present time the USSR has achieved military parity with the strongest capitalist country. Similarly, China has made rapid industrial and military progress since 1949. Although catching up with the advanced countries in labour productivity is still a matter for the distant future, the country has made substantial industrial progress and does have its own nuclear weapons and delivery systems.[6] Stalin and his successors have been successful in achieving the objectives he posed. Nevertheless, although Soviet progress up till the mid 1970s in *catching up* is clear, the apparent lack of technological creativity displayed by the USSR and the Soviet relative – and possibly absolute – stagnation of 1976–85, raise doubts as to whether the country will ever *overtake* the United States. Moreover, the achievements of Japan in catching up with the USA in the civilian sector are much more impressive than those of the USSR. Similarly, China lags behind Taiwan and South Korea,

Considered from this angle, Marxism-Leninism and Marxism-Leninism-Mao Zedong Thought appear as ideologies of state-directed industrialisation in backward countries. They correspond, *mutatis mutandis*, to liberalism in Victorian Britain. Liberalism in Victorian Britain emphasised some genuine features of reality, the existence of political freedom and the ability of the new technology combined with capitalist social relations to generate new fortunes. It ignored, however, other aspects of reality, the grotesque inequalities, the lack of democracy, and the dependence of British prosperity on the fact that the British Navy and British temporary technological leadership enabled Britain to dominate the seas and markets of the world. Similarly, Marxism-Leninism and Marxism-Leninism-Mao Zedong Thought emphasise the very real phenomena of rapid

---

[6] In 1987 a Chinese company signed a contract to launch a commercial satellite for a US company. This symbolised the extent of Chinese industrialisation.

industrialisation, the build-up of defence capacity, full employment, job security and relatively good provision of public goods. They ignore, however, the equally real phenomena of the lack of any regular process for rotation of elites in response to popular wishes, the lack of liberal political freedoms, the authoritarian nature of power relations and the strongly hierarchical nature of the socio-political system. In addition, Marxism-Leninism ignores the lack of national independence in countries such as the GDR, Poland, Czechoslovakia and Hungary (where the situation is similar, in this respect, to that in much of Latin America).

Liberalism was undermined by the rise of democracy and the labour movement. The labour movement, committed to socialism, was able to use liberal democratic institutions to reduce inequalities substantially (by taxation, transfer payments and free or subsidised state provision of education, medical care and housing). Nevertheless, the labour movement has been unable to eliminate inequality, to establish permanent full employment, or to maintain its social and political influence under recessionary conditions. Where the labour movement is not committed to socialism (as in the United States) its social achievements have been even less impressive.

Marxism-Leninism has been undermined by the economic achievements of capitalism, movements striving for national independence and the growth of a white-collar intelligentsia committed to pluralism and a different system of social differentiation. It has survived up till now in the USSR, however, because of the autocratic traditions of the Russian state, the overwhelming importance in the USSR of the national question, the service mentality of the white-collar intelligentsia, and its ability to adapt (e.g. its recognition of the merits under certain circumstances of small-scale production in agriculture, of the merits of individual and cooperative economic activity and of the need for socio-political changes if the stagnation of the late Brezhnev period is to be overcome). Other positive factors are the continued success up till now of the Soviet state in avoiding an economic catastrophe of the Polish or Mexican type, expanding Soviet world political influence, and preserving national independence. In a number of other countries, however, only external military force can maintain the veneer of Marxism-Leninism and the institutions of state socialism. Where the economic achievements of capitalism are not widely distributed, and the state socialist countries have supported the struggle against colonialism and semi-colonialism or Communist Parties have guided that struggle (e.g. the Caribbean, South East Asia, Southern Africa), then Marxism-

Leninism and Marxism-Leninism-Mao Zedong Thought have spread.

SUMMARY

This chapter considered the experience of socialist planning from the standpoint of the two issues raised in the first chapter, the creation of a higher mode of production and the need for backward countries to catch up. The first issue was considered from the standpoint of seven criteria, and it was concluded that the state socialist countries have failed to establish a higher mode of production than capitalism. As far as catching up is concerned, it was suggested that in certain periods the USSR and China have both made substantial progress in this direction, but on the whole less than that of Japan and the East Asian NICs. Nevertheless, although neither the USSR nor China show any sign in the foreseeable future of overtaking the USA in the crucial synthetic efficiency index, labour productivity, the USSR has already caught up in the decisive military field.

SUGGESTIONS FOR FURTHER READING

A. Bergson, *Productivity and social system – the USSR and the West* (Cambridge, Mass 1978).

H. Wilkens, *The two German economies* (Farnborough, England 1981).

I. L. Collier, *Connections, effective purchasing power and real product in the German Democratic Republic* (Berlin 1985).

'The Soviet growth slowdown: three views', *American Economic Review* vol. 76, no. 2 (May 1986).

R. Selucky, *Economic reforms in Eastern Europe* (New York 1972).

W. Brus, 'Political system and economic efficiency', *Journal of Comparative Economics* vol. 4, no. 1 (March 1980).

A. Chan, S. Rosen & J. Unger (eds.) *On socialist democracy and the Chinese legal system: the Li Yizhe debates* (New York 1985).

E. J. Perry & C. Wong (eds.) *The political economy of reform in post-Mao China* (Cambridge, Mass 1985).

Dong Fureng & P. Nolan (eds.) *Chinese economic reform* (Cambridge 1989).

R. Medvedev, *Socialist democracy* (London 1975).

T. Zaslavskaya, 'On the necessity for a deeper study in the USSR of the social mechanism of economic development', *Survey* (Spring 1984).

A. N. Yakovlev, 'Dostizhenie kachestvenno novogo sostoyaniya sovetskogo obshchestva i obshchestvennye nauki', *Vestnik AN SSSR* no. 6 (1987).

A. Shtromas & M. A. Kaplan (eds.) *The Soviet Union and the challenge of the future* vol. 2 (New York & London 1988).

H. H. Hohmann, A. Nove & H. Vogel, *Economics and politics in the USSR: problems of interdependence* (London 1986).

A. Becker, *The burden of Soviet defence: a political-economic essay* (Santa Monica 1981).

Soviet military-economic relations (JEC US Congress, Washington DC 1983).

P. Wiles & M. Efrat, *The economics of Soviet arms* (London 1985).

L. R. Sykes & D. M. Davis, 'The yields of Soviet strategic weapons', *Scientific American* (January 1987).

A comparative study of the South and North Korean economies (Seoul, Korea 1986).

J. Halliday, 'The economies of North and South Korea', J. Sullivan & R. Foss (eds.) *Two Koreas – one future?* (Lanham, Maryland 1987).

BIBLIOGRAPHY

This is a selective bibliography which includes only those works referred to in the text, listed at the end of the chapters or found particularly useful by the author.

NOTES

(1) Books in Russian are published in Moscow unless otherwise stated. Books in English are published in London unless otherwise stated.

(2) Russian words are transliterated into English according to the *Soviet Studies* transliteration system, with the exception that when proper names end in 'ii' the last two letters are sometimes transliterated by a 'y'.

Abalkin, L. (1987). 'Perestroika sistemy metodov planovogo upravleniya', *Planovoe khozyaistvo* no. 5.

Abdel–Fadil, M. (1976). *Development, income distribution and social change in rural Egypt (1952–1970)* (Cambridge).

Abonyi, A. & Sylvain, I. J. (1977). 'CMEA integration and policy options for Eastern Europe: A development strategy for dependent states', *Journal of Common Market Studies* vol. 16, no. 2.

Abouchar, A. (1971). *Soviet planning and spatial efficiency* (Bloomington).

  (1972). 'The new standard methodology for investment allocation', *Soviet Studies* vol. 24.

  (1979). *Economic evaluation of Soviet socialism* (New York).

Adam, J. & Nosal, M. (1982). 'Earnings differentials and household income differentials'. *Journal of Comparative Economics* vol. 6, no. 2 (June).

Adler-Karlsson, G. (1968). *Western economic warfare* (Stockholm).

  (1976). *The political economy of East–West–South cooperation* (Vienna & New York).

Amann, R. (1977). R. Amann, J. M. Cooper & R. W. Davies (eds.) *The technological level of Soviet industry* (New Haven).

  (1982). R. Amann & J. Cooper (eds.) *Industrial innovation in the Soviet Union* (New Haven).

  (1986). R. Amann & J. Cooper (eds.) *Technical progress and Soviet economic development* (Oxford).

'American' (1977). 'The American rural small-scale industry delegation', *Rural small-scale industry in the People's Republic of China* (Berkeley).

Amin, S. (1974). *Accumulation on a world scale* (New York & London).

Andrle, V. (1976). *Managerial power in the Soviet Union.*

Antal, L. (1979). 'Development – with some digression', *Acta Oeconomica* vol. 23, no. 3–4.

(1982). 'Thoughts on the further development of the Hungarian mechanism', *Acta Oeconomica* vol. 29, no. 3–4.

Arrow, K. & Hahn, F. (1971). *General competitive analysis* (San Francisco & Edinburgh).

Arutiunian, Yu. V. (1973). 'The distribution of decision-making among the rural population of the USSR', M. Yanowitch & W. A. Fisher (eds.) *Social stratification and mobility in the USSR* (New York).

Ashbrook, A. G. Jr (1975). 'China: Economic overview, 1975', *China (1975)* q.v.

Ashton, B. Hill, K., Piazza, A. & Zeitz, R. (1984). 'Famine in China, 1958–61', *Population and Development Review* vol. 10, no. 4.

Askanas, B. & Levcik, F. (1983). 'The dispersal of wages in the CMEA countries', S. F. Frowen (ed.) *Controlling industrial economies*.

Aslund, A. (1985). *Private enterprise in Eastern Europe* (London & New York).

Ausch, S. (1972). *Theory and practice of CMEA cooperation* (Budapest).

Axelrod, R. (1984). *The evolution of cooperation* (New York).

Bachurin, A. (1969). 'V. I. Lenin i sovremennye problemy planirovaniya narodnogo khozyaistva', *Planovoe khozyaistvo* no. 11.

Bagchi, A. K. (1978). 'On the political economy of technological choice and development', *Cambridge Journal of Economics* vol. 2, no. 2 (June).

Bahro, R. (1978). *The Alternative in Eastern Europe*.

Bailes, K. E. (1977). 'Alexei Gastev and the Soviet controversy over Taylorism, 1918–24', *Soviet Studies* vol. XXIX, no. 3 (July).

Balassa, B. & Tyson, L. (1986). 'Policy responses to external shocks in Hungary and Yugoslavia', *East European Economies: Slow growth in the 1980s* (JEC US Congress, Washington DC) vol. 1.

Barsov, A. A. (1969). *Balans stoimostnykh obmenov mezhdu gorodom i derevnei.*

(1974). 'Nep i vyravnivanie ekonomicheskikh otnoshenii mezhdu gorodom i derevnei', *Novaya ekonomicheskaya politika: Voprosy teorii i istorii.*

Basic (1965). *Basic principles and experiences of industrial planning in the Soviet Union* (UN New York).

Bauer, T. (1978). 'Investment cycles in planned economies', *Acta Oeconomica* vol. 21, no. 3.

(1983a). 'The Hungarian alternative to Soviet-type planning', *Journal of Comparative Economics* vol. 7, no. 3.

(1983b). 'A note on money and the consumer in Eastern Europe', *Soviet Studies* vol. XXXV, no. 3 (July).

(1984). 'The second economic reform and ownership relations', *Eastern European Economics* vol. 22, no. 3–4.

(1985). 'Reform policy in the complexity of economic policy', *Acta Oeconomica* vol. 34, no. 3–4.

(1987). 'Des cycles à la crise?', B. Chavance (ed.) *Regulation cycles en crises dans les économies socialistes* (Paris).

Baum, R. (1975a). *Prelude to revolution* (New York).

(1975b). 'Technology, economic organisation and social change: Maoism and the Chinese industrial revolution', *China in the seventies* (Wiesbaden) pp. 131–91.

Baumol, W. J. (1952). *Welfare economics and the theory of the state.*

Becker, A. (1981). *The burden of Soviet defence: a political-economic essay* (Rand, Santa Monica).

Beer, S. (1969). 'The aborting corporate plan: a cybernetic account of the interface between planning and action', E. Jantsch (ed.) *Perspectives of planning* (Paris).

Bek, A. (1971). *Novoe naznachenie* (Frankfurt).

Belkin, V. D. & Birman, I. Ya. (1964). Article in *Izvestiya* (4 December).

Belotserkovskii, V. (1977). *Svoboda, vlast' i sobstvennost'* (Achberg).

Benton, G. (1977). 'The factional struggle in the Chinese Communist Party', *Critique* no. 8.

Bergson, A. (1964). *The economics of Soviet planning* (New Haven & London).
  (1968). *Planning and productivity under Soviet socialism* (New York).
  (1978). *Productivity and the social system – the USSR and the West* (Cambridge, Mass).
  (1980). 'The geometry of Comecon trade: a note', *European Economic Review*.
  (1984). 'Income inequality under Soviet socialism', *Journal of Economic Literature* vol. XXII, no. 3 (September).

Berliner, J. (1957). *Factory and manager in the USSR* (Cambridge, Mass).
  (1964). 'The static efficiency of the Soviet economy', *American Economic Review* supplement (May).
  (1966). 'The economics of overtaking and surpassing', H. Rosovsky (ed.) *Industrialisation in two systems* (New York).
  (1976). *The innovation decision in Soviet industry* (Cambridge, Mass).

Bernstein, T. P. (1967). 'Leadership and mass mobilisation in the Soviet and Chinese collectivisation campaigns of 1929–30 and 1955–56: A comparison', *China Quarterly* no. 31.
  (1977). *Up to the mountains and down to the villages* (Yale).

Bettelheim, C. (1974a). *Les luttes de classes en URSS 1ère periode 1917–23* (Paris).
  (1974b). *Cultural revolution and industrial organisation in China* (New York).
  (1976). *Economic calculation and forms of property*.
  (1986). 'More on the nature of the Soviet system', *Monthly Review* (December).

Bhaduri, A. (1977). 'On the formation of usurious interest rates in backward agriculture', *Cambridge Journal of Economics* vol. 1, no. 4.

Birman, I. (1978). 'From the achieved level', *Soviet Studies* vol. XXX, no. 2.
  (1981). *Secret incomes of the Soviet state budget* (The Hague, Boston & London).
  (1983). *Ekonomika nedostach* (New York).
  (1986). 'A note on Soviet foreign trade gains', *Soviet Studies* (October).

Bliss, C. (1972). 'Prices, Markets and Planning', *Economic Journal* (March).

Blum, J. (1978). *The end of the old order in rural Europe* (Princeton).

Bobrowski, Cz. (1956). *Formation du Système Soviétique de Planification* (Paris). There is a Polish edition (Warsaw 1967).

Bogomolov, O. T. (1984). O. T. Bogomolov (ed.) *Agrarnye otnosheniya v stranakh sotsializma*.
  (1986). *Strany sotsializma v mezhdunarodnom razdelenii truda* 2nd edn.

Boltho, A. (1971). *Foreign trade criteria in socialist economies* (Cambridge).

Boot, P. (1982). 'The end of predominantly annual planning in the German Democratic Republic', *The ACES Bulletin* vol. XXIV, no. 3.

(1983). 'Continuity and change in the planning system of the German Democratic Republic', *Soviet Studies* vol. XXXV, no. 3.

(1984). 'Investment cycles in the German Democratic Republic', *The ACES Bulletin* vol. XXVI, no. 1 (Spring).

(1987). 'East-West trade and industrial policy: the case of the German Democratic Republic', *Soviet Studies* vol. XXXIX, no. 4 (October).

Brabant, J. P. M. van (1973). *Bilateralism and structural bilateralism in intra-CMEA trade* (Rotterdam).

(1974). *Essays on planning, trade and integration in Eastern Europe* (Rotterdam).

(1987). *Adjustment, structural change and economic efficiency* (Cambridge).

Brada, J. (1973a). 'The microallocative impact of the Hungarian economic reform of 1968: some evidence from the export sector', *Economics of Planning* vol. 13, nos. 1–2.

(1973b). 'The allocative efficiency of centrally planned foreign trade: a programming approach to the Czech case', *European Economic Review* no. 4.

(1986). 'The variability of crop production in private and socialized agriculture', *Journal of Political Economy* vol. 94, no. 3, part 1.

Brada, J. & Wädekin, K. (1988). J. Brada & K. Wädekin (eds.) *Socialist agriculture in transition* (Boulder, Co.).

Bradley, M. E. & Clark, M. G. (1972). 'Supervision and efficiency in socialized agriculture', *Soviet Studies* vol. XXIII, no. 3.

Braverman, H. (1974). *Labour and monopoly capital. The degradation of work in the twentieth century* (New York).

Brody, A. (1980). 'On the discussion about measurement – a rejoinder', *Acta Oeconomica* vol. 25, nos. 1–2.

Bromlei, Yu. (1987). 'Natsional'nye protsessy v SSSR', *Pravda* (13 February).

Brus, W. (1972). *The market in a socialist economy*.

(1973). *The economics and politics of socialism*.

(1974). 'Income distribution and economic reforms in Poland', *Il Politico* vol. XXXIX, no. 1.

(1975). *Socialist ownership and political systems*.

(1977). 'Kalecki's economics of socialism', *Oxford Bulletin of Economics and Statistics* vol. XXXIX.

(1980). 'Political system and economic efficiency', *Journal of Comparative Economics* vol. 4, no. 1.

(1985a). 'The political economy of Polish reforms', *Praxis International* vol. 5, no. 2.

(1985b). 'Socialism – feasible and viable?', *New Left Review* no. 153.

(1987). 'Market socialism', J. Eatwell, M. Milgate & P. Newman (eds.) *The new Palgrave: a dictionary of economics* vol. 3.

Brus, W. & Kowalik, T. (1983). 'Socialism and development', *Cambridge Journal of Economics* vol. 7, no. 3–4.

Bufetova, L. P. & Golland, E. B. (1977). 'Narodnokhozyaistvennaya otsenka tekhnicheskogo progressa v otrasli', *Ekonomika i organizatsiya promyshlennogo proizvodstva* no. 2.

Bukharin, N. I. (1920). *Ekonomika perekhodnogo perioda*.
Bukharin, N. I. & Preobrazhensky, E. (1969). *The ABC of Communism* (Penguin edn). This is a translation of a book first published in Russian in 1920.
Burkett, J. P. (1983). *The effects of economic reform in Yugoslavia* (Berkeley).
 (1985). 'Systemic influences on the physical quality of life', *Journal of Comparative Economics* vol. 9, no. 2.
 (1986). 'Stabilization measures in Yugoslavia', *East European Economies: Slow growth in the 1980s* (JEC US Congress, Washington DC) vol. 3.
Buzlyakov, N. I. (1969). *Metody planirovaniya povysheniya urovnya zhizni*.
Byres, T. J. (1974). 'Land reform, industrialisation and the marketed surplus in India: An essay on the power of rural bias', D. Lehmann (ed.) *Agrarian reform and agrarian reformism*.
Campbell, R. (1976). 'Technology levels in the Soviet energy sector', *East–West technological cooperation* (Brussels).
Carchedi, G. (1986). 'Comparative advantages, capital accumulation and socialism', *Economy and Society* vol. 15, no. 4.
Carillo, S. (1977). *Eurocommunism and the state*. There is a review in *New Times* no. 26.
Carr, E. H. (1939). *The 20 years' crisis*.
 (1945). *The Soviet impact on the Western world*.
 (1967). 'Some random reflections on Soviet industrialisation', C. H. Feinstein (ed.) *Socialism, capitalism and economic development* (the Dobb festschrift) (Cambridge).
Carson, R. L. (1973). *Comparative economic systems* (New York).
Chan, A., Rosen, S. & Unger, J. (1985). A. Chan, S. Rosen & J. Unger (eds.) *On socialist democracy and the Chinese legal system: the Li Yizhe debates* (New York).
Chao, K. (1970). *Agricultural production in Communist China 1949–1965* (Madison, Wis.).
Chawluk, A. (1974). 'Economic policy and economic reform', *Soviet Studies* vol. XXVI, no. 1.
Chen, C S. (1969). C. S. Chen (ed.) *Rural people's communes in Lien-chiang* (Stanford).
Chen, J. (1973). *A year in upper felicity* (New York).
Chen Yun (1961). 'An investigation of rural Qingpu', *Chinese Economic Studies* vol. XV, nos. 3–4 (Spring–Summer 1982) pp. 155–73.
Chilosi, A. (1971). 'The theory of a socialist economy of M. Kalecki', *Economics of Planning* vol. 11, no. 3.
China (1975). *China: A reassessment of the economy* (JEC US Congress, Washington DC).
China (1985). *China. Long-term development issues and options* (Baltimore). Annex 2 to this study is *China: Agriculture to the year 2000* (World Bank, Washington DC 1985).
China's (1986). *China's economy looks towards the year 2000* (JEC US Congress, Washington DC) vol. 2.
Chinese (1987). 'Chinese economic reform: how far, how fast?', *Journal of Comparative Economics* vol. 11, no. 3 (September).

Cipolla, C. (1965). *Guns and sails in the early phase of European expansion.*

Collier, I. L. (1985). *Connections, effective purchasing power and real product in the German Democratic Republic* (Berlin).

(1986). 'Effective purchasing power in a quantity constrained economy', *Review of Economics and Statistics* vol. LXVIII, no. 1.

Comparative (1986). *A comparative study of the South and North Korean economies* (Seoul, Korea 1986).

Cory, P. F. (1982). 'Industrial co-operation, joint ventures and the MNE in Yugoslavia', chapter 7 of A. M. Rugman (ed.) *New theories of the multinational enterprise.*

Crozier, M. (1964). *The bureaucratic phenomenon* (Chicago).

Csaba, L. (1985). 'Joint investments and mutual advantages in the CMEA – Retrospection and Prognosis', *Soviet Studies* vol. XXVII, no. 2.

Csaki, C. (1983). 'Economic management and organisation of Hungarian agriculture', *Journal of Comparative Economics* vol. 7, no. 3.

Davies, R. W. (1967). 'Aspects of Soviet investment policy in the 1920s', C. H. Feinstein (ed.) *Socialism, capitalism and economic growth* (Cambridge).

(1974). 'Economic planning in the USSR', M. Bornstein & D. Fusfeld (eds.) *The Soviet economy: a book of readings* (4th edn Homewood, Illinois).

(1984). R. W. Davies (ed.) *Soviet investment for planned industrialisation, 1929–1937* (Berkeley).

Davin, D. (1976). *Women-work: Women and the party in revolutionary China* (Oxford).

Davis, C. & Charemza, W. (1988). C. Davis & W. Charemza (eds.) *Modelling of disequilibrium and shortage in centrally planned economies* (London).

Deng Xiaoping (1984). *Selected Works of Deng Xiaoping (1975–1982)* (Beijing).

(1987). 'Deng calls for speedup in reform', *Beijing Review* no. 34.

Dido, M. (1971). Article in *L'espresso* (Rome 26 September). The quote in the text is taken from *Critique* no. 4, p. 23.

Dirksen, E. (1983). 'Chinese industrial productivity in an international context', *World Development* vol. 11, no. 4.

Discourses (1931). *Discourses on salt and iron* (Leiden) trans. E. M. Gale. The argument in the text can be found on p. 33.

Djilas, M. (1962). *Conversations with Stalin* (New York).

Dmitriev, V. K. (1898). *Ekonomicheskie ocherki.* The English translation of all three essays is V. K. Dmitriev, *Economic essays on value, competition and utility* (Cambridge).

Dobb, M. (1955). *On economic theory and socialism.*

(1960). *An essay on economic growth and planning.*

(1967). *Papers on capitalism, development and planning.*

Doel, H. van den (1979). *Democracy and welfare economics* (Cambridge).

Dohan, M. R. (1976). 'The economic origins of Soviet autarky 1927/28–1934', *Slavic Review* (December).

(1984). 'Foreign trade and Soviet investment strategy for planned industrialization 1928–1938', R. W. Davies (ed.) *Soviet investment for planned industrialization, 1929–1937* (Berkeley).

Dohan, M. R. & Hewett, E. (1973). *Two studies in Soviet terms of trade 1918–1970* (Bloomington, Indiana).

Domar, E. (1957). 'A Soviet model of growth', E. Domar, *Essays in the theory of economic growth* (New York).

Dong Fureng (1987). 'Socialist countries diversify ownership', *Beijing Review* no. 40.

Dong Fureng & Nolan, P. (1989). Dong Fureng & Nolan, P. (eds.) *Chinese economic reform* (Cambridge).

Donnithorne, A. (1967). *China's economic system.*

Dorner, P. (1972). *Land reform and economic development.*

Dorofeyev, V. (1976). Article in *Literaturnaya Gazeta* (31 March) p. 13.

Dovgan', L. I. (1965). *O tempakh rosta dvukh podrazdeleniya obshchestvennogo proizvodstva.*

Downs, A. (1967). *Inside bureaucracy* (Boston).

Drabek, Z. (1981). 'Demand for intermediate products and the role of product substitution and technological change in Czechoslovakia and Austria', *Greek Economic Review* vol. 3, no. 3 (December).

(1988). 'The natural resource intensity of production technology in market and planned economies', *Journal of Comparative Economics* vol. 12, no. 2 (June).

Draft (1956). *The draft programme for agricultural development in the People's Republic of China* (Peking).

Drewnowski, J. (1979). 'The central planning office on trial', *Soviet Studies* vol. XXXI, no. 1.

Drogichinsky, N. E. (1971). N. E. Drogichinsky & V. G. Starodubrovskii (eds.) *Osnovy i praktika khozyaistvennoi reformy v SSSR.*

Dudochkin, P. (1981). 'Trezvost' – norma zhizni', *Nash sovremennik* no. 8.

Dumont, R. & Mottin, M. F. (1980). *L'Afrique Etranglée* (Paris).

Eason, W. W. (1963). 'Labour force', A. Bergson & S. Kuznets (eds.) *Economic trends in the Soviet Union* (Cambridge, Mass).

East European (1977). *East European economies post-Helsinki* (JEC US Congress, Washington DC).

(1986). *East European economies: slow growth in the 1980s* (JEC US Congress, Washington DC) 3 vols.

Eastern (1986). 'Eastern imports of machinery and equipment 1960–1985', *Economic Bulletin for Europe* vol. 38, no. 4 (December).

ECE (1983). 'Exports of manufactures from Eastern Europe and the Soviet Union to the developed market economies, 1965–1981', *Economic Bulletin for Europe* vol. 35, no. 4, chapter 3.

Eckstein, A. (1968a). 'Economic fluctuations in Communist China's economic development', Ping-ti Ho & Tang Tsou (eds.) *China in crisis* vol. 1, book 2 (Chicago). This paper is reprinted in (1968b). A. Eckstein *et al.* (eds.) *Economic trends in Communist China* (Chicago)

(1971). A. Eckstein (ed.) *Comparison of economic systems* (Berkeley).

(1975). *China's economic development* (Ann Arbor).

(1977). *China's economic revolution* (Cambridge).

Economic (1965). *Economic planning in Europe* (UN Geneva).

(1975). *Economic aspects of life in the USSR* (Brussels).

Edquist, C. (1985). *Capitalism, socialism and technology*.

Eighth (1956). *The Eighth National Congress of the Communist Party of China* (Peking).

Ekonomika (1965). *Ekonomika i organizatsiya promyshlennogo proizvodstva* no. 6.

Eleventh (1977). *The eleventh national congress of the Communist Party of China* (documents) (Peking).

Ellman, M. J. (1966). 'Individual preferences and the market', *Economics of Planning* no. 3.

  (1969a). 'Aggregation as a cause of inconsistent plans', *Economica* (February).

  (1969b). *Economic reform in the Soviet Union*.

  (1973). *Planning problems in the USSR* (Cambridge).

  (1975). 'Did the agricultural surplus provide the resources for the increase in investment in the USSR during the First Five Year Plan?' *Economic Journal* (December).

  (1977). 'Seven theses on Kosyginism', *De Economist* no. 1.

  (1978). 'On a mistake on Preobrazhensky and Stalin', *Journal of Development Studies* (April).

  (1981). 'Agricultural productivity under socialism', *World Development* (September–October).

  (1983). 'Changing views on central economic planning: 1958–1983', *The ACES Bulletin* (now: *Comparative Economic Studies*) vol. XXV, no. 1.

  (1984). *Collectivisation, convergence and capitalism*.

  (1986). 'Economic reform in China', *International Affairs* vol. 62, no. 3.

  (1987). 'Economic calculation in socialist economies', *The New Palgrave: A dictionary of economics* vol. 2.

  (1988a). 'Soviet agricultural policy', *Economic and Political Weekly* (June 11).

  (1988b). 'Would economic reform improve or worsen the situation in the USSR in the short run?' A. Shtromas & Kaplan, M. A. (eds) *The Soviet Union and the challenge of the future* vol. 2 (New York & London).

Ellman, M. J. and Simatupang, B. (1982). '*Odnowa* in statistics', *Soviet Studies* (January).

Engels, F. (1878). *Anti-Dühring* (1st edn 1878, numerous later editions).

  (1894). 'The peasant question in France and Germany'. Reprinted in K. Marks & F. Engel's, *Sochineniya* 2nd edn vol. 22, (1962).

Estrin, S. (1984). *Self-management: Economic theory and Yugoslav practice* (Cambridge).

Fang Shen (1985). 'On the issue of utilizing foreign capital', *Chinese Economic Studies* (summer).

Fedorenko, N. P. (1979). *Nekotorye voprosy teorii i praktiki planirovaniya i upravleniya*.

Fehér, F., Heller, A. & Markus, G. (1983). *Dictatorship over needs* (Oxford).

Feiwel, G. R. (1975). *The intellectual capital of Michal Kalecki* (Knoxville, Tenn.).

Feldman, G. A. (1964). 'On the theory of growth rates of national income', pp. 174–99 & 304–31 of N. Spulber (ed.) *Foundations of Soviet strategy for economic growth* (Bloomington, Indiana). This is a translation of a work originally published in 1928.

Fforde, A. J. (1987). *The agrarian question in North Vietnam* (New York).

Fforde, A. & Paine, S. (1987). *The limits of national liberation.*

Fitzgerald, E. V. K. (1987). 'Planned accumulation and income distribution in the small peripheral economy', K. Martin (ed.) *Readings in capitalist and non-capitalist development strategies.*

Flaherty, D. (1982). 'Economic reform and foreign trade in Yugoslavia', *Cambridge Journal of Economics* vol. 6, no. 2.

Flakierski, H. (1979). 'Economic reform and income distribution in Hungary', *Cambridge Journal of Economics* vol. 3, no. 1.

   (1981). 'Economic reform and income distribution in Poland', *Cambridge Journal of Economics* vol. 5, no. 2.

   (1986). *Economic reform and income distribution* (New York).

Frank, A. G. (1969). *Capitalism and underdevelopment in Latin America* (2nd edn, New York & London).

Friedman, M. (1977). *Capitalism and freedom* (Chicago).

Friss, I. (1971). 'On long-term national economic planning', I. Friss, *Economic laws, policy, planning* (Budapest) pp. 112–39.

Gacs, J. & Lacko, M. (1973). 'A study of planning behaviour on the national-economic level', *Economics of Planning* vol. 13, no. 1–2.

Galasi, P. & Sziraczki, G. (1985). P. Galasi & G. Sziraczki (eds.) *Labour market and second economy in Hungary* (New York).

Garcia, R. V. (1981). R. V. Garcia (ed.) *Nature pleads not guilty* (Oxford).

Garnsey, E. (1975). 'Occupational structure in industrial society: Some notes on the convergence thesis in the light of Soviet experience', *Sociology* vol. 9, no. 3.

   (1982). 'Capital accumulation and the division of labour in the Soviet Union', *Cambridge Journal of Economics* vol. 6, no. 1.

Gerassi, J. (1968). J. Gerassi (ed.) *Venceremos! The speeches and writings of Ernesto Che Guevara* (New York).

Gerritse, R. (1982). *The realm of necessity* (PhD thesis, Amsterdam).

Gerschenkron, A. (1965). *Economic backwardness in historical perspective* (New York).

Giffen, J. (1981). 'The allocation of investment in the Soviet Union', *Soviet Studies* vol. XXXII, no. 4.

Gomulka, S. (1971). *Inventive activity, diffusion and the stages of economic growth* (Aarhus 1971).

   (1977). 'Economic factors in the democratization of socialism and the socialization of capitalism', *Journal of Comparative Economics* vol. 1, no. 4.

   (1978). 'Growth and the import of technology: Poland 1971–1980', *Cambridge Journal of Economics* vol. 2, no. 1.

   (1986). *Growth, innovation and reform in Eastern Europe* (Brighton).

Gomulka, S. & Rostowski, J. (1984). 'The reformed Polish economic system 1982–1983', *Soviet Studies* vol. XXXVI, no. 3.

   (1988). 'An international comparison of material intensity' (forthcoming).

Gomulka, S. & Sylestrowicz, J. (1976). 'Import led growth: theory and estimation', F. L. Altmann, O. Kyn & H. J. Wagener (eds.) *On the measurement of factor productivities: theoretical problems and empirical results* (Gottingen–Zurich).

Goreux, L. M. & Manne, A. S. (1973). *Multi-level planning* (Amsterdam).
Gosudarstvennyi (1972). *Gosudarstvennyi pyatletnyi plan razvitiya narodnogo kho-
    zyaistva SSSR na 1971–1975 gody.*
Gramsci, A. (1957). *The modern prince* (1957 edn).
Granick, D. (1967). *Soviet metal fabricating and economic development* (Madison,
    Milwaukee & London).
    (1975). *Enterprise guidance in Eastern Europe* (Princeton).
Gray, J. (1972), 'The Chinese model: some characteristics of Maoist policies
    for economic and social growth', A. Nove & M. Nuti (eds.) *Socialist
    economics.*
    (1973). 'The two roads: Alternative strategies of social change and
    economic growth in China', S. Schram (ed.) *Authority, Participation and
    Cultural Change in China* (Cambridge).
Gregory, P. (1981). 'Economic growth and structural change in czarist
    Russia and the Soviet Union: a long-term comparison', in S. Rosefielde
    (ed.) *Economic welfare and the economics of Soviet socialism* (Cambridge).
Gregory, P. & Leptin, G. (1977). 'Similar societies under differing economic
    systems: the case of the two Germanys', *Soviet Studies* (October).
Grossman, G. (1963). 'Notes for a theory of the Command Economy', *Soviet
    Studies* vol. XV, no. 2.
    (1977). 'The second economy of the USSR', *Problems of Communism*
    September–October, reprinted in Tanzi (1982) q.v.
    (1988). G. Grossman (ed.) *Studies in the second economy of the Communist
    countries* (Berkeley).
Group (1985). 'On the model for the reform of China's economic structure',
    Social Sciences in China vol. VI, no. 1.
Gruzinov, V. P. (1979). *The USSR's management of foreign trade* (New York).
Guidelines (1972). *Guidelines for project evaluation* (UNIDO).
Gunsteren, H. R. van (1976). *The quest for control.*
    (1980). 'Planning in de verzorgingsstaat', J. K. M. Gevers & R. J. in 't
    Veld (eds.) *Planning als maatschappelijke vormgeving* (Deventer).
Gustafson, T. (1981). *Reform in Soviet politics* (Cambridge).
Habr, J. (1967). 'From central planning to socialist marketing: problems of
    information systems', *Bulletin of the International Statistical Institute* vol. 42,
    pp. 979–88
Hahn, F. (1973). 'The winter of our discontent', *Economica* (August).
    (1974). 'Back to square one', *Cambridge Review* (November).
Hall, J. B. (1986). 'Plan bargaining in the Hungarian economy', *Comparative
    Economic Studies* vol. XXVIII, no. 2.
Halliday, J. (1987). 'The economies of North and South Korea', J. Sullivan
    & R. Foss (eds.) *Two Koreas – one future?* (Lanham, Maryland).
Hamermesh, D. & Portes, R. (1972). 'The labour market under central
    planning', *Oxford Economic Papers* vol. 24.
Handy, L. J. (1971). 'National job evaluation: the Soviet Union and Poland',
    mimeo (DAE, Cambridge).
Hanlon, J. (1984). *Mozambique: the revolution under fire.*
Hanson, P. (1968). *The consumer in the Soviet economy.*
    (1970). 'Acquisitive dissent', *New Society* (29 October). This article is

reprinted in P. Barker (ed.) *One for sorrow, Two for joy: Ten years of New Society* (1972).

(1971). 'East–West comparisons and comparative economic systems', *Soviet Studies* vol. 22.

(1974). *Advertising and socialism.*

(1981). *Trade and technology in Soviet–Western relations.*

(1982). 'The end of import-led growth?' *Journal of Comparative Economics* vol. 6, no. 2.

(1983). 'Success indicators revisited', *Soviet Studies* vol. XXXV, no. 1.

(1987). *Soviet industrial espionage: some new information.*

(1988). *Western economic statecraft in East–West relations.*

Haraszi, M. (1975). 'I have heard the iron cry', *New Left Review* no. 91.

Hare, P., Radice, H. & Swain, N. (1981). P. Hare, H. Radice & N. Swain (eds.) *Hungary: A decade of economic reform.*

Harrison, M. (1988). 'Resource mobilisation for World War II', *Economic History Review* vol. XLI, no. 2 (May).

Hartford, K. (1985). 'Hungarian agriculture: A model for the socialist world?' *World Development* (January).

Hayden, E. W. (1976). *Technology transfer to East Europe. US corporate experience* (New York).

Hayek, F. (1935). F. Hayek (ed.) *Collectivist economic planning.*

(1937). 'Economics and knowledge', *Economica* vol. IV, no. 13.

(1945). 'The use of knowledge in society', *American Economic Review* vol. XXXV, no. 4.

(1973 & 1978). *Law, legislation and liberty* vols. 1 & 2 (Chicago).

Hegedus, A. (1970). 'Marxist theories of political leadership and bureaucracy', R. B. Farrell (ed.) *Political leadership in Eastern Europe and the Soviet Union.*

(1976a). *Socialism and bureaucracy.*

(1976b). A. Hegedus, M. Markus & M. Vajda (eds.) *The humanisation of socialism.*

Hewett, E. A. (1974). *Foreign trade prices in the Council for Mutual Economic Assistance* (Cambridge).

(1976). 'A gravity model of CMEA trade', J. Brada (ed.) *Quantitative and analytical studies in East–West economic relations* (Bloomington).

Hitch, C. J. & McKean, R. N. (1960). *The economics of defence in the nuclear age* (Cambridge, Mass).

Hoffman, C. (1967). *Work incentive practices and policies in the People's Republic of China* (New York).

(1974). *The Chinese worker* (Albany).

Höhmann, H. H., Nove, A. & Vogel, H. (1986). *Economics and politics in the USSR: problems of interdependence.*

Holesovsky, V. (1968). 'Planning reforms in Czechoslovakia', *Soviet Studies* (April).

Holloway, D. (1983). *The Soviet Union and the arms race* (New Haven & London).

Holzman, F. (1960). 'Soviet inflationary pressures 1928–57: causes and cures', *Quarterly Journal of Economics* vol. LXXIV, no. 2.

(1974). *Foreign trade under central planning* (Cambridge, Mass).

(1985). 'Comecon: A "trade destroying" customs union?', *Journal of Comparative Economics* vol. 9, no. 4.

(1986). 'The significance of Soviet subsidies to Eastern Europe', *Comparative Economic Studies* vol. XXVIII, no. 1.

Horvat, B. (1958). 'The optimum rate of investment', *Economic Journal*.

(1964). *Towards a theory of planned economy* (Belgrade).

(1965). 'The optimum rate of investment reconsidered', *Economic Journal* (September).

(1974). 'Welfare of the common man in various countries', *World Development* vol. 2, no. 7.

Howe, C. (1971). *Employment and economic growth in urban China, 1949–1957* (Cambridge).

(1973a). *Wage patterns and wage policy in modern China 1919–1972* (Cambridge).

(1973b). 'Labour organisation and incentives in industry, before and after the Cultural Revolution', Schram (1973) q.v.

(1978). *China's economy*.

Howe, C. & Walker, K. R. (1977). 'The economist', D. Wilson (ed.) *Mao Tse-tung in the scales of history* (Cambridge).

Hsu, R. C. (1986). 'The political economy of guidance planning in post-Mao China', *Weltwirtschaftliches Archiv* vol. 122, no. 2.

Huberman, L. & Sweezy, P. M. (1969). *Socialism in Cuba* (New York & London).

Huenemann, R. (1966). 'Urban rationing in Communist China', *China Quarterly* no. 26.

Hunt, E. K. & Schwartz, J. G. (1972). E. K. Hunt & J. G. Schwartz (eds.) *A critique of economic theory*.

Hussain, A. & Tribe, K. (1983). *Marxism and the agrarian question*.

(1984). A. Hussain & K. Tribe (eds.) *Paths of development in capitalist agriculture*.

Hymer, S. & Resnick, K. (1971). 'International trade and uneven development', J. N. Bhagwati, R. W. Jones, R. A. Mundell & J. Vanek (eds.) *Trade, balance of payments and growth* (Amsterdam).

Incomes (1967). *Incomes in postwar Europe* (UN ECE *Economic Survey of Europe in 1965* Part II, chapters 7–11, Geneva).

Investment (1965). *Investment appraisal* (National Economic Development Office) 1st edn. 1965, 2nd edn 1967.

Irvin, G. (1983). 'Nicaragua: establishing the state as the centre of accumulation', *Cambridge Journal of Economics* vol. 7, no. 2.

Ishikawa, S. (1967). *Economic development in Asian perspective* (Tokyo).

(1972). 'A note on the choice of technology in China', *Journal of Development Studies* vol. 9.

Jánossy, F. (1970). 'The origins of contradictions in our economy and the path to their solution', *Eastern European Economics* vol. VIII, no. 4.

Jiménez, A. C. (1987). 'Worker incentives in Cuba', *World Development* (January).

Johansen, L. (1979). 'The bargaining society and the inefficiency of bargaining', *Kyklos* vol. XXXII, no. 3.

Kalecki, M. (1943). 'Political aspects of full employment', *Political Quarterly*.
   (1972a). *Selected essays on the economic growth of the socialist and the mixed economy* (Cambridge).
   (1972b). 'Outline of a method of constructing a perspective plan', pp. 213–22 of A. Nove & D. M. Nuti (eds.) *Socialist economics*.
   (1986). *Selected essays on economic planning* (Cambridge).
Kantorovich, L. V. (1965). *The best use of economic resources* (Oxford).
Kantorovich, L. V. (1970). L. V. Kantorovich, N. I. Cheshenko, Iu. M. Zorin & G. I. Shepelev, 'On the use of optimization methods in automated management systems for economic ministries', *Matekon* vol. XV, no. 4.
   (1987). L. V. Kantorovich, M. Albegov & V. Bezrukov, 'Towards the wider use of optimizing methods in the national economy', *Problems of Economics* vol. XXIX, no. 10.
Karavaev, V. P. (1979). *Integratsiya i investitsii: problemy sotrudnichestva stran SEV*.
Kaser, M. (1967). *Comecon* (2nd edn Oxford).
Katsenelinboigen, A. (1977). 'Coloured markets in the Soviet Union', *Soviet Studies* (January).
Keren, M. (1976). 'The GDR's "Economic Miracle"', *Problems of Communism* (January–February).
Keynes, M. M. (1937). 'The general theory of employment', *Quarterly Journal of Economics* vol. 51.
Khanin, G. I. (1967). 'Ekonomicheskii rost i vybor', *Novyi mir* no. 12.
   (1984). 'Puti sovershenstvovaniya ... ', *Izvestiya AN SSSR: Seriya ekonomicheskaya* no. 3.
Khozyaistvennaya (1968). *Khozyaistvennaya reforma i problemy realizatsii*.
Kirichenko, V. N. (1974a). *Dolgosrochnyi plan razvitiya narodnogo khozyaistva*.
   (1974b). V. N. Kirichenko (ed.) *Kompleksnye programmy v sisteme perspektivnogo narodnokhozyaistvennogo planirovaniya*.
Kirstein, T. (1984). 'The Ural–Kuznetsk Combine', in Davies (1984) q.v.
Kiser, J. W. III (1976). 'Technology is not a one-way street', *Foreign Policy* no. 23.
Klochko, M. A. (1964). *Soviet scientist in China*.
Knaack, R. (1984). 'Dynamic comparative economics', A. Zimbalist (ed.) *Comparative economic systems* (Boston).
   (1985). 'Ekonomische hervormingen in China', *Tijdschrift voor politieke ekonomie* vol. 9, no. 2 (December).
Komorov, B. (n.d.). *The destruction of nature in the Soviet Union* (1980?).
Koopmans, T. & Montias, J. M. (1971). 'On the description and comparison of economic systems', in Eckstein (1971) q.v.
Kornai, J. (1959). *Overcentralization in economic administration*.
   (1967). *Mathematical planning of structural decisions* (Amsterdam). There is a second edn (Amsterdam 1975).
   (1970). 'A general descriptive model of planning processes', *Economics of Planning* nos. 1–2.
   (1971). *Anti-equilibrium: On economic systems and the tasks of research* (Amsterdam & London).
   (1972). *Rush versus harmonic growth* (Amsterdam).

(1979). 'Appraisal of project appraisal', M. J. Boskin (ed.) *Economics and human welfare* (New York).

(1980). *Economics of shortage* 2 vols. (Amsterdam).

(1985). *Contradictions and dilemmas* (Budapest).

(1986). 'The Hungarian reform process', *Journal of Economic Literature* vol. XXIV, no. 4.

(1988). 'Individual freedom and reform of the socialist economy', *European Economic Review* vol. 32, no. 2/3 (March).

Korzec, M. (1988). 'New labour laws in the People's Republic of China', *Comparative Economic Studies* vol. XXX, no. 2 (Summer).

Korzec, M. & Whyte, M. K. (1981). 'Reading notes: the Chinese wage system', *China Quarterly* 86.

Kostakov, V. G. (1987). 'Polnaya zanyatost'. Kak my yeyo ponimaem?' *Kommunist* no. 14.

Kostakov, V. G. & Litvyakov, P. P. (1970). *Balans truda* (2nd edn).

Krasikov, A. (1977). 'Commodity Number One' (Part 1), R. Medvedev (ed.) *Samizdat Register I*.

(1981). 'Commodity Number One' (Part 2), R. Medvedev (ed.) *Samizdat Register II*.

Krasovsky, V. P. (1967). *Problemy ekonomiki kapital'nykh vlozhenii*.

Kritsman, L. (1921). *O edinom khozyaistvennom plane*.

(1924). *Geroicheskii period Velikoi Russkoi Revolyutsii*.

Krylov, P. (1969). 'Tsentralizirovanoe planirovanie v novykh usloviyakh', *Ekonomicheskaya Gazeta* no. 45.

Kudrov, V. M. (1972). 'Pyatidesyatiletie SSSR i ekonomicheskoe sorevnovanie dvukh sistem', *Mirovaya Ekonomika i Mezhdunarodnye Otnosheniya* no. 10.

(1973). 'Sovremennyi etap v ekonomicheskom sorevnovanii SSSR i SShA', *Sorevnovanie dvukh sistem*. vol. 6.

(1976). 'Sovremennyi etap ekonomicheskogo sorevnovaniya dvukh mirovykh sistem', *Izvestiya Akademii nauk SSSR: Seriya Ekonomicheskaya* no. 4.

(1977). 'Sotsializm v mirnom ekonomicheskom sorevnovanii s kapitalizmom', *Izvestiya Akademii nauk SSSR: Seriya Ekonomicheskaya* no. 5.

Kueh, Y. Y. (1984). 'A weather index for analysing grain yield instability in China, 1952–81', *China Quarterly* no. 97.

(1986). 'Weather cycles and agricultural instability in China', *Journal of Agricultural Economics* vol. XXXVII, no. 1.

Kurashvili, B. P. (1982). 'Gosudarstvennoe upravlenie narodnym khozyaistvom: perspektivy razvitiya', *Sovetskoe gosudarstvo i pravo* no. 6.

(1983a). 'Sud'by otraslevogo upravleniya', *EKO* no. 10.

(1983b). 'Ob''ektivnye zakony gosudarstvennogo upravleniya', *Sovetskoe gosudarstvo i pravo* no. 10.

(1985). 'Kontory vozmozhnoi perestroiki', *EKO* no. 5.

Kushnirsky, F. I. (1982). *Soviet economic planning, 1965–1980* (Boulder Co.).

Kuznetsov, V. L. (1976). *Economic integration: two approaches*.

Laky, T. (1980). 'The hidden mechanism of recentralization in Hungary', *Acta Oeconomica* vol. 24, no. 1/2.

Lane, D. (1982). *The end of social inequality?*

(1986). D. Lane (ed.) *Labour and employment in the USSR* (Brighton).

Lane, D. & O'Dell, F. (1978). *Soviet industrial workers.*

Lange, O. (1937). 'On the economic theory of socialism', *Review of Economic Studies* (February).

  (1962). O. Lange (ed.) *Problems of political economy of socialism* (New Delhi).

Lardy, N. R. (1978). N. Lardy (ed.) *Chinese economic planning* (New York).

  (1983). *Agriculture in China's modern economic development* (Cambridge).

Lavigne, M. (1973). *Le comecon* (Paris).

Lebedinskii, N. P. (1980). N. P. Lebedinskii (ed.) *Avtomatizirovannaya sistema planovykh raschetov.*

Lebita, R. & Orfeev, Yu. (1984). 'Otbrosiv effekt bumazhnyi', *Pravda* (2 February).

Lee (1978). Lee Yu See, *Three essays on the new mandarins* (Hong Kong n.d. 1978?).

Lehmann, D. (1974). 'Agrarian reforms in Chile, 1965–1972: An essay in contradictions', D. Lehmann (ed.) *Agrarian reform and agrarian reformism.*

Lenin, V. I. (1917). *IMPERIALISM, the latest stage of capitalism* (numerous editions, first published in Russian in Petrograd in 1917).

  (1921). Speech at the 3rd all-Russian food conference, reprinted in *Pol'noe sobranie sochinenii* 5th edn vol. 43 (1963). The quotation is from p. 359.

  (1956 edn). *The development of capitalism in Russia* (Moscow).

Leontief, W. (1966). *Input-output economics* (New York).

  (1971). 'The trouble with Cuban socialism', *New York Review of Books* (7 January).

Leptin, G. & Melzer, M. (1977). *Economic reform in East German industry* (Oxford).

Lerner, A. Ya (1975). *Fundamentals of cybernetics* (New York). This is a translation of *Nachala Kibernetiki* (1967).

Levcik, F. (1977). 'Migration and employment of foreign workers in the CMEA countries and their problems', *East European economies post-Helsinki* (JEC US Congress, Washington DC).

Levcik, F. & Stankovsky, I. (1979). *Industrial cooperation between East and West* (New York).

Levin, A. I. & Yarkin, A. P. (1976). *Platezhesposobnyi spros naseleniya.*

Levine, H. S. (1959). 'The centralised planning of supply in Soviet industry', *Comparisons of the United States and Soviet economies* (JEC US Congress, Washington DC).

Lewin, M. (1973). 'The disappearance of planning in the plan', *Slavic Review* vol. 32, no. 2 (June).

  (1974). '"Taking grain": Soviet policies of agricultural procurements before the War', C. Abramsky (ed.) *Essays in honour of E. H. Carr.*

  (1985). *The making of the Soviet system* (New York).

Lewis, R. (1979). *Science and industrialization in the USSR.*

Li, Choh-Ming (1962). *The statistical system of Communist China* (Chicago).

Liberman, E. G. (1950). *Khozyaistvennyi raschet mashinostroitel'nogo zavoda.*

  (1970). *Ekonomicheskie metody povysheniya effektivnosti proizvodstva.* The English translation is *Economic methods and the effectiveness of production* (New York).

Lichtheim, G. (1961). *Marxism.*
  (1970). *A short history of socialism.*
Lippit, V. D. (1975). *Land reform and economic development in China* (New York).
Lipton, M. (1974). 'Towards a theory of land reform', D. Lehmann (ed.)
  Agrarian reform and agrarian reformism.
Litvyakov, P. P. (1969). *Nauchnye osnovy ispol'zovanie trudovykh resursov.*
Liu Guoguang & Wang Ruisun (1984). 'Restructuring of the economy',
  chapter II of Yu Guangyuan (ed.) *China's socialist modernization* (Beijing).
Liu (1987). Liu Guoguang *et al.*, 'Economic reform and macroeconomic
  management', *Chinese Economic Studies* vol. XX, no. 3.
Loasby, B. J. (1976). *Choice, complexity and ignorance* (Cambridge).
Luo Hanxian (1985). *Economic change in rural China* (Beijing).
Lydall, H. (1984). *Yugoslav socialism* (Oxford).
Lyovin, A. I. (1967). *Ekonomicheskoe regulirovanie vnutrennogo rynka.*
Ma Hong (1983). *New strategy for China's economy* (Beijing).
Shu-yun Ma (1986). 'Recent changes in China's pure trade theory', *China
  Quarterly* 106.
Mack, R. P. (1971). *Planning on uncertainty* (New York).
Macpherson, C. B. (1973). *Democratic theory: essays in retrieval* (Oxford).
Mahalanobis, P. C. (1953). 'Some observations on the process of growth of
  national income', *Sankhya* 1953.
Mandeville, B. (1724). *The fable of the bees.* There is a Penguin 1970 edn.
Manevich, E. L. (1980). *Voprosy truda v SSSR.*
Mannheim, K. (1936). *Ideology and utopia.*
Manoilesco, M. (1931). *The theory of protectionism and of international trade.*
Manual (1968–69). Little, I. & Mirrlees, J. *Manual of industrial project analysis in
  developing countries* 2 vols. (OECD, Paris).
Mao Tse-tung (1954–61). *Selected Works* 4 vols. (Peking).
  (1974a). S. Schram (ed.) *Mao Tse-tung unrehearsed.*
  (1974b). *Miscellany of Mao Tse Tung thought* (Joint Publications Research
  Service, Arlington, Virginia).
  (1977a). *On the ten major relationships* (Peking).
  (1977b). *Selected Works* vol. 5 (Peking).
Marer, P. (1972). *Postwar pricing and price patterns in socialist foreign trade
  1946–1971* (Indiana).
  (1974). 'Soviet economic policy in Eastern Europe', *Reorientation and
  commercial relations of the economies of Eastern Europe* (JEC US Congress,
  Washington DC).
  (1985). *Dollar GNPS of the USSR and Eastern Europe* (Baltimore).
Marx, K. (1961). *Capital* vol. 1 (Moscow).
Marx, K. & Engels, F. (1848). *The Communist Manifesto.*
  (1973). *Fuerbach: Opposition of the Materialist and idealist outlooks* (the first part
  of *The German Ideology*). This is a translation of the Soviet 1965–66 edition.
Matejko, A. (1974). *Social change and stratification in Eastern Europe* (New York).
Matthews, M. (1975). 'Top incomes in the USSR: towards a definition of the
  Soviet elite', *Survey* vol. 21, no. 3.
  (1978). *Privilege in the Soviet Union.*
  (1986). *Poverty in the Soviet Union* (Cambridge).

McAuley, A. (1977). 'The distribution of earnings and incomes in the Soviet Union', *Soviet Studies* (April).

(1979). *Economic welfare in the Soviet Union.*

(1981). *Women's work and wages in the Soviet Union.*

McAuley, M. (1969). *Settling labour disputes in Soviet Russia* (Oxford).

McMillan, C. H. (1979). 'Soviet investment in the industrialized Western economies and the developing countries of the third world', *Soviet economy in a time of change* (JEC US Congress, Washington DC) vol. 2.

Medvedev, R. (1975). *Socialist democracy.*

(1979). 'Russia under Brezhnev', *New Left Review* no. 117.

Medvedev, R. A. & Zh, A. (1977). *Khrushchev. The years in power* (Oxford).

Mesa-Lago, C. (1968). *The labour sector and socialist distribution in Cuba* (New York).

Metodicheskie (1969). *Metodicheskie ukazaniya k sostavleniyu gosudarstvennogo plana razvitiya narodnogo khozyaistva SSSR.* The second edition is *Metodicheskie* (1974).

(1974). *Metodicheskie ukazaniya k razrabotke gosudarstvennykh planov razvitiya narodogo khozyaistva SSSR.* The third edition is *Metodicheskie* (1980).

(1980). *Metodicheskie ukazaniya k razrabotke gosudarstvennykh planov ekonomi-cheskogo i sotsial'nogo razvitiya SSSR.*

Mieczkowski, B. (1975). *Personal and social consumption in Eastern Europe* (New York).

Mikulski, K. I. (1983). *Ekonomicheskii rost pri sotsializme.*

Miliband, R. (1975). 'Bettelheim and Soviet experience', *New Left Review* 91. (1977). *Marxism and politics* (Oxford).

Mill, J. S. (1891). *Principles of political economy.* Book 1, chapter 9 and Book II, chapters 6 & 7.

Millar, J. R. (1977). 'The prospects for Soviet agriculture', *Problems of Communism* (May–June).

Mises, L. von (1920). 'Economic calculation in the socialist commonwealth' in Hayek (1935). This essay is a translation of a work first published in 1920.

Mishan, E. J. (1971a). 'Pangloss on pollution', *The Swedish Journal of Economics* (March). Reprinted in P. Bohm & A. V. Kneese (eds.) *The economics of environment* (1971).

(1971b). 'The postwar literature on externalities', *Journal of Economic Literature* (March).

Moise, E. E. (1983). *Land reform in China and Vietnam* (Chapel Hill, NC).

Montias, J. M. (1976). *The structure of economic systems* (New Haven).

Moore, B. (1966). *Social origins of dictatorship and democracy* (Boston).

Morishima, M. (1982). *Why has Japan 'succeeded'?* (Cambridge).

Morrison, C. (1984). 'Income distribution in East European and Western countries', *Journal of Comparative Economics* vol. 8, no. 2.

Mouly, J. (1977). 'Employment: a concept in need of renovation', *International Labour Review* vol. 116, no. 1.

National (1960). *National programme for agricultural development 1956–1967* (Peking).

Nesterikhin, Yu. E. (1982). 'Vychislitelnaya tekhnika: vozmozhnosti i bar'ery', *EKO* no. 10.

Neuberger, E. & Duffy, W. J. (1976). *Comparative economic systems: a decision-making approach* (Boston).

Neumann, J. von & Morgenstern, O. (1944). *Theory of games and economic behaviour* (Princeton).

Nickum, J. E. (1978). 'Labour accumulation in rural China and its role since the cultural revolution', *Cambridge Journal of Economics*, vol. 2, no. 3.

Nolan, P. (1976). 'Collectivisation in China – some comparisons with the USSR', *Journal of Peasant Studies* vol. 3, no. 2.

  (1983). 'Decollectivisation of agriculture in China', *Cambridge Journal of Economics* vol. 7, no. 3/4.

Nolan, P. & Paine, S. (1986). 'Towards an appraisal of the impact of rural reform in China, 1978–85', *Cambridge Journal of Economics* (March).

Nove, A. (1958). 'The problem of success indicators in Soviet industry', *Economica*.

  (1964). 'Occupational patterns in the USSR and Great Britain', chapter 15 of A. Nove, *Was Stalin really necessary?*

  (1968). *The Soviet economy* (3rd edn).

  (1977). *The Soviet economic system*.

  (1979). *Political economy and Soviet socialism*.

  (1983). *The economics of feasible socialism*.

  (1987). ' "Radical reform", Problems and prospects', *Soviet Studies* vol. XXXIX, no. 3.

Nove, A. & Nuti, D. M. (1972). *Socialist economics* (Penguin edn).

Novozhilov, V. V. (1926). 'Nedostatok tovarov', *Vestnik Finansov* no. 2.

  (1959). 'Izmerenie zatrat i ikh rezul'tatov v sotsialisticheskom kho-zyaistve', V. S. Nemchinov (ed.) *Primenenie matematiki v ekonomicheskikh issledovaniyakh* (1959). The English translation is A. Nové (ed.) *The use of mathematics in economics* (Edinburgh 1964).

Nuti, D. M. (1971). 'Social choice and the Polish consumer', *Cambridge Review* (28 May).

  (1977). 'Large corporations and the reform of Polish industry', *Jahrbuch der Wirtschaft Osteuropas* vol. 7 (Munich).

  (1979). 'The contradictions of socialist economies: a Marxist interpretation', R. Miliband & J. Saville (eds.) *The Socialist Register 1979*.

  (1986a). 'Hidden and repressed inflation in Soviet-type economies', *Contributions to Political Economy* vol. 5.

  (1986b). 'Michal Kalecki's contribution to the theory and practice of socialist planning', *Cambridge Journal of Economics* vol. 10, no. 4.

  (1986c). 'Economic planning in market economies: scope, instruments, institutions', P. Nolan & S. Paine (eds.) *Rethinking socialist economics* (Cambridge).

Oi, J. C. (1986). 'Peasant grain marketing and state procurement', *China Quarterly* no. 106.

Oksenberg, M. (1982). 'Economic policy making in China: summer 1981', *China Quarterly* 90.

Paine, S. (1976a). 'Balanced development: Maoist conception and Chinese practice', *World Development* vol. 4, no. 4.

(1976b). 'Development with growth: A quarter century of socialist transformation in China', *Economic and Political Weekly* special issue (August).

Parkin, F. (1972). *Class, Inequality and political order.*

Pasqualini, J. (1975). J. Pasqualini & R. Chelminskii, *Prisoner of Mao.*

Patel, S. J. (1961). 'Rates of industrial growth in the last century, 1860–
1958', *Economic development and cultural change.*

Perakh, M. (1977). 'Utilization of Western technological advances in Soviet
industry', *East-West technological co-operation* (Brussels).

Perlmutter, H. V. (1969). 'Emerging East-West ventures: The transideologi-
cal enterprise', *Columbia Journal of World Business* (September–October).

(1972). 'Towards research on and development of nations, unions and firms
as worldwide institutions', H. Gunter (ed.) *Transnational industrial relations.*

Perry, E. J. & Wong, C. (1985). E. J. Perry & C. Wong (eds.) *The political
economy of reform in post-Mao China* (Cambridge, Mass).

Pésci, K. (1981). *The future of socialist economic integration* (New York).

Petrakov, N. Ya. (1974). *Kiberneticheskie problemy upravleniya ekonomikoi.*

Petras, J. (1984). *Capitalist and socialist crises in the late twentieth century* (Totowa,
NJ).

Pigou, A. C. (1937). *Socialism versus capitalism.*

Planning (1975). *Planning of manpower in the Soviet Union* (Moscow).

Plekhanov, G. V. (1883). *Sotzialism i politicheskaya borba* (Geneva). This is
reprinted in *Sochineniya* 3rd edn (n.d.) vol. 2. The passage quoted in the
text is on p. 81.

Podkaminer, L. (1982). 'Estimates of the disequilibria in Poland's consumer
markets, 1965–1978', *The Review of Economics and Statistics* vol. LXIV,
no. 3 (August).

(1986). 'Persistent disequilibrium in Poland's consumer markets: some
hypothetical explanations', *Comparative Economic Studies* vol. XXVIII,
no. 3 (Fall).

(1987). 'On Polish disequilibrium once again', *Soviet Studies* vol. XXXIX,
no. 3 (July).

(1988). 'Disequilibrium on Poland's consumer markets', *Journal of Comparative Economics* vol. 12, no. 1 (March).

Pohl, R. (1979). R. Pohl (ed.) *Handbook of the economy of the German Democratic
Republic* (Farnborough, England).

Political Economy (1957). *Political Economy. A textbook issued by the Institute of
Economics of the Academy of Sciences of the USSR* (Moscow). This is an
English translation of the second Russian edition, published in 1956.

Pollitt, B. (1971). 'Some notes on Soviet economic debate in the 1920s',
Discussion Paper no. 129, Economic Growth Centre, Yale University,
Appendix A.

Ponchaud, F. (1978). *Cambodia year zero.*

Portes, R. (1979). 'Internal and external balance in a centrally planned
economy', *Journal of Comparative Economics* vol. 3.

(1983). 'Central planning and monetarism: fellow travellers?' in P. Desai
(ed.) *Marxism, central planning and the Soviet economy* (Cambridge, Mass).

Portes, R. & Winter, D. (1977). 'The supply of consumption goods in
centrally planned economies', *Journal of Comparative Economics* vol. 1.

(1978). 'The demand for money and for consumption goods in centrally planned economies', *Review of Economics and Statistics* vol. 60.

(1980). 'Disequilibrium estimates for consumption goods markets in centrally planned economies', *Review of Economic Studies* vol. 47.

Portes, R., Quandt, R., Winter, D. & Yeo, S. (1984). 'Planning the consumption goods market: preliminary disequilibrium estimates for Poland 1955–80', in P. Malgronge, & P. A. Muet, (eds.) *Contemporary macroeconomic modelling* (Oxford).

Portes, R. & Santorum, A. (1987). 'Money and the consumption goods market in China', *Journal of Comparative Economics* vol. 11, no. 3 (September).

Pryor, F. L. (1963). *The Communist foreign trade system* (Cambridge, Mass).

(1968). 'Discussion' in A. Brown & E. Neuberger (eds.) *International trade and central planning* (Berkeley).

(1973). *Property and industrial organisation in communist and capitalist nations* (Bloomington, Indiana).

(1977). 'Some costs and benefits of markets: An empirical study', *Quarterly Journal of Economics* (February).

Raj, K. N. (1967). 'Role of the "machine-tools" sector in economic growth', C. H. Feinstein (ed.) *Socialism, capitalism and economic growth* (Cambridge).

Raj, K. N. & Sen, A. K. (1961). 'Alternative patterns of growth under conditions of stagnant export earnings', *Oxford Economic Papers*.

Rakovski, M. (1977). 'Marxism and Soviet societies', *Capital and Class* no. 1.

(1978). *Towards an East European Marxism*.

Ramsey, F. (1928). 'A mathematical theory of saving', *Economic Journal*.

Reforma (1968). *Reforma stavit problemy* compilers Yu. V. Yakovlets & L. S. Blyakhman.

Richman, B. (1969). *Industrial society in Communist China* (New York).

Rimashevskaya, N. M. (1987). 'Neobkhodimost' novykh podkhodov', *Kommunist* no. 13.

Riskin, C. (1973). 'Maoism and motivation: work incentives in China', *Bulletin of Concerned Asian Scholars* vol. 5, no. 1.

(1975). 'Workers' incentives in Chinese industry', *China* (1975) q.v.

(1987). *China's political economy*.

Roberts, P. C. (1970). 'War Communism: A re-examination', *Slavic Review* (June).

(1971). *Alienation and the Soviet economy* (Albuquerque, N. Mex.).

Robinson, J. (1960). *Exercises in economic analysis*.

(1964a). 'Chinese agricultural communes', *Coexistence* (May).

(1964b). 'Consumer's sovereignty in a planned economy', *On political economy and econometrics* (Warsaw).

(1966). *The new mercantilism* (Cambridge).

(1975). *Economic management in China*. 2nd edn 1976.

(1977). 'Employment and the choice of technique', K. S. Krishnaswamy, A. Mitra, J. G. Patel, K. N. Raj & M. N. Srivinas (eds.) *Society and Change* (Bombay).

Rode, R. & Jacobsen, H.-O. (1985). *Economic warfare or detente* (Boulder & London).

Rumer, B. Z. (1981). 'The "second" agriculture in the USSR', *Soviet Studies* (October).

(1984). *Investment and Reindustrialization in the Soviet economy* (Boulder, Co.).

Runciman, W. G. & Sen, A. K. (1965). 'Games, Justice and the General Will', *Mind*.

Rutland, P. (1985). *The myth of the plan*.

Rychard, A. (1980). *Economic reform. A sociological analysis of the links between politics and economics* (Wroclaw, in Polish). The text quotation is taken from Brus (1985) p. 205.

Sah, R. K. & Stiglitz, J. E. (1984). 'The economics of price scissors', *American Economic Review* vol. 74, no. 1.

Sakharov, A. (1969). *Reflections on progress, peaceful coexistence and intellectual freedom*.

Sapir, A. (1980). 'Economic growth and factor substitution: what happened to the Yugoslav economic miracle?', *Economic Journal* (June).

Sartre, J. P. (1974). 'Czechoslovakia: the socialism that came in from the cold', J. P. Sartre, *Between existentialism and Marxism* (New York).

Sau, R. (1978). *Unequal exchange, imperialism and underdevelopment* (Calcutta).

Saunders, C. T. (1977). C. T. Saunders (ed.) *East–West cooperation in business: Inter-firm studies* (Vienna & New York).

Schram, S. (1973). S. Schram (ed.) *Authority, participation and cultural change in China* (Cambridge).

Schran, P. (1969). *The development of Chinese agriculture* (Illinois).

Scott, H. (1974). *Does socialism liberate women?* (Boston).

Seers, D. (1976). 'A system of Social and Demographic statistics: A Review note', *Economic Journal* (September).

Segal, B. M. (1967). *Alkogolizm*.

Selucky, R. (1972). *Economic reforms in Eastern Europe* (New York).

(1979). *Marxism, socialism, freedom*.

Selyunin, V. (1968). 'Vedomstvennyi bar'er', *Ekonomicheskaya Gazeta* no. 25.

Selyunin, V. & Khanin, G. (1987). 'Lukavaya tsifra', *Novyi Mir* no. 2.

Sen, A. K. (1961). 'On optimising the rate of saving', *Economic Journal*.

(1968). *Choice of technique* (3rd edn Oxford).

(1983). 'Development: which way now?', *Economic Journal* (December).

(1985). 'The moral standing of the market', *Social philosophy and policy* vol. 2, no. 2.

Senin, M. (1973). *Problemy optimal'nogo vneshneekonomicheskikh svyazei*.

Shagalov, G. L. (1973). *Problemy optimal'nago planirovaniya vneshnyeekonomicheskikh svyazei*.

Shanin, T. (1972). *The awkward class* (Oxford).

Sheng Yuming (1986). 'Resource flows and terms of trade between farm and non-farm sectors in China, 1953–1983' (mimeo, Cambridge).

Shirk, S. L. (1984). 'The decline of virtuocracy in China', J. L. Watson (ed.) *Class and social stratification in post-revolutionary China* (Cambridge).

Shtromas, A. (1977). 'Crime, law and penal practice in the USSR', *Review of socialist law* vol. 3, issue 3.

Shtromas, A. & Kaplan, M. A. (1988). A. Shtromas & M. A. Kaplan (eds.) *The Soviet Union and the challenge of the future* vol. 2 (New York and London).

Sigurdson, J. (1977). *Rural industrialisation in China* (Cambridge, Mass).

Sik, O. (1972). *The bureaucratic economy* (New York).

Silverman, B. (1971). *Man and socialism in Cuba: The great debate* (New York).

Simatupang, B. (1981). 'Polish agriculture in the 1970s and the prospects for the early 1980s', *European Review of Agricultural Economics* no. 4.

(1988). 'Economic crisis and full employment: The Polish case', *The Journal of Communist Studies* (September).

Simes, D. K. (1975). 'The Soviet parallel market', *Survey* vol. 21, no. 3.

Simon, H. (1976). *Administrative behaviour* 3rd edn (New York).

Sinha, R. P. (1976). *Food and poverty.*

Sirc, L. (1979). *The Yugoslav economy under self-management.*

Skurski, R. (1972). 'The buyers' market and Soviet consumer goods distribution', *Slavic Review* (December).

Slama, J. (1986). 'An international comparison of sulphur dioxide emissions', *Journal of Comparative Economics* vol. 10, no. 3.

Smekhov, B. M. (1968). 'Khozyaistvennaya reforma i stabil'nost' planov', B. M. Smekhov (edn.) *Problemy sovershenstvovaniya planirovaniya.*

Smil, V. (1986). 'Food production and quality of diet in China', *Population and Development Review* vol. 12, no. 1.

Solzhenitsyn, A. (1970 ed.). *The first circle.*

Soos, K. A. (1976). 'Causes of investment fluctuations in the Hungarian economy', *Eastern European Economics* vol. XIV, no. 2.

Sorokin, G. M. & Alampiev, P. M. (1970). G. M. Sorokin & P. M. Alampiev (eds.) *Problemy ekonomicheskoi integratsii stran – chlenov SEV.*

Soviet (1972). *Soviet planning: principles and techniques* (Moscow).

Soviet (1983). *Soviet military–economic relations* (JEC US Congress, Washington DC).

Soviet (1986). 'The Soviet growth slowdown: three views', *American Economic Review* vol. 76, no. 2 (May).

Spraos, J. (1983). *Inequalising trade* (Oxford).

Spulber, N. (1964). *Foundations of Soviet strategy for economic growth* (Bloomington, Indiana).

(1979). *Organisational alternatives in Soviet-type economies* (Cambridge).

Stalin, J. (1927). 'Interview with the first American workers' delegation', reprinted in *Sochineniya* vol. 10.

(1929). 'On the right deviation in the AUCP(b)', printed in full in Stalin (1955a).

(1931). 'New circumstances – new tasks of economic construction', speech of 23 July 1931, reprinted in *Sochineniya* vol. 13.

(1954). *Works* vol. 11 (Moscow).

(1955a). *Works* vol. 12 (Moscow).

(1955b). *Works* vol. 13 (Moscow).

(1972). *Economic problems of socialism in the USSR* (Peking). The first edition was published in Moscow in 1952.

'Standard' (1960). 'The standard method for determining the economic efficiency of investment and new technology in the national economy', *Problems of economics* vol. III, no. 6.

(1970). 'The standard method for determining the economic efficiency of investment', *Matekon* vol. VIII, no. 1.

(1978). 'Standard methodology for calculations to optimize the development and location of production in the long run', *Matekon* vol. XV, no. 1.

Steedman, I. (1979). *Trade among growing economies* (Cambridge).

Steinbruner, J. D. (1974). *The cybernetic theory of decisions* (Princeton).

Strauss, E. (1969). *Soviet agriculture in perspective*.

Strumilin, S. G. (1924). 'Khozyaistvennoe znachenie obrazovaniya', *Planovoe khozyaistvo* no. 9–10. Reprinted in S. G. Strumilin, *Problemy ekonomiki truda* (1957 & 1964).

(1931). Paper reprinted on pp. 587–601 of *Problemy ekonomiki truda* (1957).

Sturm, P. H. (1977). 'The system component in differences in per capita output between East and West Germany', *Journal of Comparative Economics* vol. 1.

Sun Yefang (1980). 'What is the origin of the law of value?', *Social Sciences in China* vol. 1, no. 3.

Sutton, A. C. (1968). *Western technology and Soviet economic development 1917 to 1930* (Stanford, California).

(1971). *Western technology and Soviet economic development 1930 to 1945* (Stanford, California).

(1973). *Western technology and Soviet economic development 1945 to 1965* (Stanford, California).

(1974). *Wall Street and the Bolshevik revolution* (New York).

Swain, N. (1985). *Collective farms which work?* (Cambridge).

(1987). 'Hungarian agriculture in the early 1980s', *Soviet Studies* vol. XXXIX, no. 1.

Swianiewicz, S. (1965). *Forced labour and economic development* (Oxford).

Sykes, L. R. & Davies, D. M. (1987). 'The yields of Soviet strategic weapons', *Scientific American* (January).

Szalai, E. (1982). 'The new stage of the reform process in Hungary and the large enterprises', *Acta Oeconomica* vol. 24, nos. 1–2.

Szamuely, L. (1974). *First models of socialist economic systems* (Budapest).

Szelenyi, I. (1972). 'Housing system and socialist structure', *The Sociological Review Monograph* vol. XVII (February). Repr. *The social structure of Eastern Europe* (ed.) B. L. Faber (New York 1976).

Talmon, J. L. (1952). *The origins of totalitarian democracy*.

(1957). *Utopianism and politics*.

(1960). *Political Messianism: the romantic phase*.

Taniuchi, Y. (1981). 'A note on the Ural-Siberian method', *Soviet Studies* (October).

Tannenbaum, A. S. *et al.* (1974). *Hierarchy in organisations* (San Francisco).

Tanzi, V. (1982). *The underground economy in the United States and abroad* (Lexington).

Tardos, H. (1983). 'The hidden mechanism of recentralization in Hungary', *Acta Oeconomica* vol. XXI, no. 3–4, vol. XXII, no. 1.

Teng Weizao (1982). 'Socialist modernisation and the pattern of foreign trade', Xu Dixin *et al. China's search for economic growth* (Beijing).

Tickin, H. (1973). 'Towards a political economy of the USSR', *Critique* 1.
  (1975). 'The current crisis and the decline of a superpower', *Critique* no. 5.
  (1976a). 'The contradictions of Soviet society and Professor Bettelheim', *Critique* no. 6.
  (1976b). 'The USSR: the beginning of the end', *Critique* no. 7.

Timar, J. (1966). *Planning the labour force in Hungary* (New York).
  (1983). 'Problems of full employment', *Acta Oeconomica* vol. 31.

Togliyatti, P. (1964). 'Pamyatnaya zapiska Pal'miro Tol'yatti', *Pravda* (10 September).

Toranska, T. (1987). *Oni. Stalin's Polish puppets.*

Toruno, M. C. (1988). 'Appraisals and rational reconstructions of general competitive equilibrium theory', *Journal of Economic Issues* vol. XXII, no. 1 (March).

Travers, S. Lee (1982). 'Bias in Chinese economic statistics', *China Quarterly* 91.

Treml, V. G. (1982). *Alcohol in the USSR: A statistical study.* (Durham, NC).

Treml, V. G. & Hardt, J. P. (1972). V. Treml & J. P. Hardt (eds) *Soviet economic statistics* (Durham, NC).

Tretyakova, A. & Birman, I. Ya. (1976). 'Input-output analysis in the USSR', *Soviet studies* vol. XXVIII, no. 2.

Trotsky, L. D. (1930). *Permanentnaya revolyutsia* (Berlin). Italics added.

Turcan, J. R. (1977). 'Some observations on retail distribution in Poland', *Soviet Studies* vol. XXIX, no. 1.

Tyson, L. (1981). *The Yugoslav economic system and its performance in the 1970s* (Berkeley).

Unger, J. (1984). 'The class system in rural China', J. L. Watson (ed.) *Class and social stratification in post-revolution China* (Cambridge).

Use (1965). *Use of systems of models in planning* (UN, New York).

Vacić, A. M. (1986). 'Why the development of Yugoslavia deviated from the socialist self-management market economy', *Eastern European economics* vol. XXV, no. 2.

Vainshtein, A. L. (1969). *Narodnyi dokhod rossii i SSSR.*

Val'tukh, K. K. (1977). 'Intensifikatsiya proizvodstva i sovershenstvovanie planirovaniya', *EKO* no. 2.

Vanous, J. (1986). 'Macroeconomic adjustment in Eastern Europe in 1981–83', *East European Economies: slow growth in the 1980s* (JEC US Congress, Washington DC) vol. 1.

Vermeer, E. B. (1977). *Water conservancy and irrigation in China* (Leiden).
  (1970). 'Social welfare provisions and the limits of inequality in contemporary China', *Asian Survey* vol. 19, no. 9.
  (1982). 'Income differentials in rural China', *China Quarterly* 89.

Vogel, E. F. (1969). *Canton under Communism* (Cambridge Mass).

Volkonsky, V. A. (1981). *Problemy sovershenstvovaniya khozyaistvennogo mekhanizma.*

Vortmann, H. (1979). 'Incomes', R. Pohl, (ed.) *Handbook of the economy of the German Democratic Republic* (Farnborough, England).

Voslensky, M. (1984). *Nomenklatura.*

Wädekin, K. E. (1973). *The private sector in Soviet agriculture* (Berkeley).
  (1982). *Agrarian policies in Communist Europe* (Totowa, NJ).
Walder, A. G. (1986). *Communist neo-traditionalism – work and authority in Chinese industry* (Berkeley).
  (1987). 'Wage reform and the web of factory interests', *China Quarterly* 109.
Walker, K. R. (1984). *Food grain consumption and procurement in China* (Cambridge).
Wang Jue, Han Kang & Lu Zhongyuan (1987). 'On China's system of a socialist planned market and the way to its realization', *Social Sciences in China* vol. VIII, no. 2.
Wang Liming & Li Shirong (1987). 'Probing the question of the state's right of ownership by the whole people', *Social Sciences in China* vol. VIII, no. 2.
Wang Zheng (1981). 'Some questions of right and wrong in statistics work must be clarified', *Chinese Economic Studies* vol. XV, no. 1.
Wariner, D. (1969). *Land reform in principle and practice*.
Watanbe, S. (1974). 'Reflections on current policies for promoting small enterprises and sub-contracting', *International Labour Review* (November).
Watson, A. (1975). *Living in China*.
Watson, J. L. (1984). J. L. Watson (ed.) *Class and social stratification in post-revolution China* (Cambridge).
Weintraub, E. R. (1985). *General equilibrium analysis* (Cambridge).
Weitzman, P. (1974). 'Soviet long-term consumption planning: distribution according to rational need', *Soviet Studies* (July).
Wheatcroft, S. G., Davies, R. W. & Cooper, J. M. (1986). 'Soviet industrialization reconsidered', *Economic History Review* (May).
Wheelwright, E. L. & McFarlane, B. (1970). *The Chinese road to socialism*.
White book (1951). *White book on aggressive activities by the Governments of the USSR, Poland, Czechoslovakia, Hungary, Rumania, Bulgaria and Albania towards Yugoslavia* (Belgrade).
Whyte, L. T. (1977). 'Deviance, modernization, rations and household registers in urban China', A. Wilson, S. L. Greenblatt & R. W. Wilson (eds.) *Deviance and social control in Chinese society* (New York).
Whyte, M. K. (1975). 'Inequality and stratification in China', *China Quarterly* (December).
Wilczynski, J. (1965). 'The theory of comparative costs and centrally planned economies', *Economic Journal* (March).
  (1976). *The multinationals and East–West relations*.
Wiles, P. (1962). *The political economy of Communism* (Oxford).
  (1968). *Communist international economics* (Oxford).
  (1972). 'Soviet unemployment on US definitions', *Soviet Studies* vol. 23.
  (1974a). *Distribution of income: East and West* (Amsterdam).
  (1974b). 'La lotta contro l'inflazione nelle economie collectiviste: una valutazione', *Rivista di Politica Economica* (December).
  (1974c). 'The control of inflation in Hungary', *Economie appliquée* vol. 27, pp. 119–48.
  (1982). 'Are there any Communist economic cycles?' *ACES Bulletin* vol. 24, no. 2.

Wiles, P. & Efrat, M. (1985). *The economics of Soviet arms.*

Wilhelm, J. H. (1985). 'The Soviet Union has an administered, not a planned, economy', *Soviet Studies* vol. XXXVII, no. 1.

Wilkens, H. (1981). *The two German economies* (Farnborough).

Williamson, O. (1975). *Markets and hierarchies* (New York).

Winiecki, J. (1986). 'Central planning and export orientation', *Eastern European Economics* vol. XXIV, no. 4.

Wittfogel, K. (1971). 'Communist and non-Communist agrarian systems', In W. A. Douglas Jackson (ed.) *Agrarian policies and problems in Communist and non-Communist countries* (Seattle).

Wuyts, M. (1985). 'Money, planning and rural transformation in Mozambique', *Journal of Development Studies* vol. 22, no. 1.

Xu Dixin (1982a). 'Opening speech at the symposium on the theory of overall balance of the national economy', *Chinese Economic Studies* vol. XVI, no. 1.

   (1982b). *China's search for economic growth* (Beijing).

Xue Muqiao (1981). *China's socialist economy* (Beijing).

   (1983). 'An inquiry into the problems concerning the reform of the economic system', *Chinese Economic Studies* vol. XVII, no. 2.

   (1986). *China's socialist economy* rev. edn (Beijing).

Yakovlev, A. N. (1987). 'Dostizhenie kachestvenno novogo sostoyaniya sovetskogo obshchestva i obshchestvennye nauki', *Vestnik AN SSSR* no. 6.

Yuan-li Wu (1967). 'Planning, management and economic development in Communist China', *An economic profile of Mainland China* (JEC US Congress, Washington DC).

Zafanolli, W. (1985). 'A brief outline of China's second economy', *Asian Survey* vol. XXV, no. 7.

Zaleski, E. (1971). *Planning for economic growth in the Soviet Union 1918–32* (Chapel Hill, NC).

   (1980). *Stalinist planning for economic growth, 1933–52* (Chapel Hill, NC).

Zaslavskaya, T. (1984). 'On the necessity for a deeper study in the USSR of the social mechanism of economic development', *Survey* (Spring).

   (1987). 'Creative activity of the masses: social reserves of growth', *Problems of Economics* vol. XXIX, no. 11.

Zhou Qiren & Du Ying (1985). 'A study on specialised households', Wang Guichen *et al. Smashing the communal pot* (Beijing).

Zielinski, J. (1967). 'On the theory of success indicators', *Economics of Planning* no. 1.

   (1970). 'Planification et gestion au niveau de la branche industrielle en Europe de l'Est', *Revue de l'Est* vol. 1, no. 1.

   (1973). *Economic reforms in Polish industry.*

Zimon, H. A. (1979). 'Regional inequalities in Poland: 1960–1975', *Economic Geography* vol. 55.

Zubkov, A. I. (1979). *Toplivno-syrevaya problema v usloviyakh sotsialisticheskoi ekonomicheskoi integratsii.*

Županov, J. (1983). *Marginalia o društvennoj krizi* (Zagreb).

INDEX

Abalkin, L., 27–8
alcohol, 74, 261–3
Andropov, Yu., 74, 192, 244
Antal, L., 81
Austrian school, 82–3, 255–6

Bahro, R.
  obstacle to dynamism in the
    traditional model on, 27
  state ownership on, 323
Bauer, T., 64–5, 131, 163–4, 227
Bender, O., 225, 255
Bergson, A.
  on waste in the traditional model, 26,
    31
  efficiency of the two systems on,
    299–311
Bettelheim, C., 48, 191
Birman, I. Ya., 43, 175, 237
Brezhnev, L. I., 44, 53, 109, 138, 259,
    282, 329
Brus, W.
  main features of traditional model
    on, 18–19
  need for reform argued by, 53, 59
  non-implementation of reform on, 60
  socialisation on, 84, 322
  role of planning in reformed model
    analysed by, 85–6
  ideology of administrative methods
    on, 195
  etatist model on, 313
  limitations of self-management on,
    314
Bukharin, N. I.
  The economics of the transition period
    cited, 104, 195, 256
  opposes administrative methods in
    agriculture, 105
Bukharin, N. I and Preobrazhensky,
    E. A.
  ABC of Communism quoted from, 9–10
bureaucratic degeneration, 322

bureaucratisation, 26–7, 46–7, 103, 323

Carillo, S., vi
Chen Yun, 102
China
  Marco Polo favourably impressed by,
    10
  adopts traditional model, 18
  Constitution quoted from, 21
  attempt to abolish second economy
    in, 33
  economic reform in, 69–73
  decollectivisation in, 71, 101, 117–18,
    211
  relation between agriculture and
    industry in, 119
  1961–2 depression in, 163
  unemployment in, 180–1
  labour process in, 191–2
  allocation of labour in, 69–70, 196–8,
    214
  distribution according to need in,
    210–11
  income distribution in, 222–7
  consumption plan in, 234
  dynamic efficiency of, 307–8
CMEA
  cooperation in production of
    computers by, 44
  aspects of, 274–89
coercion
  in Soviet agriculture, 104–10
  in Chinese labour policy, 181, 195–6
  in organisation of labour, 194–6
  in foreign trade, 273–4
  reduction in USSR after 1953 of, 315
Collier, I. L., 254–5, 304–6
corruption, 72–3, 212, 221
costs of revolution, 256
Cuba
  traditional model in, 18, 49
  fall in labour productivity in the
    1960s in, 46

359

consumption in, 256–7
economic assistance from USSR, 274
position in CMEA, 274, 276

Deng Xiaoping, 72, 92, 102, 308–9,
    325
dictatorship over needs, 26–31
dictatorship, political, 19, 21–3, 87
Discourses on salt and iron, 28
Dobb, M., 153–6, 233

Engels, F.
    *The peasant question in France and
        Germany* quoted from, 92
entrepreneurship, 82–3

famine
    in USSR, 106, 108, 125
    in China, 111, 116
    in Ireland, 116
feedback, 21, 40, 54, 246
Feldman, G. A., 142–7

German Democratic Republic,
    not a backward country, 11
    economic reform in, 66–9
    cycles in, 164
    trade unions in, 215
    income distribution in, 216
    cost of shortages in, 254–5
    burden of reparations on, 273
    foreign workers in, 284
    efficiency of in comparison with FRG,
        304–6
Glittering Future, 22, 49, 325
Gorbachev, M. S.
    reaction to 'non-labour incomes'
        campaign of, 22
    price increases threatened by, 67
    economic reform on, 73
    agricultural changes under, 127
    nationalities policy of, 188
    discipline drive of, 192
    wage differentials under, 210
    anti-alcohol campaign of, 263
    international trade and, 271
    social changes under, 315, 318
Granick, D., 55, 58–9, 67, 196, 202, 215
Grossman, G., 18–19, 244

Hanson, P., 80, 239
Holzman, F., 212, 290
Horvat, B., 135–6, 258–9
Hungary

economic reform in, 63–5
agriculture in, 122–4
investment tension in, 162
informal sector in, 177–8
housing in, 220, 227
income distribution in, 228–9
sumptuary laws in, 229
prices in foreign trade of, 281
discussion of foreign trade criteria in,
    288–9

IMF, 62, 71, 293
industrial safety, 178, 206
inflation, 55–7, 72, 78, 212
Ishikawa, S., 119–20, 157

Kalecki, M.
    views of adherents of, 3
    warns about implications of grain
        policy, 37
    economic reform and economic policy
        on, 62–3
    overinvestment on, 136–7
    choice of techniques on, 155–6
Kampuchea, 33, 180, 226, 319, 320, 324
Keynes, J. M., 3, 39, 131, 182
Khanin, G. I., 28, 303
Khrushchev, N. S.
    abandons 'dictatorship of the
        proletariat', 21
    report to 20th Congress of, 59
    speech to 22nd Congress of, 73
    reduces hours of work, 177
    international planning and, 277–8
    typical 'pushed up one', 312
    dismissal of, 318
Korea, 304, 318, 328
Kornai, J.
    waste in the traditional model on, 26
    need for reform argued by, 53
    Hungarian economic system
        described by, 65
    criteria for assessing performance of
        socialist economies on, 68
    alternative economic mechanisms on,
        80, 253–4
    regulation illusion on, 81
    investment planning on, 82, 131–2,
        134–5, 138, 149–50, 161, 163
    rationality criteria on, 182
    behavioural explanation of shortages
        by, 247–9
Kritsman, L.
    on bureaucratisation, 26

on inefficiency of administrative
    methods, 29–30, 47–8
Kudrov, V. M., 301–4

Lenin, V. I.
    on uninterrupted revolution, 11
    on need for 'using barbarous methods
        in fighting barbarism', vi, 12
    introduction of NEP by, 78
    capitalist agriculture on, 93
    Taylorism on, 189–90
    position of party leader established
        by, 317
    premature attempts to build socialism
        on, 322, 326
Liberman, E. G., 34

Mandeville, 1, 8
Mao Zedong
    need for policy changes recognised
        by, 69
    agriculture on, 110–14
    priority for heavy industry on, 140
    small scale industries and, 157
    advantages of repression on, 195–6
    attitude to democracy of, 319
    officially criticised by CCP, 321
market socialism, 85
Marx, K.
    analysis of 10 hours Act, 2
    writes *Address of the Central Committee of
        the Communist League*, 11
    General Law of Capitalist
        Accumulation in agriculture, 95
    analyses original accumulation, 104
    industrial reserve army on, 179
    market under socialism on, 194–5
    foreign trade on, 266
Marxism–Leninism
    new developments in, xi, 10, 103–4,
        250
    inadequacy of theory of decision
        making in, 34–5
    weakness of planning theory of, 40
    foreign trade theory of, 266–70
    role of, 328–9
Marxism–Leninism–Mao Zedong
    Thought, 328–30
McAuley, A., 176, 217–18
monetary reform, 250–1

national income accounting, 20, 302–3
nomenklatura, 23, 60, 75, 84
Nove, A., 28, 31

ownership of the means of production,
    19–21, 83–5, 193, 201, 321–4

Pajestka, J., 239–40
Podkaminer, L., 241, 245
Poland
    privileges of leaders in, 20–1
    partial ignorance of leaders in, 38
    economic reform in, 59–63
    comparison of socialist and private
        agriculture in, 121
    working class opposition in, 186, 229
    labour morale in, 200
    trade unions in, 202
    inflation in, 212, 245
    repression in, 216
    worsening of shortages in, 243
    distribution in, 246–7
    negotiations with IMF by, 293
    liberal censorship in, 317
    pluralism in, 318
Portes, R., 199, 244–5
Preobrazhensky, E., 105, 107, 174
prisoners' dilemma, 5–7, 315–20
propaganda of success, 303
Pryor, F. L., 177, 188, 216, 289

'rational low wage policy', 186
rationing, 70, 72, 235, 251–4
Robinson, J., 99, 156
Romania
    repays debt quickly, 68
    direction of labour in, 196
    labour morale in, 200
    opposes CMEA supranational
        planning, 278

Sen, A., 136, 153–6, 225
Smith, A., 1, 2, 3, 7, 8, 55, 104, 213
social indicators, 258–60
Stalin, J. V.
    need for rapid industrialisation on,
        12–13
    characterisation of planning by, 24
    profit on, 25, 182
    surprised by German invasion, 36
    suspicion of specialists of, 37
    perception of agricultural situation
        by, 37–8
    sources of accumulation on, 96–7, 102
    launches dekulakisation,
        collectivisation and taking grain,
        105
    priority for producer goods on, 140

political economy on, 152–3
criticised, 158, 321
shortages on, 242–4
two world markets on, 270
success of, 328
statistics
partymindedness of, 23, 260
falsified in Poland, 23
non-comparability of Soviet
consumption, 237
unreliability of CMEA
macro-economic, 303
Strumilin, S. G., 175

Taylorism, 189–92, 312
trade unions, 38, 178, 186, 202, 214–15
Trotsky
'permanent revolution' on, 11, 319
'self-exploitation of the working class'
on, 107
allocation of labour by the state on,
195

USSR
traditional model developed in, 17
economic reform in, 73–6
passport system in, 179–80
unemployment benefit introduced in,
193
labour balances in, 204
labour coefficients worked out for,
205
inflation in, 212
job evaluation in, 213
income distribution in, 217–22
comprehensive programmes in, 235–6

shortages in, 243–4
reintegration into world market of,
271
socialist imperialism by, 272–3

Vietnam
traditional model in, 18, 49
full employment not attained in, 193
monetary reform in, 250–1
gains from CMEA by, 274
accepts Soviet criticism, 276

Wiles, P., 163, 216–18, 256, 272, 274

Xu Dixin, 156
Xue Muqiao
low quality on, 29
instability of the plans on, 32
need for reform on, 53
choice of technique on, 156
labour morale on, 201
comparison of socialism and
capitalism by, 298

Yakovlev, A. N., vi, 323
Yugoslavia
economic reform in, 54–9
decollectivisation in, 102
Soviet–Yugoslav joint stock
companies in, 272
model, 313–14

Zaleski, E., 48
Zaslavskaya, T. I., 53, 76–7
Zhou Enlai, 38
Zhou Ziyang, 86–7